KERORO GUNSO

ENCOUNTER 1 - ENTER THE SERGEANT

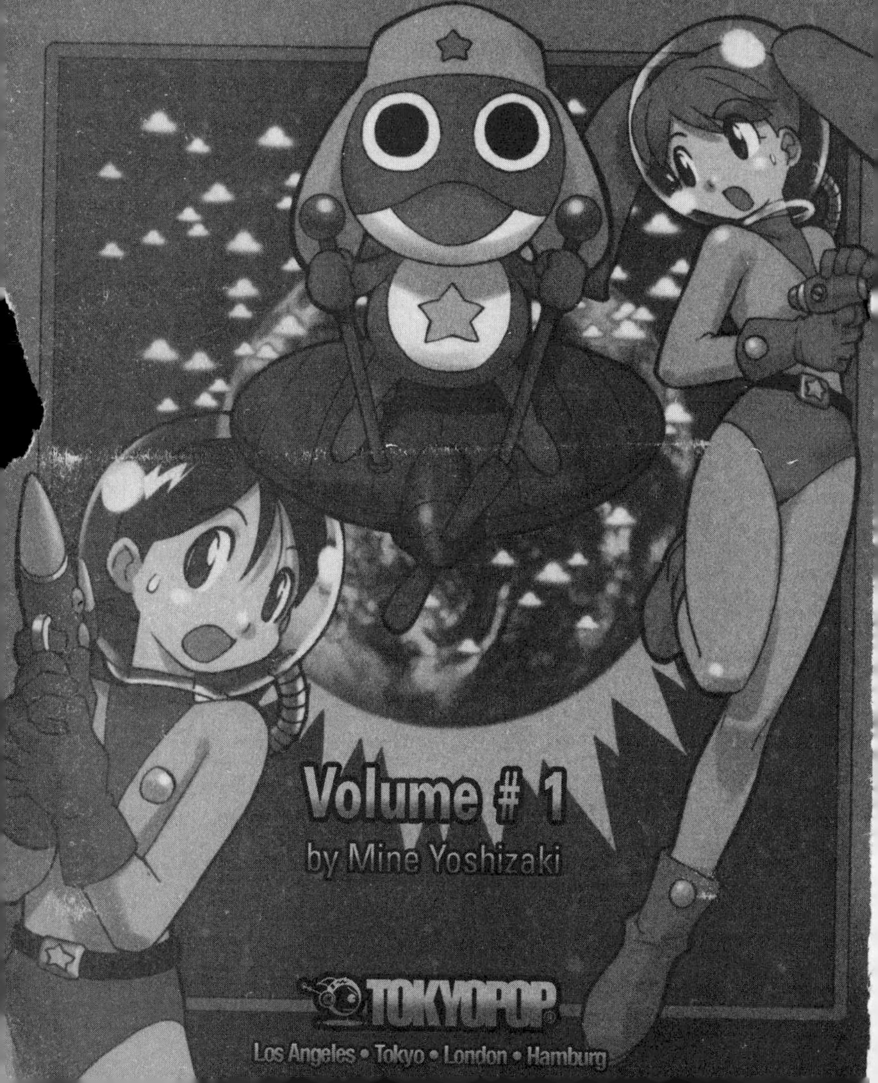
Volume # 1
by Mine Yoshizaki
TOKYOPOP
Los Angeles • Tokyo • London • Hamburg

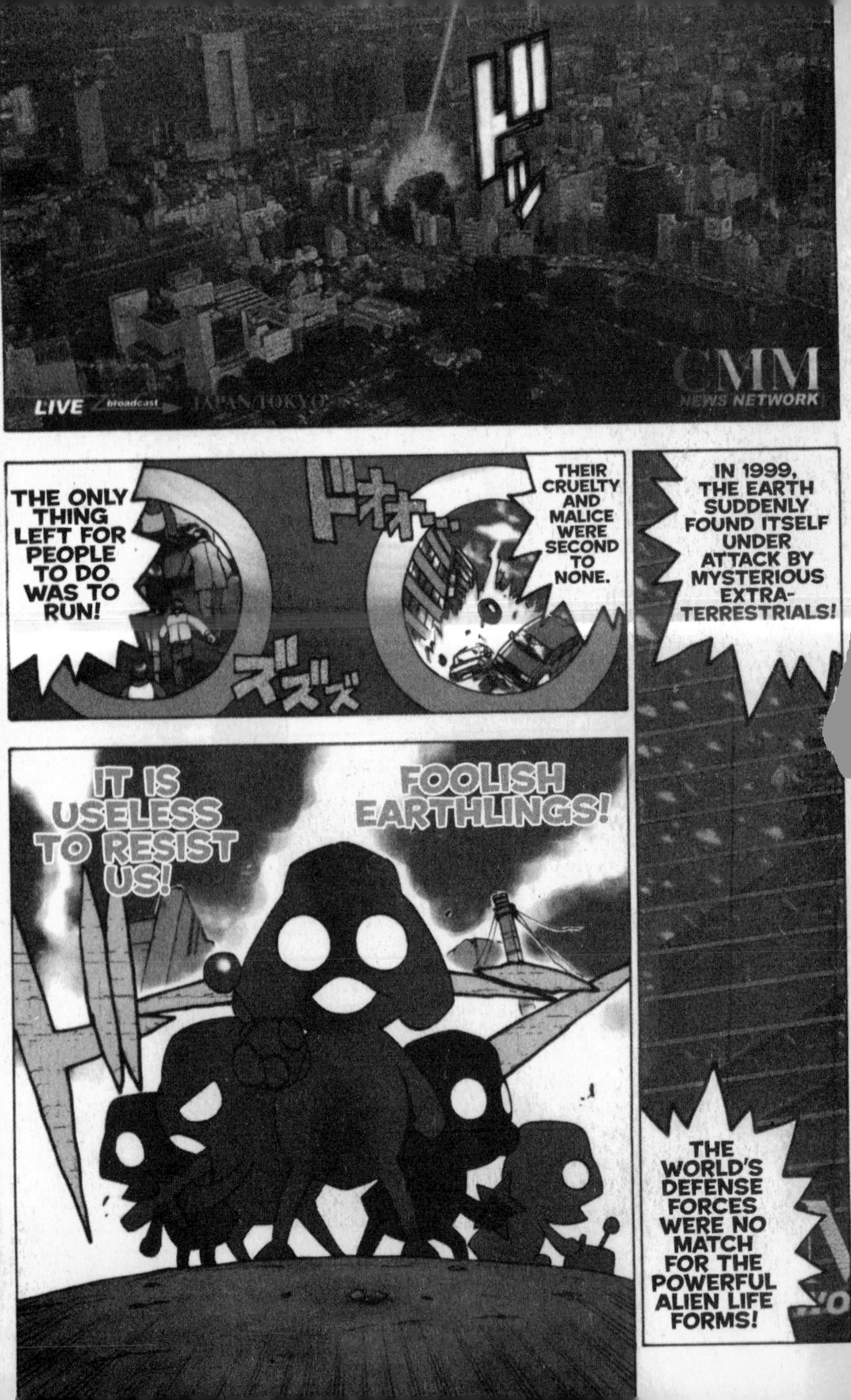

LIVE
broadcast
JAPAN TOKYO
CMM
NEWS NETWORK
IN 1999, THE EARTH SUDDENLY FOUND ITSELF UNDER ATTACK BY MYSTERIOUS EXTRA-TERRESTRIALS!
THE WORLD'S DEFENSE FORCES WERE NO MATCH FOR THE POWERFUL ALIEN LIFE FORMS!
THEIR CRUELTY AND MALICE WERE SECOND TO NONE.
ドオオ…
THE ONLY THING LEFT FOR PEOPLE TO DO WAS TO RUN!
ズズズ
FOOLISH EARTHLINGS!
IT IS USELESS TO RESIST US!

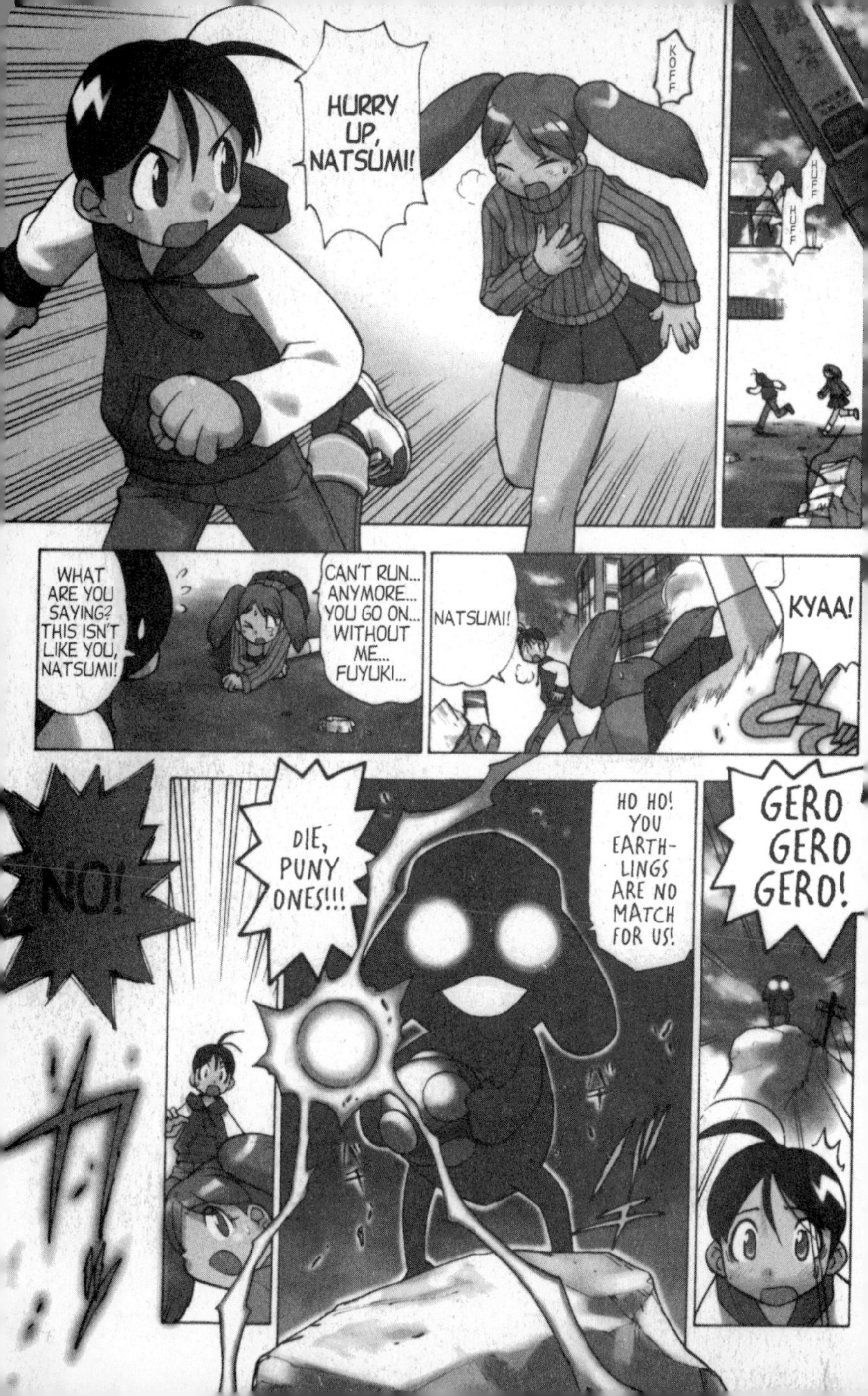
HUFF
HUFF
KOFF
HURRY UP, NATSUMI!
KYAA!
NATSUMI!
CAN'T RUN... ANYMORE... YOU GO ON... WITHOUT ME... FUYUKI...
WHAT ARE YOU SAYING? THIS ISN'T LIKE YOU, NATSUMI!
GERO GERO GERO!
HO HO! YOU EARTH-LINGS ARE NO MATCH FOR US!
DIE, PUNY ONES!!!
NO!

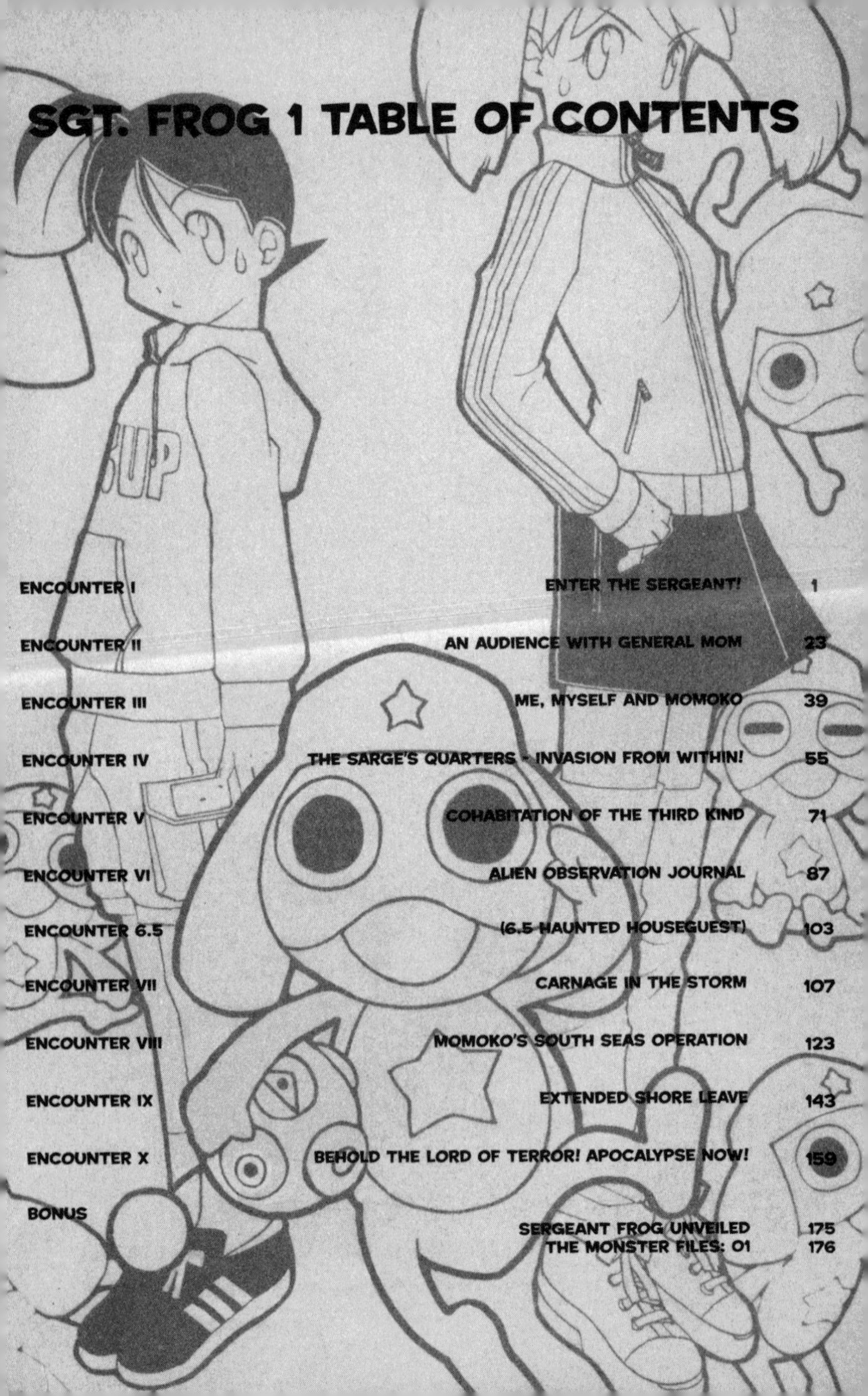
SUP

SGT. FROG 1 TABLE OF CONTENTS

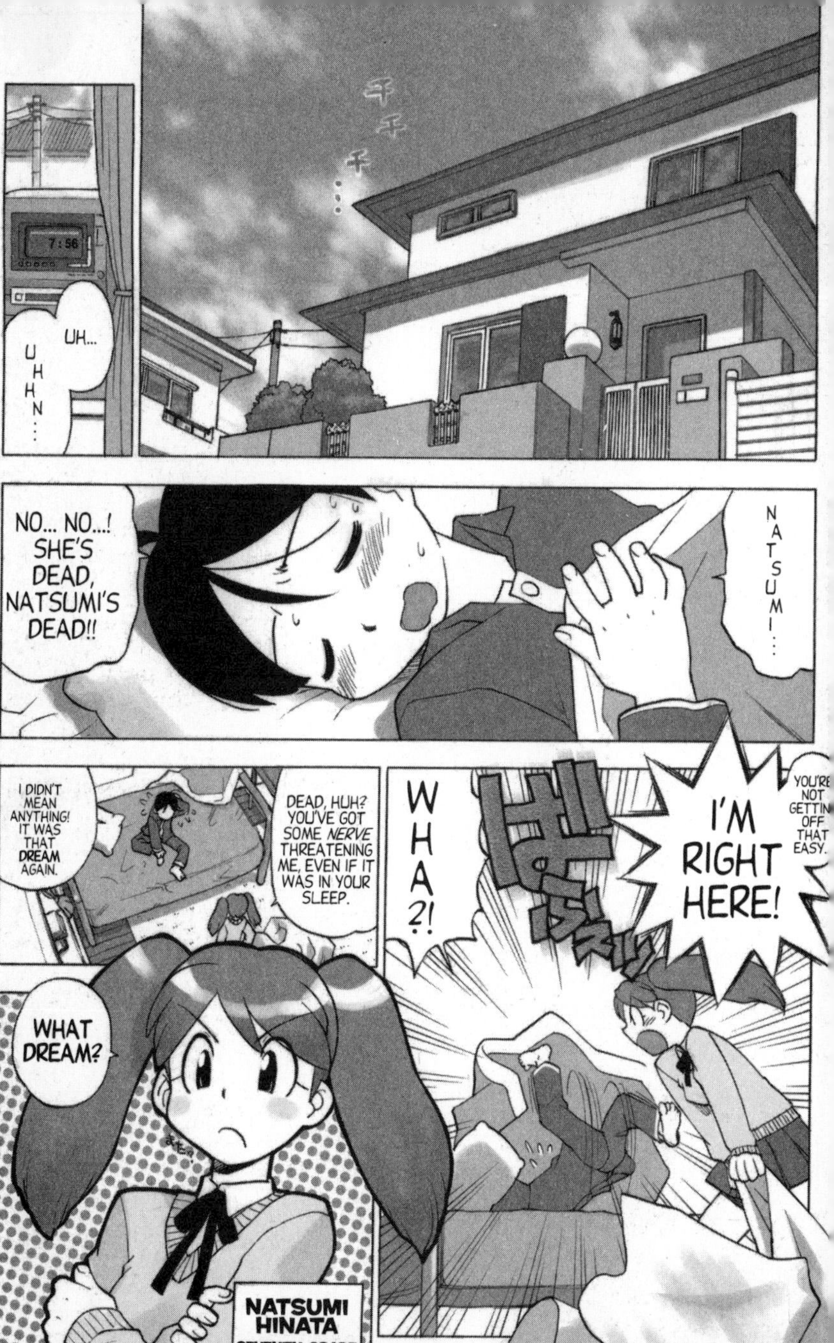

チチチ...
UH... UHHN...
NATSUMI...
NO... NO...! SHE'S DEAD, NATSUMI'S DEAD!!
YOU'RE NOT GETTIN OFF THAT EASY.
I'M RIGHT HERE!
WHA?!
DEAD, HUH? YOU'VE GOT SOME NERVE THREATENING ME, EVEN IF IT WAS IN YOUR SLEEP.
I DIDN'T MEAN ANYTHING! IT WAS THAT DREAM AGAIN.
WHAT DREAM?
NATSUMI HINATA
SEVENTH GRADE

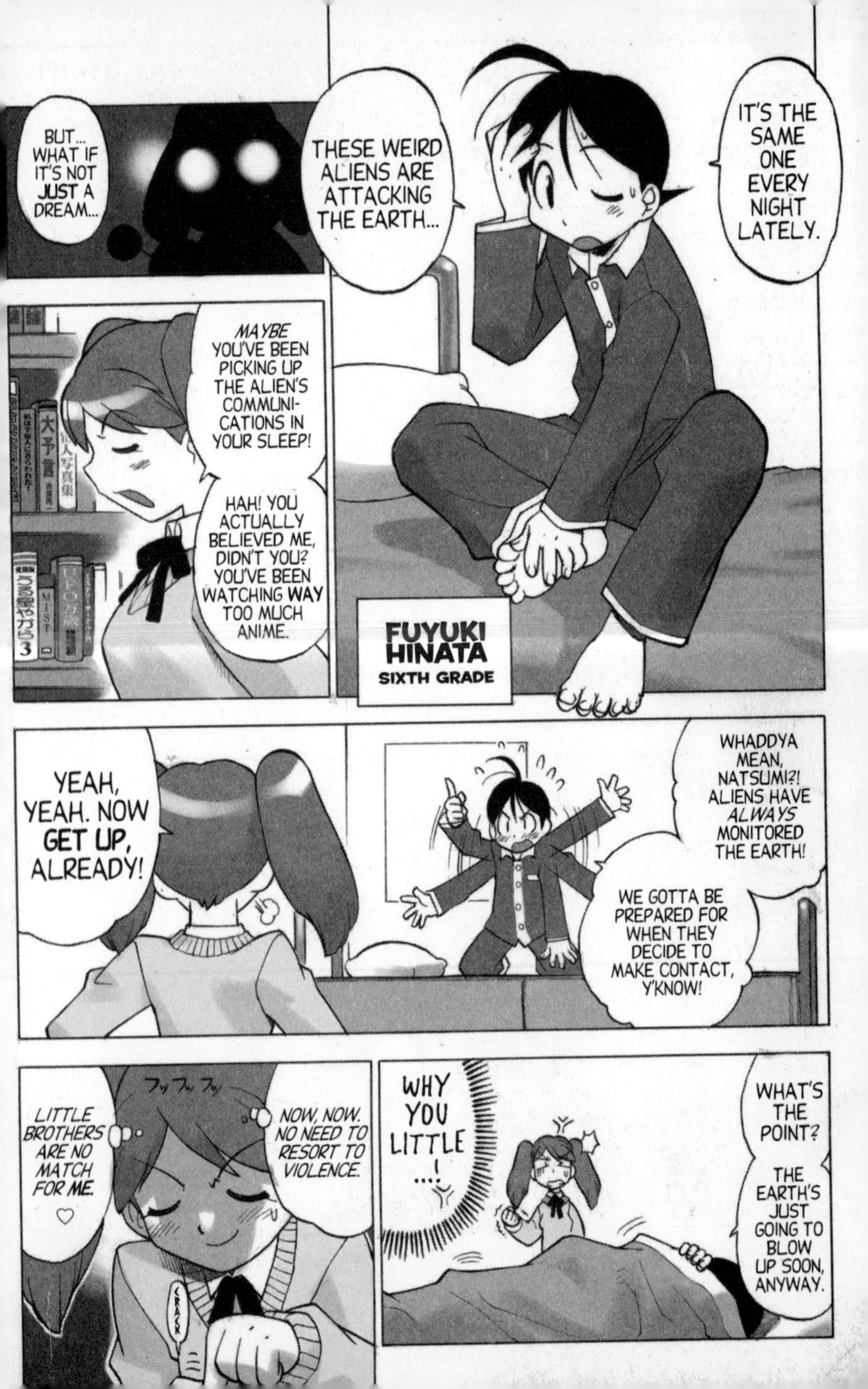
IT'S THE SAME ONE EVERY NIGHT LATELY.
THESE WEIRD ALIENS ARE ATTACKING THE EARTH...
FUYUKI HINATA SIXTH GRADE
BUT... WHAT IF IT'S NOT JUST A DREAM...
MAYBE YOU'VE BEEN PICKING UP THE ALIEN'S COMMUNI-CATIONS IN YOUR SLEEP!
HAH! YOU ACTUALLY BELIEVED ME, DIDN'T YOU? YOU'VE BEEN WATCHING WAY TOO MUCH ANIME.
WHADDYA MEAN, NATSUMI?! ALIENS HAVE ALWAYS MONITORED THE EARTH!
WE GOTTA BE PREPARED FOR WHEN THEY DECIDE TO MAKE CONTACT, Y'KNOW!
YEAH, YEAH. NOW GET UP, ALREADY!
WHAT'S THE POINT?
THE EARTH'S JUST GOING TO BLOW UP SOON, ANYWAY.
WHY YOU LITTLE...!
フッフッフッ
NOW, NOW. NO NEED TO RESORT TO VIOLENCE.
LITTLE BROTHERS ARE NO MATCH FOR ME. ♡
CRACK

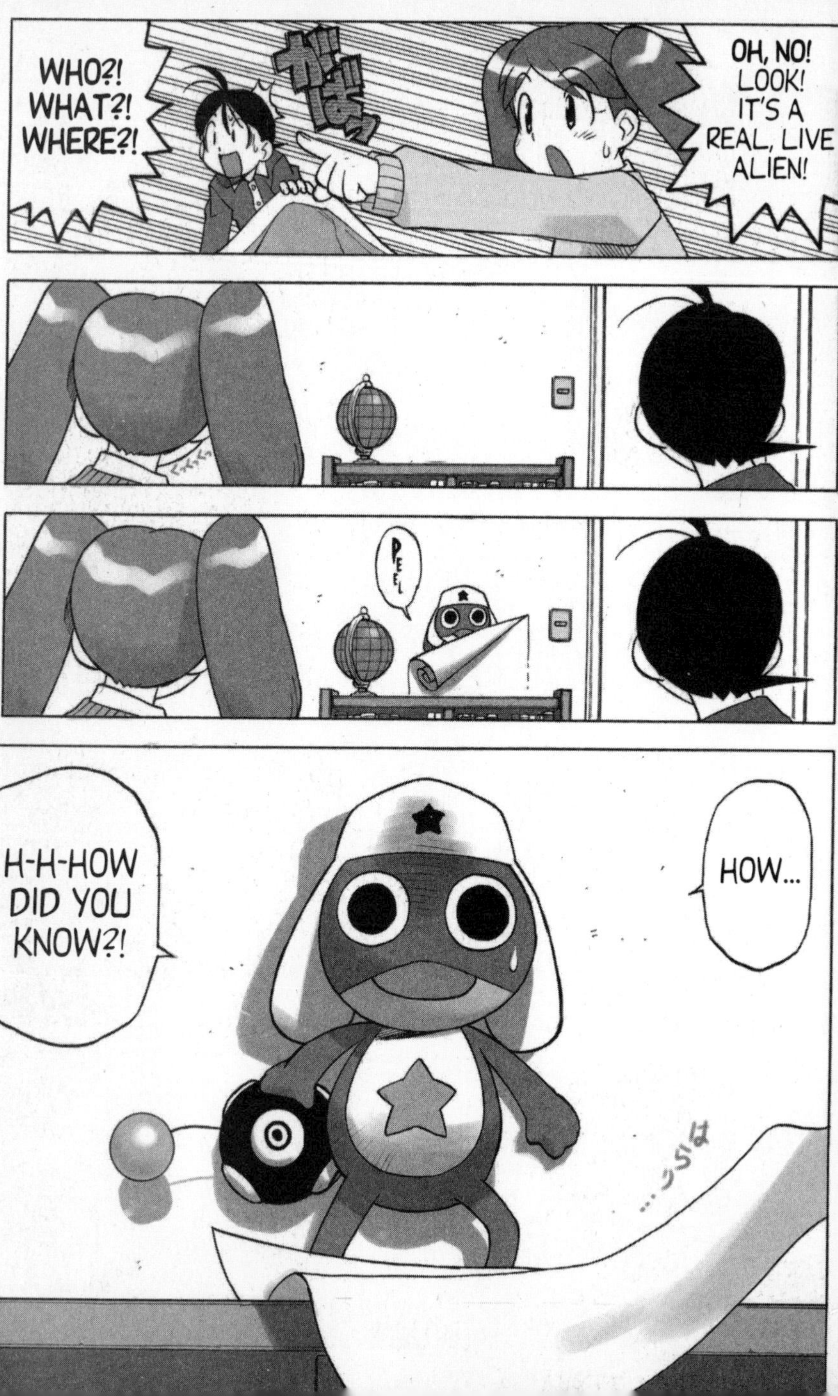
OH, NO! LOOK! IT'S A REAL, LIVE ALIEN!
WHO?! WHAT?! WHERE?!
PEEL
HOW...
H-H-HOW DID YOU KNOW?!

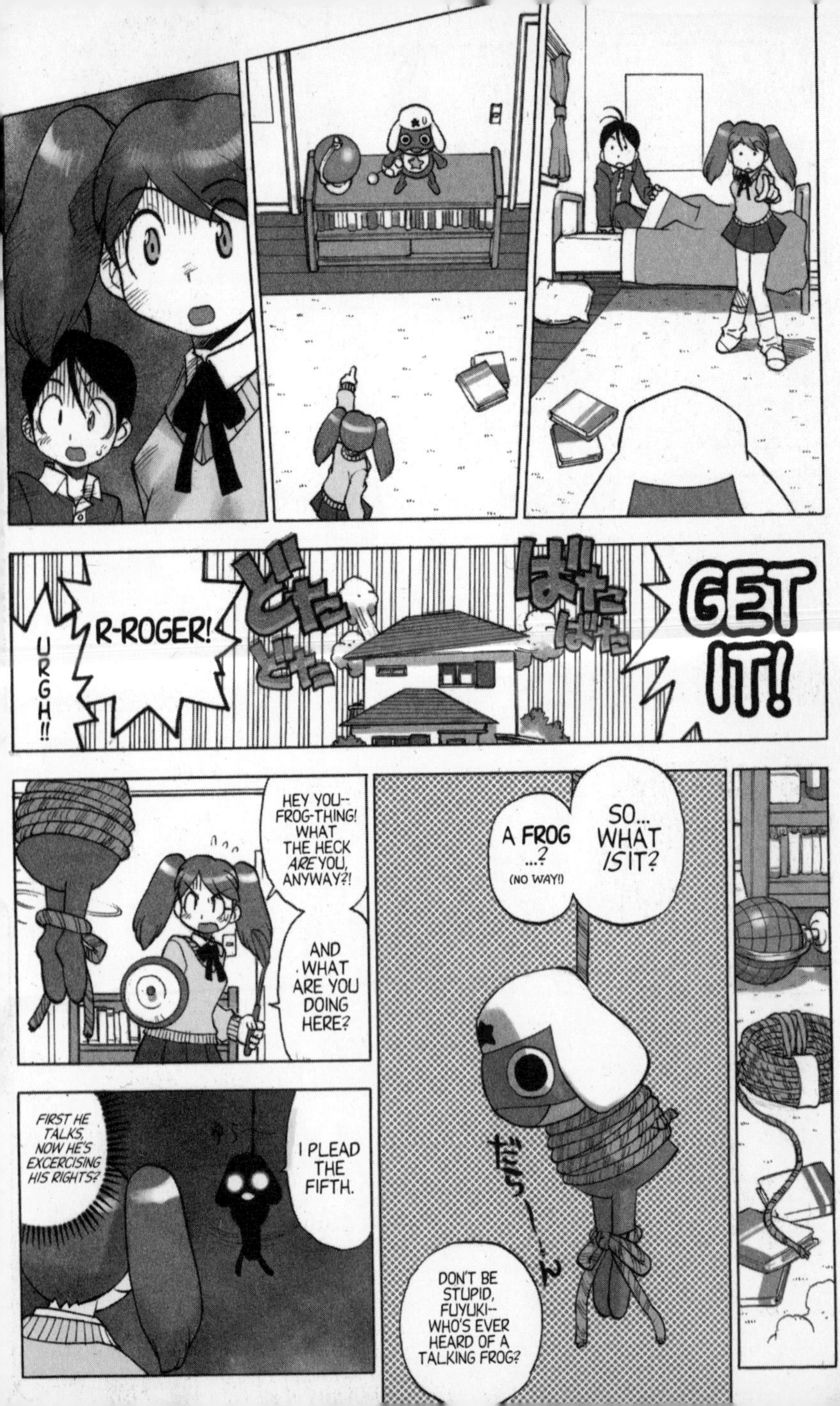
GET IT!
ばたばた
どたどた
R-ROGER!
URGH!!
SO... WHAT IS IT?
A FROG ...? (NO WAY!)
DON'T BE STUPID, FUYUKI-- WHO'S EVER HEARD OF A TALKING FROG?
HEY YOU-- FROG-THING! WHAT THE HECK ARE YOU, ANYWAY?!
AND WHAT ARE YOU DOING HERE?
I PLEAD THE FIFTH.
FIRST HE TALKS, NOW HE'S EXCERCISING HIS RIGHTS?

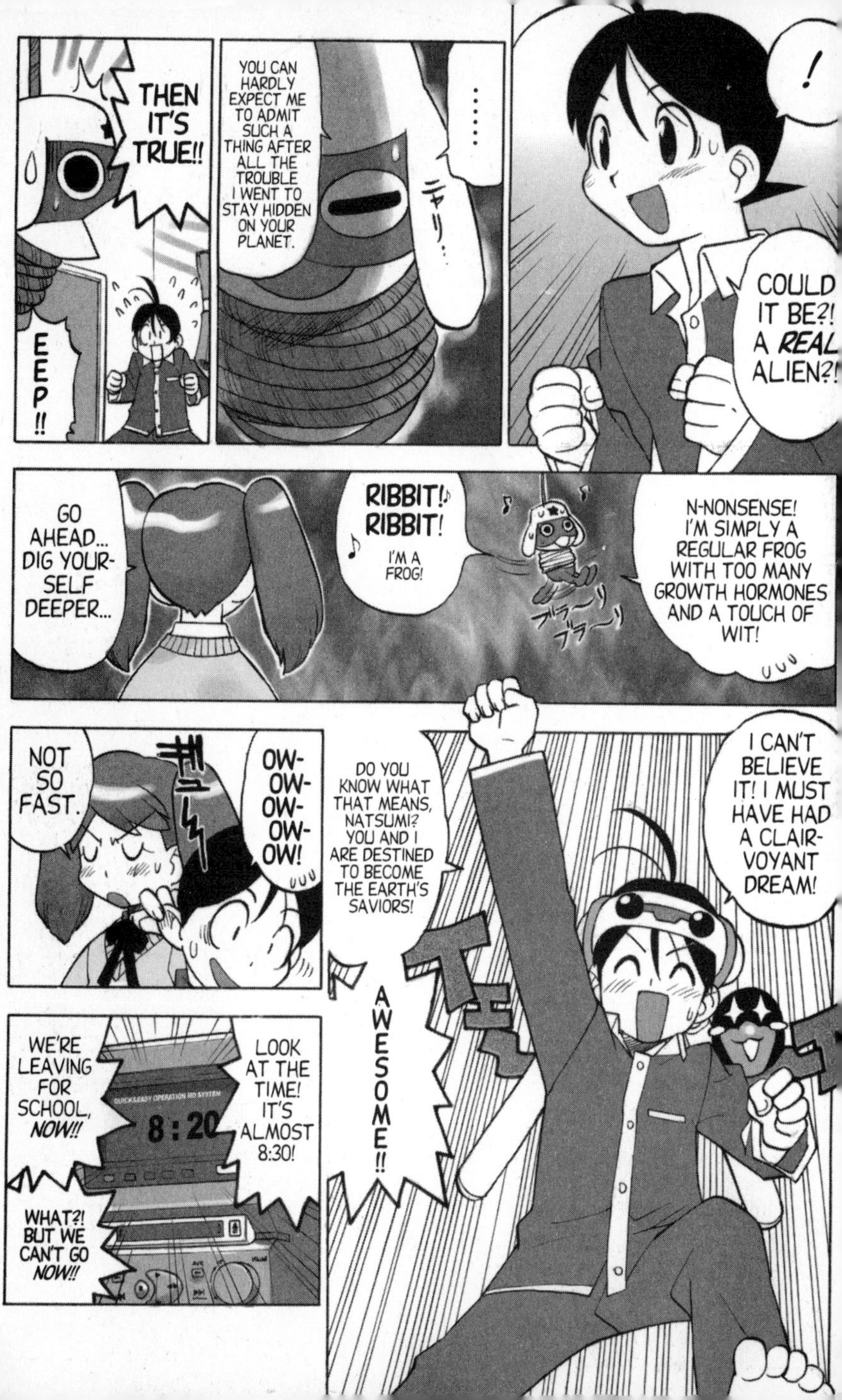
!
COULD IT BE?! A REAL ALIEN?!
......
YOU CAN HARDLY EXPECT ME TO ADMIT SUCH A THING AFTER ALL THE TROUBLE I WENT TO STAY HIDDEN ON YOUR PLANET.
THEN IT'S TRUE!!
EEP!!
N-NONSENSE! I'M SIMPLY A REGULAR FROG WITH TOO MANY GROWTH HORMONES AND A TOUCH OF WIT!
RIBBIT! RIBBIT!
I'M A FROG!
GO AHEAD... DIG YOURSELF DEEPER...
I CAN'T BELIEVE IT! I MUST HAVE HAD A CLAIRVOYANT DREAM!
DO YOU KNOW WHAT THAT MEANS, NATSUMI? YOU AND I ARE DESTINED TO BECOME THE EARTH'S SAVIORS!
AWESOME!!
OW-OW-OW-OW-OW!
NOT SO FAST.
LOOK AT THE TIME! IT'S ALMOST 8:30!
8 : 20
WE'RE LEAVING FOR SCHOOL, NOW!!
WHAT?! BUT WE CAN'T GO NOW!!

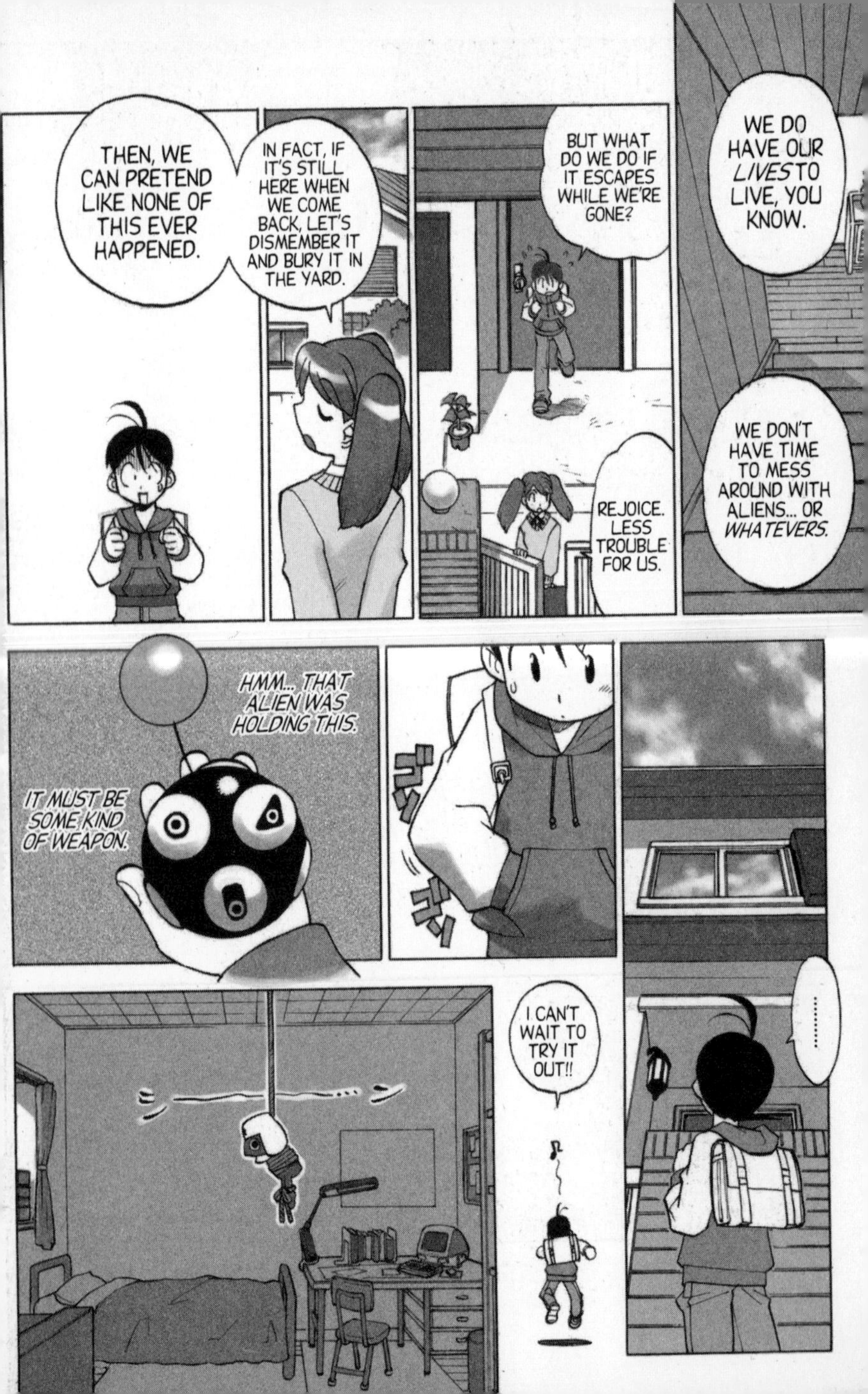
WE DO HAVE OUR *LIVES* TO LIVE, YOU KNOW.
WE DON'T HAVE TIME TO MESS AROUND WITH ALIENS... OR *WHATEVERS.*
BUT WHAT DO WE DO IF IT ESCAPES WHILE WE'RE GONE?
REJOICE. LESS TROUBLE FOR US.
IN FACT, IF IT'S STILL HERE WHEN WE COME BACK, LET'S DISMEMBER IT AND BURY IT IN THE YARD.
THEN, WE CAN PRETEND LIKE NONE OF THIS EVER HAPPENED.
......
HMM... THAT ALIEN WAS HOLDING THIS.
IT MUST BE SOME KIND OF WEAPON.
I CAN'T WAIT TO TRY IT OUT!!

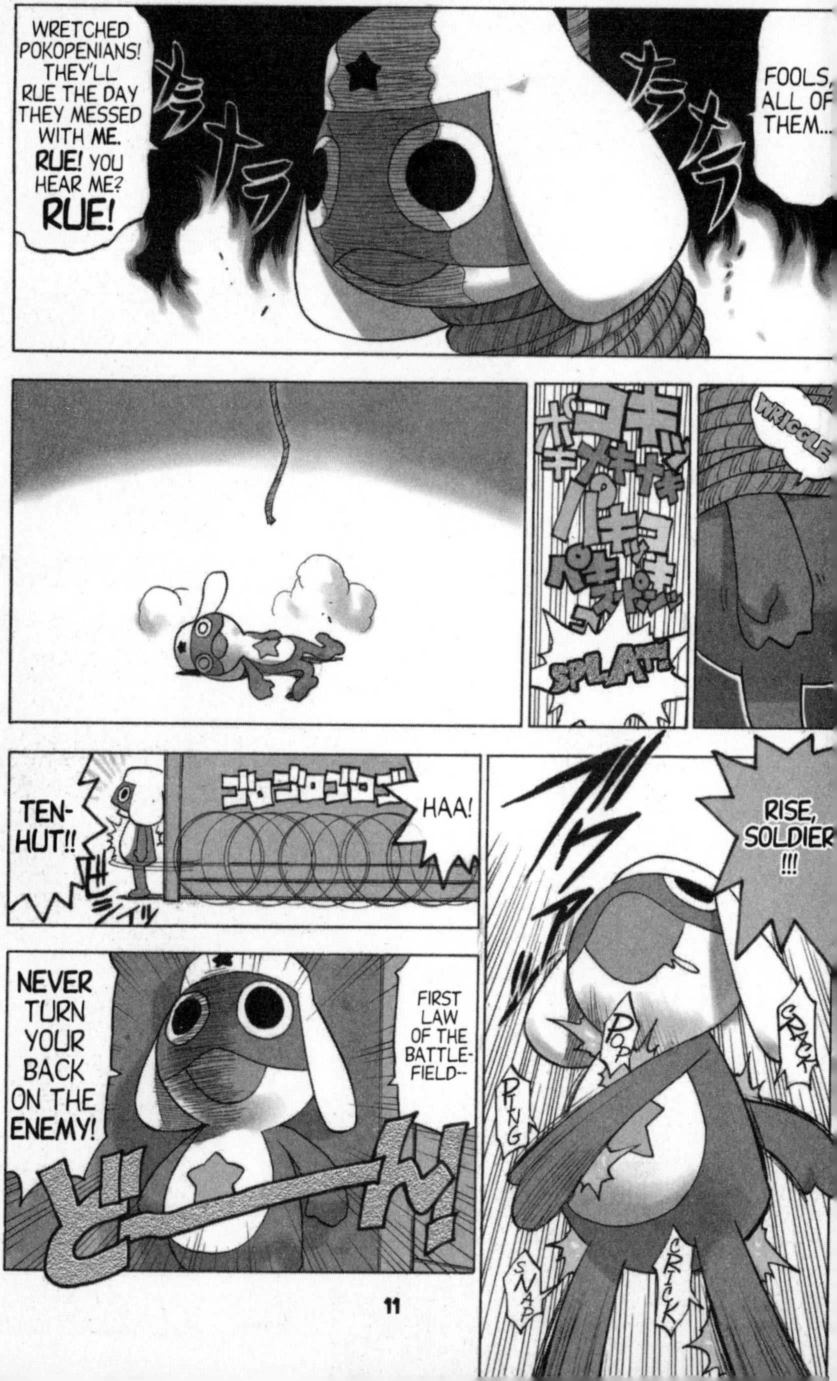
FOOLS, ALL OF THEM...
WRETCHED POKOPENIANS! THEY'LL RUE THE DAY THEY MESSED WITH ME. RUE! YOU HEAR ME? RUE!
WRIGGLE
SPLAT!!
RISE, SOLDIER!!!
CRACK
POP
PING
CRICK
SNAP
HAA!
TEN-HUT!!
FIRST LAW OF THE BATTLE-FIELD--
NEVER TURN YOUR BACK ON THE ENEMY!

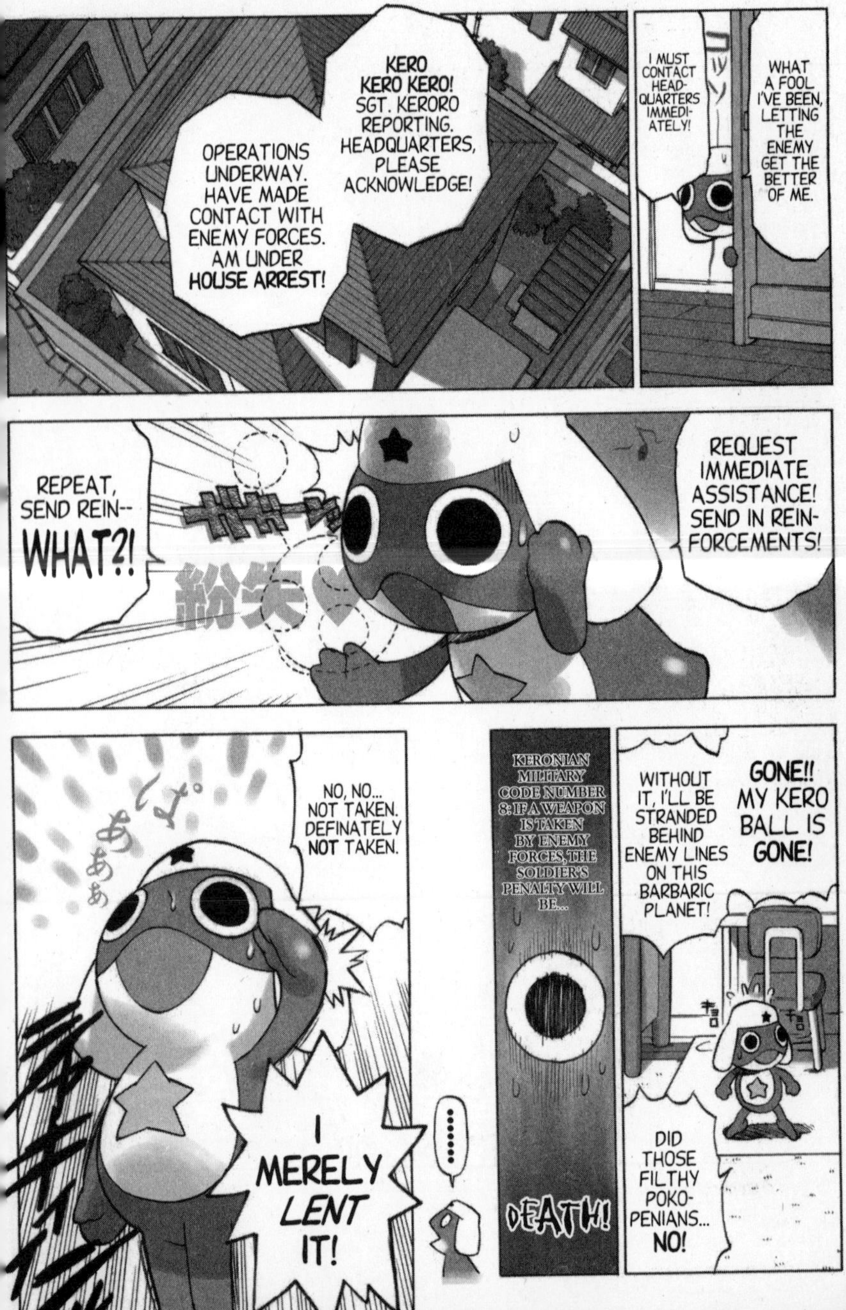
WHAT A FOOL I'VE BEEN, LETTING THE ENEMY GET THE BETTER OF ME.
I MUST CONTACT HEAD-QUARTERS IMMEDI-ATELY!
KERO KERO KERO! SGT. KERORO REPORTING. HEADQUARTERS, PLEASE ACKNOWLEDGE!
OPERATIONS UNDERWAY. HAVE MADE CONTACT WITH ENEMY FORCES. AM UNDER HOUSE ARREST!
REQUEST IMMEDIATE ASSISTANCE! SEND IN REIN-FORCEMENTS!
REPEAT, SEND REIN-- WHAT?!
紛失
GONE!! MY KERO BALL IS GONE!
WITHOUT IT, I'LL BE STRANDED BEHIND ENEMY LINES ON THIS BARBARIC PLANET!
DID THOSE FILTHY POKO-PENIANS... NO!
KERONIAN MILITARY CODE NUMBER 8: IF A WEAPON IS TAKEN BY ENEMY FORCES, THE SOLDIER'S PENALTY WILL BE...
DEATH!
NO, NO... NOT TAKEN. DEFINATELY NOT TAKEN.
I MERELY LENT IT!
......

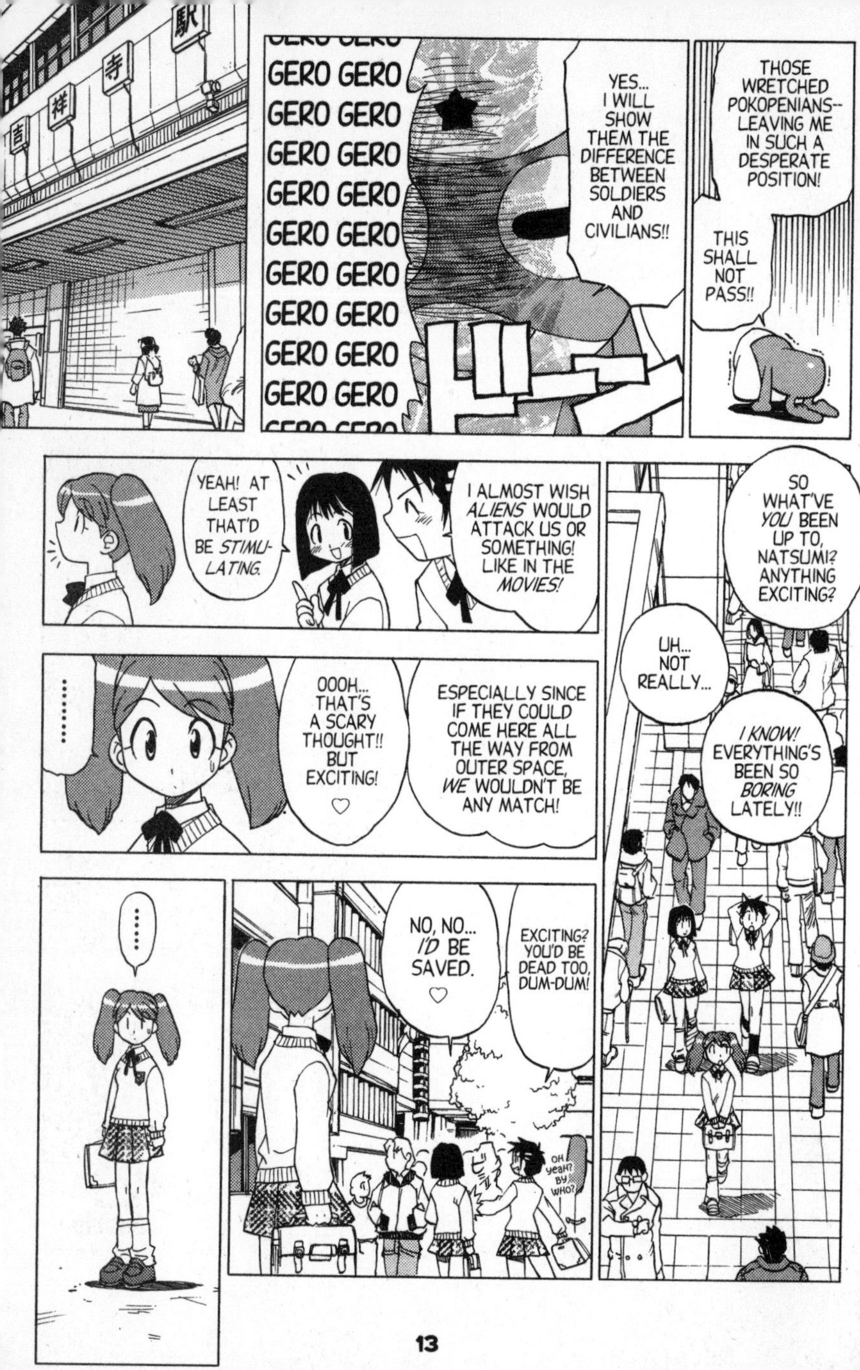
THOSE WRETCHED POKOPENIANS-- LEAVING ME IN SUCH A DESPERATE POSITION!
THIS SHALL NOT PASS!!
YES... I WILL SHOW THEM THE DIFFERENCE BETWEEN SOLDIERS AND CIVILIANS!!
GERO GERO
GERO GERO
GERO GERO
GERO GERO
GERO GERO
GERO GERO
GERO GERO
GERO GERO
GERO GERO
GERO GERO
吉祥寺駅
SO WHAT'VE *YOU* BEEN UP TO, NATSUMI? ANYTHING EXCITING?
UH... NOT REALLY...
I KNOW! EVERYTHING'S BEEN SO *BORING* LATELY!!
I ALMOST WISH *ALIENS* WOULD ATTACK US OR SOMETHING! LIKE IN THE *MOVIES!*
YEAH! AT LEAST THAT'D BE *STIMULATING.*
ESPECIALLY SINCE IF THEY COULD COME HERE ALL THE WAY FROM OUTER SPACE, *WE* WOULDN'T BE ANY MATCH!
OOOH... THAT'S A SCARY THOUGHT!! BUT EXCITING! ♡
....
EXCITING? YOU'D BE DEAD TOO, DUM-DUM!
NO, NO... *I'D* BE SAVED. ♡
OH YEAH? BY WHO?
......

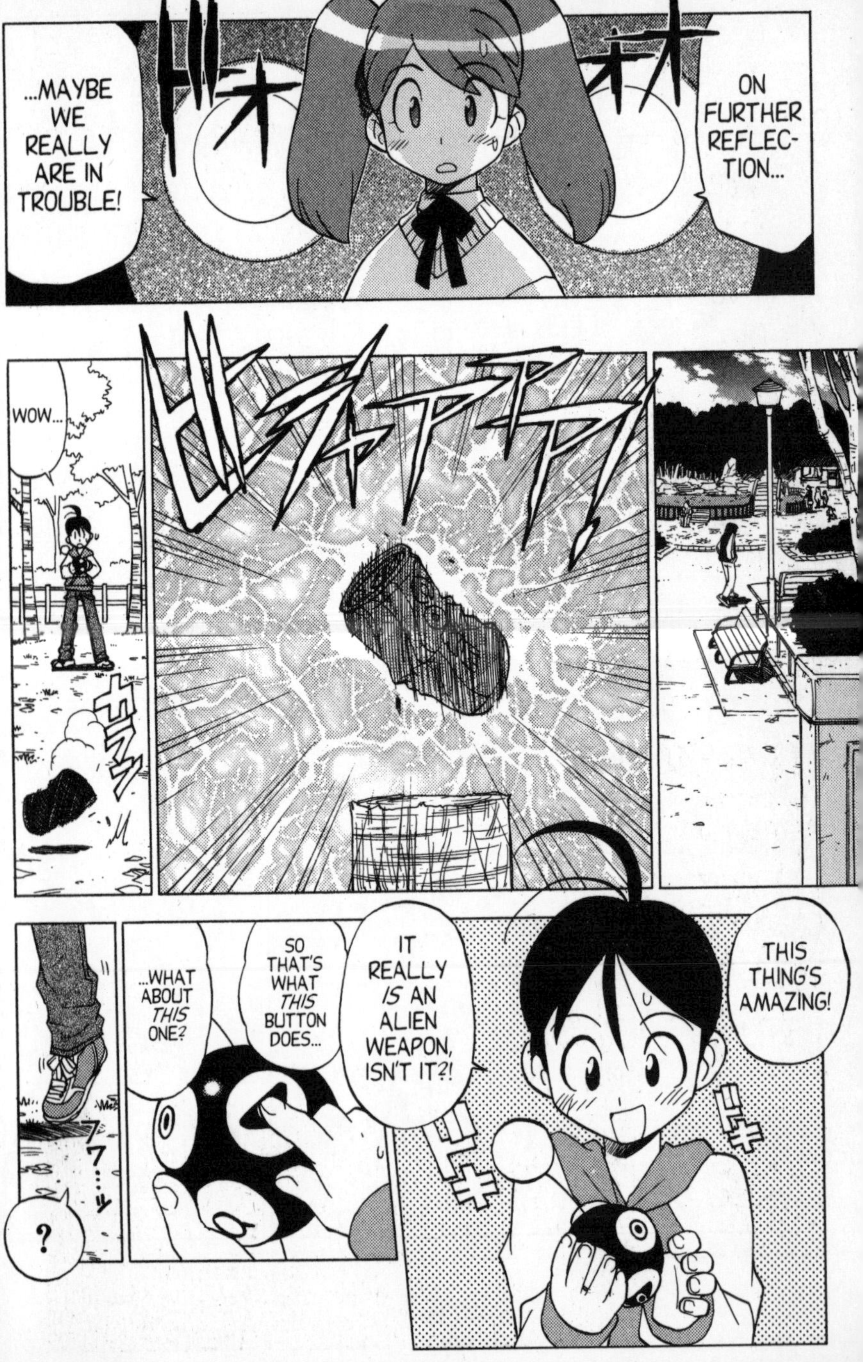
ON FURTHER REFLECTION...
...MAYBE WE REALLY ARE IN TROUBLE!
WOW...
THIS THING'S AMAZING!
IT REALLY *IS* AN ALIEN WEAPON, ISN'T IT?!
SO THAT'S WHAT *THIS* BUTTON DOES...
...WHAT ABOUT *THIS* ONE?
?

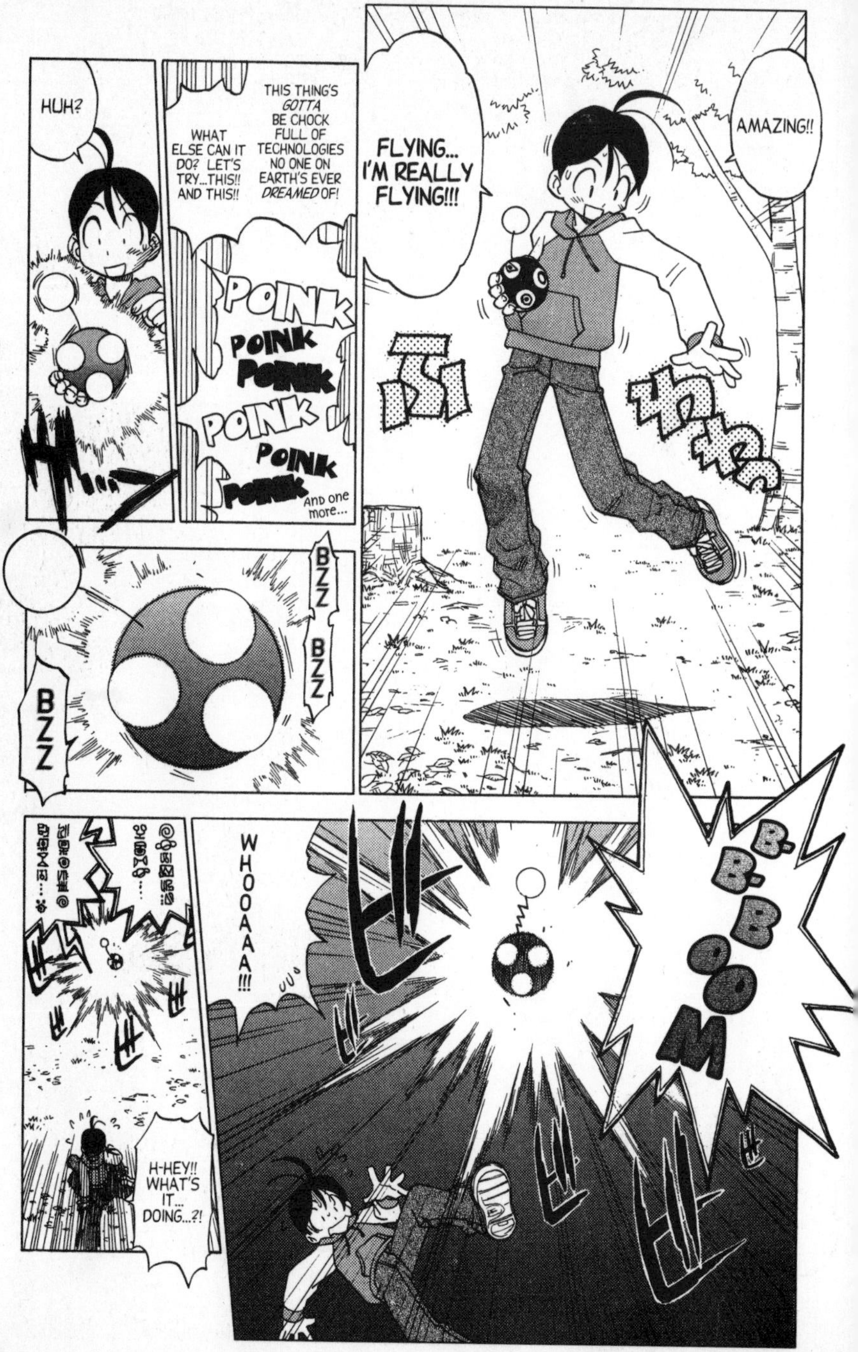
AMAZING!!
FLYING... I'M REALLY FLYING!!!
THIS THING'S GOTTA BE CHOCK FULL OF TECHNOLOGIES NO ONE ON EARTH'S EVER DREAMED OF!
WHAT ELSE CAN IT DO? LET'S TRY...THIS!! AND THIS!!
POINK POINK POINK POINK POINK POINK
And one more...
HUH?
BZZ BZZ
BZZ
B-B-BOOOM
WHOOOAAA!!!
H-HEY!! WHAT'S IT... DOING...?!

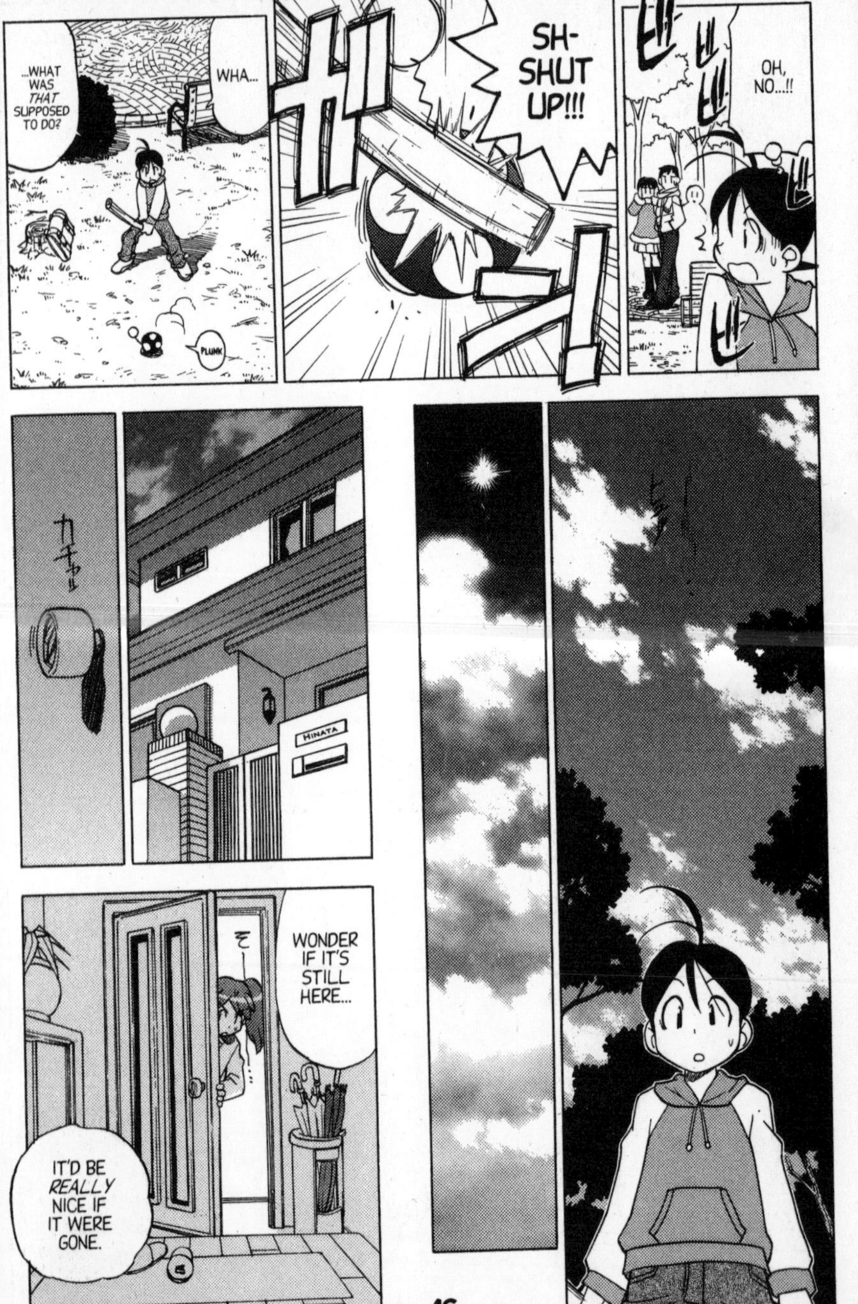
OH, NO...!!
SH-SHUT UP!!!
WHA...
...WHAT WAS *THAT* SUPPOSED TO DO?
PLUNK
HINATA
WONDER IF IT'S STILL HERE...
IT'D BE *REALLY* NICE IF IT WERE GONE.

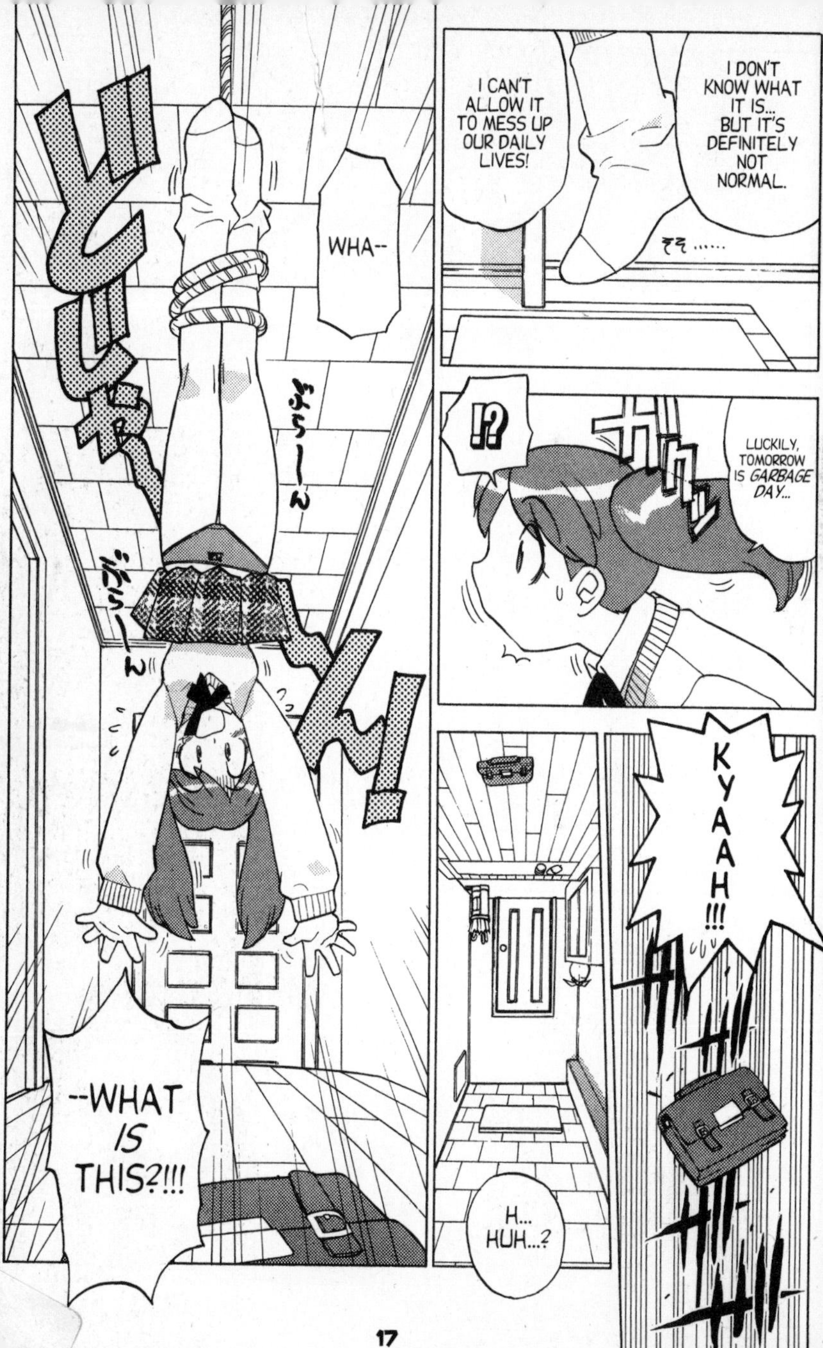

I DON'T KNOW WHAT IT IS... BUT IT'S DEFINITELY NOT NORMAL.
I CAN'T ALLOW IT TO MESS UP OUR DAILY LIVES!
LUCKILY, TOMORROW IS GARBAGE DAY...
!?
KYAAH!!!
H... HUH...?
WHA--
--WHAT IS THIS?!!!

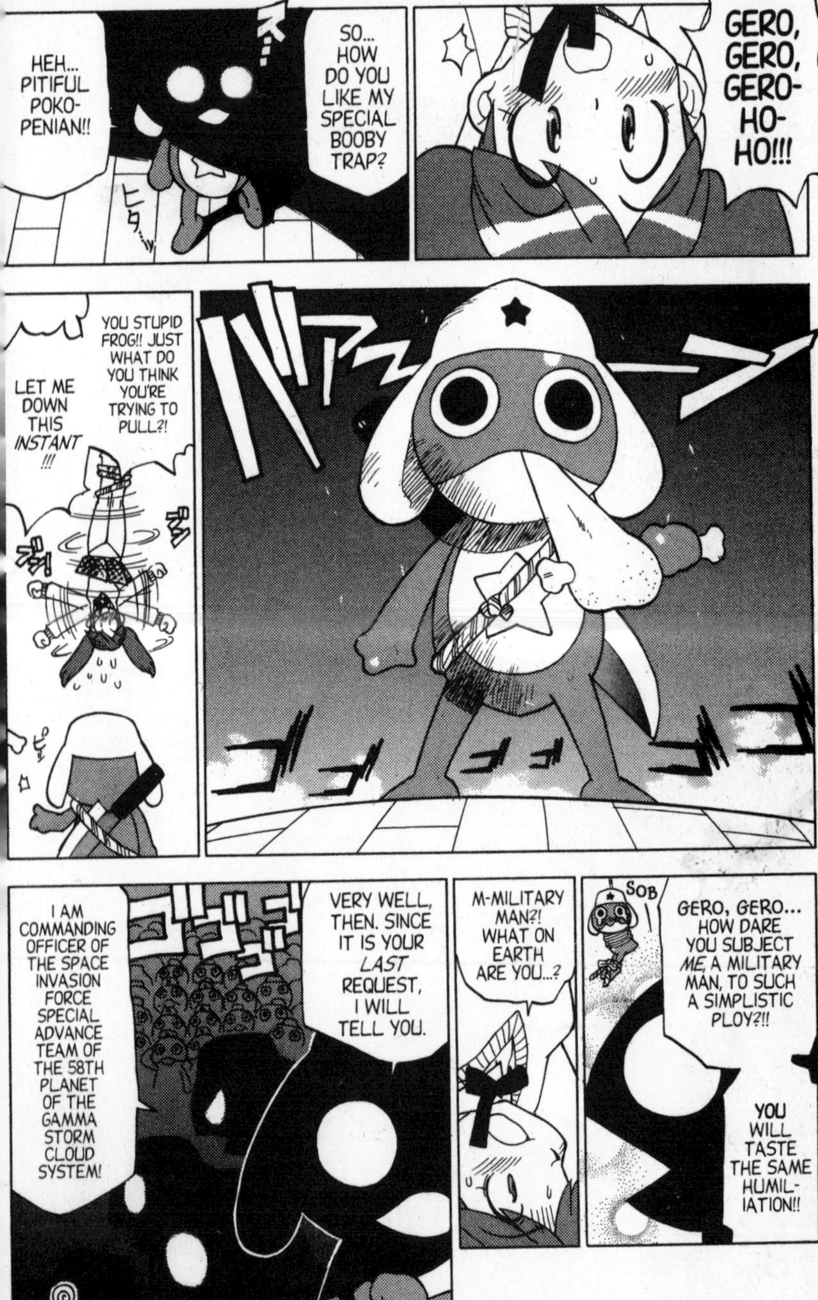
GERO, GERO, GERO-HO-HO!!!
SO... HOW DO YOU LIKE MY SPECIAL BOOBY TRAP?
HEH... PITIFUL POKO-PENIAN!!
YOU STUPID FROG!! JUST WHAT DO YOU THINK YOU'RE TRYING TO PULL?!
LET ME DOWN THIS INSTANT!!!
SOB
GERO, GERO... HOW DARE YOU SUBJECT ME, A MILITARY MAN, TO SUCH A SIMPLISTIC PLOY?!!
YOU WILL TASTE THE SAME HUMILIATION!!
M-MILITARY MAN?! WHAT ON EARTH ARE YOU...?
VERY WELL, THEN. SINCE IT IS YOUR LAST REQUEST, I WILL TELL YOU.
I AM COMMANDING OFFICER OF THE SPACE INVASION FORCE SPECIAL ADVANCE TEAM OF THE 58TH PLANET OF THE GAMMA STORM CLOUD SYSTEM!

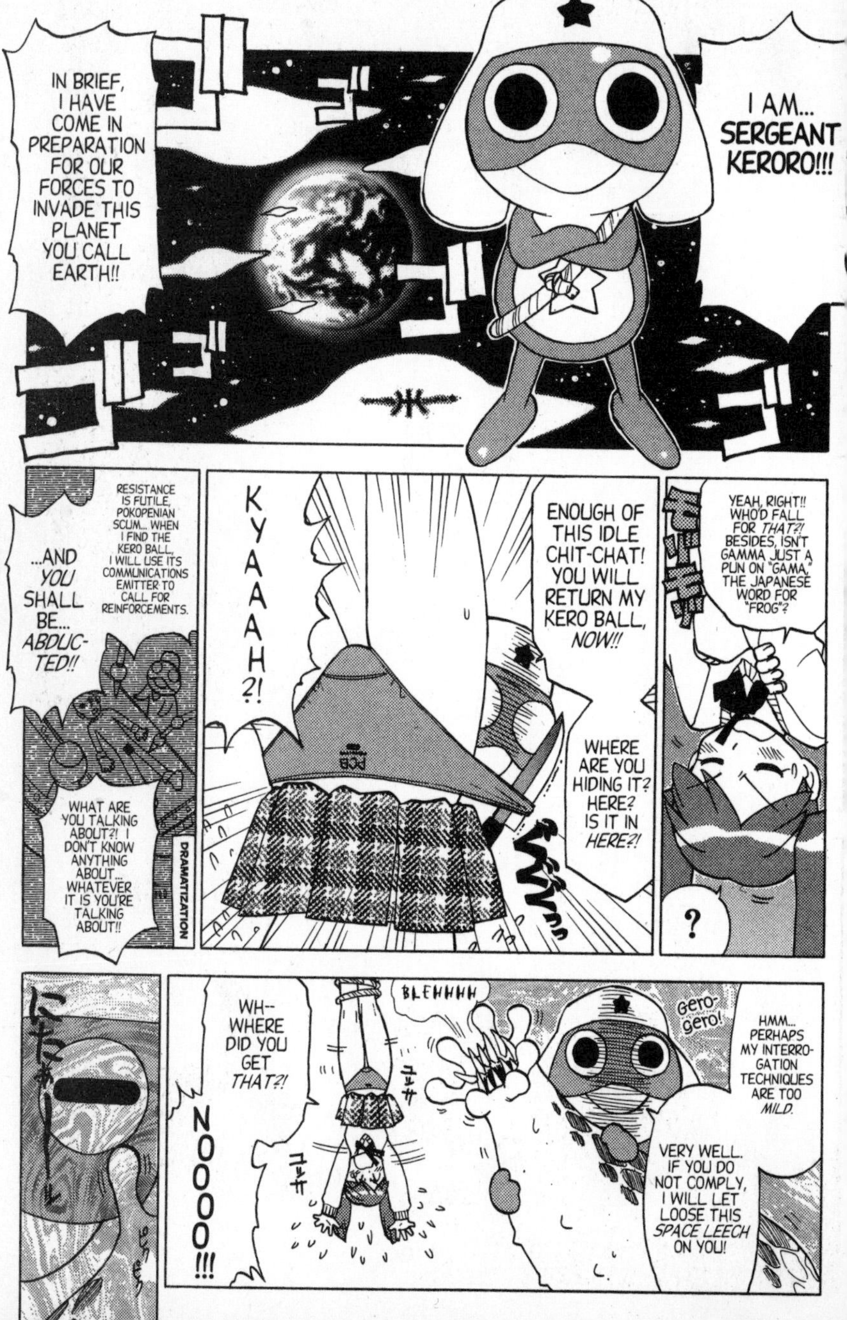
I AM... SERGEANT KERORO!!!
IN BRIEF, I HAVE COME IN PREPARATION FOR OUR FORCES TO INVADE THIS PLANET YOU CALL EARTH!!
YEAH, RIGHT!! WHO'D FALL FOR THAT?! BESIDES, ISN'T GAMMA JUST A PUN ON "GAMA," THE JAPANESE WORD FOR "FROG"?
?
ENOUGH OF THIS IDLE CHIT-CHAT! YOU WILL RETURN MY KERO BALL, NOW!!
WHERE ARE YOU HIDING IT? HERE? IS IT IN HERE?!
KYAAAAH?!
RESISTANCE IS FUTILE, POKOPENIAN SCUM... WHEN I FIND THE KERO BALL, I WILL USE ITS COMMUNICATIONS EMITTER TO CALL FOR REINFORCEMENTS.
...AND YOU SHALL BE... ABDUCTED!!
WHAT ARE YOU TALKING ABOUT?! I DON'T KNOW ANYTHING ABOUT... WHATEVER IT IS YOU'RE TALKING ABOUT!!
DRAMATIZATION
HMM... PERHAPS MY INTERROGATION TECHNIQUES ARE TOO MILD.
Gero-gero!
BLEHHHH
VERY WELL. IF YOU DO NOT COMPLY, I WILL LET LOOSE THIS SPACE LEECH ON YOU!
WH-- WHERE DID YOU GET THAT?!
NOOOOO!!!

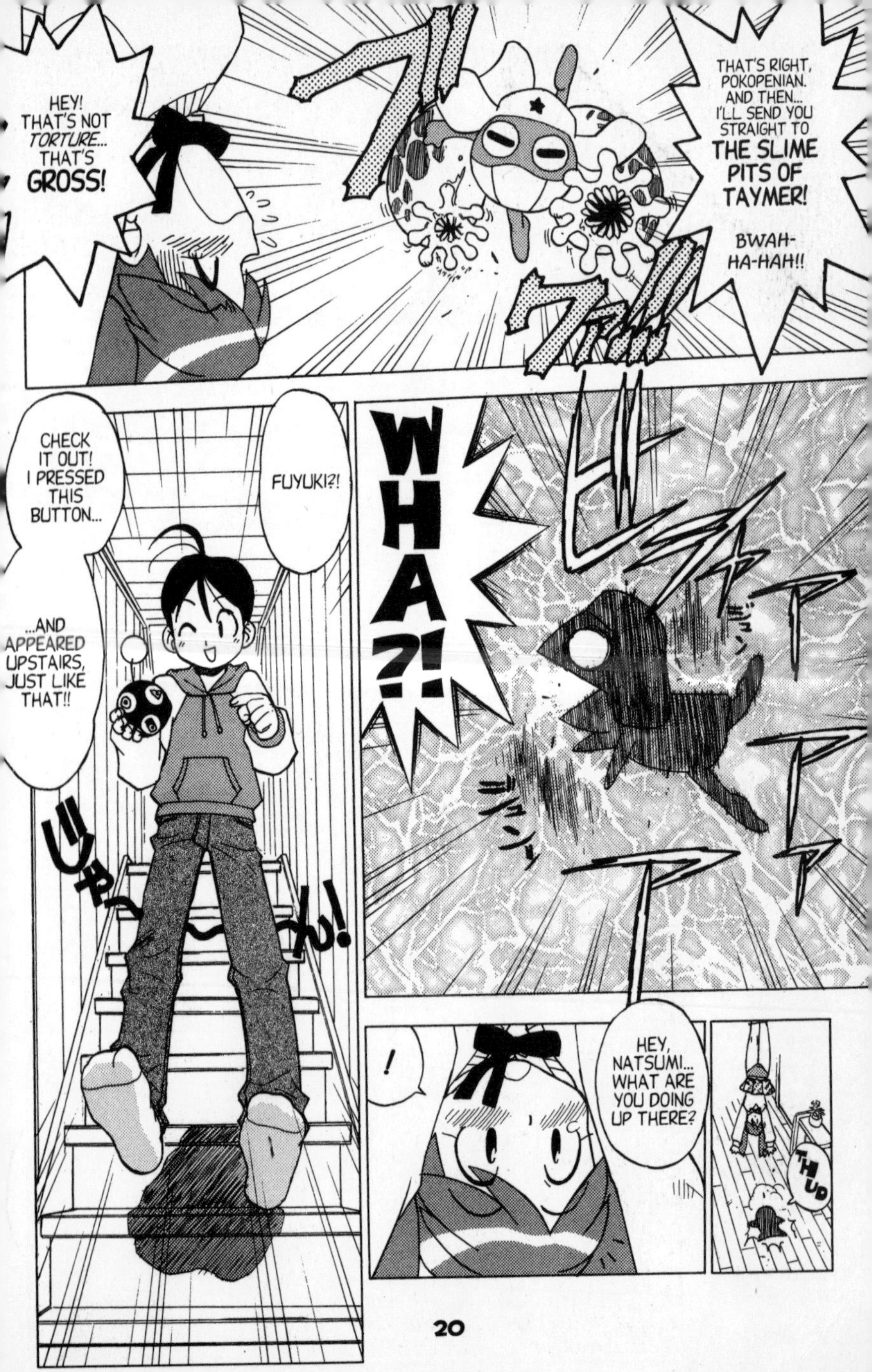
THAT'S RIGHT, POKOPENIAN. AND THEN... I'LL SEND YOU STRAIGHT TO THE SLIME PITS OF TAYMER!
BWAH-HA-HAH!!
HEY! THAT'S NOT TORTURE... THAT'S GROSS!
WHA?!
THUD
HEY, NATSUMI... WHAT ARE YOU DOING UP THERE?
!
FUYUKI?!
CHECK IT OUT! I PRESSED THIS BUTTON...
...AND APPEARED UPSTAIRS, JUST LIKE THAT!!

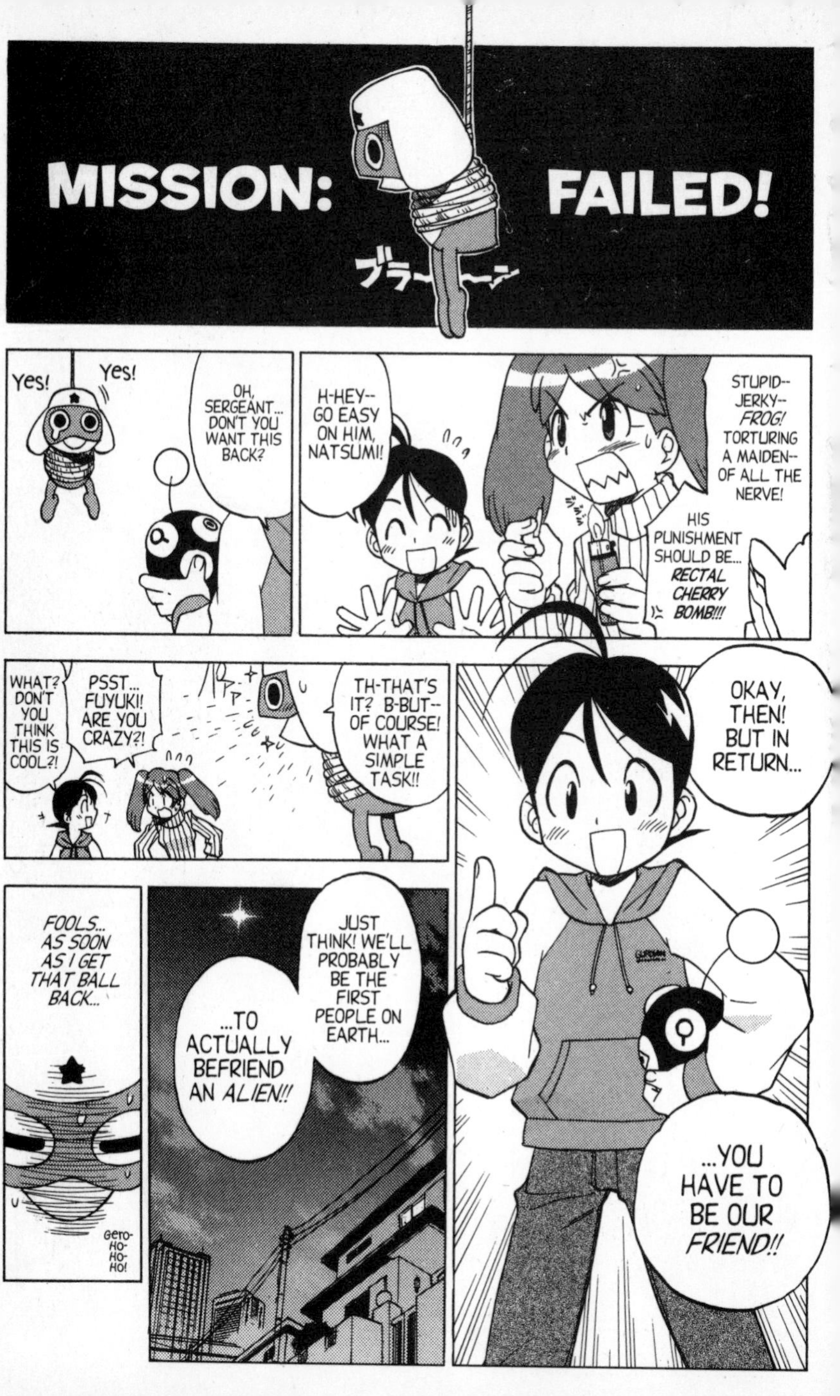
MISSION: FAILED!
ブラ〜〜ン
STUPID-- JERKY-- *FROG!* TORTURING A MAIDEN-- OF ALL THE NERVE!
HIS PUNISHMENT SHOULD BE... *RECTAL CHERRY BOMB!!!*
H-HEY-- GO EASY ON HIM, NATSUMI!
OH, SERGEANT... DON'T YOU WANT THIS BACK?
Yes!
Yes!
OKAY, THEN! BUT IN RETURN...
...YOU HAVE TO BE OUR *FRIEND!!*
TH-THAT'S IT? B-BUT-- OF COURSE! WHAT A SIMPLE TASK!!
PSST... FUYUKI! ARE YOU CRAZY?!
WHAT?! DON'T YOU THINK THIS IS COOL?!
JUST THINK! WE'LL PROBABLY BE THE FIRST PEOPLE ON EARTH...
...TO ACTUALLY BEFRIEND AN *ALIEN!!*
FOOLS... AS SOON AS I GET THAT BALL BACK...
GERO-HO-HO-HO!

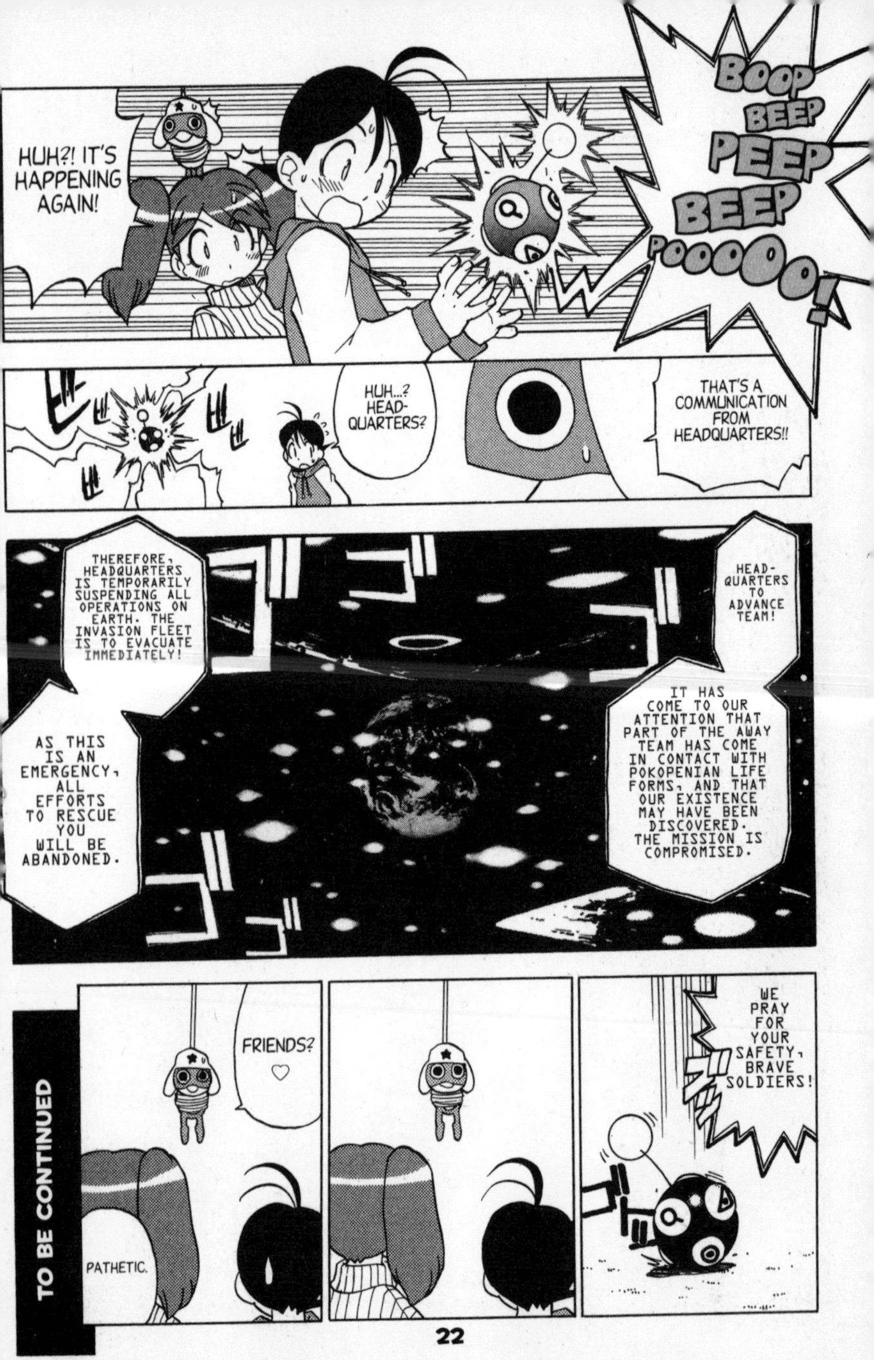
BOOP BEEP PEEP BEEP POOOOOO!
HUH?! IT'S HAPPENING AGAIN!
THAT'S A COMMUNICATION FROM HEADQUARTERS!!
HUH...? HEAD-QUARTERS?
HEAD-QUARTERS TO ADVANCE TEAM!
IT HAS COME TO OUR ATTENTION THAT PART OF THE AWAY TEAM HAS COME IN CONTACT WITH POKOPENIAN LIFE FORMS, AND THAT OUR EXISTENCE MAY HAVE BEEN DISCOVERED. THE MISSION IS COMPROMISED.
THEREFORE, HEADQUARTERS IS TEMPORARILY SUSPENDING ALL OPERATIONS ON EARTH. THE INVASION FLEET IS TO EVACUATE IMMEDIATELY!
AS THIS IS AN EMERGENCY, ALL EFFORTS TO RESCUE YOU WILL BE ABANDONED.
WE PRAY FOR YOUR SAFETY, BRAVE SOLDIERS!
FRIENDS? ♡
PATHETIC.
TO BE CONTINUED

ENCOUNTER 11

AN AUDIENCE WITH GENERAL MOM

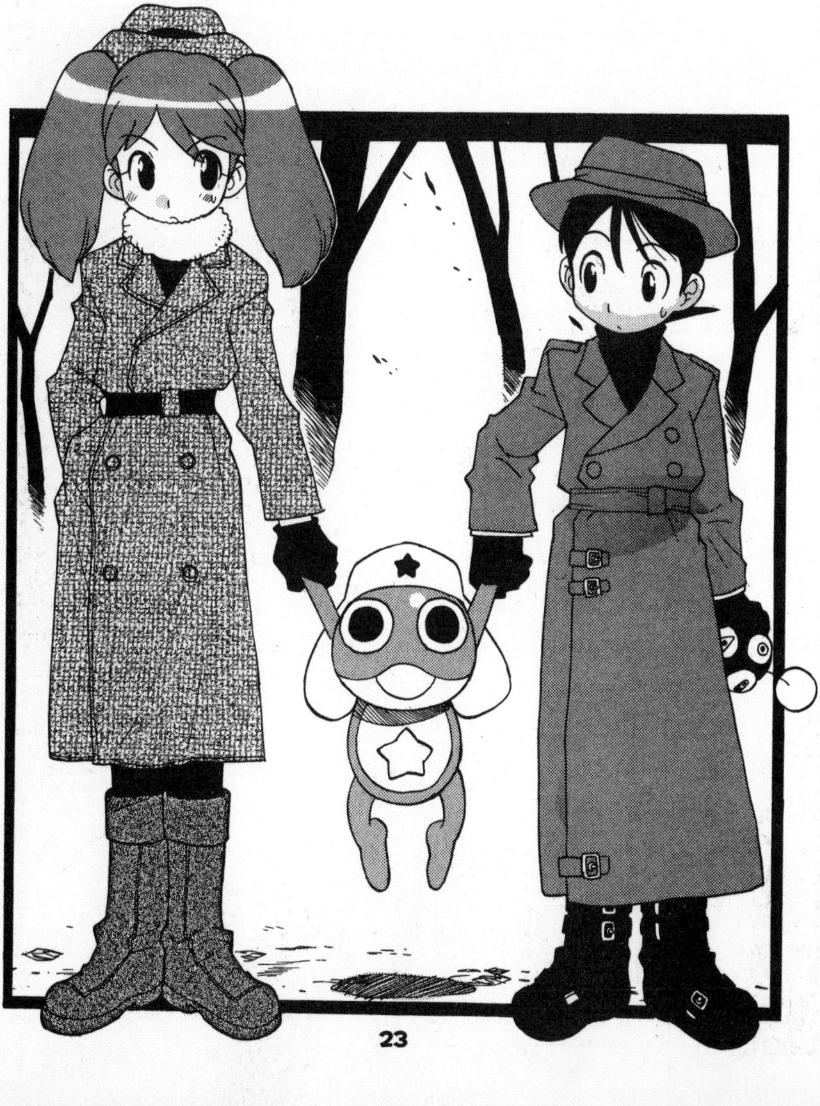

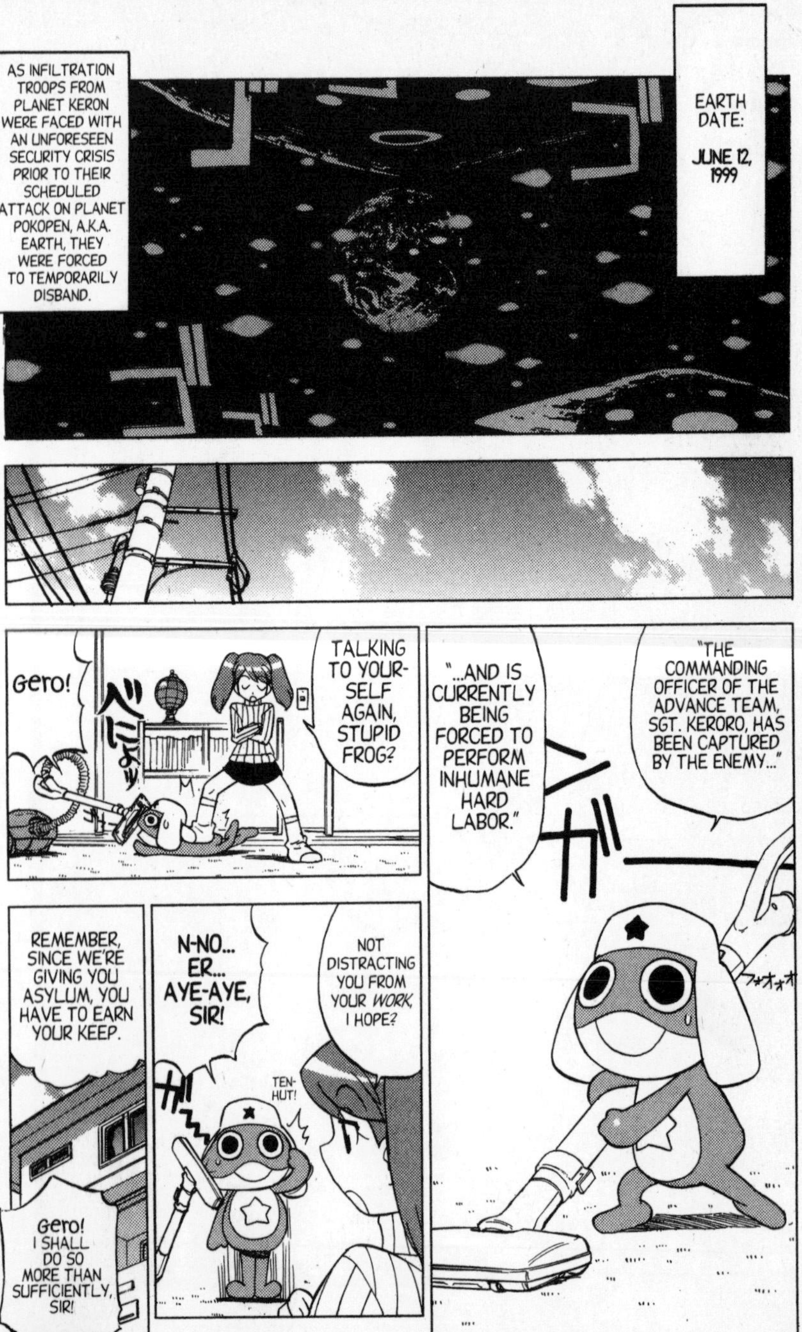
EARTH DATE:
JUNE 12, 1999
AS INFILTRATION TROOPS FROM PLANET KERON WERE FACED WITH AN UNFORESEEN SECURITY CRISIS PRIOR TO THEIR SCHEDULED ATTACK ON PLANET POKOPEN, A.K.A. EARTH, THEY WERE FORCED TO TEMPORARILY DISBAND.
"THE COMMANDING OFFICER OF THE ADVANCE TEAM, SGT. KERORO, HAS BEEN CAPTURED BY THE ENEMY..."
"...AND IS CURRENTLY BEING FORCED TO PERFORM INHUMANE HARD LABOR."
ガー
フォオオオ
TALKING TO YOURSELF AGAIN, STUPID FROG?
Gero!
べにょッ
NOT DISTRACTING YOU FROM YOUR *WORK*, I HOPE?
N-NO... ER... AYE-AYE, SIR!
TEN-HUT!
REMEMBER, SINCE WE'RE GIVING YOU ASYLUM, YOU HAVE TO EARN YOUR KEEP.
Gero! I SHALL DO SO MORE THAN SUFFICIENTLY, SIR!

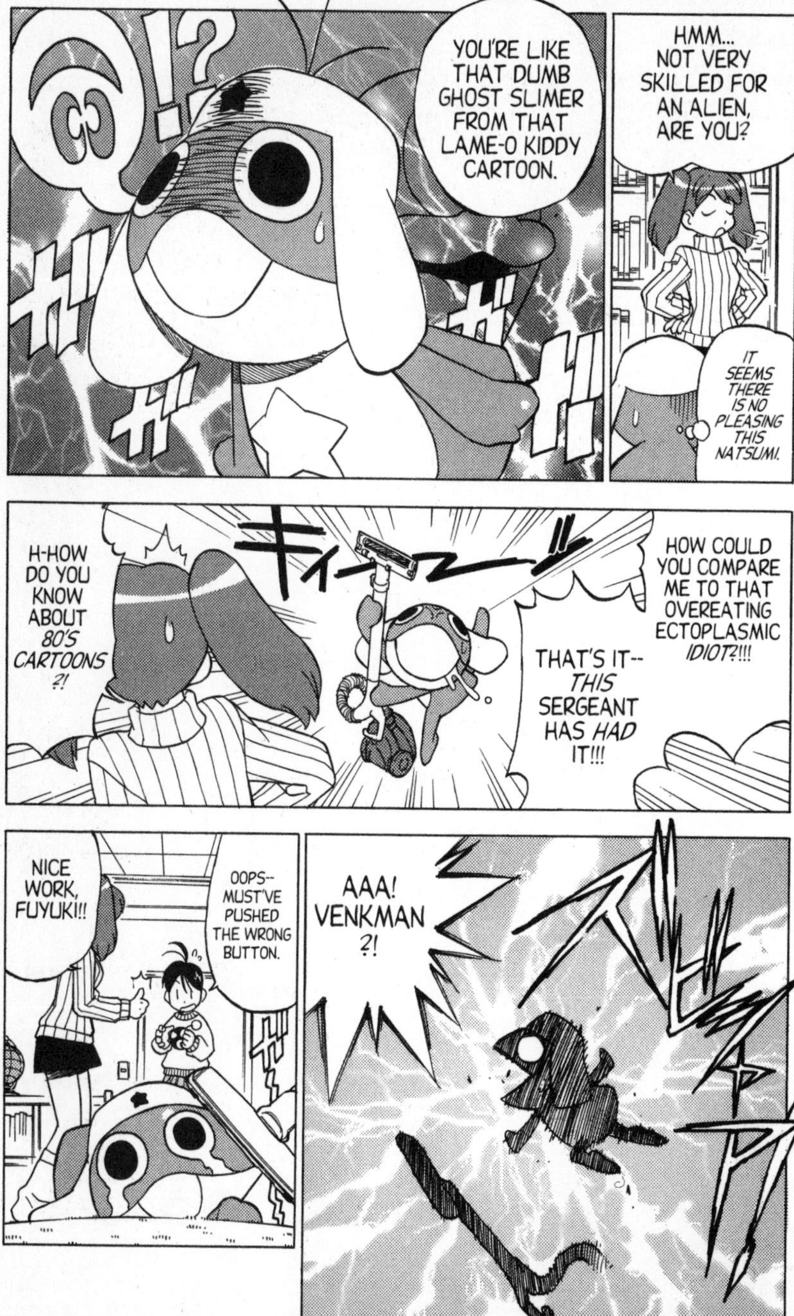
HMM... NOT VERY SKILLED FOR AN ALIEN, ARE YOU?
IT SEEMS THERE IS NO PLEASING THIS NATSUMI.
YOU'RE LIKE THAT DUMB GHOST SLIMER FROM THAT LAME-O KIDDY CARTOON.
!?
HOW COULD YOU COMPARE ME TO THAT OVEREATING ECTOPLASMIC IDIOT?!!!
THAT'S IT-- THIS SERGEANT HAS HAD IT!!!
H-HOW DO YOU KNOW ABOUT 80'S CARTOONS ?!
AAA! VENKMAN ?!
OOPS-- MUST'VE PUSHED THE WRONG BUTTON.
NICE WORK, FUYUKI!!

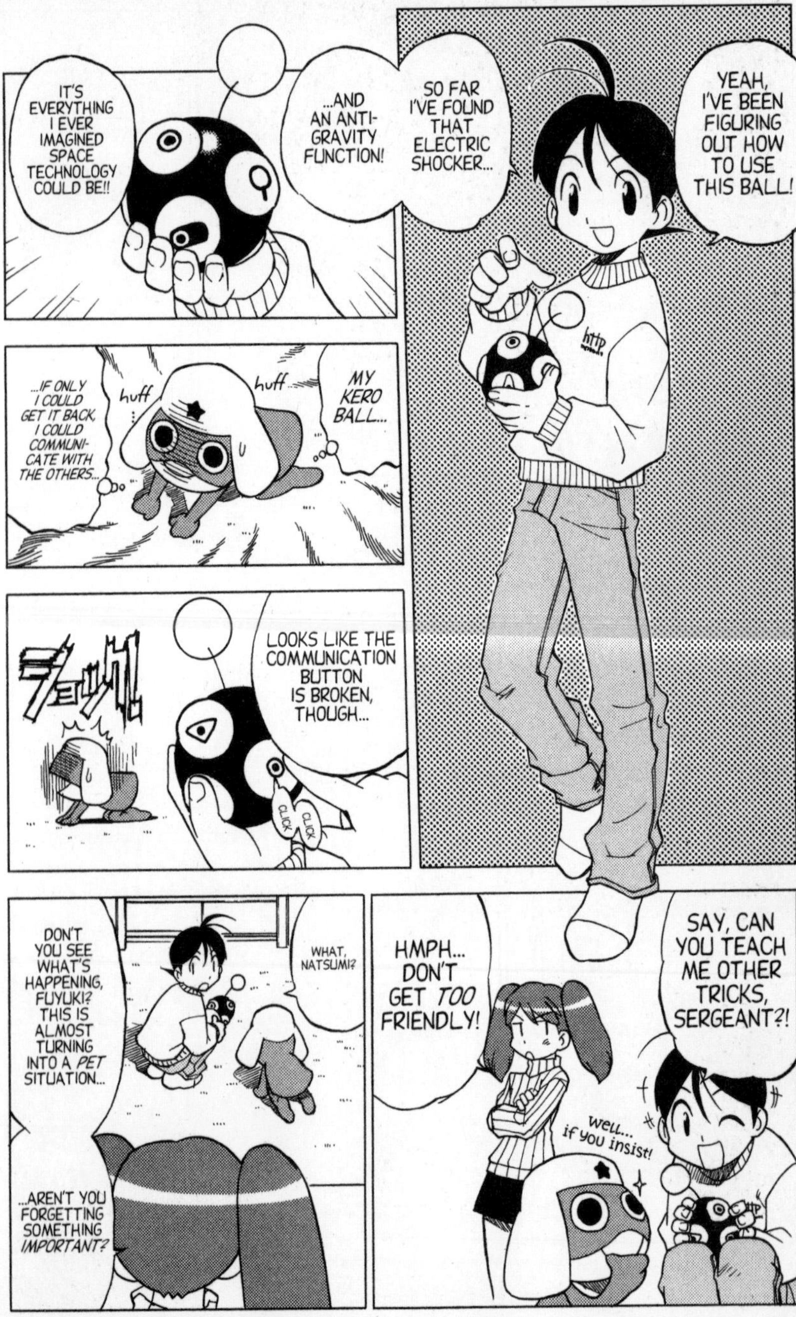
YEAH, I'VE BEEN FIGURING OUT HOW TO USE THIS BALL!
SO FAR I'VE FOUND THAT ELECTRIC SHOCKER...
...AND AN ANTI-GRAVITY FUNCTION!
IT'S EVERYTHING I EVER IMAGINED SPACE TECHNOLOGY COULD BE!!
MY KERO BALL...
huff huff
...IF ONLY I COULD GET IT BACK, I COULD COMMUNICATE WITH THE OTHERS...
LOOKS LIKE THE COMMUNICATION BUTTON IS BROKEN, THOUGH...
CLICK CLICK
ショック!
SAY, CAN YOU TEACH ME OTHER TRICKS, SERGEANT?!
well... if you insist!
HMPH... DON'T GET *TOO* FRIENDLY!
WHAT, NATSUMI?
DON'T YOU SEE WHAT'S HAPPENING, FUYUKI? THIS IS ALMOST TURNING INTO A *PET* SITUATION...
...AREN'T YOU FORGETTING SOMETHING *IMPORTANT*?

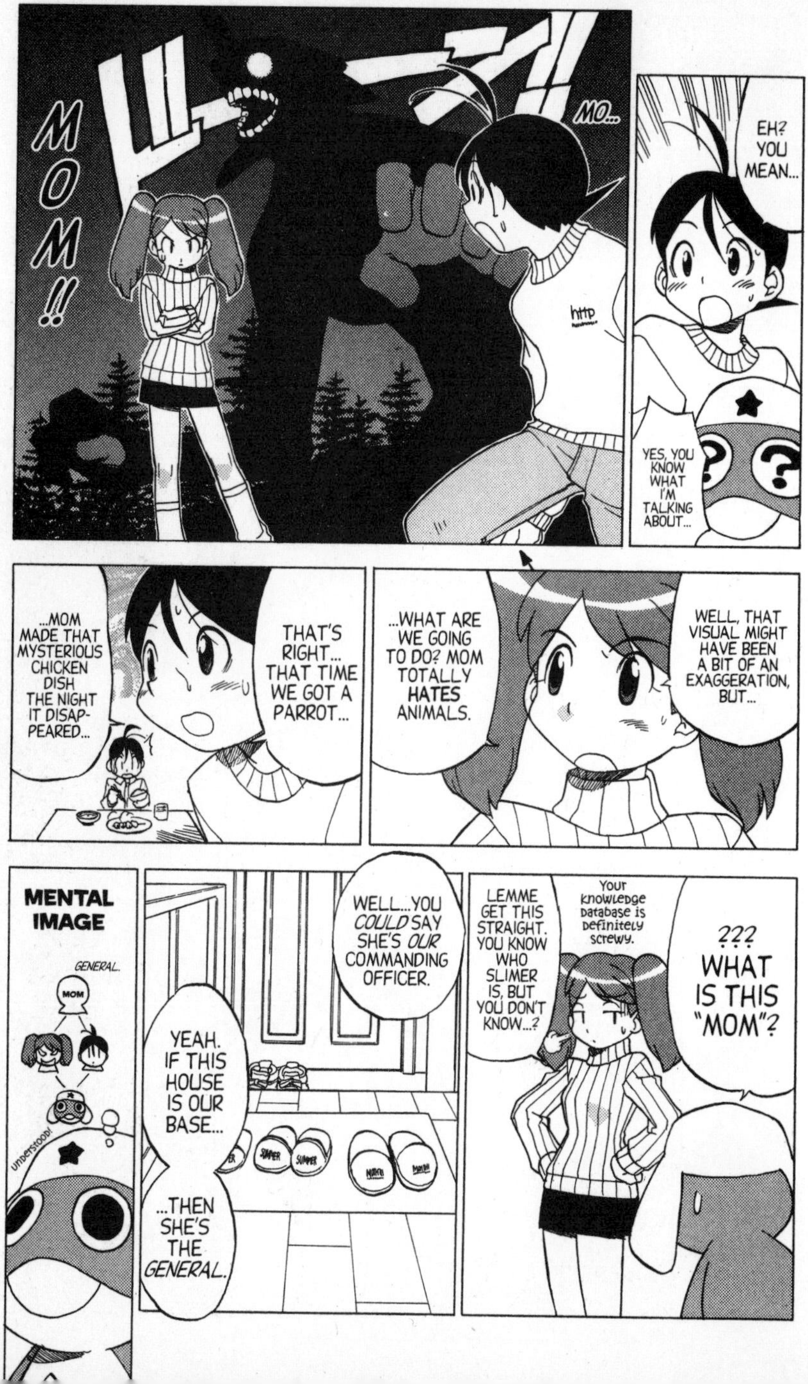
EH? YOU MEAN...
YES, YOU KNOW WHAT I'M TALKING ABOUT...
MO...
MOM!!
WELL, THAT VISUAL MIGHT HAVE BEEN A BIT OF AN EXAGGERATION, BUT...
...WHAT ARE WE GOING TO DO? MOM TOTALLY HATES ANIMALS.
THAT'S RIGHT... THAT TIME WE GOT A PARROT...
...MOM MADE THAT MYSTERIOUS CHICKEN DISH THE NIGHT IT DISAPPEARED...
??? WHAT IS THIS "MOM"?
Your knowledge database is definitely screwy.
LEMME GET THIS STRAIGHT. YOU KNOW WHO SLIMER IS, BUT YOU DON'T KNOW...?
WELL...YOU COULD SAY SHE'S OUR COMMANDING OFFICER.
YEAH. IF THIS HOUSE IS OUR BASE...
...THEN SHE'S THE GENERAL.
MENTAL IMAGE
GENERAL.
MOM
UNDERSTOOD!

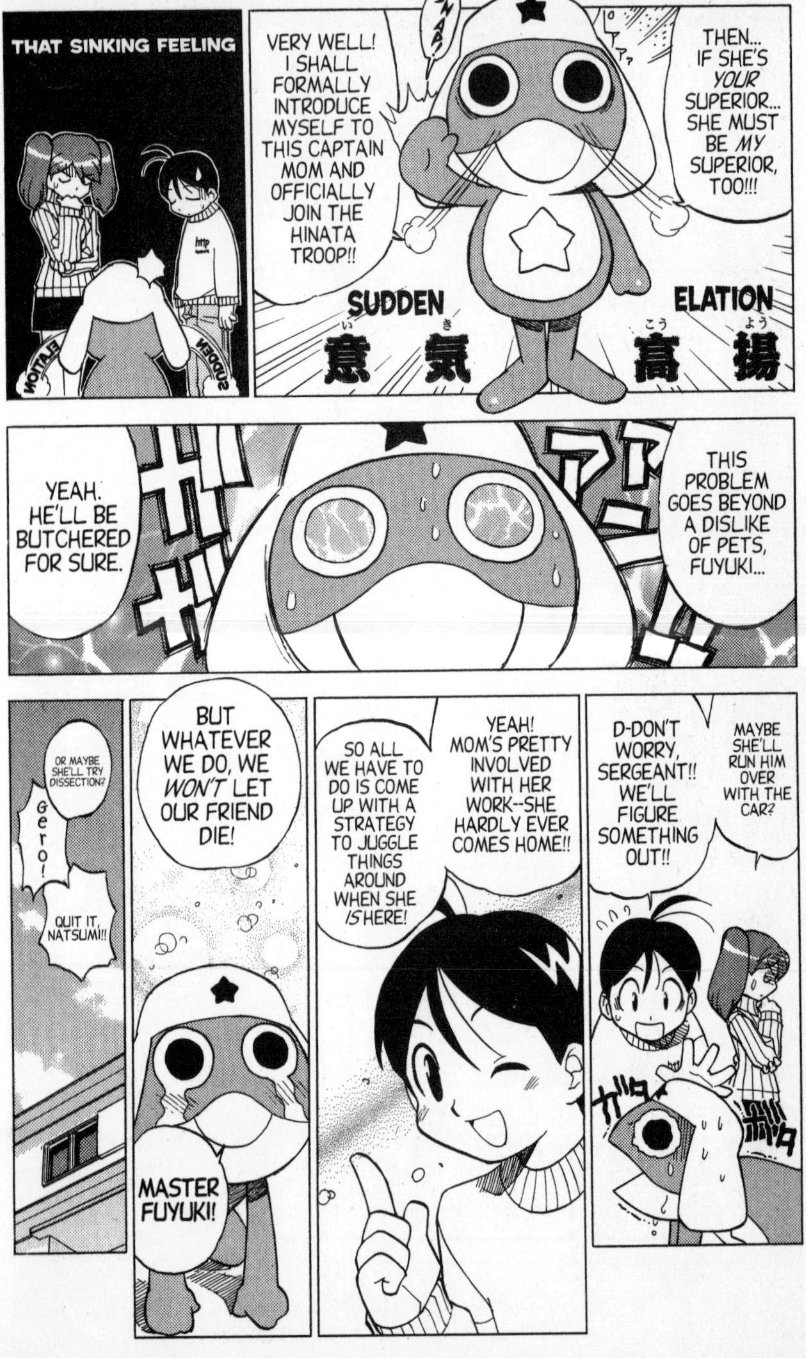
THEN... IF SHE'S *YOUR* SUPERIOR... SHE MUST BE *MY* SUPERIOR, TOO!!!
SNAP!
VERY WELL! I SHALL FORMALLY INTRODUCE MYSELF TO THIS CAPTAIN MOM AND OFFICIALLY JOIN THE HINATA TROOP!!
SUDDEN ELATION
意気高揚
THAT SINKING FEELING
SUDDEN
ELATION
THIS PROBLEM GOES BEYOND A DISLIKE OF PETS, FUYUKI...
YEAH. HE'LL BE BUTCHERED FOR SURE.
MAYBE SHE'LL RUN HIM OVER WITH THE CAR?
D-DON'T WORRY, SERGEANT!! WE'LL FIGURE SOMETHING OUT!!
YEAH! MOM'S PRETTY INVOLVED WITH HER WORK--SHE HARDLY EVER COMES HOME!!
SO ALL WE HAVE TO DO IS COME UP WITH A STRATEGY TO JUGGLE THINGS AROUND WHEN SHE *IS* HERE!
BUT WHATEVER WE DO, WE *WON'T* LET OUR FRIEND DIE!
MASTER FUYUKI!
OR MAYBE SHE'LL TRY DISSECTION?
Gero!
QUIT IT, NATSUMI!!

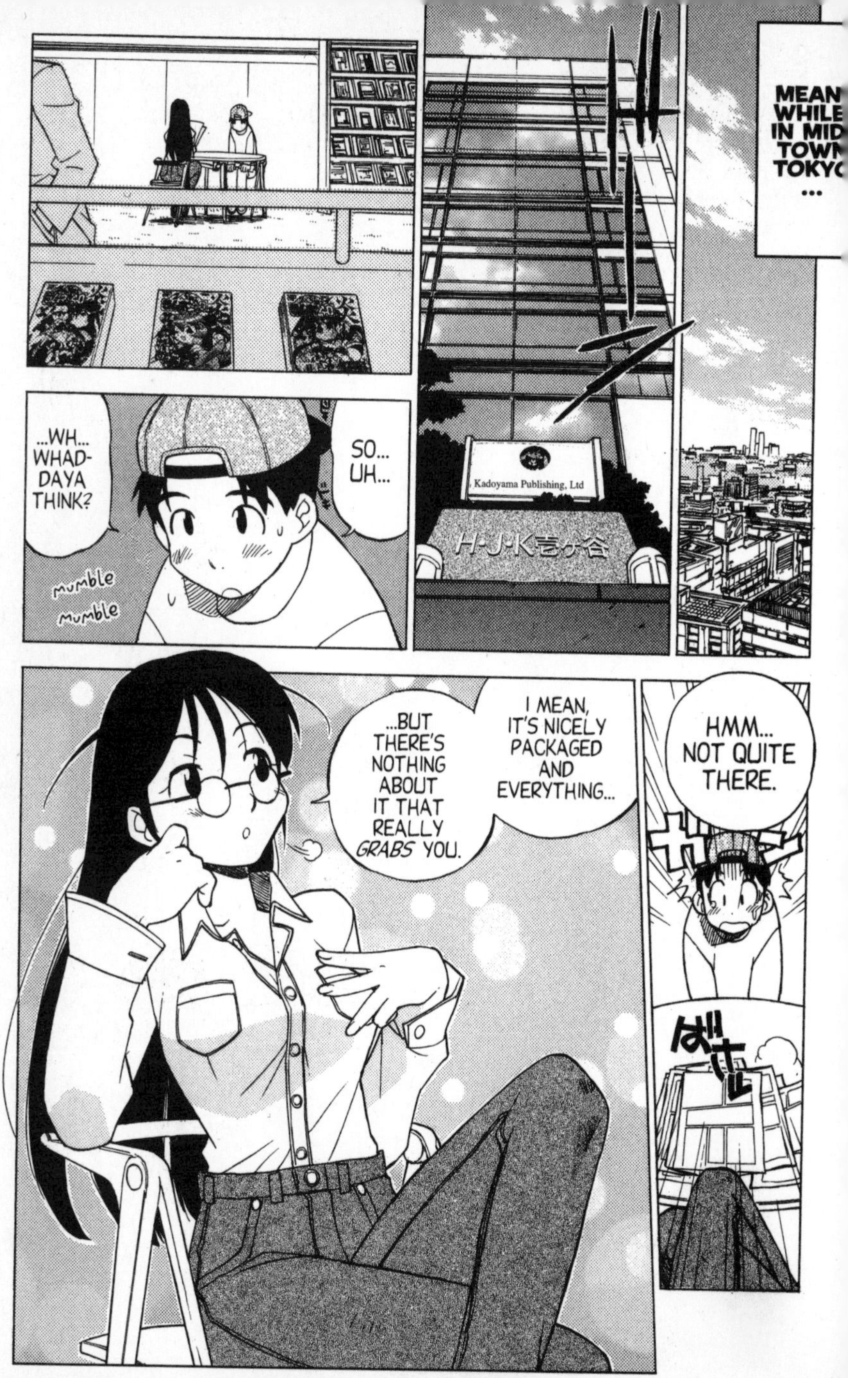
MEAN
WHILE
IN MID
TOWN
TOKYO
...
Kadoyama Publishing, Ltd
SO... UH...
...WH... WHAD-DAYA THINK?
mumble mumble
HMM... NOT QUITE THERE.
I MEAN, IT'S NICELY PACKAGED AND EVERYTHING...
...BUT THERE'S NOTHING ABOUT IT THAT REALLY *GRABS* YOU.

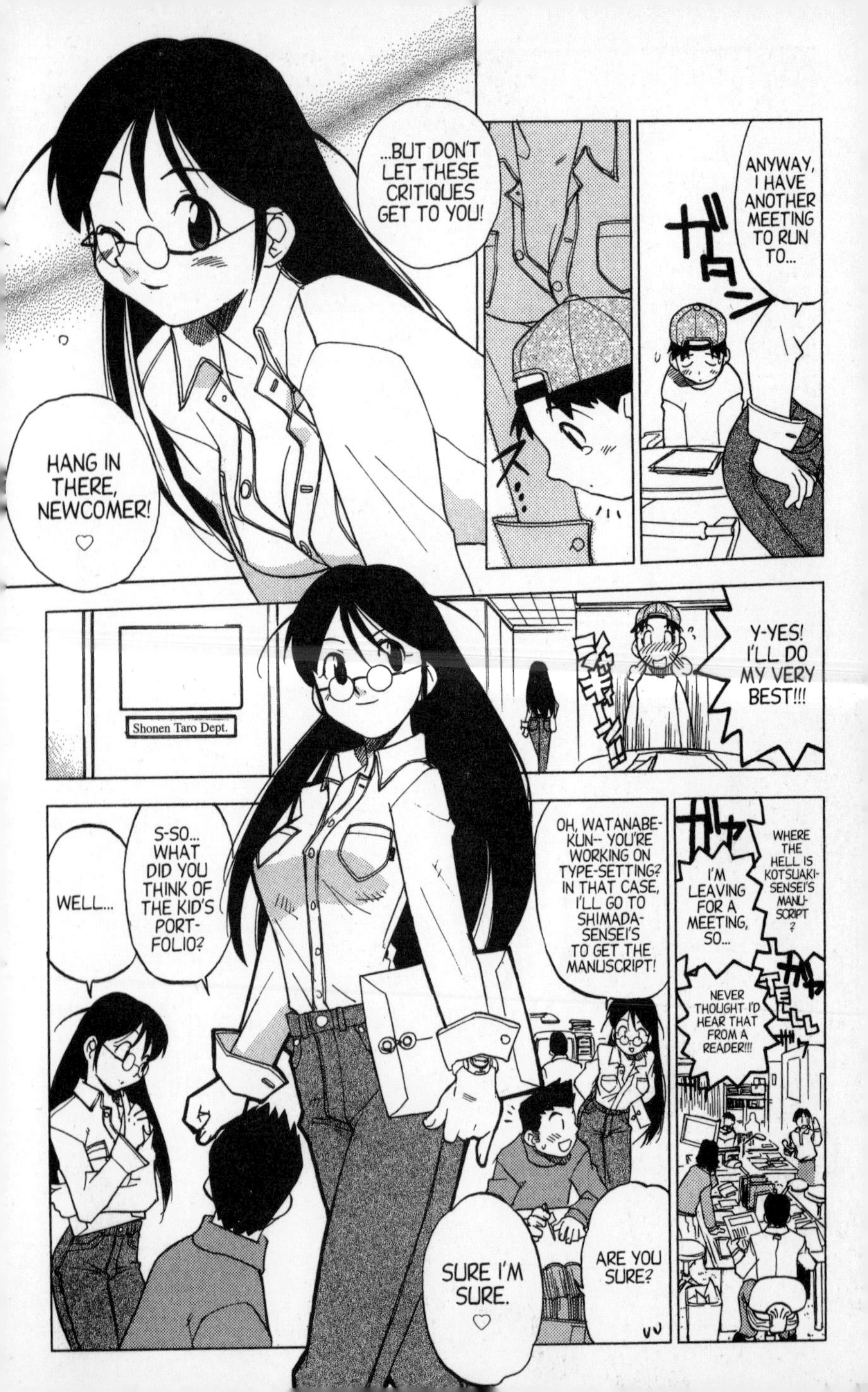
ANYWAY, I HAVE ANOTHER MEETING TO RUN TO...
...BUT DON'T LET THESE CRITIQUES GET TO YOU!
HANG IN THERE, NEWCOMER! ♡
Y-YES! I'LL DO MY VERY BEST!!!
Shonen Taro Dept.
WHERE THE HELL IS KOTSUAKI-SENSEI'S MANUSCRIPT?
I'M LEAVING FOR A MEETING, SO...
NEVER THOUGHT I'D HEAR THAT FROM A READER!!!
OH, WATANABE-KUN-- YOU'RE WORKING ON TYPE-SETTING? IN THAT CASE, I'LL GO TO SHIMADA-SENSEI'S TO GET THE MANUSCRIPT!
ARE YOU SURE?
SURE I'M SURE. ♡
S-SO... WHAT DID YOU THINK OF THE KID'S PORT-FOLIO?
WELL...

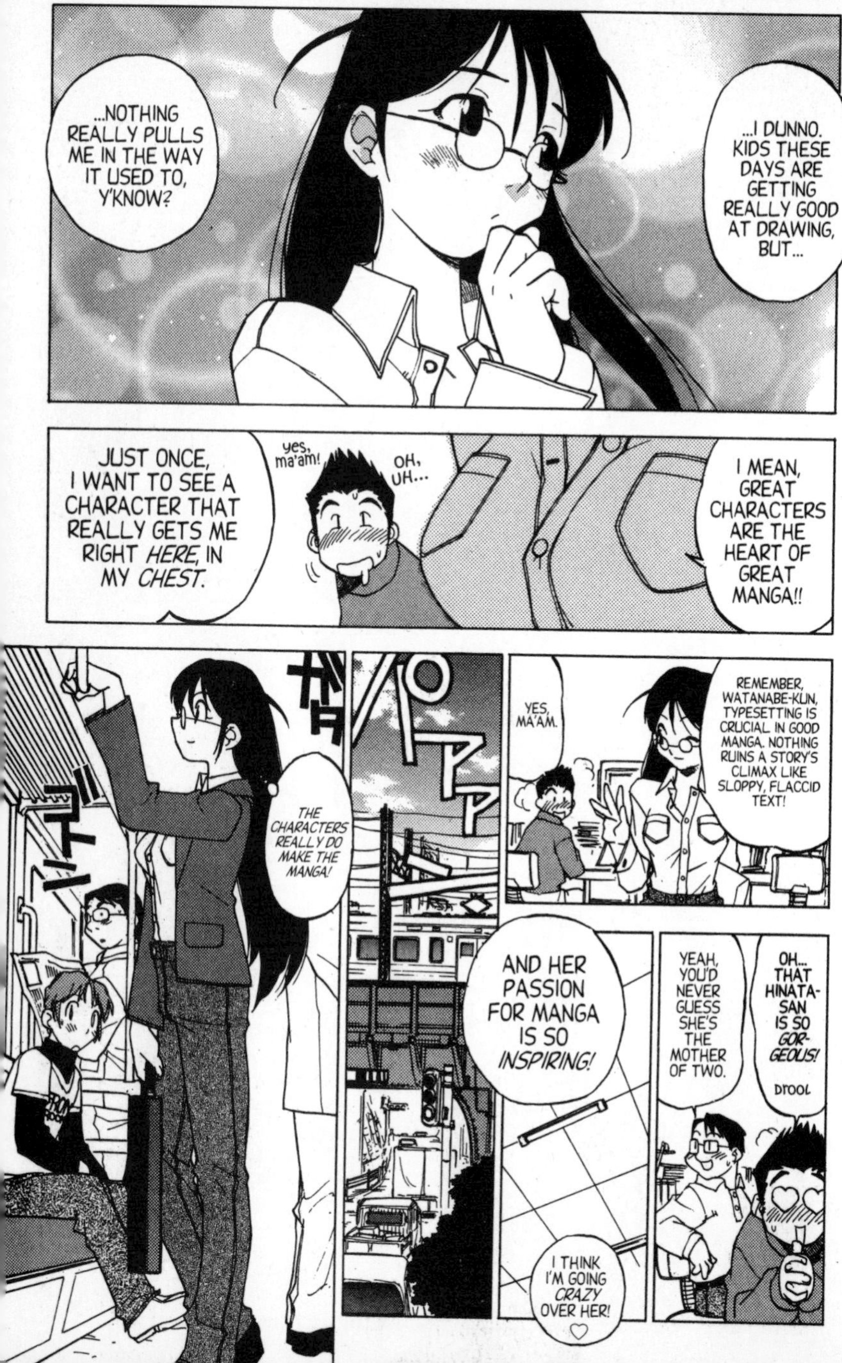
...I DUNNO. KIDS THESE DAYS ARE GETTING REALLY GOOD AT DRAWING, BUT...
...NOTHING REALLY PULLS ME IN THE WAY IT USED TO, Y'KNOW?
I MEAN, GREAT CHARACTERS ARE THE HEART OF GREAT MANGA!!
OH, UH...
yes, ma'am!
JUST ONCE, I WANT TO SEE A CHARACTER THAT REALLY GETS ME RIGHT *HERE*, IN MY *CHEST*.
REMEMBER, WATANABE-KUN, TYPESETTING IS CRUCIAL IN GOOD MANGA. NOTHING RUINS A STORY'S CLIMAX LIKE SLOPPY, FLACCID TEXT!
YES, MA'AM.
OH... THAT HINATA-SAN IS SO *GOR-GEOUS!*
DROOL
YEAH, YOU'D NEVER GUESS SHE'S THE MOTHER OF TWO.
AND HER PASSION FOR MANGA IS SO *INSPIRING!*
I THINK I'M GOING *CRAZY* OVER HER! ♡
THE CHARACTERS REALLY DO MAKE THE MANGA!

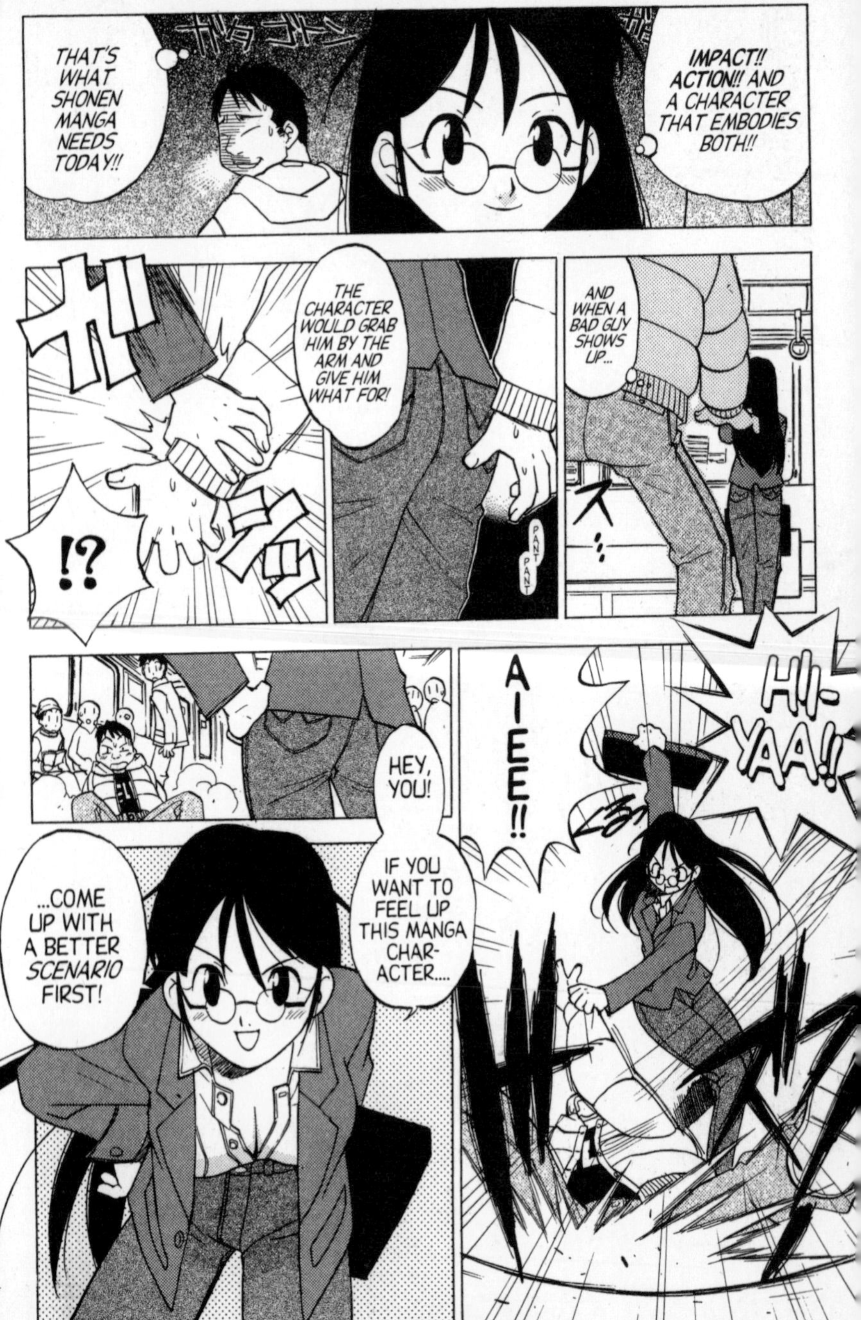
IMPACT!! ACTION!! AND A CHARACTER THAT EMBODIES BOTH!!
THAT'S WHAT SHONEN MANGA NEEDS TODAY!!
AND WHEN A BAD GUY SHOWS UP...
THE CHARACTER WOULD GRAB HIM BY THE ARM AND GIVE HIM WHAT FOR!
PANT PANT
!?
HI-YAA!!
AIEE!!
HEY, YOU!
IF YOU WANT TO FEEL UP THIS MANGA CHAR-ACTER....
...COME UP WITH A BETTER SCENARIO FIRST!

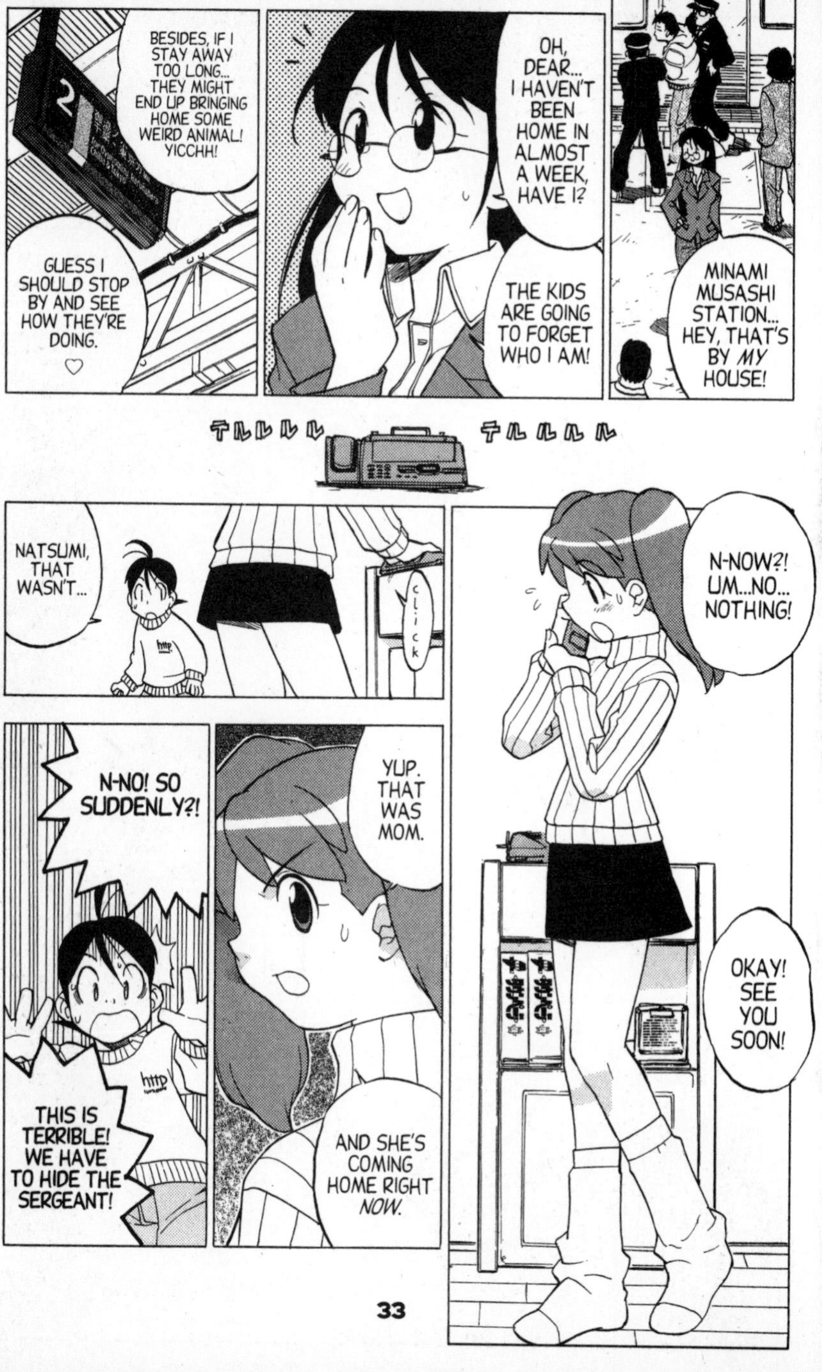
MINAMI MUSASHI STATION... HEY, THAT'S BY *MY* HOUSE!
OH, DEAR... I HAVEN'T BEEN HOME IN ALMOST A WEEK, HAVE I?
THE KIDS ARE GOING TO FORGET WHO I AM!
BESIDES, IF I STAY AWAY TOO LONG... THEY MIGHT END UP BRINGING HOME SOME WEIRD ANIMAL! YICCHH!
GUESS I SHOULD STOP BY AND SEE HOW THEY'RE DOING. ♡
テルルルル
テルルルル
N-NOW?! UM...NO... NOTHING!
OKAY! SEE YOU SOON!
click
NATSUMI, THAT WASN'T...
YUP. THAT WAS MOM.
AND SHE'S COMING HOME RIGHT *NOW*.
N-NO! SO SUDDENLY?!
THIS IS TERRIBLE! WE HAVE TO HIDE THE SERGEANT!

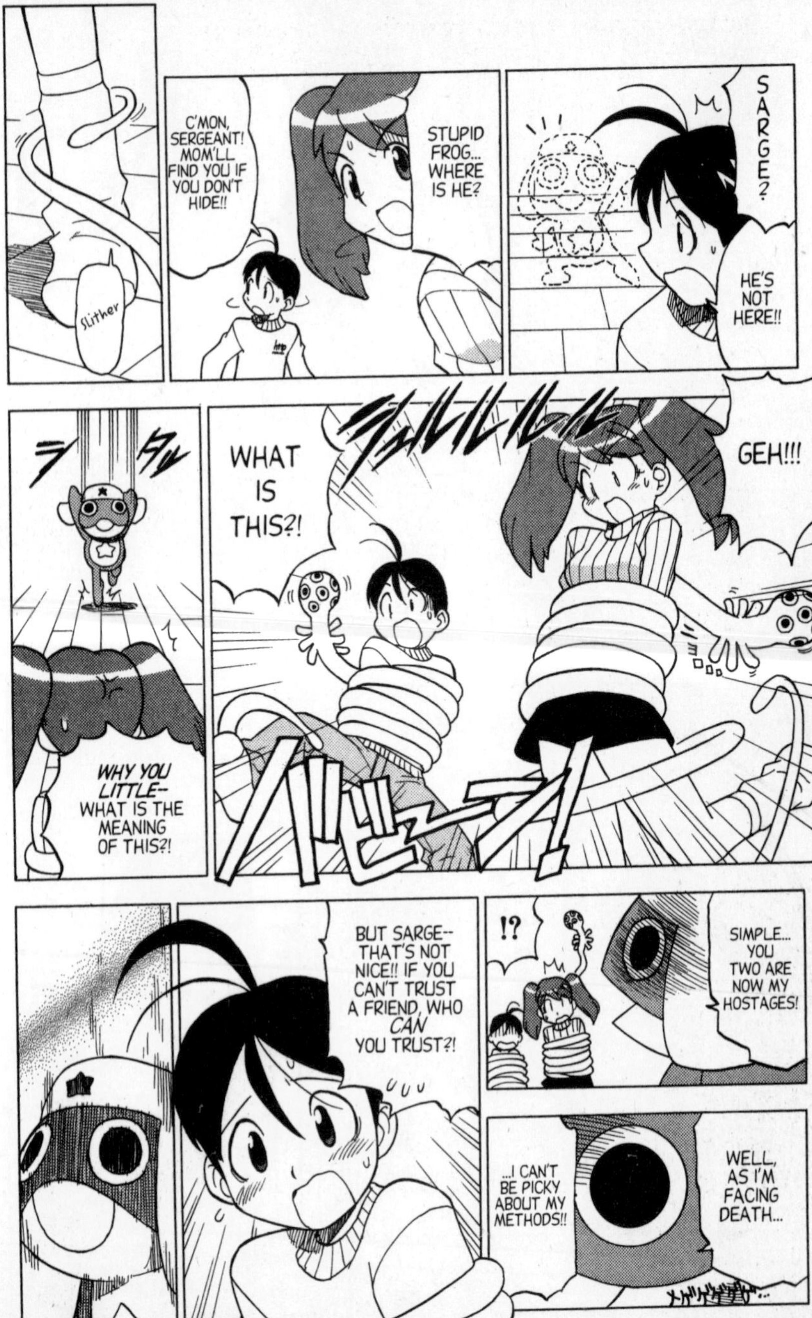
SARGE?
HE'S NOT HERE!!
STUPID FROG... WHERE IS HE?
C'MON, SERGEANT! MOM'LL FIND YOU IF YOU DON'T HIDE!!
Slither
GEH!!!
WHAT IS THIS?!
WHY YOU LITTLE-- WHAT IS THE MEANING OF THIS?!
SIMPLE... YOU TWO ARE NOW MY HOSTAGES!
!?
WELL, AS I'M FACING DEATH...
...I CAN'T BE PICKY ABOUT MY METHODS!!
BUT SARGE-- THAT'S NOT NICE!! IF YOU CAN'T TRUST A FRIEND, WHO *CAN* YOU TRUST?!

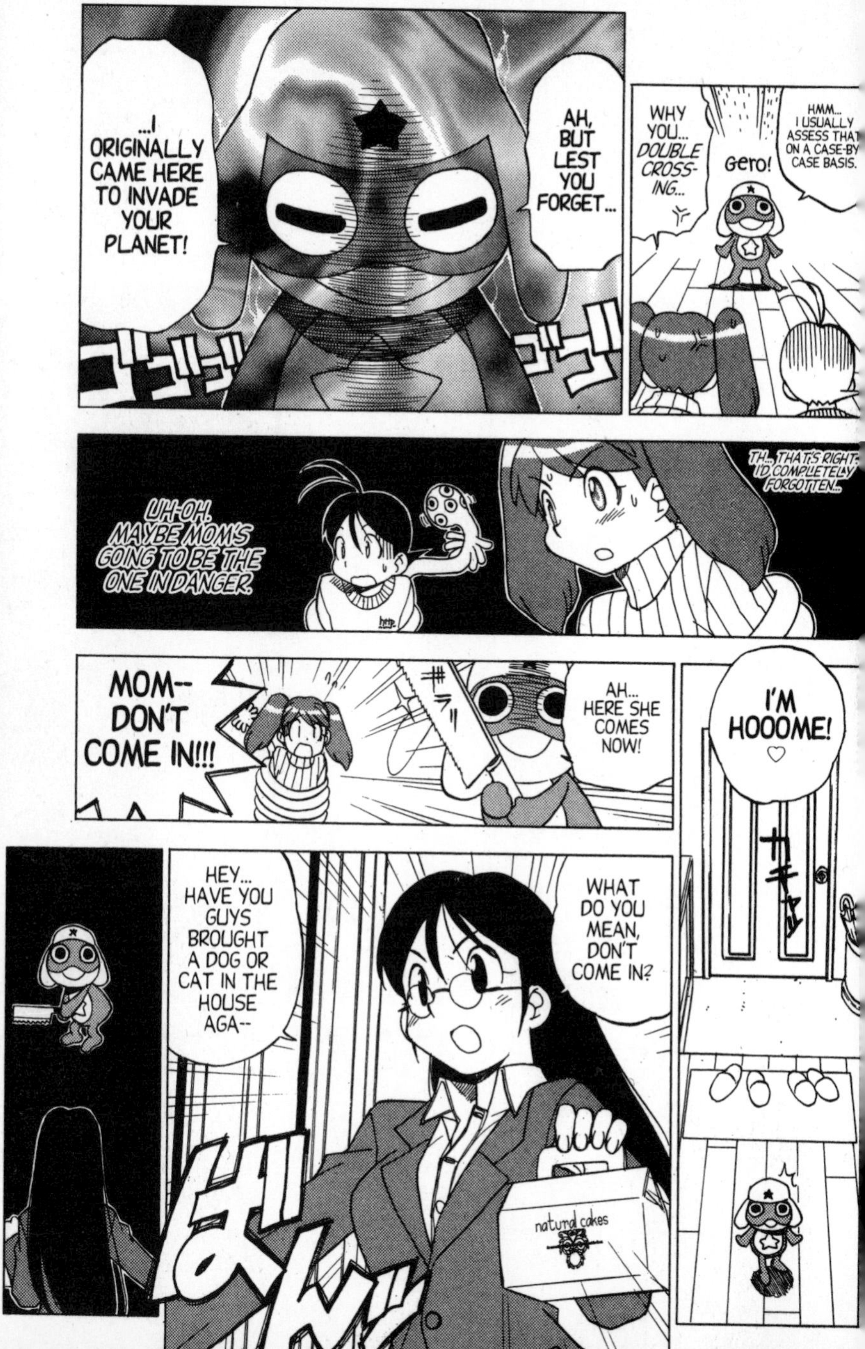

HMM... I USUALLY ASSESS THAT ON A CASE-BY CASE BASIS.
Gero!
WHY YOU... DOUBLE CROSSING...
AH, BUT LEST YOU FORGET...
...I ORIGINALLY CAME HERE TO INVADE YOUR PLANET!
TH... THAT'S RIGHT. I'D COMPLETELY FORGOTTEN...
UH-OH. MAYBE MOM'S GOING TO BE THE ONE IN DANGER.
I'M HOOOME! ♡
AH... HERE SHE COMES NOW!
MOM-- DON'T COME IN!!!
WHAT DO YOU MEAN, DON'T COME IN?
HEY... HAVE YOU GUYS BROUGHT A DOG OR CAT IN THE HOUSE AGA--
natural cakes

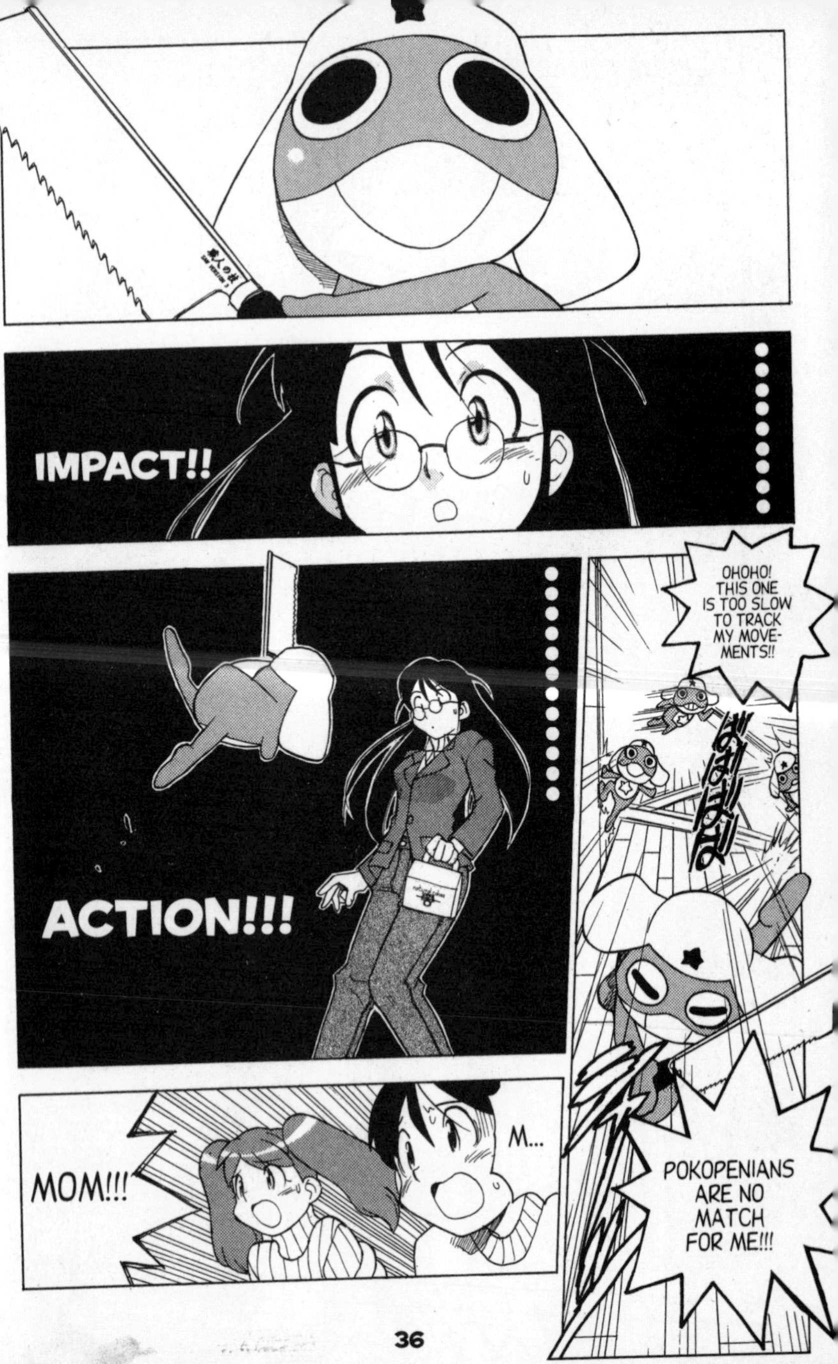
IMPACT!!
OHOHO! THIS ONE IS TOO SLOW TO TRACK MY MOVEMENTS!!
POKOPENIANS ARE NO MATCH FOR ME!!!
ACTION!!!
M...
MOM!!!

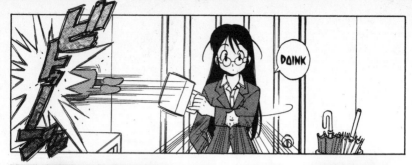

DOINK
ズズ…
WHOOOA...
ポカーン…
THEY DON'T CALL HER AN AIKIDO MASTER FOR NOTHING.
LOOKS LIKE MOM'S OUR SAVIOR THIS TIME...
AT A HINATA FAMILY EMERGENCY MEETING, FUYUKI HINATA BRIEFED "GENERAL" MOM ON THE SITUATION.
SO... THAT'S WHAT HAPPENED.
AND, UH...WE'RE NOT CRAZY. IN CASE YOU WERE WONDERING.
カタ
カタ
*TREMBLE
むんずっ
yeek!
じ
WE'RE SORRY, MOM!!
I'LL GET RID OF HIM RIGHT AWAY! JUST PLEASE... SPARE HIS LIFE!!

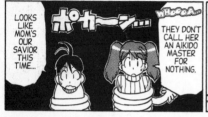

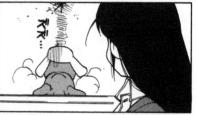

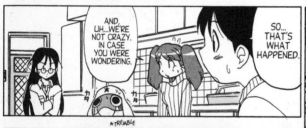

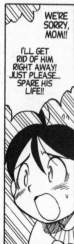

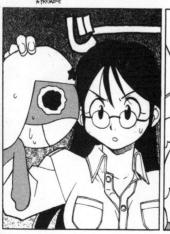

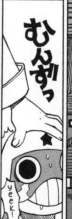

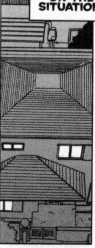

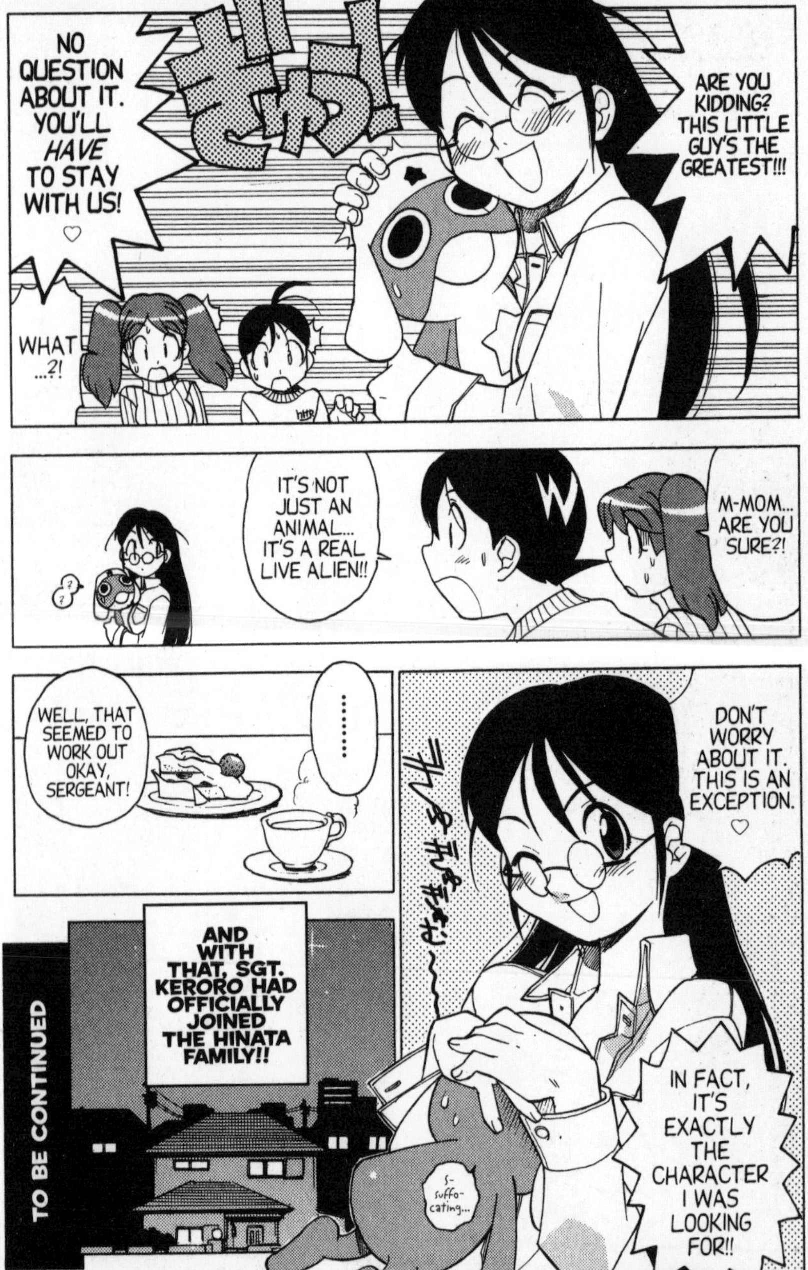
ARE YOU KIDDING? THIS LITTLE GUY'S THE GREATEST!!!
NO QUESTION ABOUT IT. YOU'LL *HAVE* TO STAY WITH US! ♡
WHAT ...?!
M-MOM... ARE YOU SURE?!
IT'S NOT JUST AN ANIMAL... IT'S A REAL LIVE ALIEN!!
? ?
DON'T WORRY ABOUT IT. THIS IS AN EXCEPTION. ♡
IN FACT, IT'S EXACTLY THE CHARACTER I WAS LOOKING FOR!!
S-suffocating...
WELL, THAT SEEMED TO WORK OUT OKAY, SERGEANT!
....
AND WITH THAT, SGT. KERORO HAD OFFICIALLY JOINED THE HINATA FAMILY!!
TO BE CONTINUED

ENCOUNTER III
ME, MYSELF AND MOMOKO

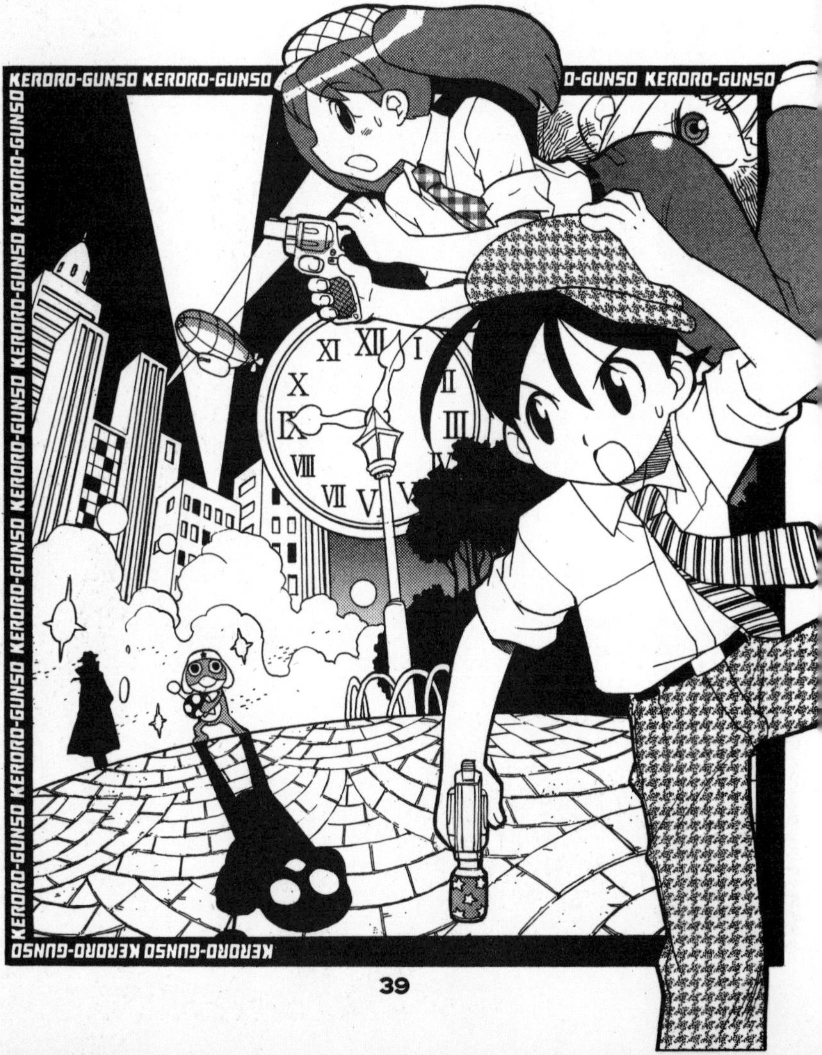
KERORO-GUNSO KERORO-GUNSO
O-GUNSO KERORO-GUNSO
KERORO-GUNSO KERORO-GUNSO KERORO-GUNSO KERORO-GUNSO KERORO-GUNSO
KERORO-GUNSO KERORO-GUNSO

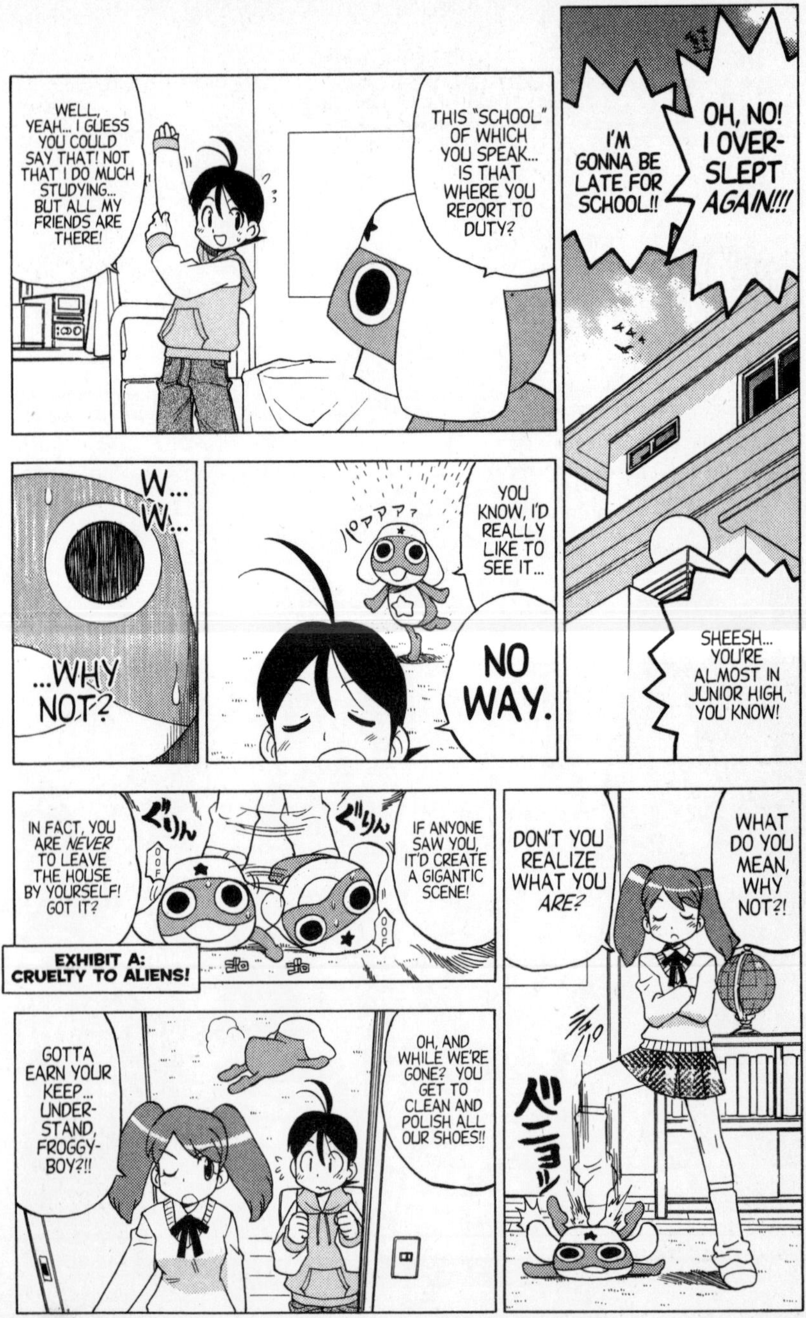
OH, NO! I OVER-SLEPT AGAIN!!!
I'M GONNA BE LATE FOR SCHOOL!!
SHEESH... YOU'RE ALMOST IN JUNIOR HIGH, YOU KNOW!
THIS "SCHOOL" OF WHICH YOU SPEAK... IS THAT WHERE YOU REPORT TO DUTY?
WELL, YEAH... I GUESS YOU COULD SAY THAT! NOT THAT I DO MUCH STUDYING... BUT ALL MY FRIENDS ARE THERE!
YOU KNOW, I'D REALLY LIKE TO SEE IT...
NO WAY.
W... W...
...WHY NOT?
WHAT DO YOU MEAN, WHY NOT?!
DON'T YOU REALIZE WHAT YOU ARE?
IF ANYONE SAW YOU, IT'D CREATE A GIGANTIC SCENE!
ぐりん
OOF
ぐりん
OOF
IN FACT, YOU ARE NEVER TO LEAVE THE HOUSE BY YOURSELF! GOT IT?
EXHIBIT A: CRUELTY TO ALIENS!
OH, AND WHILE WE'RE GONE? YOU GET TO CLEAN AND POLISH ALL OUR SHOES!!
GOTTA EARN YOUR KEEP... UNDER-STAND, FROGGY-BOY?!!

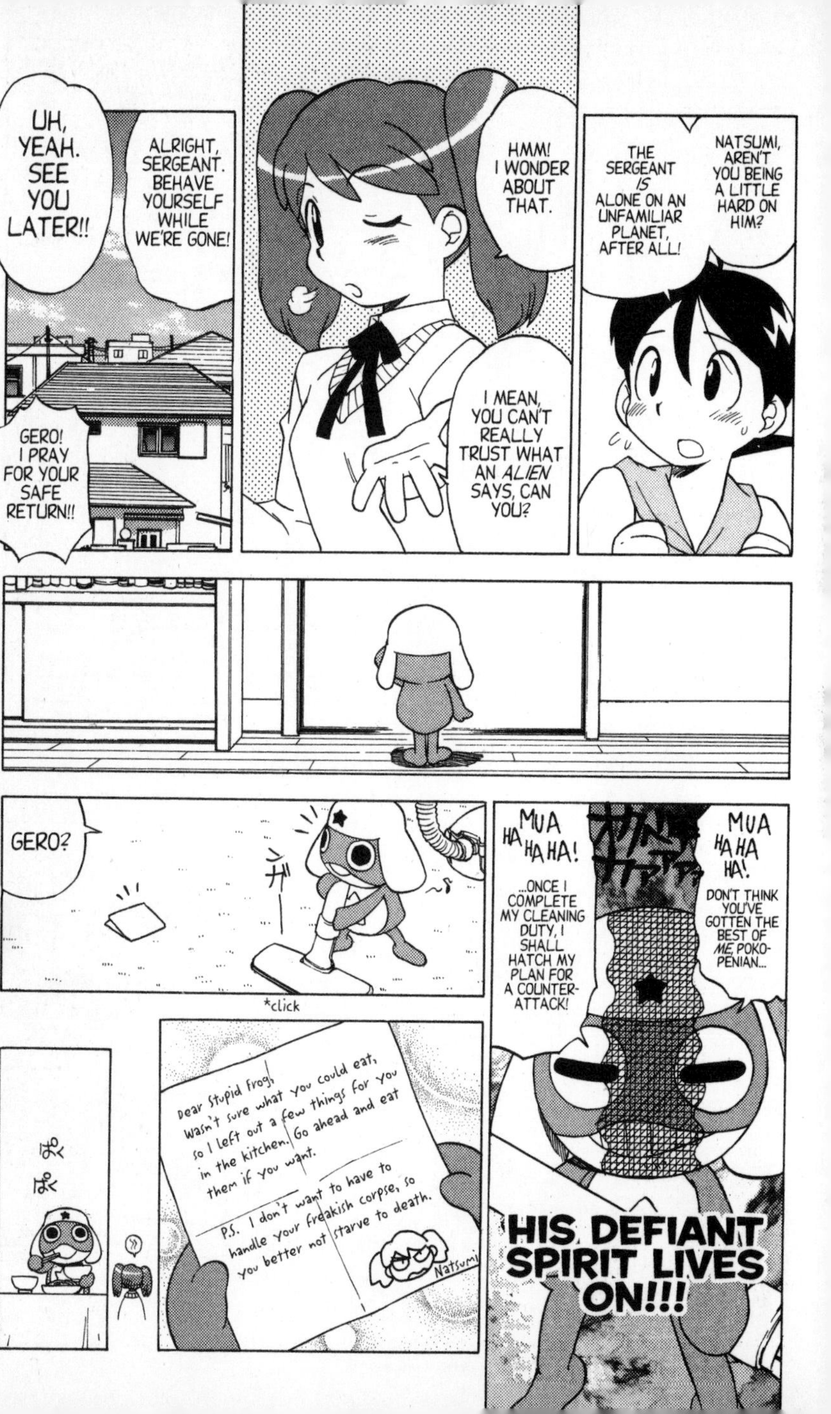

NATSUMI, AREN'T YOU BEING A LITTLE HARD ON HIM?
THE SERGEANT *IS* ALONE ON AN UNFAMILIAR PLANET, AFTER ALL!
HMM! I WONDER ABOUT THAT.
I MEAN, YOU CAN'T REALLY TRUST WHAT AN *ALIEN* SAYS, CAN YOU?
ALRIGHT, SERGEANT. BEHAVE YOURSELF WHILE WE'RE GONE!
UH, YEAH. SEE YOU LATER!!
GERO! I PRAY FOR YOUR SAFE RETURN!!
MUA HA HA HA!
DON'T THINK YOU'VE GOTTEN THE BEST OF *ME*, POKOPENIAN...
MUA HA HA HA!
...ONCE I COMPLETE MY CLEANING DUTY, I SHALL HATCH MY PLAN FOR A COUNTER-ATTACK!
HIS DEFIANT SPIRIT LIVES ON!!!
ガー
GERO?
*click
Dear Stupid Frog,
Wasn't sure what you could eat, so I left out a few things for you in the kitchen. Go ahead and eat them if you want.
P.S. I don't want to have to handle your freakish corpse, so you better not starve to death.
Natsumi
ぱく
ぱく

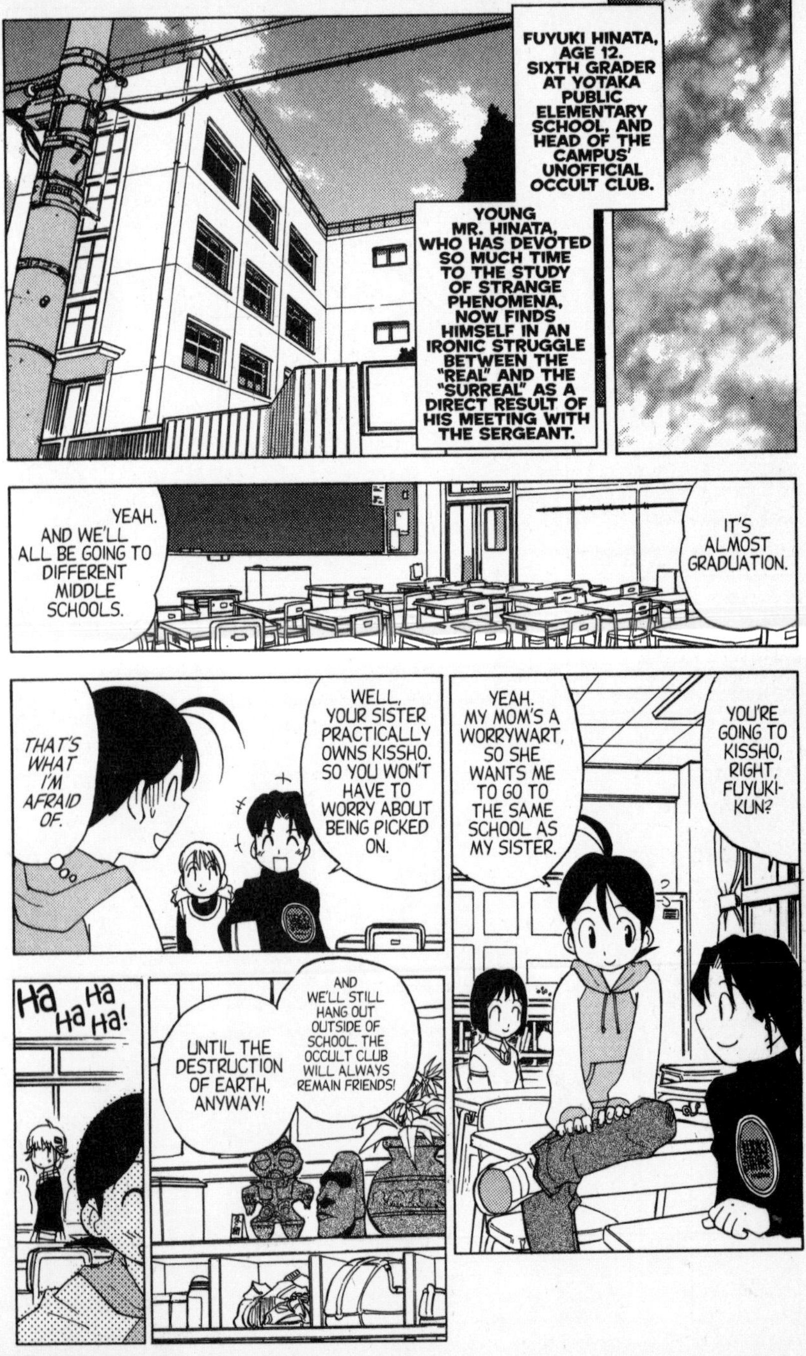
FUYUKI HINATA, AGE 12. SIXTH GRADER AT YOTAKA PUBLIC ELEMENTARY SCHOOL, AND HEAD OF THE CAMPUS' UNOFFICIAL OCCULT CLUB.
YOUNG MR. HINATA, WHO HAS DEVOTED SO MUCH TIME TO THE STUDY OF STRANGE PHENOMENA, NOW FINDS HIMSELF IN AN IRONIC STRUGGLE BETWEEN THE "REAL" AND THE "SURREAL" AS A DIRECT RESULT OF HIS MEETING WITH THE SERGEANT.
IT'S ALMOST GRADUATION.
YEAH. AND WE'LL ALL BE GOING TO DIFFERENT MIDDLE SCHOOLS.
YOU'RE GOING TO KISSHO, RIGHT, FUYUKI-KUN?
YEAH. MY MOM'S A WORRYWART, SO SHE WANTS ME TO GO TO THE SAME SCHOOL AS MY SISTER.
WELL, YOUR SISTER PRACTICALLY OWNS KISSHO. SO YOU WON'T HAVE TO WORRY ABOUT BEING PICKED ON.
THAT'S WHAT I'M AFRAID OF.
AND WE'LL STILL HANG OUT OUTSIDE OF SCHOOL. THE OCCULT CLUB WILL ALWAYS REMAIN FRIENDS!
UNTIL THE DESTRUCTION OF EARTH, ANYWAY!
Ha Ha Ha Ha!

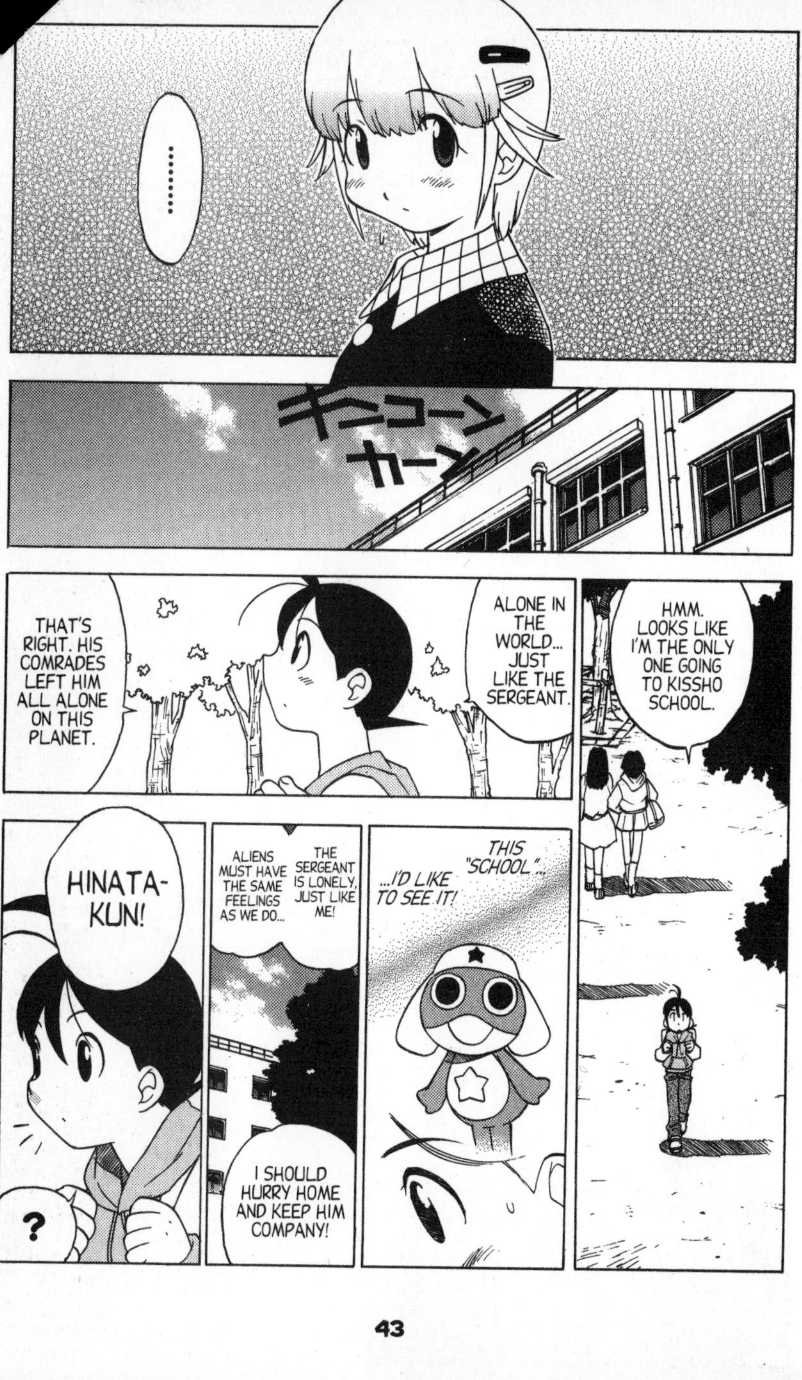

......
キ～ンコーン
カーン
HMM. LOOKS LIKE I'M THE ONLY ONE GOING TO KISSHO SCHOOL.
ALONE IN THE WORLD... JUST LIKE THE SERGEANT.
THAT'S RIGHT. HIS COMRADES LEFT HIM ALL ALONE ON THIS PLANET.
THIS "SCHOOL"...
...I'D LIKE TO SEE IT!
THE SERGEANT IS LONELY, JUST LIKE ME!
ALIENS MUST HAVE THE SAME FEELINGS AS WE DO...
I SHOULD HURRY HOME AND KEEP HIM COMPANY!
HINATA-KUN!
?

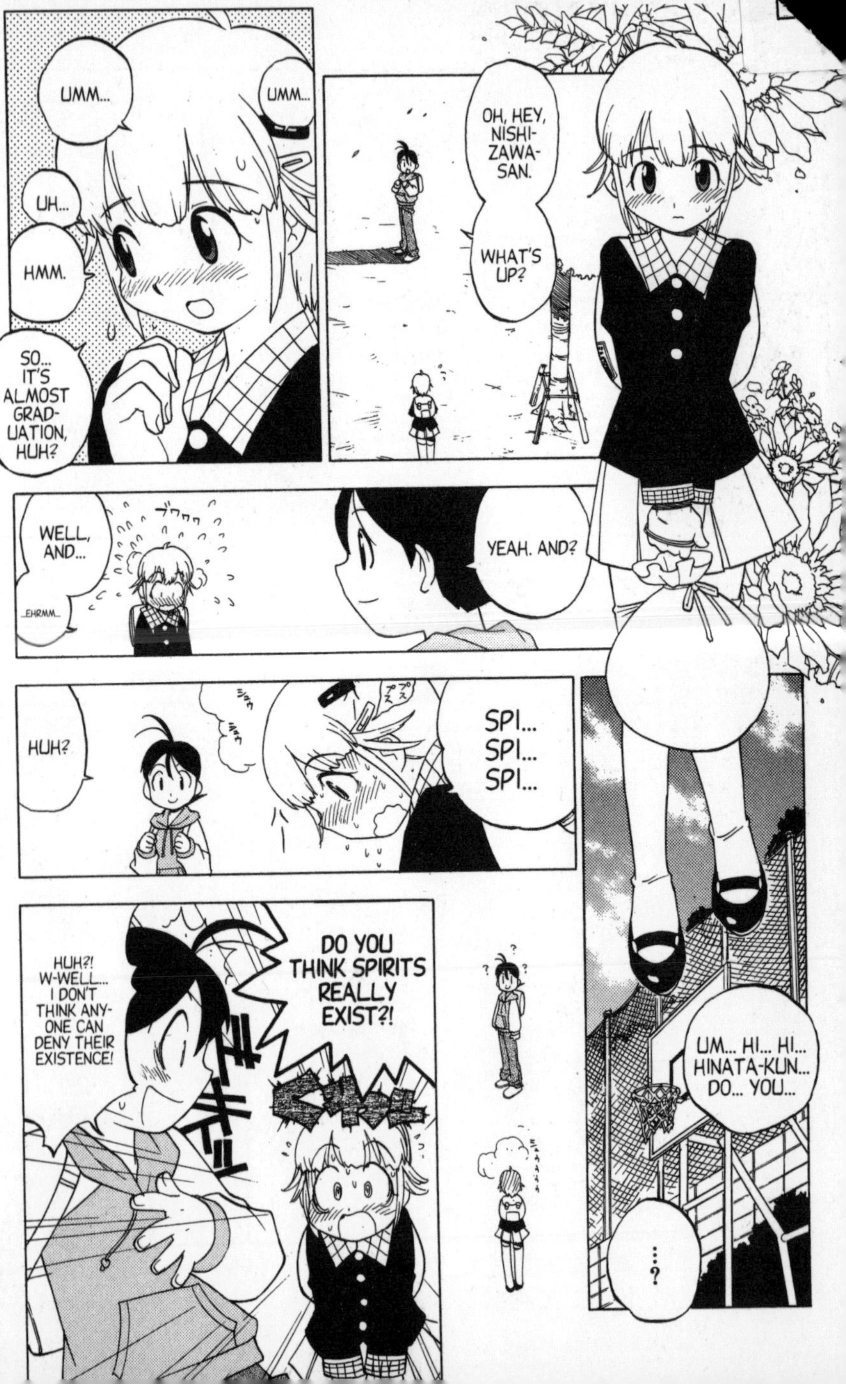
UM... HI... HI... HINATA-KUN... DO... YOU...
...?
OH, HEY, NISHIZAWA-SAN.
WHAT'S UP?
UMM...
UMM...
UH...
HMM.
SO... IT'S ALMOST GRADUATION, HUH?
YEAH. AND?
WELL, AND...
EHRMM
SPI... SPI... SPI...
HUH?
DO YOU THINK SPIRITS REALLY EXIST?!
HUH?! W-WELL... I DON'T THINK ANYONE CAN DENY THEIR EXISTENCE!

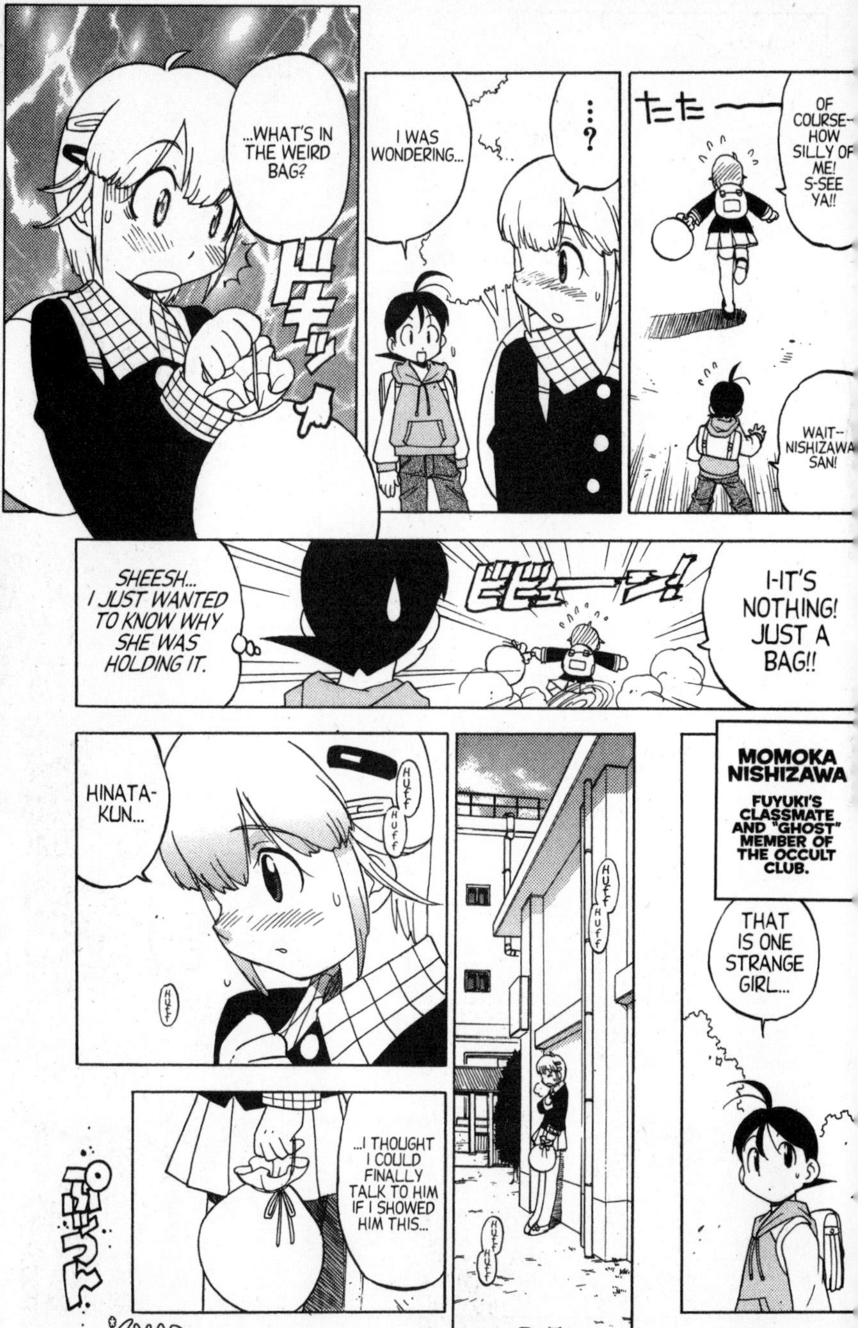
OF COURSE--HOW SILLY OF ME! S-SEE YA!!
たたーー
WAIT-- NISHIZAWA-SAN!
...?
I WAS WONDERING...
...WHAT'S IN THE WEIRD BAG?
ドキッ
I-IT'S NOTHING! JUST A BAG!!
ビビューン!
SHEESH... I JUST WANTED TO KNOW WHY SHE WAS HOLDING IT.
MOMOKA NISHIZAWA
FUYUKI'S CLASSMATE AND "GHOST" MEMBER OF THE OCCULT CLUB.
THAT IS ONE STRANGE GIRL...
HUFF HUFF
HUFF HUFF
HINATA-KUN...
HUFF HUFF
HUFF
...I THOUGHT I COULD FINALLY TALK TO HIM IF I SHOWED HIM THIS...
*SNAP

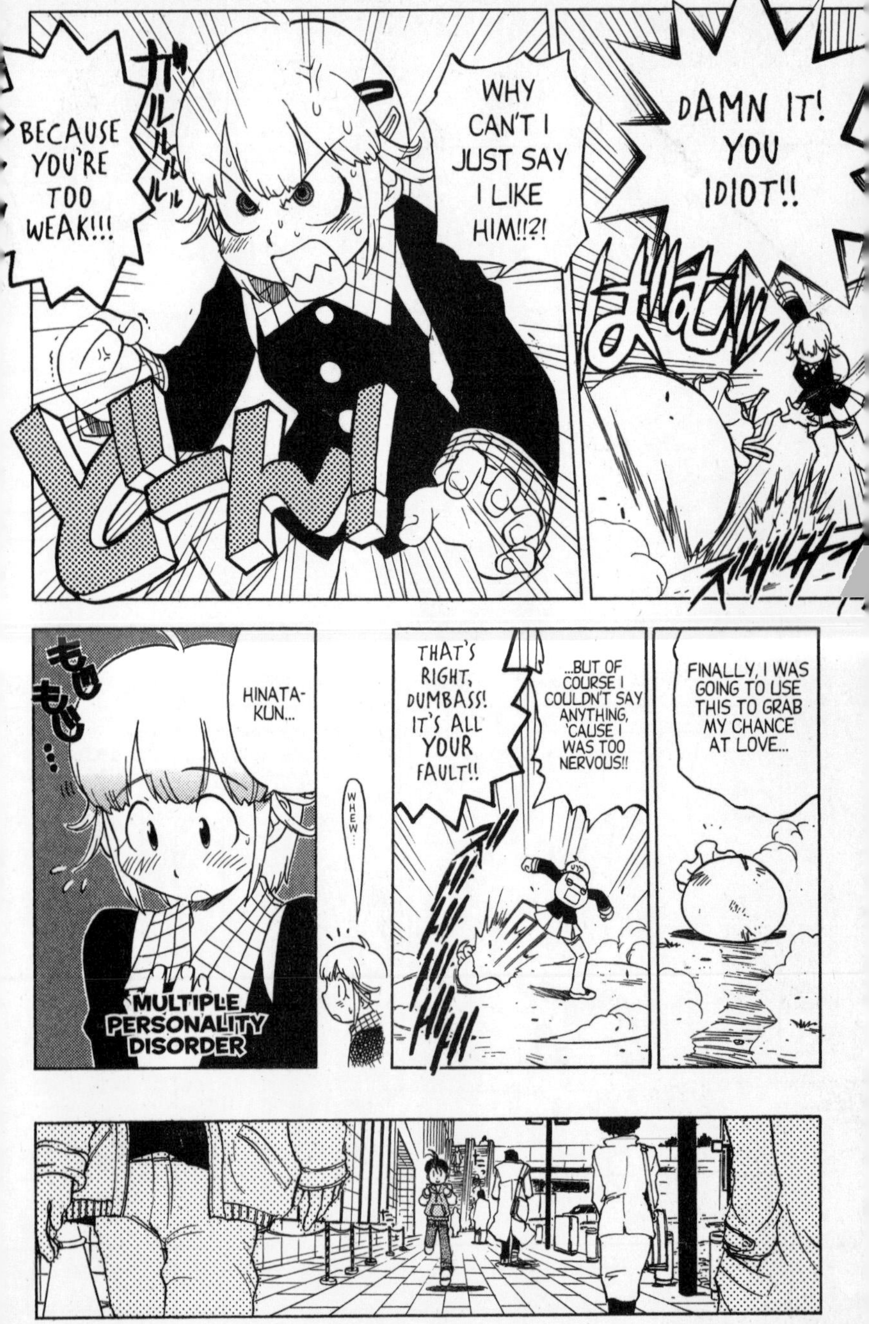
DAMN IT! YOU IDIOT!!
WHY CAN'T I JUST SAY I LIKE HIM!!?!
BECAUSE YOU'RE TOO WEAK!!!
FINALLY, I WAS GOING TO USE THIS TO GRAB MY CHANCE AT LOVE...
...BUT OF COURSE I COULDN'T SAY ANYTHING, 'CAUSE I WAS TOO NERVOUS!!
THAT'S RIGHT, DUMBASS! IT'S ALL YOUR FAULT!!
HINATA-KUN...
WHEW...
MULTIPLE PERSONALITY DISORDER

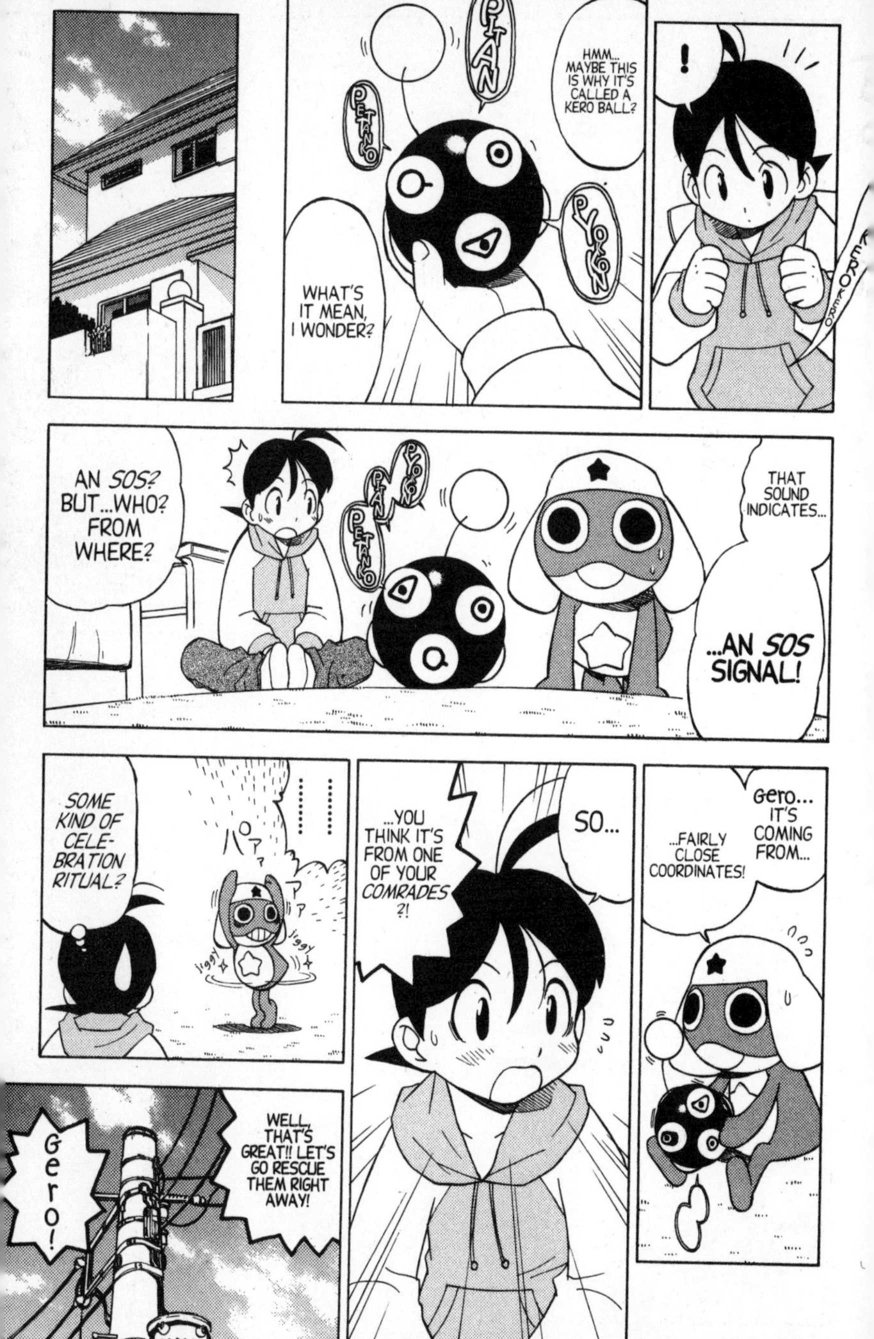
!
KEROKERO
HMM... MAYBE THIS IS WHY IT'S CALLED A KERO BALL?
PITAN
PYOYON
PETANKO
WHAT'S IT MEAN, I WONDER?
THAT SOUND INDICATES...
...AN *SOS* SIGNAL!
PYOYON
PITAN
PETANKO
AN *SOS*? BUT...WHO? FROM WHERE?
Gero... IT'S COMING FROM...
...FAIRLY CLOSE COORDINATES!
SO...
...YOU THINK IT'S FROM ONE OF YOUR *COMRADES*?!
....
....
パァァァ
SOME KIND OF CELEBRATION RITUAL?
jiggy
jiggy
WELL, THAT'S GREAT!! LET'S GO RESCUE THEM RIGHT AWAY!
Gero!

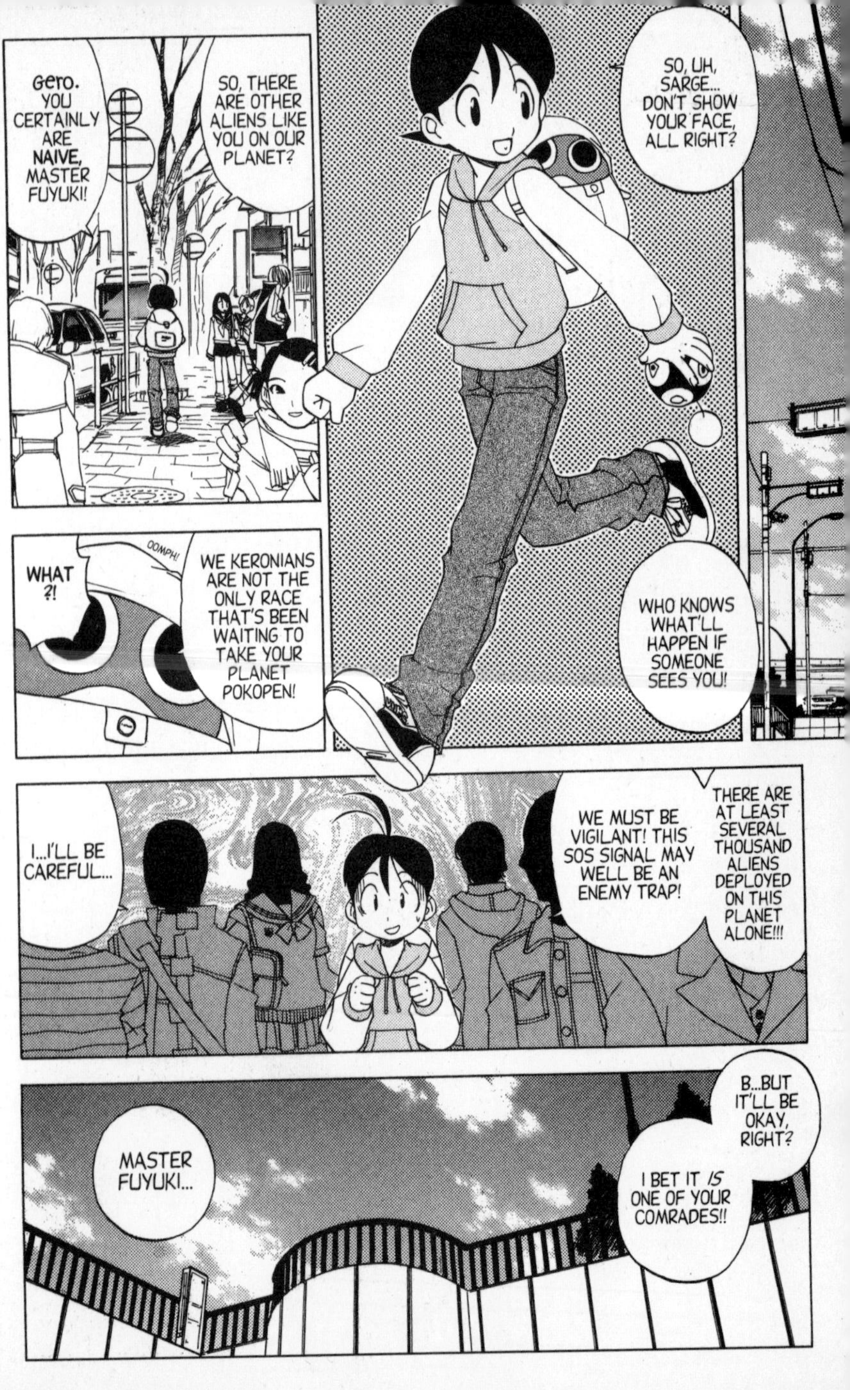

SO, UH, SARGE... DON'T SHOW YOUR FACE, ALL RIGHT?
WHO KNOWS WHAT'LL HAPPEN IF SOMEONE SEES YOU!
SO, THERE ARE OTHER ALIENS LIKE YOU ON OUR PLANET?
Gero. YOU CERTAINLY ARE NAIVE, MASTER FUYUKI!
OOMPH!
WE KERONIANS ARE NOT THE ONLY RACE THAT'S BEEN WAITING TO TAKE YOUR PLANET POKOPEN!
WHAT ?!
WE MUST BE VIGILANT! THIS SOS SIGNAL MAY WELL BE AN ENEMY TRAP!
THERE ARE AT LEAST SEVERAL THOUSAND ALIENS DEPLOYED ON THIS PLANET ALONE!!!
I...I'LL BE CAREFUL...
B...BUT IT'LL BE OKAY, RIGHT?
I BET IT *IS* ONE OF YOUR COMRADES!!
MASTER FUYUKI...

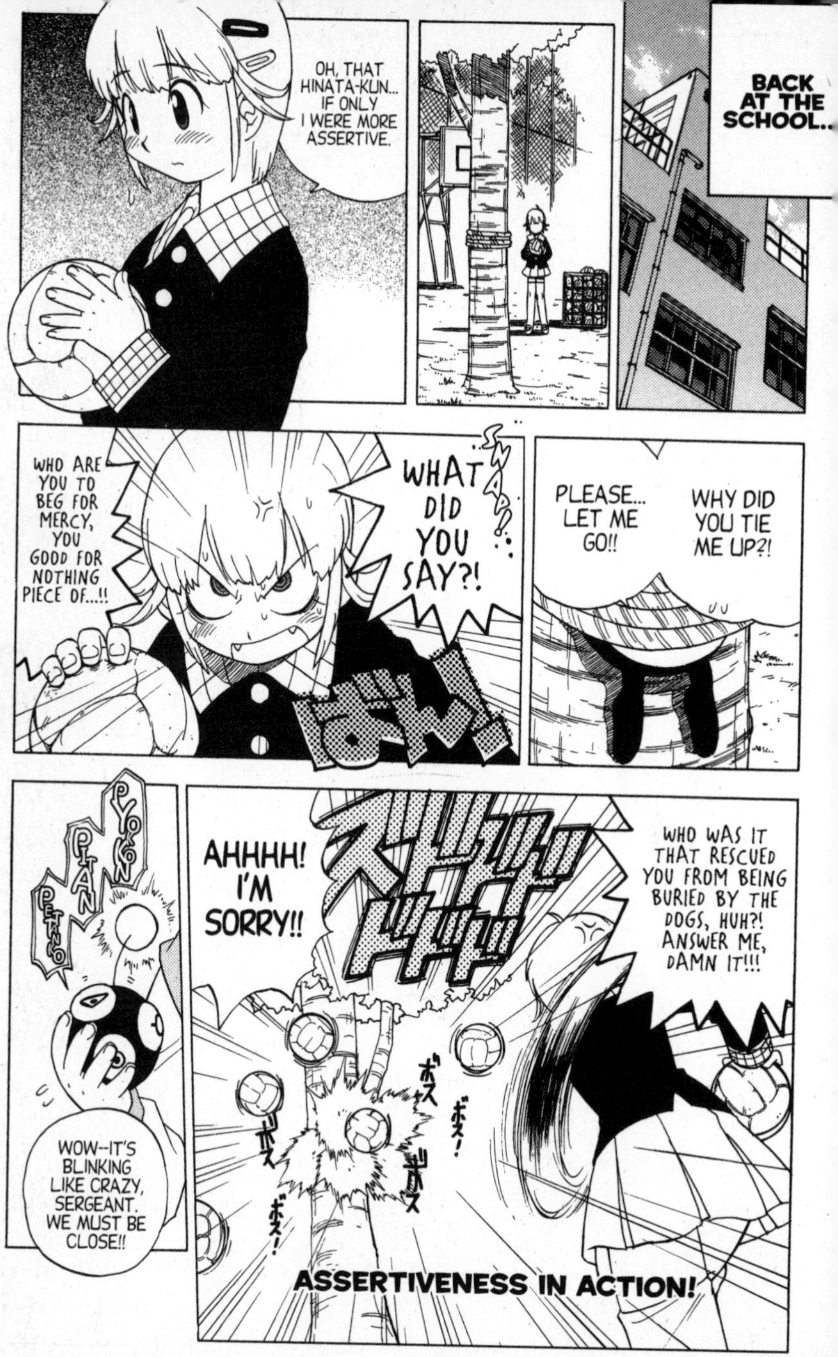
BACK AT THE SCHOOL..
OH, THAT HINATA-KUN... IF ONLY I WERE MORE ASSERTIVE.
WHY DID YOU TIE ME UP?!
PLEASE... LET ME GO!!
SNAP!
WHAT DID YOU SAY?!
WHO ARE YOU TO BEG FOR MERCY, YOU GOOD FOR NOTHING PIECE OF...!!
WHO WAS IT THAT RESCUED YOU FROM BEING BURIED BY THE DOGS, HUH?! ANSWER ME, DAMN IT!!!
AHHHH! I'M SORRY!!
ボス!
ボス!
ボス
ボス!
ASSERTIVENESS IN ACTION!
PYOKON
PITAN
PETAKO
WOW--IT'S BLINKING LIKE CRAZY, SERGEANT. WE MUST BE CLOSE!!

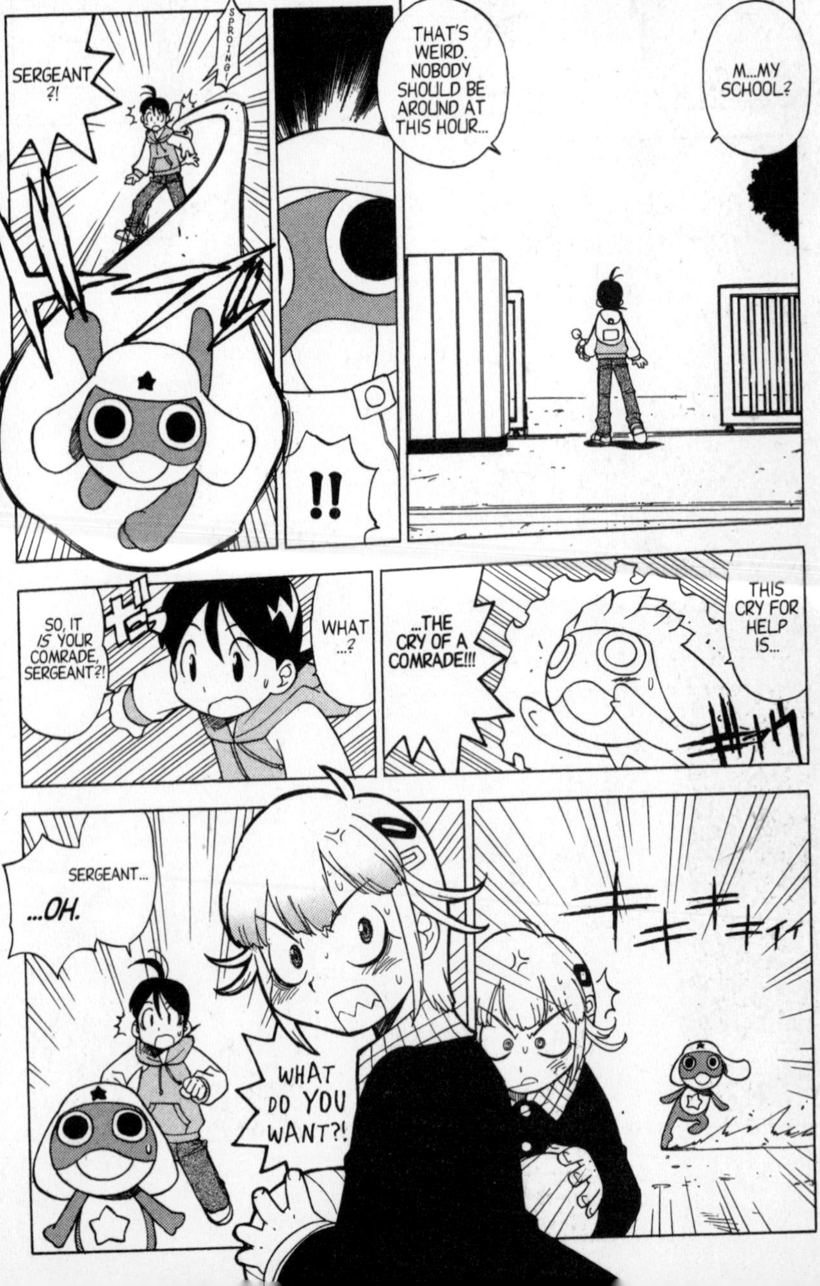
M...MY SCHOOL?
THAT'S WEIRD. NOBODY SHOULD BE AROUND AT THIS HOUR...
!!
SPROING!
SERGEANT?!
THIS CRY FOR HELP IS...
...THE CRY OF A COMRADE!!!
WHAT...?
SO, IT IS YOUR COMRADE, SERGEANT?!
WHAT DO YOU WANT?!
SERGEANT...
...OH.

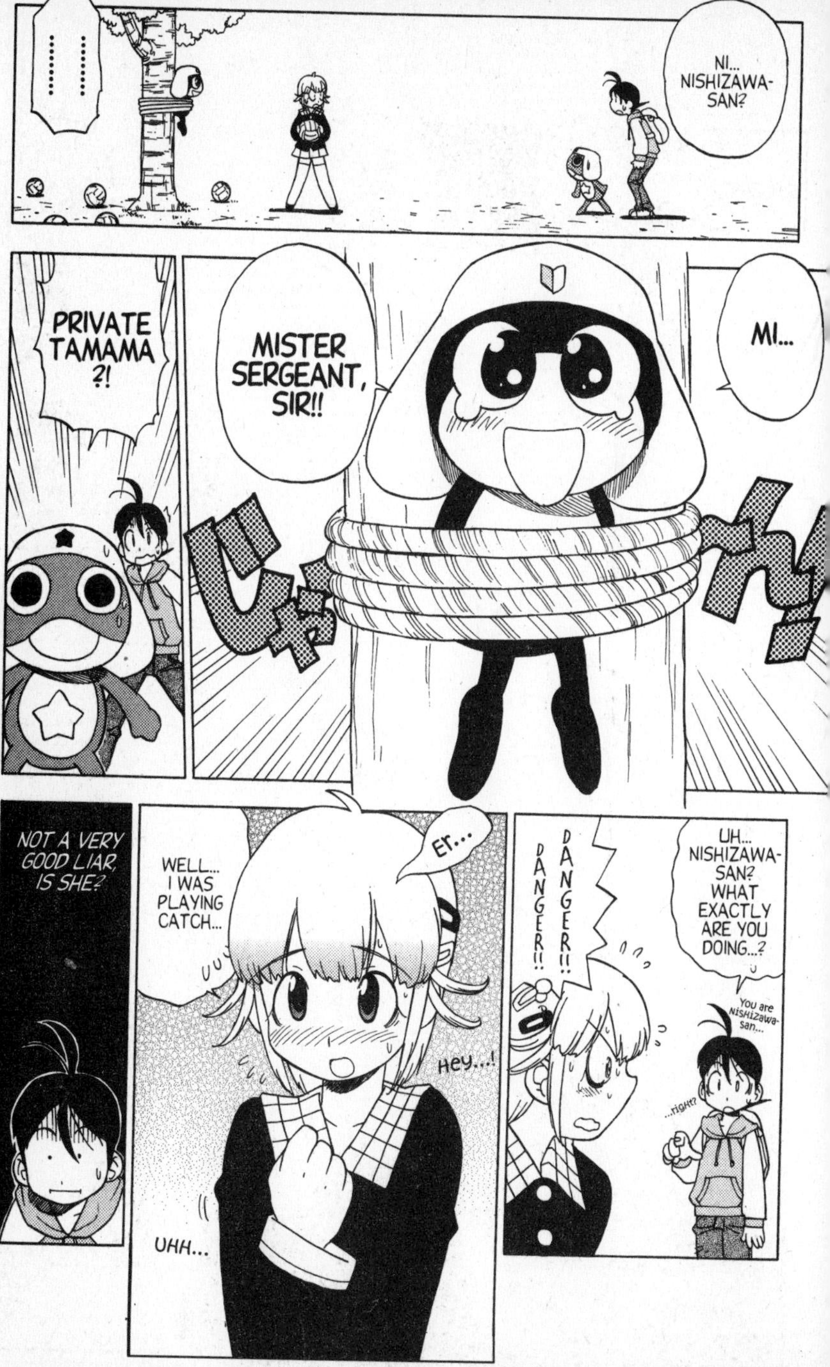
NI... NISHIZAWA-SAN?
......
MI...
MISTER SERGEANT, SIR!!
じゃん!!
PRIVATE TAMAMA ?!
UH... NISHIZAWA-SAN? WHAT EXACTLY ARE YOU DOING...?
You are NISHIZAWA-san...
...right?
DANGER!! DANGER!!
Er...
WELL... I WAS PLAYING CATCH...
Hey...!
UHH...
NOT A VERY GOOD LIAR, IS SHE?

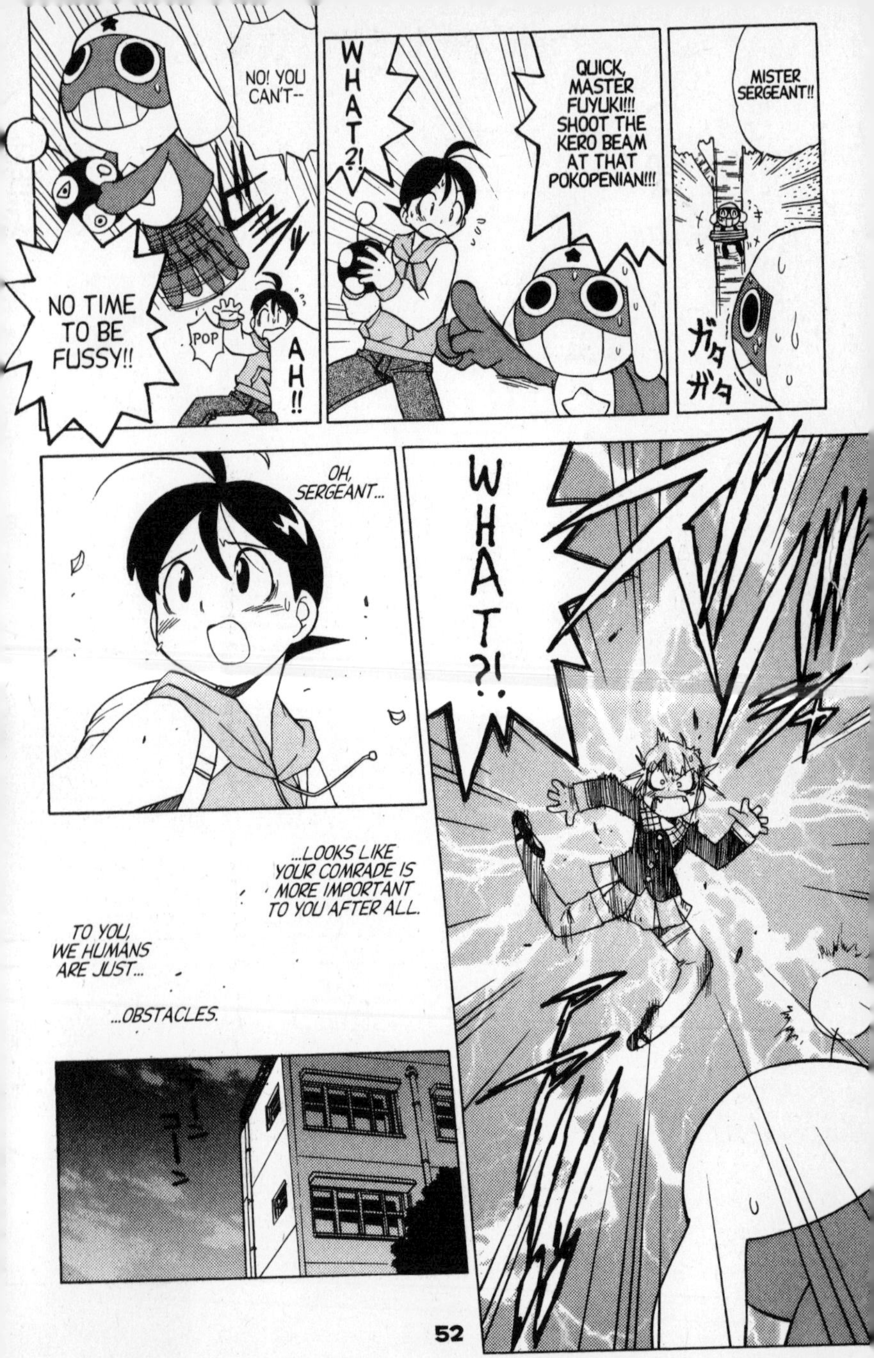
MISTER SERGEANT!!
ガタガタ
QUICK, MASTER FUYUKI!!! SHOOT THE KERO BEAM AT THAT POKOPENIAN!!!
WHAT?!
NO! YOU CAN'T--
NO TIME TO BE FUSSY!!
POP
AH!!
WHAT?!
OH, SERGEANT...
...LOOKS LIKE YOUR COMRADE IS MORE IMPORTANT TO YOU AFTER ALL.
TO YOU, WE HUMANS ARE JUST...
...OBSTACLES.

THE ALIENS' TALE

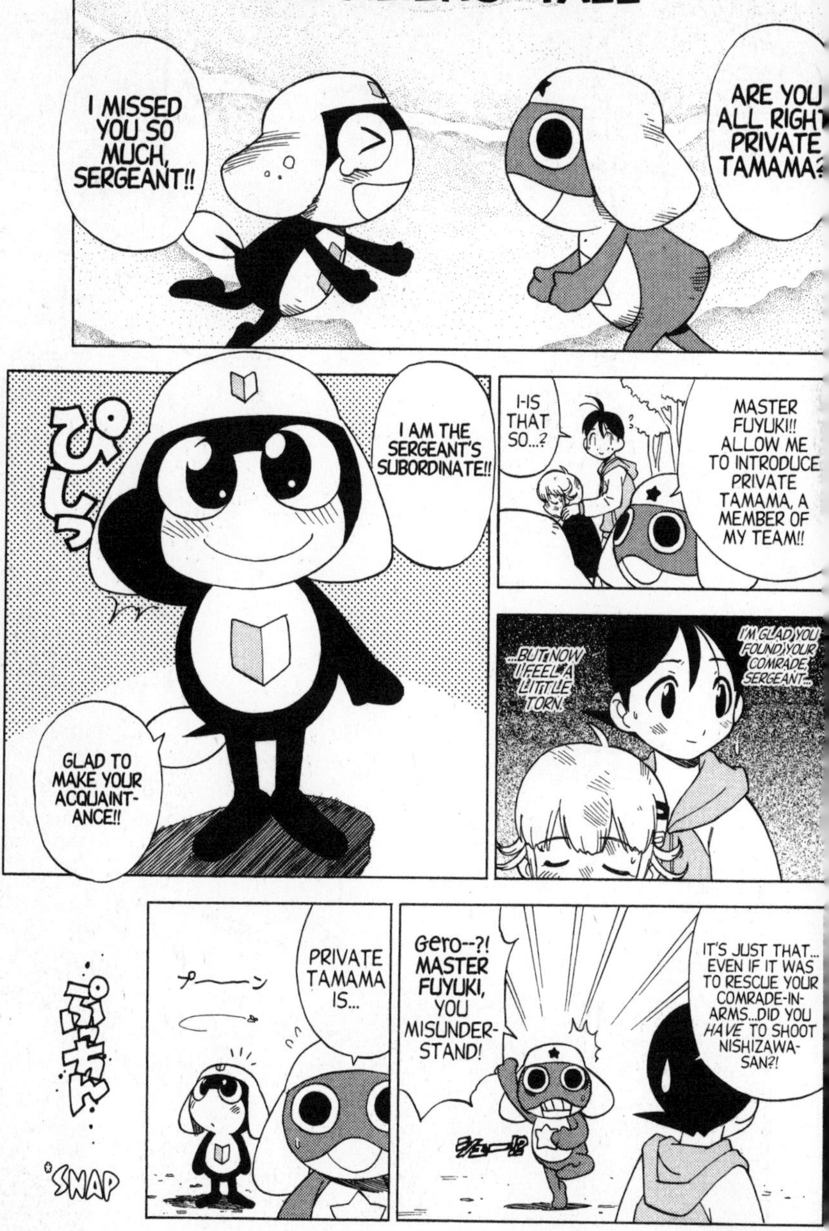
ARE YOU ALL RIGHT PRIVATE TAMAMA?
I MISSED YOU SO MUCH, SERGEANT!!
MASTER FUYUKI!! ALLOW ME TO INTRODUCE PRIVATE TAMAMA, A MEMBER OF MY TEAM!!
I-IS THAT SO...?
I'M GLAD YOU FOUND YOUR COMRADE, SERGEANT...
...BUT NOW I FEEL A LITTLE TORN.
I AM THE SERGEANT'S SUBORDINATE!!
ぴしっ
GLAD TO MAKE YOUR ACQUAINT-ANCE!!
IT'S JUST THAT... EVEN IF IT WAS TO RESCUE YOUR COMRADE-IN-ARMS...DID YOU *HAVE* TO SHOOT NISHIZAWA-SAN?!
Gero--?! MASTER FUYUKI, YOU MISUNDER-STAND!
PRIVATE TAMAMA IS...
プーーン
ぷっちん
*SNAP

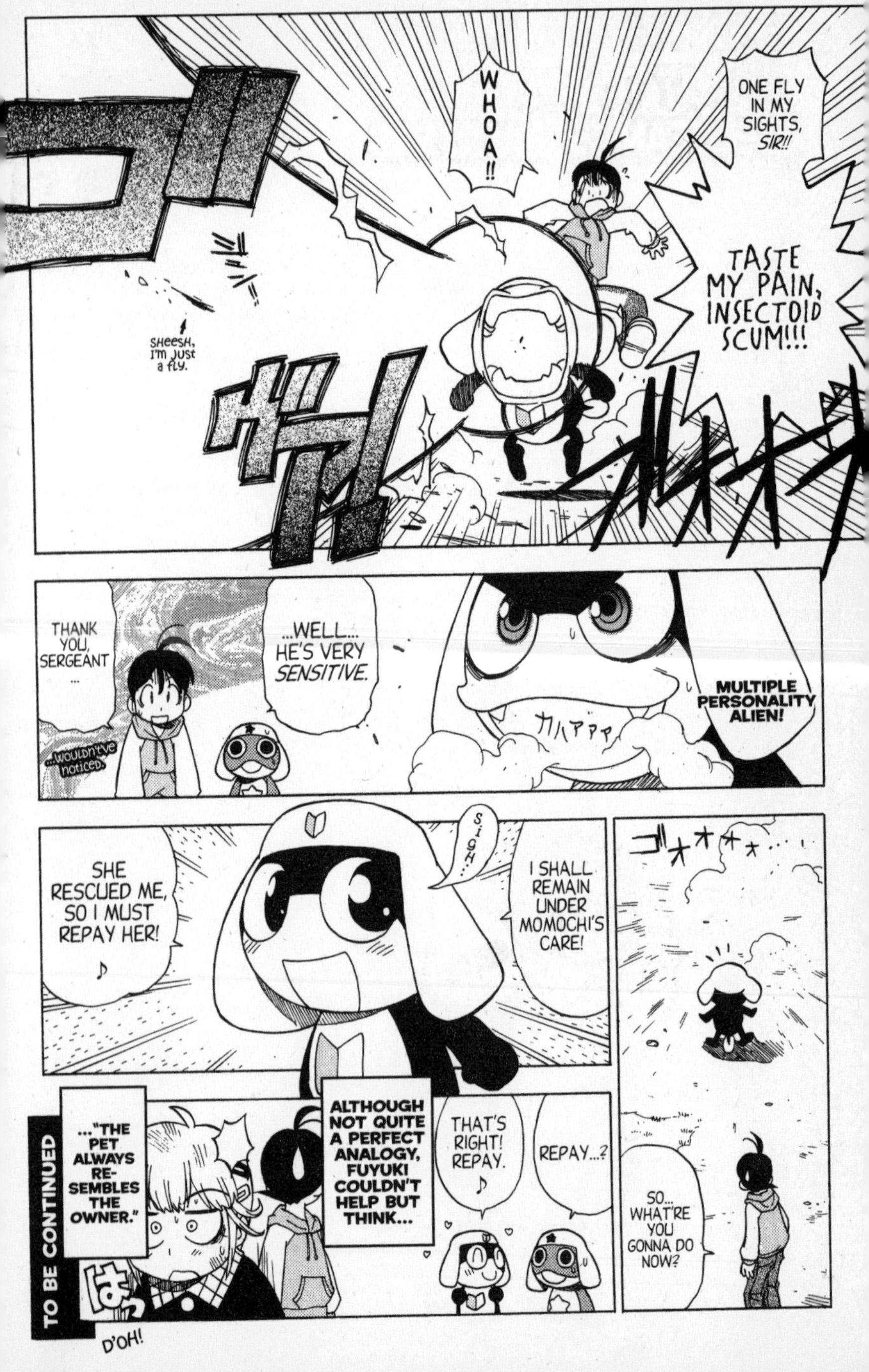
ONE FLY IN MY SIGHTS, SIR!!
TASTE MY PAIN, INSECTOID SCUM!!!
WHOA!!
SHEESH, I'm just a fly.
MULTIPLE PERSONALITY ALIEN!
...WELL... HE'S VERY SENSITIVE.
THANK YOU, SERGEANT ...
...wouldn't've noticed.
SO... WHAT'RE YOU GONNA DO NOW?
I SHALL REMAIN UNDER MOMOCHI'S CARE!
SIGH...
SHE RESCUED ME, SO I MUST REPAY HER! ♪
REPAY...?
THAT'S RIGHT! REPAY. ♪
ALTHOUGH NOT QUITE A PERFECT ANALOGY, FUYUKI COULDN'T HELP BUT THINK...
..."THE PET ALWAYS RE-SEMBLES THE OWNER."
D'OH!
TO BE CONTINUED

ENCOUNTER IV
A VISIT TO THE SERGEANT'S QUARTERS

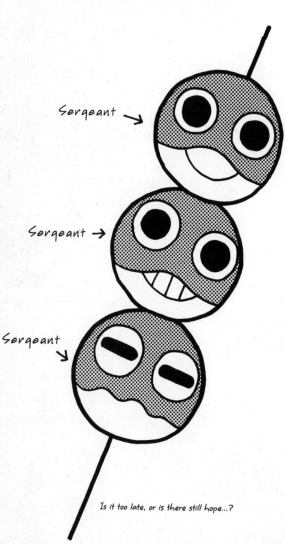

Sergeant →

Sergeant →

Sergeant →

Is it too late, or is there still hope...?

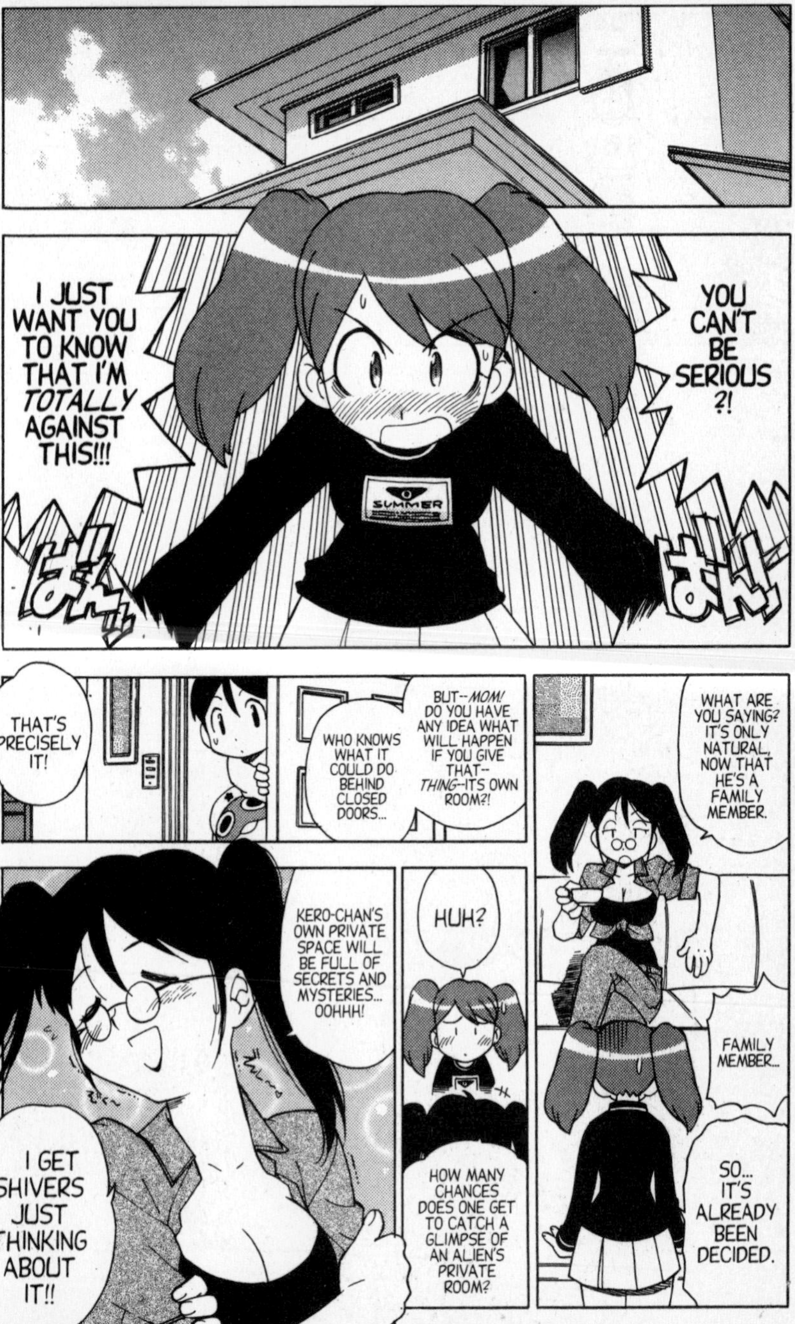
YOU CAN'T BE SERIOUS?!
I JUST WANT YOU TO KNOW THAT I'M *TOTALLY* AGAINST THIS!!!
WHAT ARE YOU SAYING? IT'S ONLY NATURAL, NOW THAT HE'S A FAMILY MEMBER.
FAMILY MEMBER...
SO... IT'S ALREADY BEEN DECIDED.
BUT--*MOM!* DO YOU HAVE ANY IDEA WHAT WILL HAPPEN IF YOU GIVE THAT--*THING*--ITS OWN ROOM?!
WHO KNOWS WHAT IT COULD DO BEHIND CLOSED DOORS...
THAT'S PRECISELY IT!
HUH?
HOW MANY CHANCES DOES ONE GET TO CATCH A GLIMPSE OF AN ALIEN'S PRIVATE ROOM?
KERO-CHAN'S OWN PRIVATE SPACE WILL BE FULL OF SECRETS AND MYSTERIES... OOHHH!
I GET SHIVERS JUST THINKING ABOUT IT!!

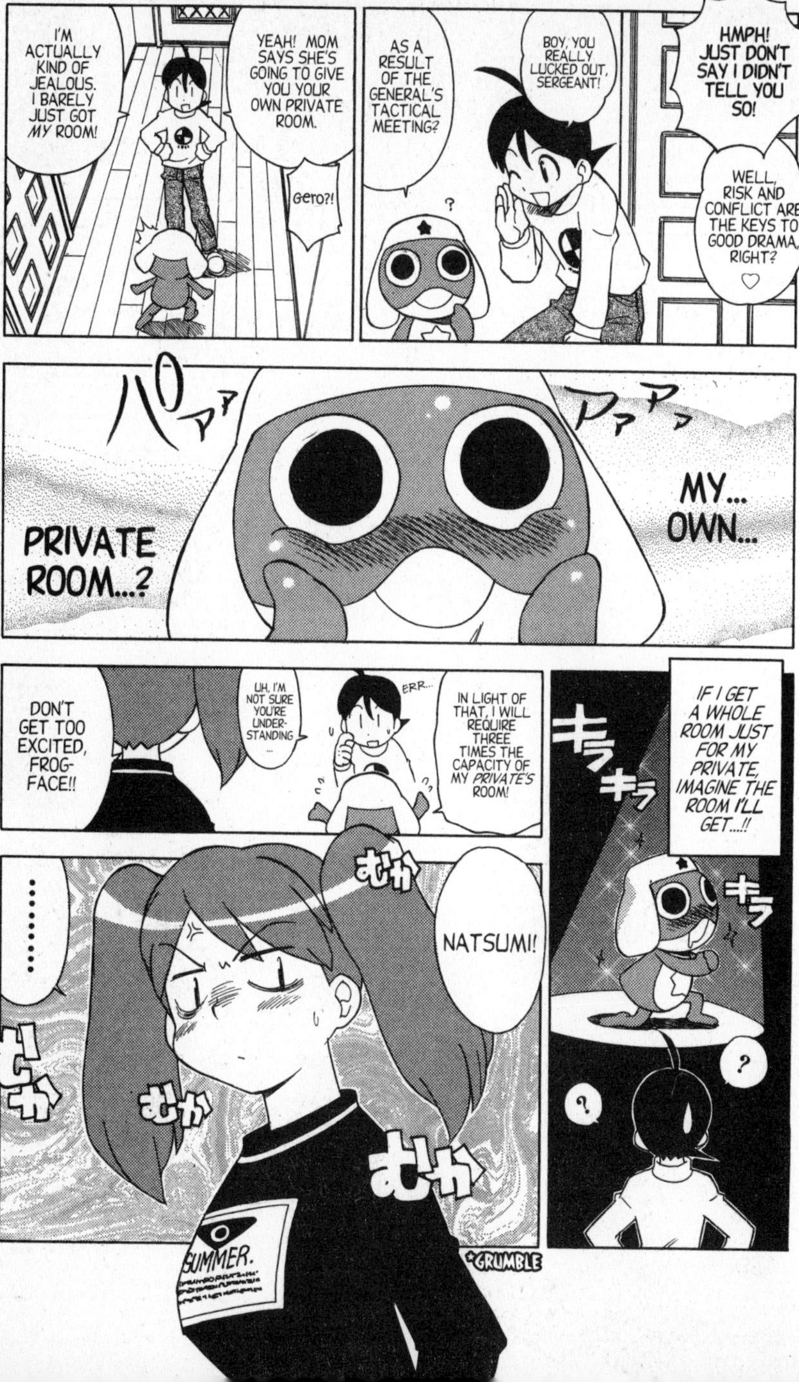
HMPH! JUST DON'T SAY I DIDN'T TELL YOU SO!
BOY, YOU REALLY LUCKED OUT, SERGEANT!
AS A RESULT OF THE GENERAL'S TACTICAL MEETING?
?
WELL, RISK AND CONFLICT ARE THE KEYS TO GOOD DRAMA, RIGHT? ♡
YEAH! MOM SAYS SHE'S GOING TO GIVE YOU YOUR OWN PRIVATE ROOM.
I'M ACTUALLY KIND OF JEALOUS. I BARELY JUST GOT MY ROOM!
Gero?!
MY... OWN...
PRIVATE ROOM...?
IF I GET A WHOLE ROOM JUST FOR MY PRIVATE, IMAGINE THE ROOM I'LL GET...!!
キラ キラ
キラ
?
?
IN LIGHT OF THAT, I WILL REQUIRE THREE TIMES THE CAPACITY OF MY PRIVATE'S ROOM!
ERR...
UH, I'M NOT SURE YOU'RE UNDER-STANDING...
DON'T GET TOO EXCITED, FROG-FACE!!
NATSUMI!
むか
......
むか
むか
むか
SUMMER.
*GRUMBLE

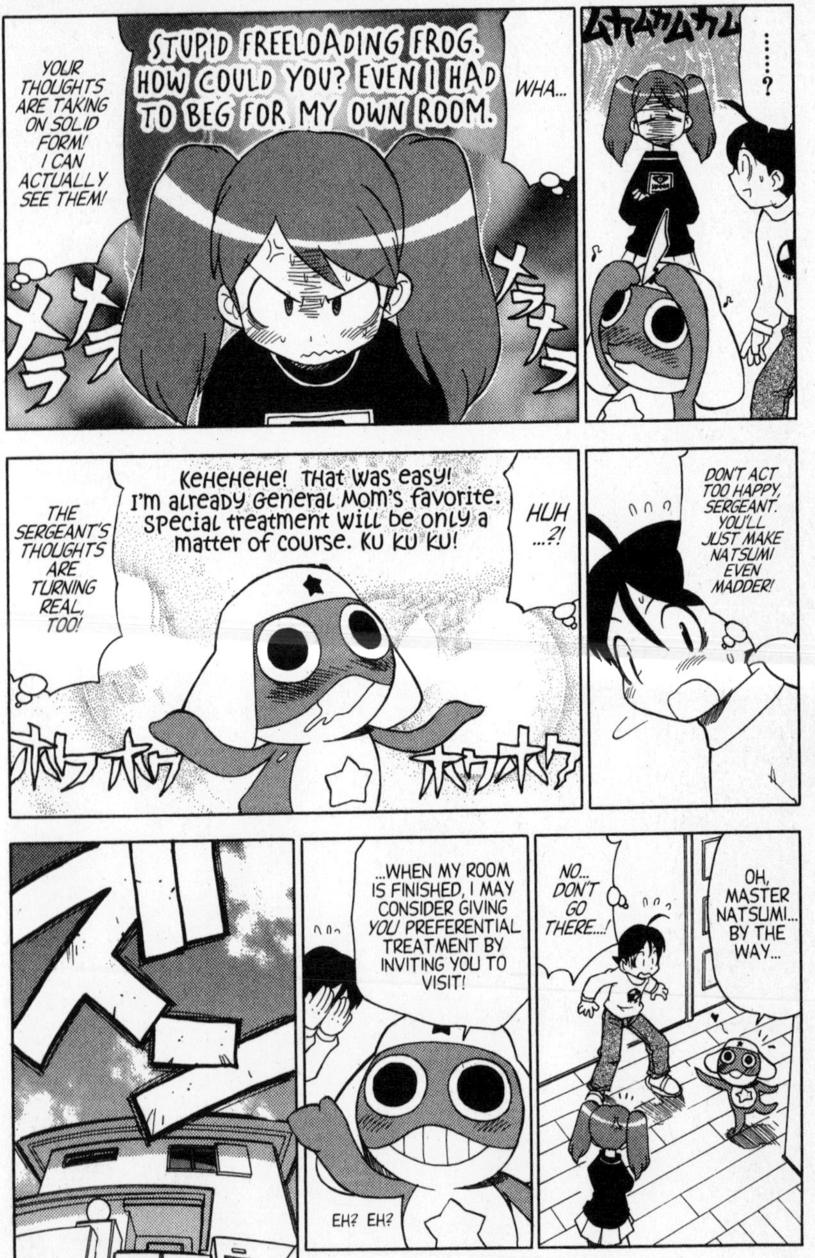
ムカムカムカム
......?
WHA...
STUPID FREELOADING FROG. HOW COULD YOU? EVEN I HAD TO BEG FOR MY OWN ROOM.
YOUR THOUGHTS ARE TAKING ON SOLID FORM! I CAN ACTUALLY SEE THEM!
DON'T ACT TOO HAPPY, SERGEANT. YOU'LL JUST MAKE NATSUMI EVEN MADDER!
HUH ...?!
KEHEHEHE! THAT WAS EASY! I'M ALREADY GENERAL MOM'S FAVORITE. SPECIAL TREATMENT WILL BE ONLY A MATTER OF COURSE. KU KU KU!
THE SERGEANT'S THOUGHTS ARE TURNING REAL, TOO!
ホワホワ
ホワホワ
OH, MASTER NATSUMI... BY THE WAY...
NO... DON'T GO THERE...!
...WHEN MY ROOM IS FINISHED, I MAY CONSIDER GIVING YOU PREFERENTIAL TREATMENT BY INVITING YOU TO VISIT!
EH? EH?

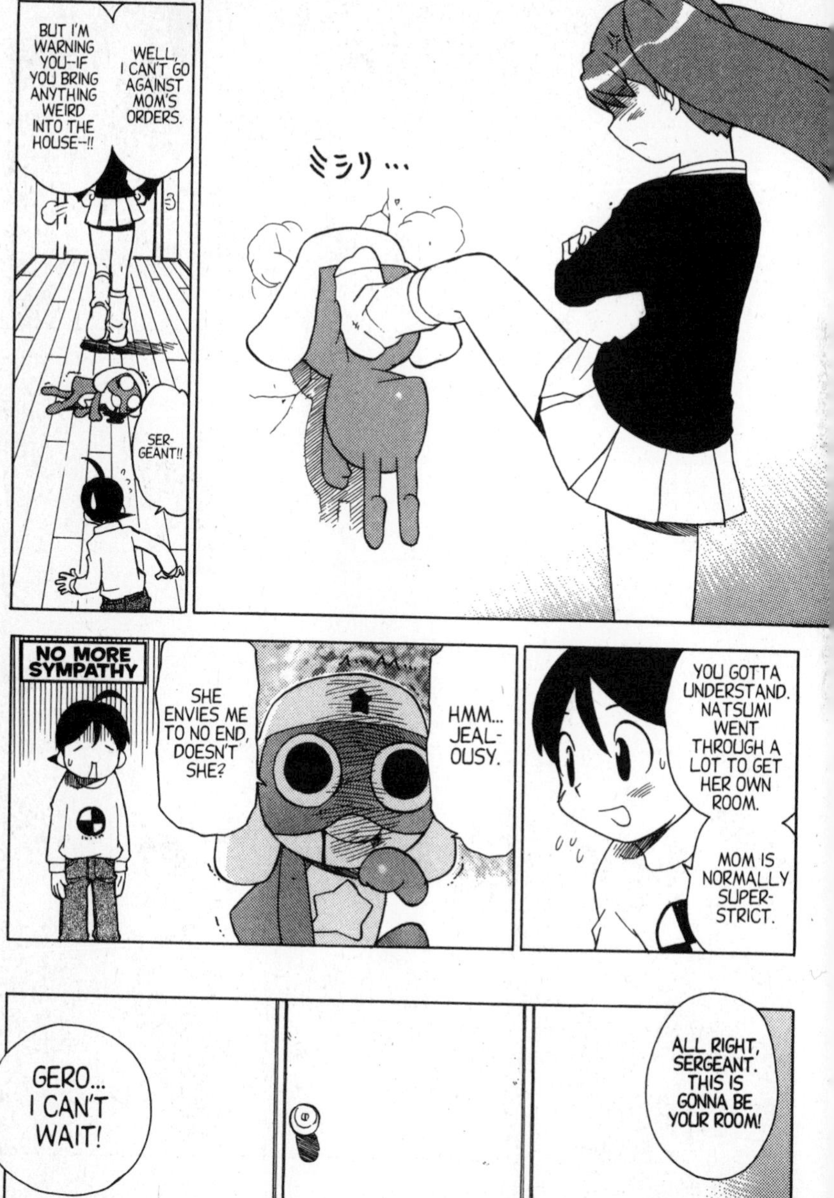
ミシリ…
WELL, I CAN'T GO AGAINST MOM'S ORDERS.
BUT I'M WARNING YOU--IF YOU BRING ANYTHING WEIRD INTO THE HOUSE--!!
SER-GEANT!!
YOU GOTTA UNDERSTAND. NATSUMI WENT THROUGH A LOT TO GET HER OWN ROOM.
MOM IS NORMALLY SUPER-STRICT.
HMM... JEAL-OUSY.
SHE ENVIES ME TO NO END, DOESN'T SHE?
NO MORE SYMPATHY
ALL RIGHT, SERGEANT. THIS IS GONNA BE YOUR ROOM!
GERO... I CAN'T WAIT!

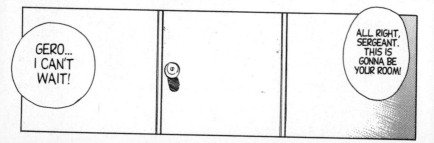

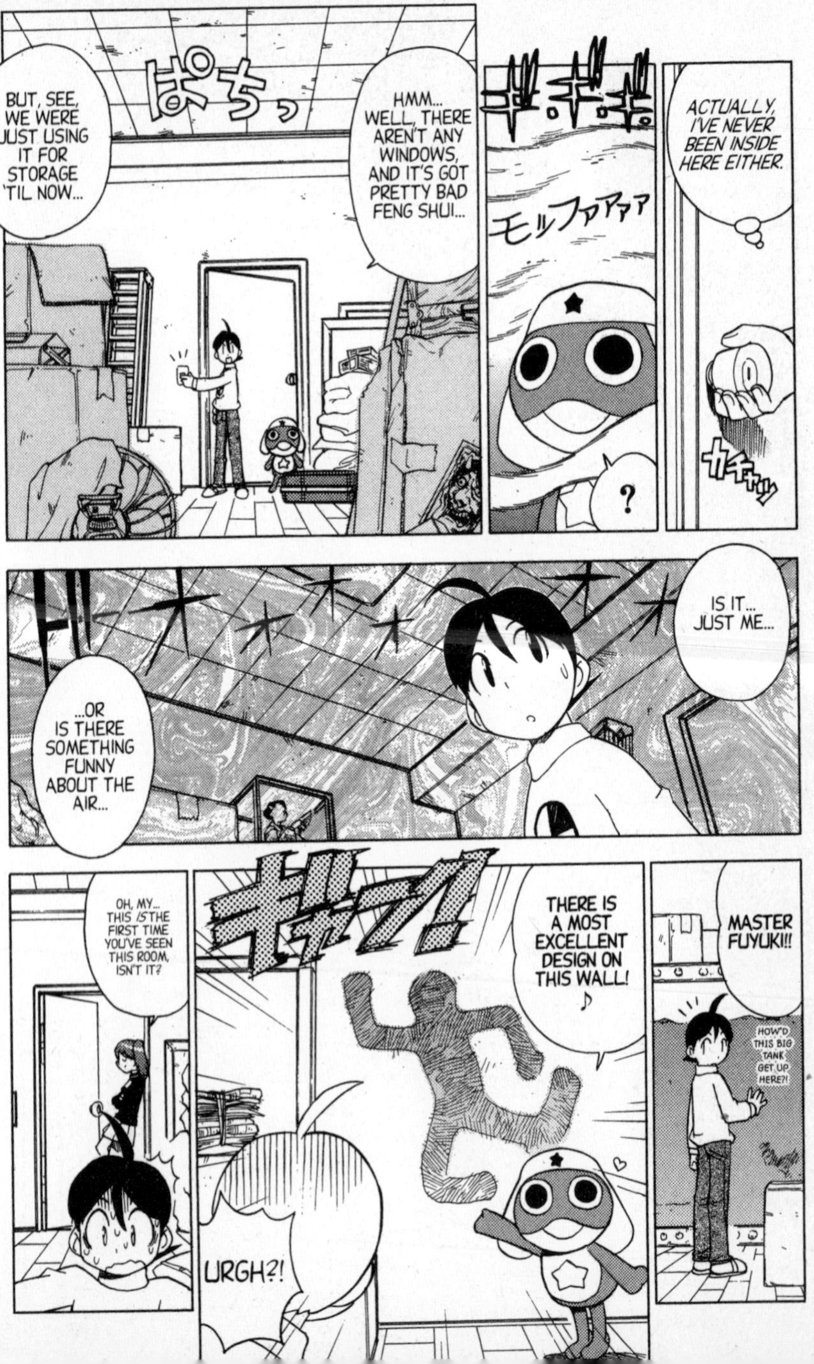
ACTUALLY, I'VE NEVER BEEN INSIDE HERE EITHER.
カチャッ
モルファアアア
?
HMM... WELL, THERE AREN'T ANY WINDOWS, AND IT'S GOT PRETTY BAD FENG SHUI...
ぱちっ
BUT, SEE, WE WERE JUST USING IT FOR STORAGE 'TIL NOW...
IS IT... JUST ME...
...OR IS THERE SOMETHING FUNNY ABOUT THE AIR...
MASTER FUYUKI!!
HOW'D THIS BIG TANK GET UP HERE?!
THERE IS A MOST EXCELLENT DESIGN ON THIS WALL! ♪
URGH?!
OH, MY... THIS *IS* THE FIRST TIME YOU'VE SEEN THIS ROOM, ISN'T IT?

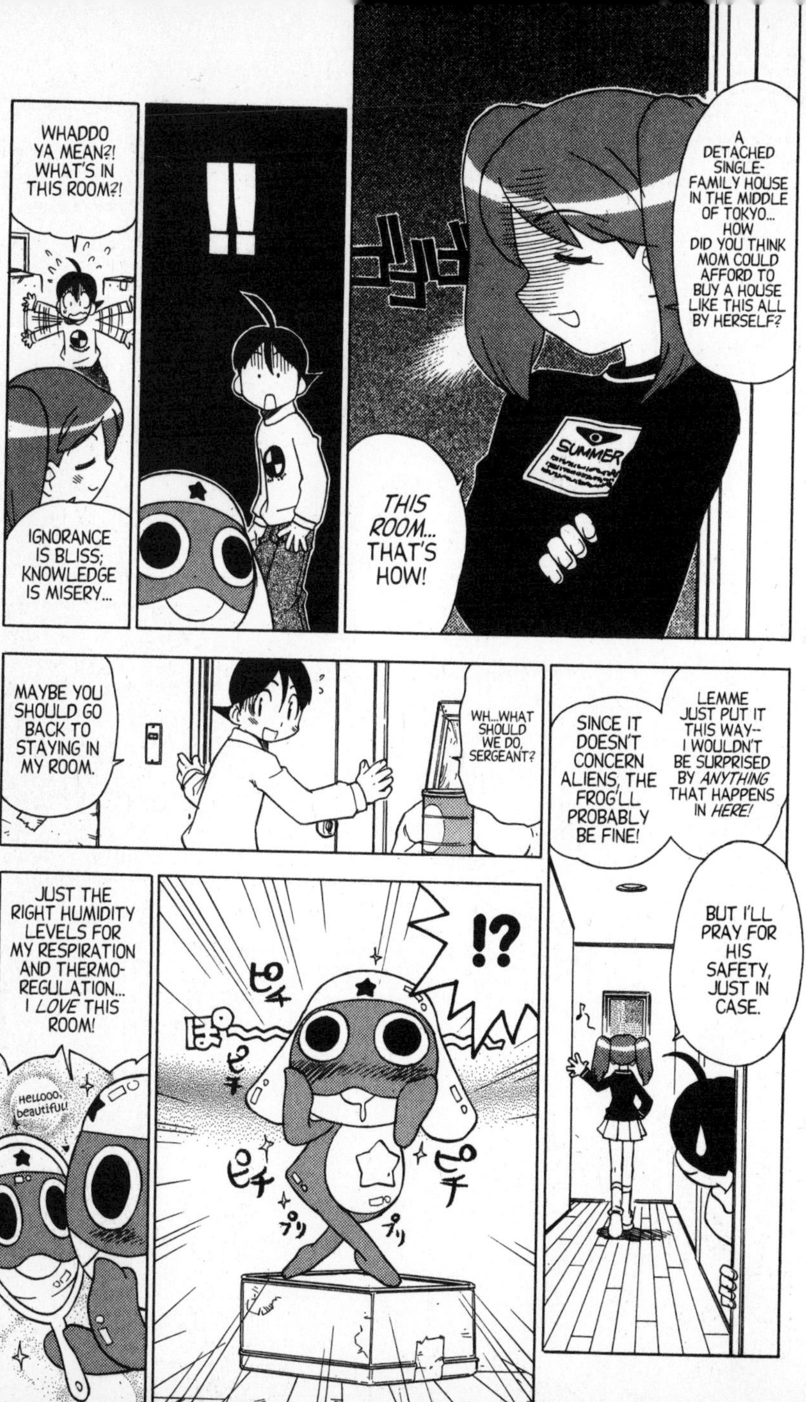
A DETACHED SINGLE-FAMILY HOUSE IN THE MIDDLE OF TOKYO... HOW DID YOU THINK MOM COULD AFFORD TO BUY A HOUSE LIKE THIS ALL BY HERSELF?
THIS ROOM... THAT'S HOW!
!!
WHADDO YA MEAN?! WHAT'S IN THIS ROOM?!
IGNORANCE IS BLISS; KNOWLEDGE IS MISERY...
LEMME JUST PUT IT THIS WAY-- I WOULDN'T BE SURPRISED BY *ANYTHING* THAT HAPPENS IN *HERE!*
SINCE IT DOESN'T CONCERN ALIENS, THE FROG'LL PROBABLY BE FINE!
BUT I'LL PRAY FOR HIS SAFETY, JUST IN CASE.
WH...WHAT SHOULD WE DO, SERGEANT?
MAYBE YOU SHOULD GO BACK TO STAYING IN MY ROOM.
!?
ピチ
ぽ
ピチ
ピチ
ピチ
プリ
プリ
JUST THE RIGHT HUMIDITY LEVELS FOR MY RESPIRATION AND THERMO-REGULATION... I *LOVE* THIS ROOM!
Hellooo, beautiful!

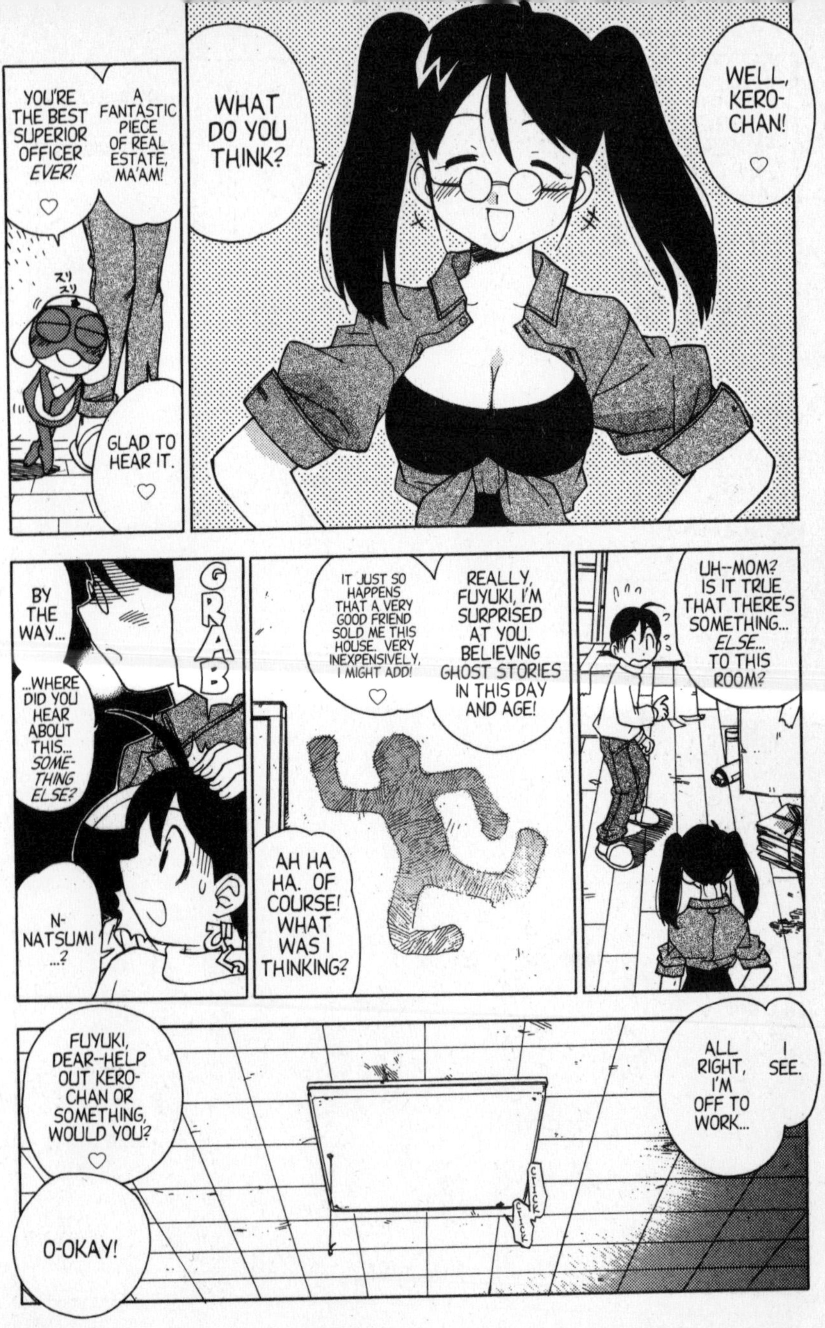
WELL, KERO-CHAN! ♡
WHAT DO YOU THINK?
A FANTASTIC PIECE OF REAL ESTATE, MA'AM!
YOU'RE THE BEST SUPERIOR OFFICER *EVER!* ♡
ズリズリ
GLAD TO HEAR IT. ♡
UH--MOM? IS IT TRUE THAT THERE'S SOMETHING... *ELSE*... TO THIS ROOM?
REALLY, FUYUKI, I'M SURPRISED AT YOU. BELIEVING GHOST STORIES IN THIS DAY AND AGE!
IT JUST SO HAPPENS THAT A VERY GOOD FRIEND SOLD ME THIS HOUSE. VERY INEXPENSIVELY, I MIGHT ADD! ♡
AH HA HA. OF COURSE! WHAT WAS I THINKING?
GRAB
BY THE WAY...
...WHERE DID YOU HEAR ABOUT THIS... *SOMETHING ELSE?*
N-NATSUMI ...?
I SEE.
ALL RIGHT, I'M OFF TO WORK...
FUYUKI, DEAR--HELP OUT KERO-CHAN OR SOMETHING, WOULD YOU? ♡
O-OKAY!
CLICK
CLICK

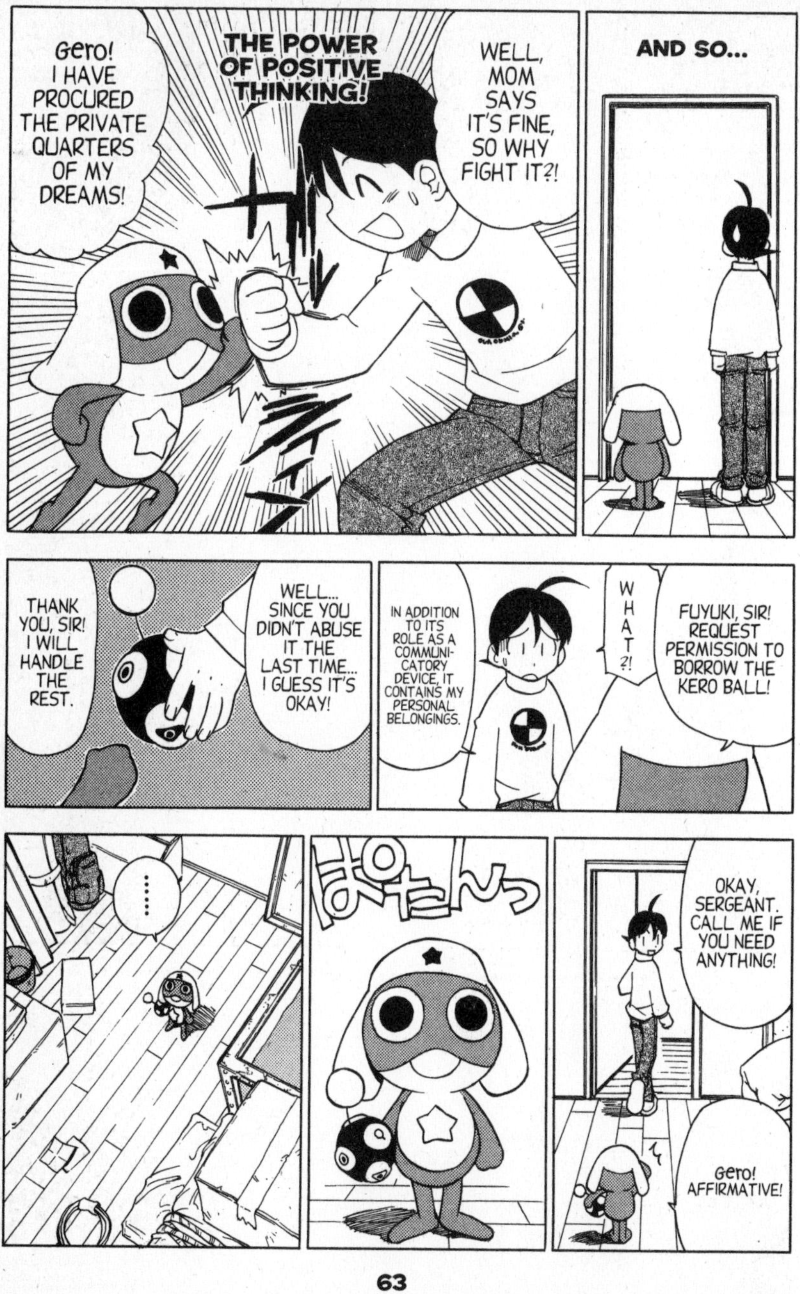
AND SO...
WELL, MOM SAYS IT'S FINE, SO WHY FIGHT IT?!
THE POWER OF POSITIVE THINKING!
Gero! I HAVE PROCURED THE PRIVATE QUARTERS OF MY DREAMS!
FUYUKI, SIR! REQUEST PERMISSION TO BORROW THE KERO BALL!
WHAT?!
IN ADDITION TO ITS ROLE AS A COMMUNICATORY DEVICE, IT CONTAINS MY PERSONAL BELONGINGS.
WELL... SINCE YOU DIDN'T ABUSE IT THE LAST TIME... I GUESS IT'S OKAY!
THANK YOU, SIR! I WILL HANDLE THE REST.
OKAY, SERGEANT. CALL ME IF YOU NEED ANYTHING!
Gero! AFFIRMATIVE!
ぱたんっ
......

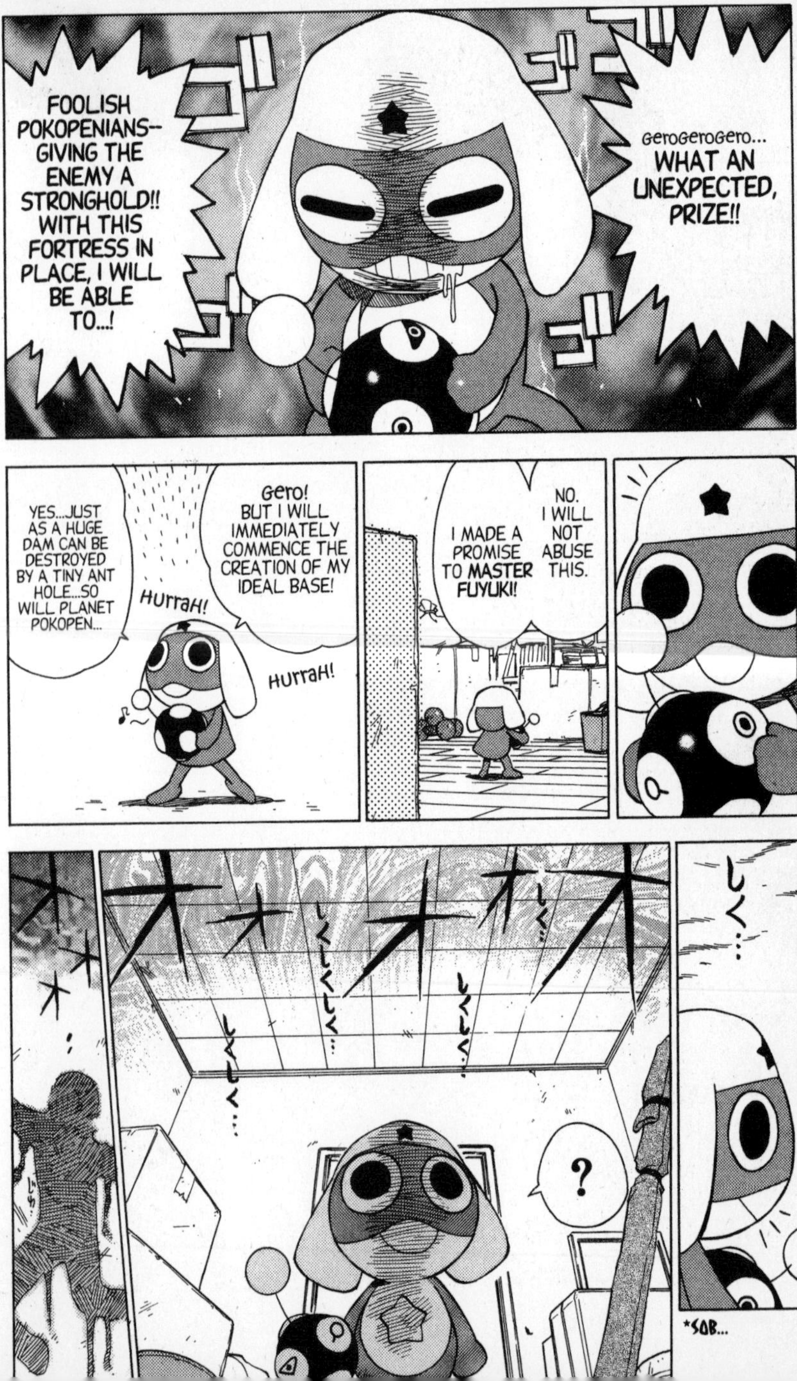
GeroGeroGero... WHAT AN UNEXPECTED, PRIZE!!
FOOLISH POKOPENIANS-GIVING THE ENEMY A STRONGHOLD!! WITH THIS FORTRESS IN PLACE, I WILL BE ABLE TO...!
NO. I WILL NOT ABUSE THIS.
I MADE A PROMISE TO MASTER FUYUKI!!
Gero! BUT I WILL IMMEDIATELY COMMENCE THE CREATION OF MY IDEAL BASE!
YES...JUST AS A HUGE DAM CAN BE DESTROYED BY A TINY ANT HOLE...SO WILL PLANET POKOPEN...
HurraH!
HurraH!
しく…
しく…
しくしく…
しくしくしく…
しくしく…
?
*SOB...

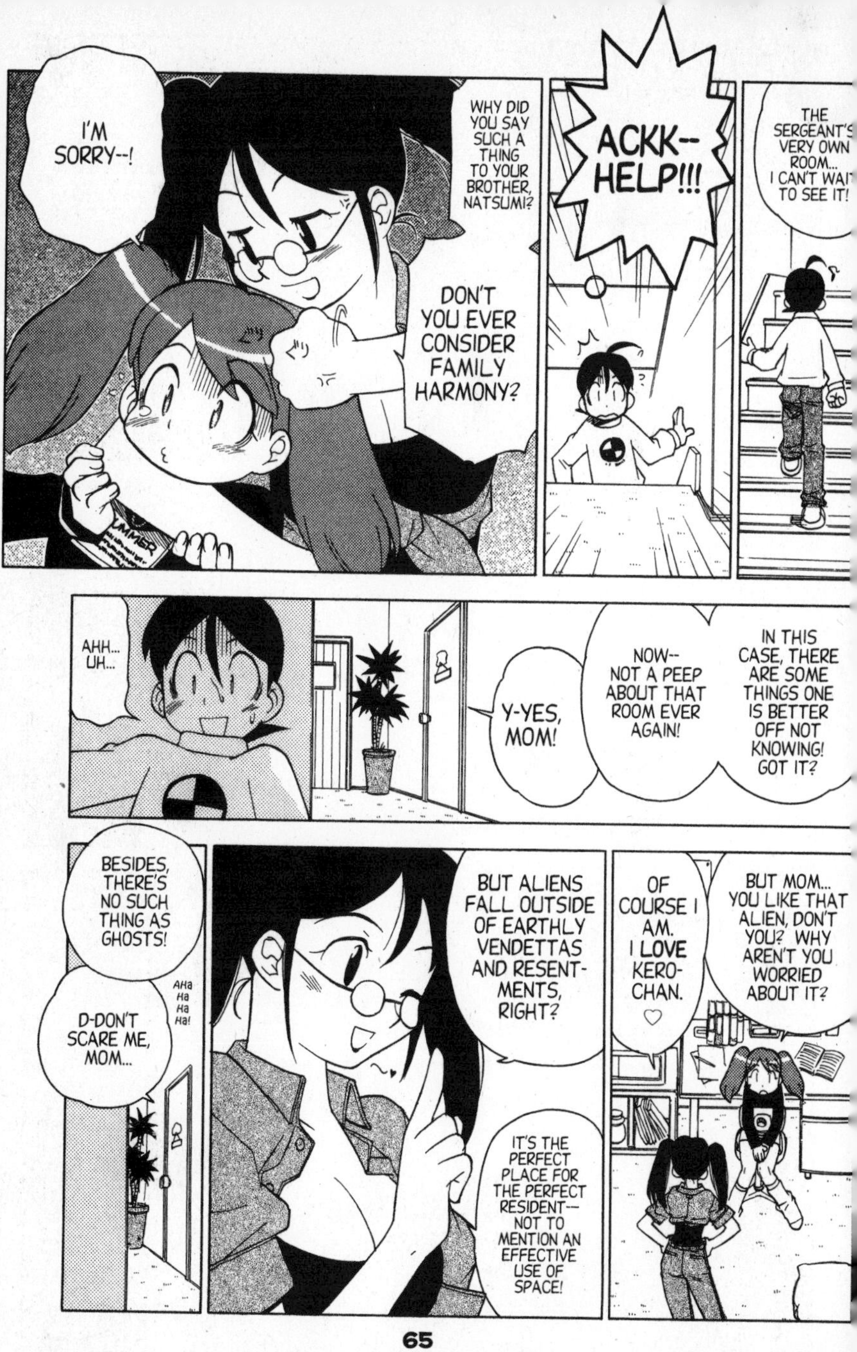
THE SERGEANT'S VERY OWN ROOM... I CAN'T WAIT TO SEE IT!
ACKK-- HELP!!!
WHY DID YOU SAY SUCH A THING TO YOUR BROTHER, NATSUMI?
DON'T YOU EVER CONSIDER FAMILY HARMONY?
I'M SORRY--!
IN THIS CASE, THERE ARE SOME THINGS ONE IS BETTER OFF NOT KNOWING! GOT IT?
NOW-- NOT A PEEP ABOUT THAT ROOM EVER AGAIN!
Y-YES, MOM!
AHH... UH...
BUT MOM... YOU LIKE THAT ALIEN, DON'T YOU? WHY AREN'T YOU WORRIED ABOUT IT?
OF COURSE I AM. I LOVE KERO-CHAN. ♡
BUT ALIENS FALL OUTSIDE OF EARTHLY VENDETTAS AND RESENT-MENTS, RIGHT?
IT'S THE PERFECT PLACE FOR THE PERFECT RESIDENT-- NOT TO MENTION AN EFFECTIVE USE OF SPACE!
BESIDES, THERE'S NO SUCH THING AS GHOSTS!
AHA HA HA HA!
D-DON'T SCARE ME, MOM...

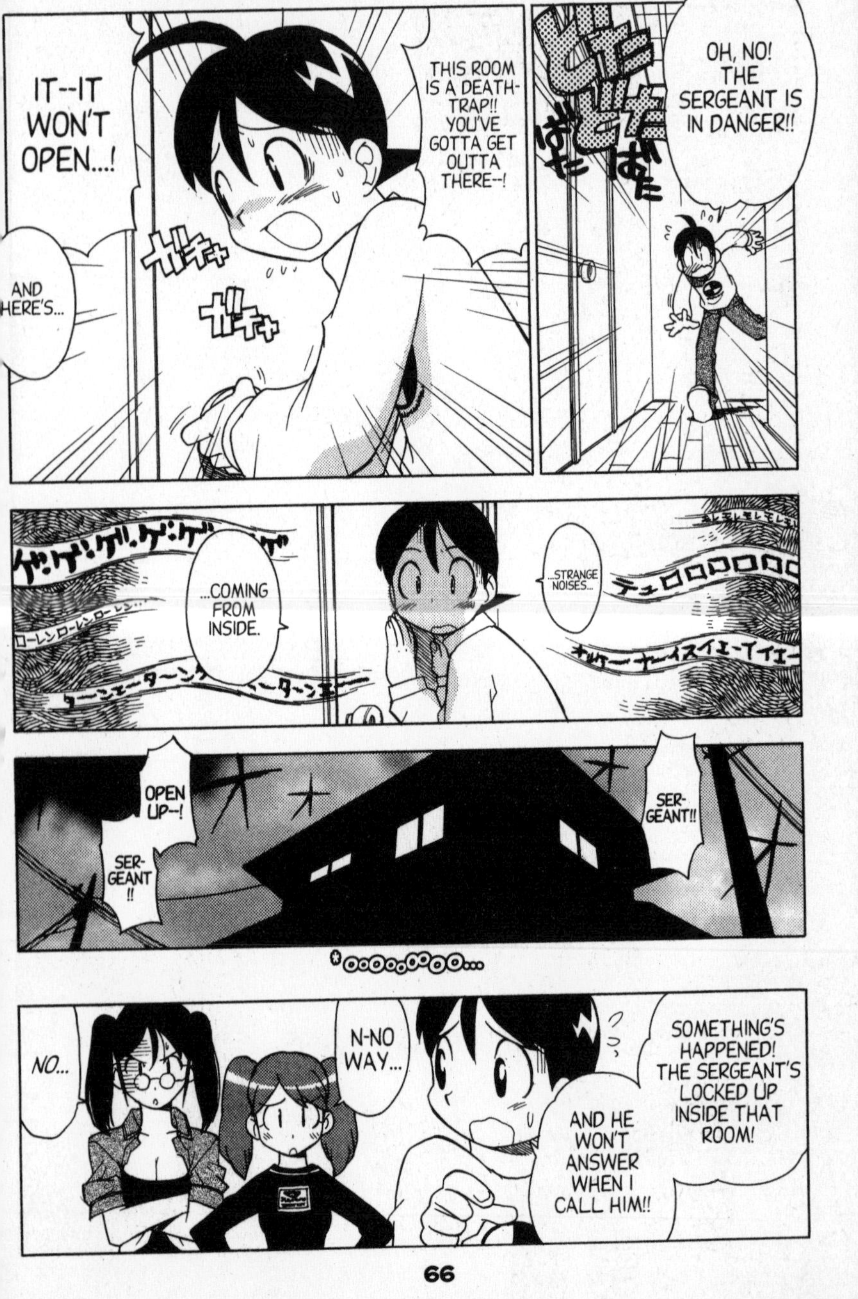
OH, NO! THE SERGEANT IS IN DANGER!!
THIS ROOM IS A DEATH-TRAP!! YOU'VE GOTTA GET OUTTA THERE--!
IT--IT WON'T OPEN...!
ガチャ
ガチャ
AND HERE'S...
...STRANGE NOISES...
...COMING FROM INSIDE.
SER-GEANT!!
OPEN UP--!
SER-GEANT !!
SOMETHING'S HAPPENED! THE SERGEANT'S LOCKED UP INSIDE THAT ROOM!
AND HE WON'T ANSWER WHEN I CALL HIM!!
N-NO WAY...
NO...

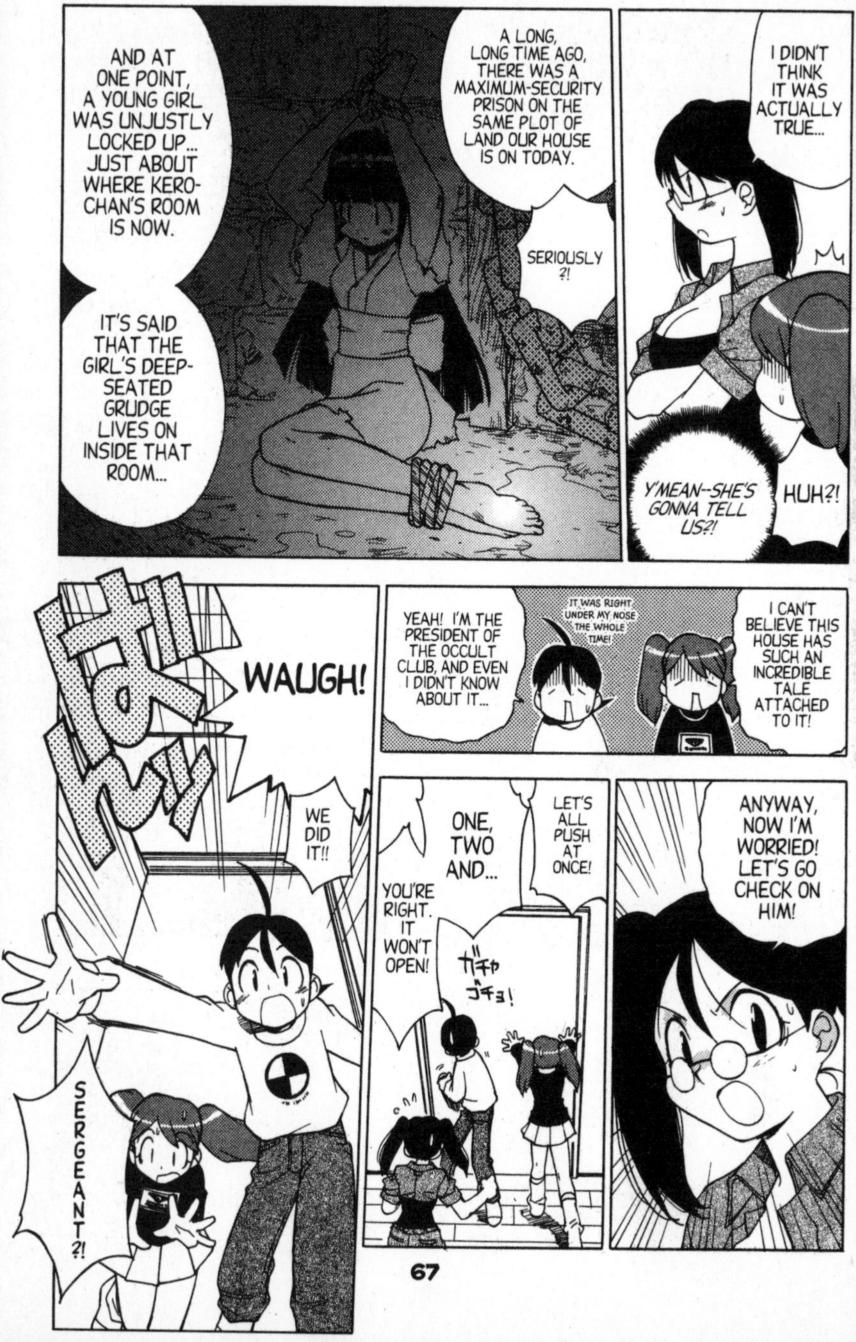
I DIDN'T THINK IT WAS ACTUALLY TRUE...
HUH?!
Y'MEAN--SHE'S GONNA TELL US?!
A LONG, LONG TIME AGO, THERE WAS A MAXIMUM-SECURITY PRISON ON THE SAME PLOT OF LAND OUR HOUSE IS ON TODAY.
AND AT ONE POINT, A YOUNG GIRL WAS UNJUSTLY LOCKED UP... JUST ABOUT WHERE KERO-CHAN'S ROOM IS NOW.
SERIOUSLY?!
IT'S SAID THAT THE GIRL'S DEEP-SEATED GRUDGE LIVES ON INSIDE THAT ROOM...
I CAN'T BELIEVE THIS HOUSE HAS SUCH AN INCREDIBLE TALE ATTACHED TO IT!
IT WAS RIGHT UNDER MY NOSE THE WHOLE TIME!
YEAH! I'M THE PRESIDENT OF THE OCCULT CLUB, AND EVEN I DIDN'T KNOW ABOUT IT...
ANYWAY, NOW I'M WORRIED! LET'S GO CHECK ON HIM!
LET'S ALL PUSH AT ONCE!
ONE, TWO AND...
YOU'RE RIGHT. IT WON'T OPEN!
ガチャ ゴチョ!
WAUGH!
WE DID IT!!
SERGEANT?!

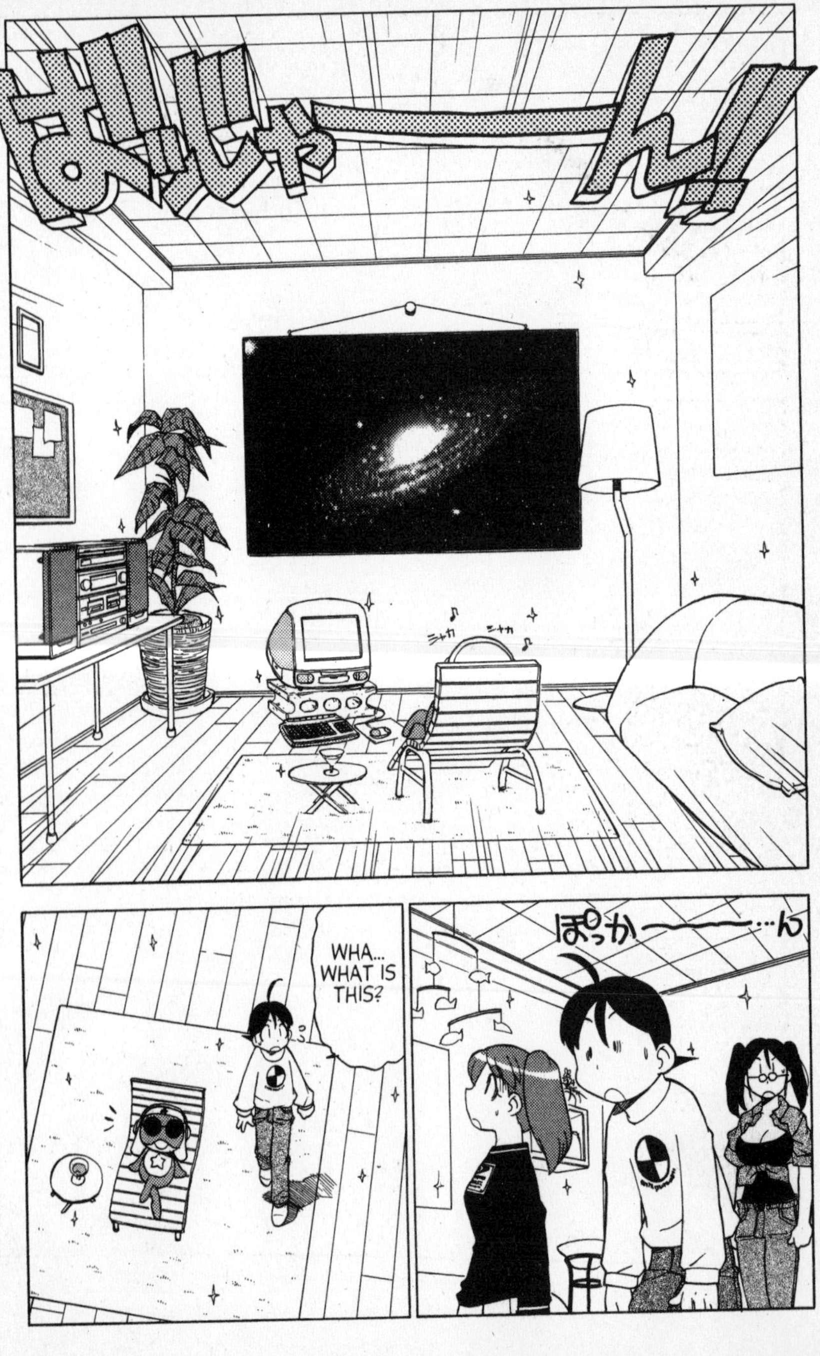
シャカ
シャカ
ぽっかーーーー…ん
WHA... WHAT IS THIS?

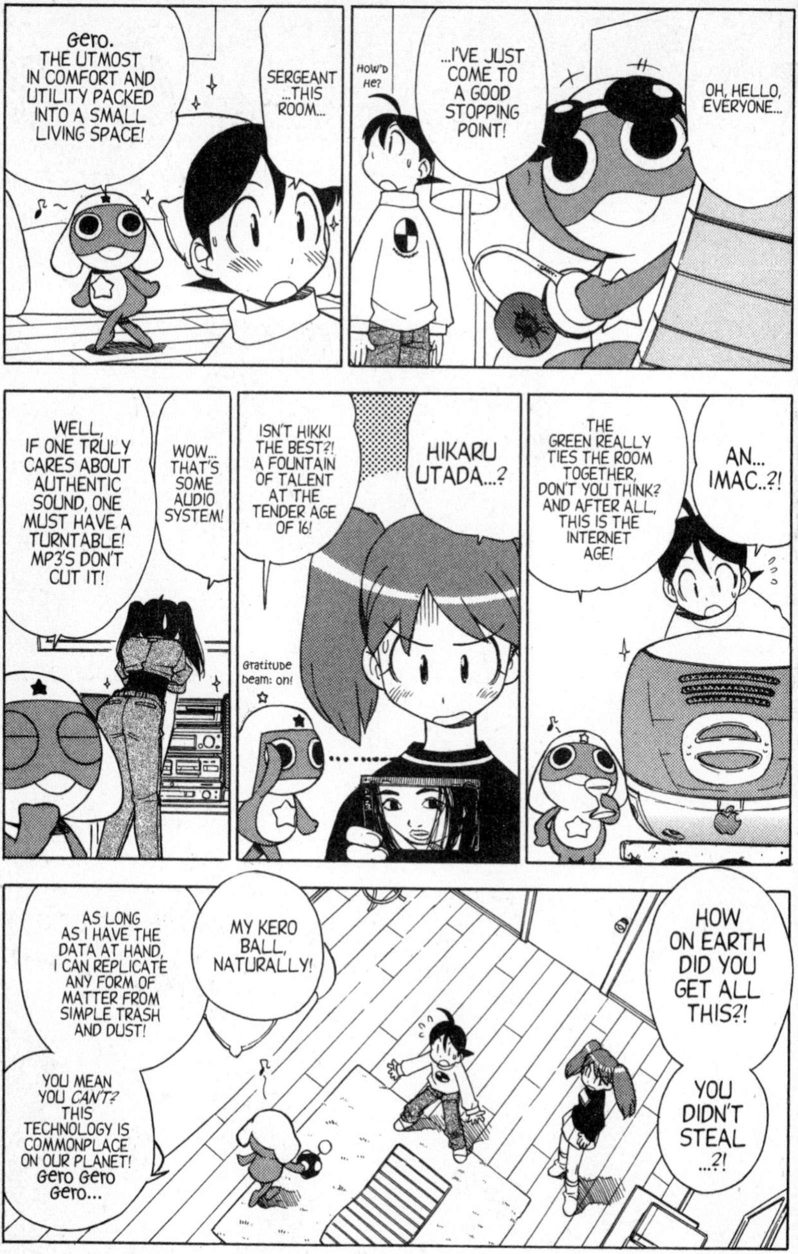
OH, HELLO, EVERYONE...
...I'VE JUST COME TO A GOOD STOPPING POINT!
HOW'D HE?
SERGEANT ...THIS ROOM...
Gero. THE UTMOST IN COMFORT AND UTILITY PACKED INTO A SMALL LIVING SPACE!
AN... IMAC..?!
THE GREEN REALLY TIES THE ROOM TOGETHER, DON'T YOU THINK? AND AFTER ALL, THIS IS THE INTERNET AGE!
HIKARU UTADA...?
ISN'T HIKKI THE BEST?! A FOUNTAIN OF TALENT AT THE TENDER AGE OF 16!
Gratitude beam: on!
WOW... THAT'S SOME AUDIO SYSTEM!
WELL, IF ONE TRULY CARES ABOUT AUTHENTIC SOUND, ONE MUST HAVE A TURNTABLE! MP3'S DON'T CUT IT!
HOW ON EARTH DID YOU GET ALL THIS?!
YOU DIDN'T STEAL ...?!
MY KERO BALL, NATURALLY!
AS LONG AS I HAVE THE DATA AT HAND, I CAN REPLICATE ANY FORM OF MATTER FROM SIMPLE TRASH AND DUST!
YOU MEAN YOU CAN'T? THIS TECHNOLOGY IS COMMONPLACE ON OUR PLANET! Gero Gero Gero...

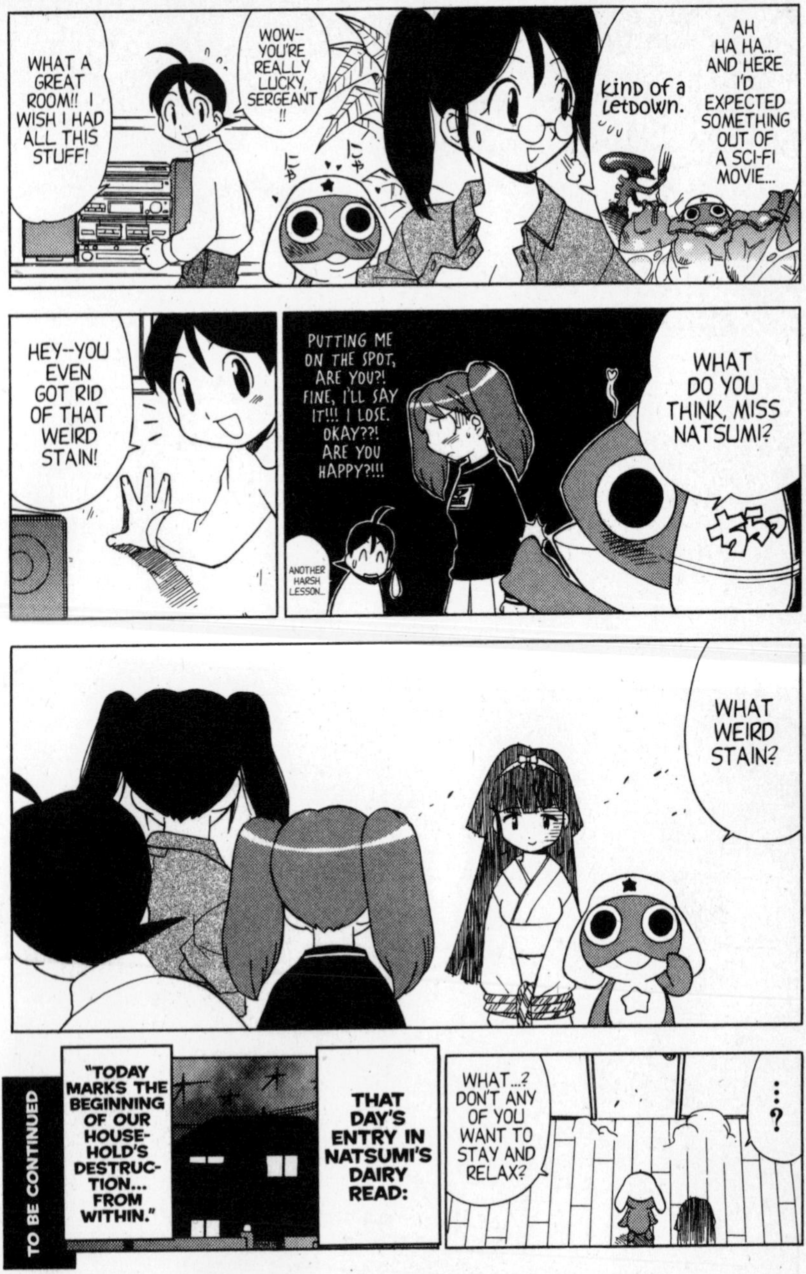
AH HA HA... AND HERE I'D EXPECTED SOMETHING OUT OF A SCI-FI MOVIE...
Kind of a letdown.
WOW-- YOU'RE REALLY LUCKY, SERGEANT!!
にゃ
にゃ
WHAT A GREAT ROOM!! I WISH I HAD ALL THIS STUFF!
WHAT DO YOU THINK, MISS NATSUMI?
ちらっ
PUTTING ME ON THE SPOT, ARE YOU?! FINE, I'LL SAY IT!!! I LOSE. OKAY??! ARE YOU HAPPY?!!!
ANOTHER HARSH LESSON...
HEY--YOU EVEN GOT RID OF THAT WEIRD STAIN!
WHAT WEIRD STAIN?
...?
WHAT...? DON'T ANY OF YOU WANT TO STAY AND RELAX?
THAT DAY'S ENTRY IN NATSUMI'S DAIRY READ:
"TODAY MARKS THE BEGINNING OF OUR HOUSEHOLD'S DESTRUCTION... FROM WITHIN."
TO BE CONTINUED

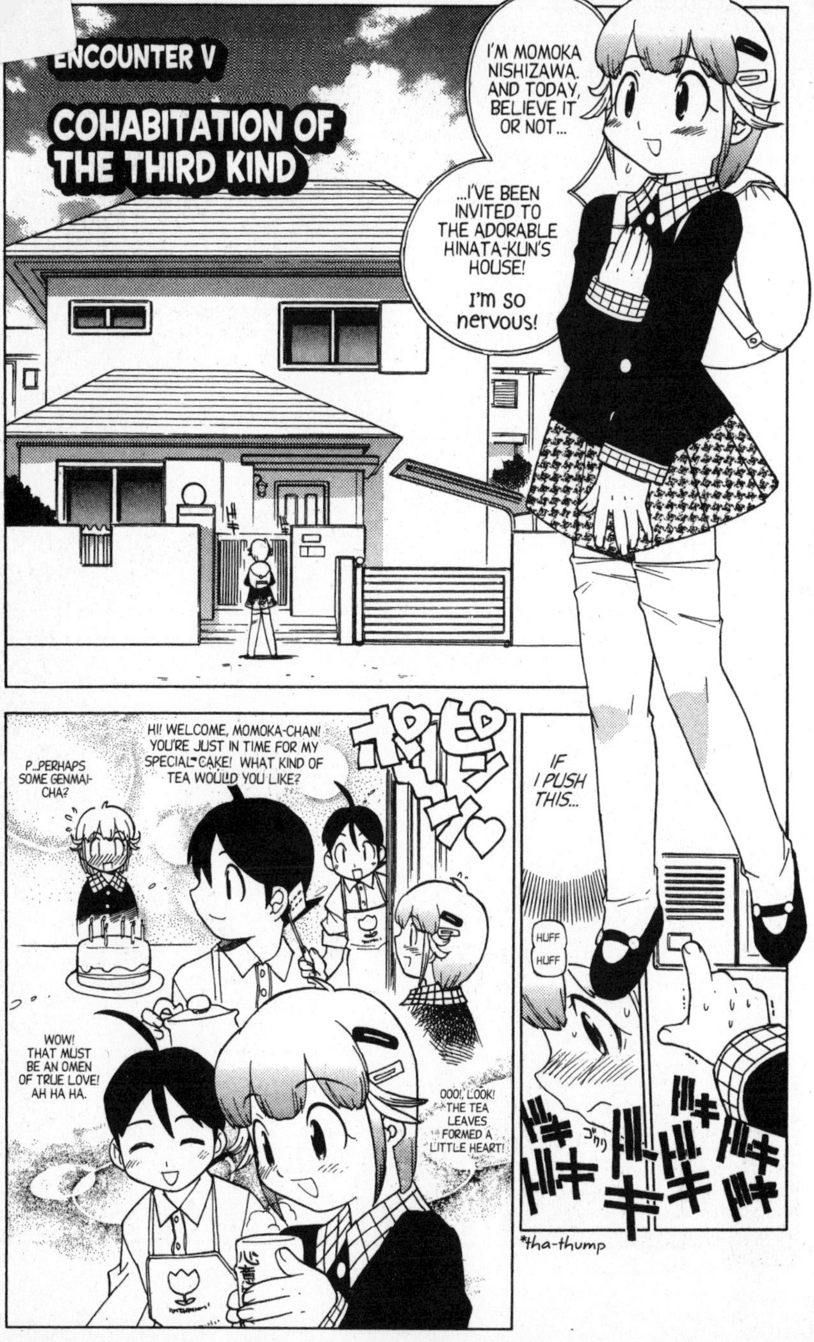
ENCOUNTER V
COHABITATION OF THE THIRD KIND
I'M MOMOKA NISHIZAWA. AND TODAY, BELIEVE IT OR NOT...
...I'VE BEEN INVITED TO THE ADORABLE HINATA-KUN'S HOUSE!
I'm so nervous!
IF I PUSH THIS...
HUFF
HUFF
*tha-thump
HI! WELCOME, MOMOKA-CHAN! YOU'RE JUST IN TIME FOR MY SPECIAL CAKE! WHAT KIND OF TEA WOULD YOU LIKE?
P...PERHAPS SOME GENMAI-CHA?
OOO!, LOOK! THE TEA LEAVES FORMED A LITTLE HEART!
WOW! THAT MUST BE AN OMEN OF TRUE LOVE! AH HA HA.

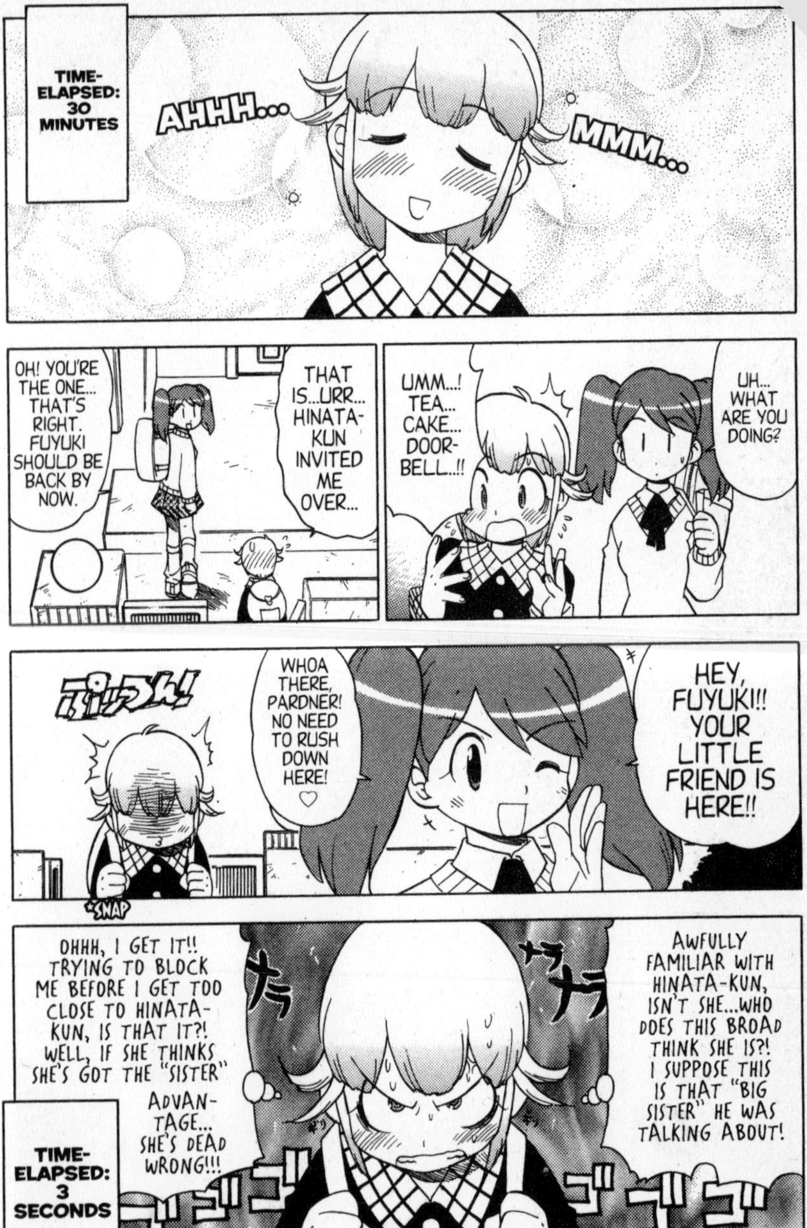
MMM...
AHHH...
TIME-ELAPSED: 30 MINUTES
UH... WHAT ARE YOU DOING?
UMM...! TEA... CAKE... DOOR-BELL...!!
THAT IS...URR... HINATA-KUN INVITED ME OVER...
OH! YOU'RE THE ONE... THAT'S RIGHT. FUYUKI SHOULD BE BACK BY NOW.
HEY, FUYUKI!! YOUR LITTLE FRIEND IS HERE!!
WHOA THERE, PARDNER! NO NEED TO RUSH DOWN HERE! ♡
ぷっつん!
*SNAP
AWFULLY FAMILIAR WITH HINATA-KUN, ISN'T SHE...WHO DOES THIS BROAD THINK SHE IS?! I SUPPOSE THIS IS THAT "BIG SISTER" HE WAS TALKING ABOUT!
OHHH, I GET IT!! TRYING TO BLOCK ME BEFORE I GET TOO CLOSE TO HINATA-KUN, IS THAT IT?! WELL, IF SHE THINKS SHE'S GOT THE "SISTER"
ADVAN-TAGE... SHE'S DEAD WRONG!!!
TIME-ELAPSED: 3 SECONDS

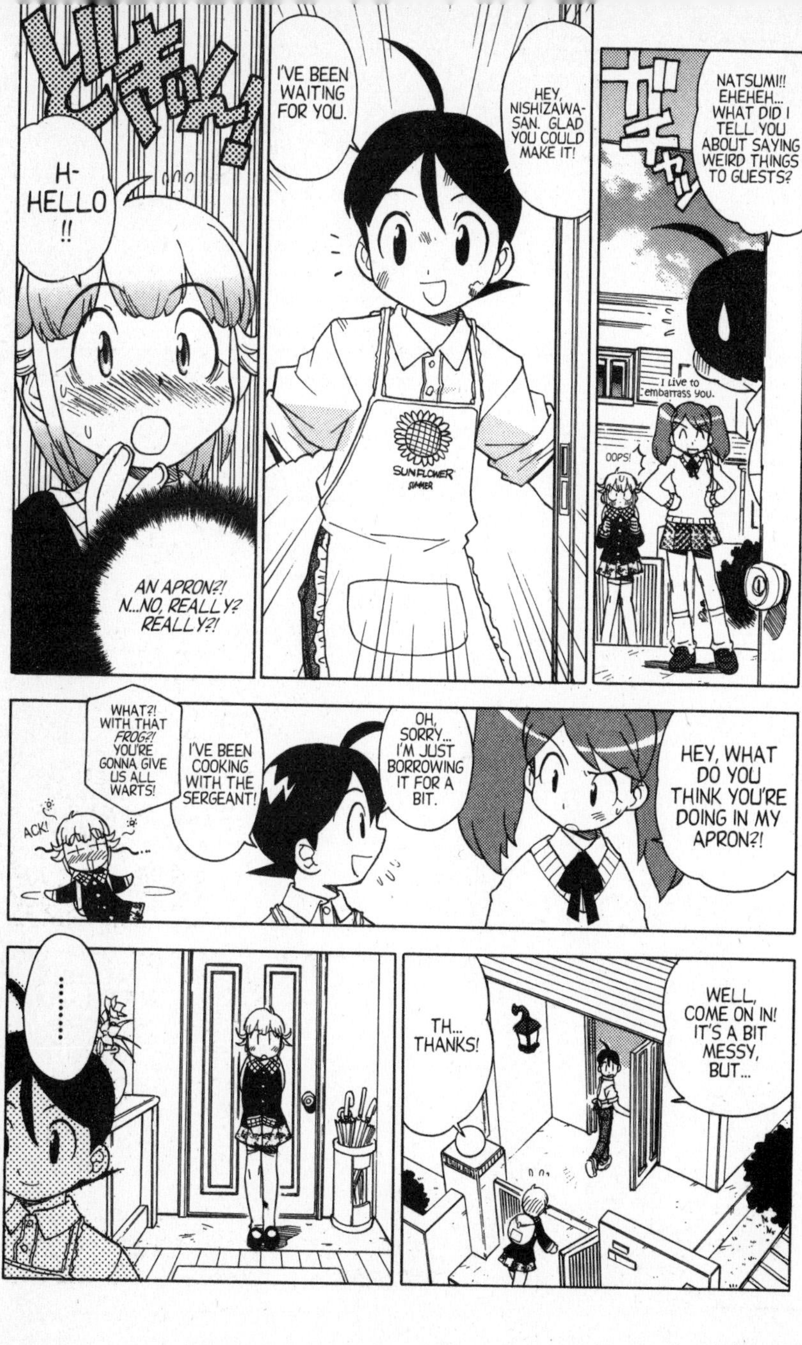
ガチャッ
NATSUMI!! EHEHEH... WHAT DID I TELL YOU ABOUT SAYING WEIRD THINGS TO GUESTS?
I live to embarrass you.
OOPS!
HEY, NISHIZAWA-SAN. GLAD YOU COULD MAKE IT!
I'VE BEEN WAITING FOR YOU.
SUNFLOWER
H-HELLO!!
AN APRON?! N...NO, REALLY? REALLY?!
HEY, WHAT DO YOU THINK YOU'RE DOING IN MY APRON?!
OH, SORRY... I'M JUST BORROWING IT FOR A BIT.
I'VE BEEN COOKING WITH THE SERGEANT!
WHAT?! WITH THAT FROG?! YOU'RE GONNA GIVE US ALL WARTS!
ACK!
WELL, COME ON IN! IT'S A BIT MESSY, BUT...
TH... THANKS!
....

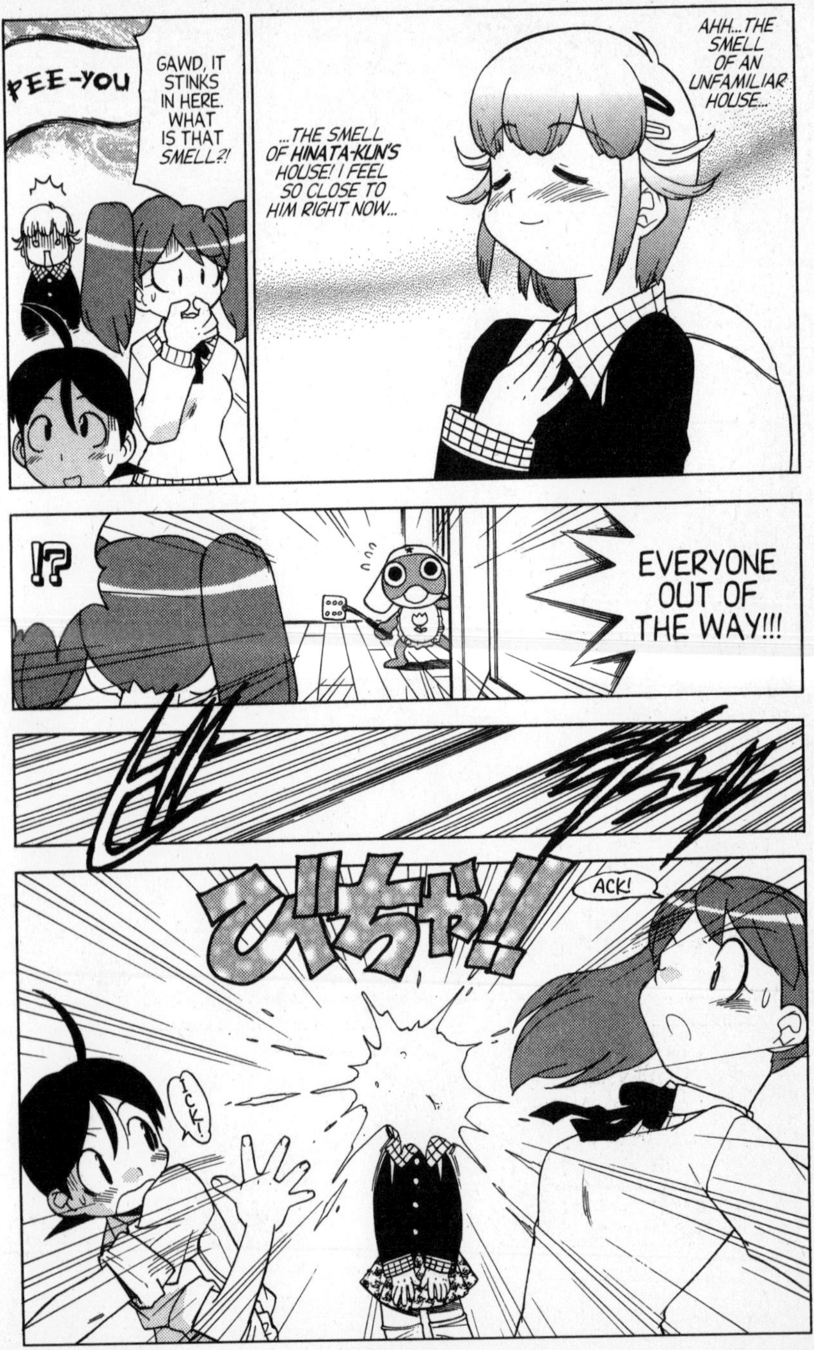
AHH...THE SMELL OF AN UNFAMILIAR HOUSE...
...THE SMELL OF HINATA-KUN'S HOUSE! I FEEL SO CLOSE TO HIM RIGHT NOW...
GAWD, IT STINKS IN HERE. WHAT IS THAT SMELL?!
PEE-YOU
EVERYONE OUT OF THE WAY!!!
!?
びちゃ!!
ACK!
ICK!

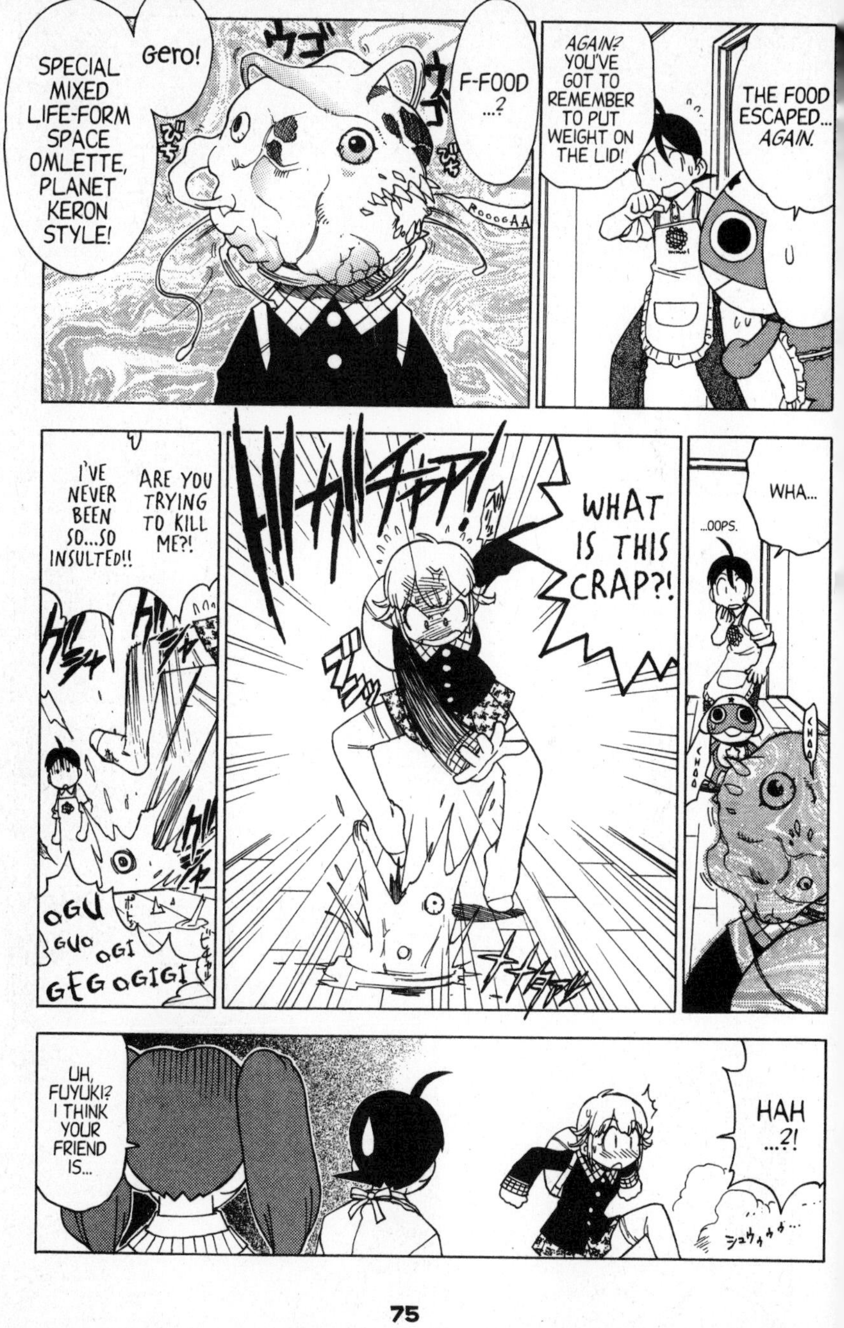
THE FOOD ESCAPED... AGAIN.
AGAIN? YOU'VE GOT TO REMEMBER TO PUT WEIGHT ON THE LID!
F-FOOD ...?
Gero!
SPECIAL MIXED LIFE-FORM SPACE OMLETTE, PLANET KERON STYLE!
ROOOGAA
WHA...
...OOPS.
WHAT IS THIS CRAP?!
ARE YOU TRYING TO KILL ME?!
I'VE NEVER BEEN SO...SO INSULTED!!
OGU GUO OGI GEGOGIGI
HAH ...?!
UH, FUYUKI? I THINK YOUR FRIEND IS...

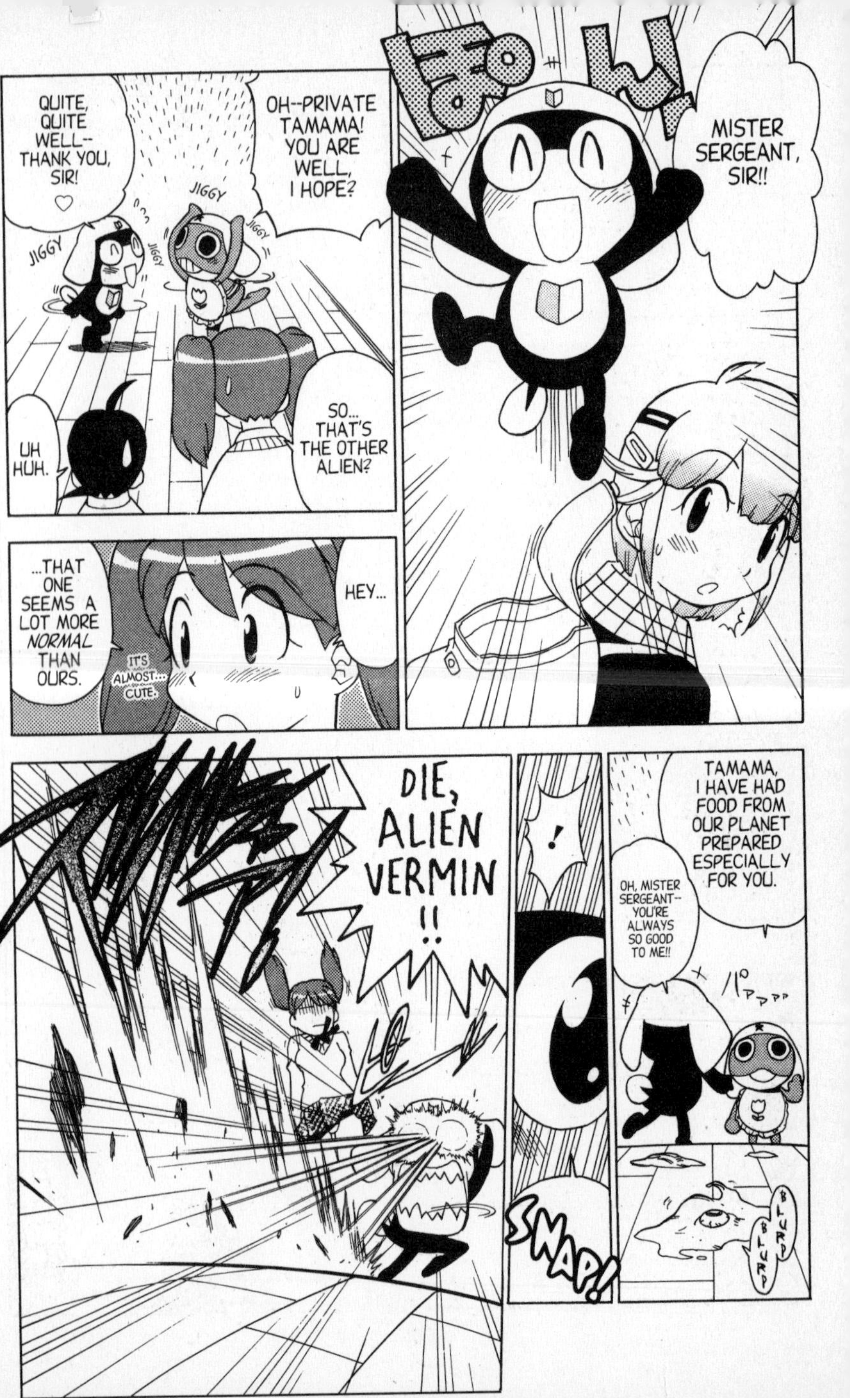
MISTER SERGEANT, SIR!!
OH--PRIVATE TAMAMA! YOU ARE WELL, I HOPE?
QUITE, QUITE WELL--THANK YOU, SIR! ♡
JIGGY
JIGGY
JIGGY
JIGGY
SO... THAT'S THE OTHER ALIEN?
UH HUH.
HEY...
...THAT ONE SEEMS A LOT MORE *NORMAL* THAN OURS.
IT'S ALMOST... CUTE.
TAMAMA, I HAVE HAD FOOD FROM OUR PLANET PREPARED ESPECIALLY FOR YOU.
OH, MISTER SERGEANT--YOU'RE ALWAYS SO GOOD TO ME!!
BLURP
BLURP
!
SNAP!
DIE, ALIEN VERMIN!!

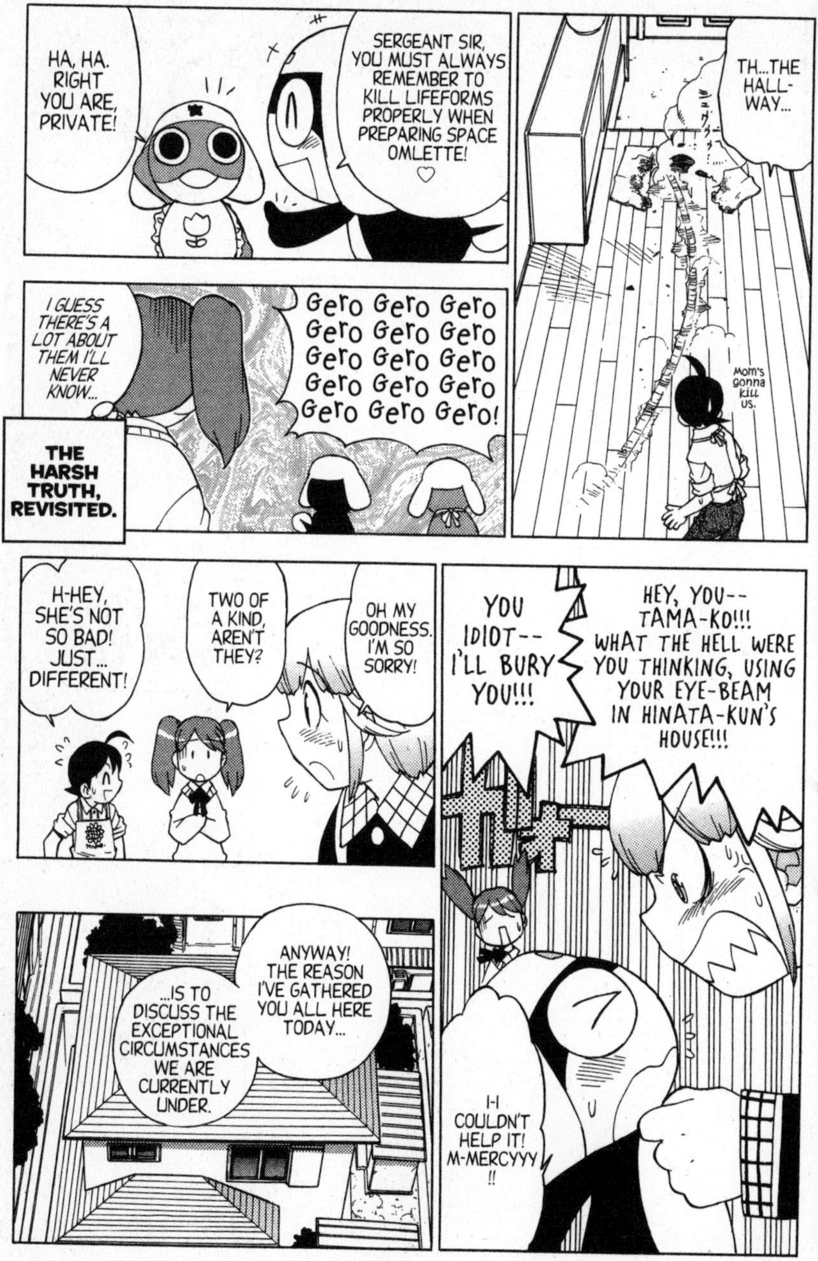
TH...THE HALL-WAY...
Mom's gonna kill us.
SERGEANT SIR, YOU MUST ALWAYS REMEMBER TO KILL LIFEFORMS PROPERLY WHEN PREPARING SPACE OMLETTE! ♡
HA, HA. RIGHT YOU ARE, PRIVATE!
Gero Gero Gero Gero Gero Gero Gero Gero Gero Gero Gero Gero Gero Gero Gero!
I GUESS THERE'S A LOT ABOUT THEM I'LL NEVER KNOW...
THE HARSH TRUTH, REVISITED.
HEY, YOU-- TAMA-KO!!! WHAT THE HELL WERE YOU THINKING, USING YOUR EYE-BEAM IN HINATA-KUN'S HOUSE!!!
YOU IDIOT-- I'LL BURY YOU!!!
I-I COULDN'T HELP IT! M-MERCYYY !!
OH MY GOODNESS. I'M SO SORRY!
TWO OF A KIND, AREN'T THEY?
H-HEY, SHE'S NOT SO BAD! JUST... DIFFERENT!
ANYWAY! THE REASON I'VE GATHERED YOU ALL HERE TODAY...
...IS TO DISCUSS THE EXCEPTIONAL CIRCUMSTANCES WE ARE CURRENTLY UNDER.

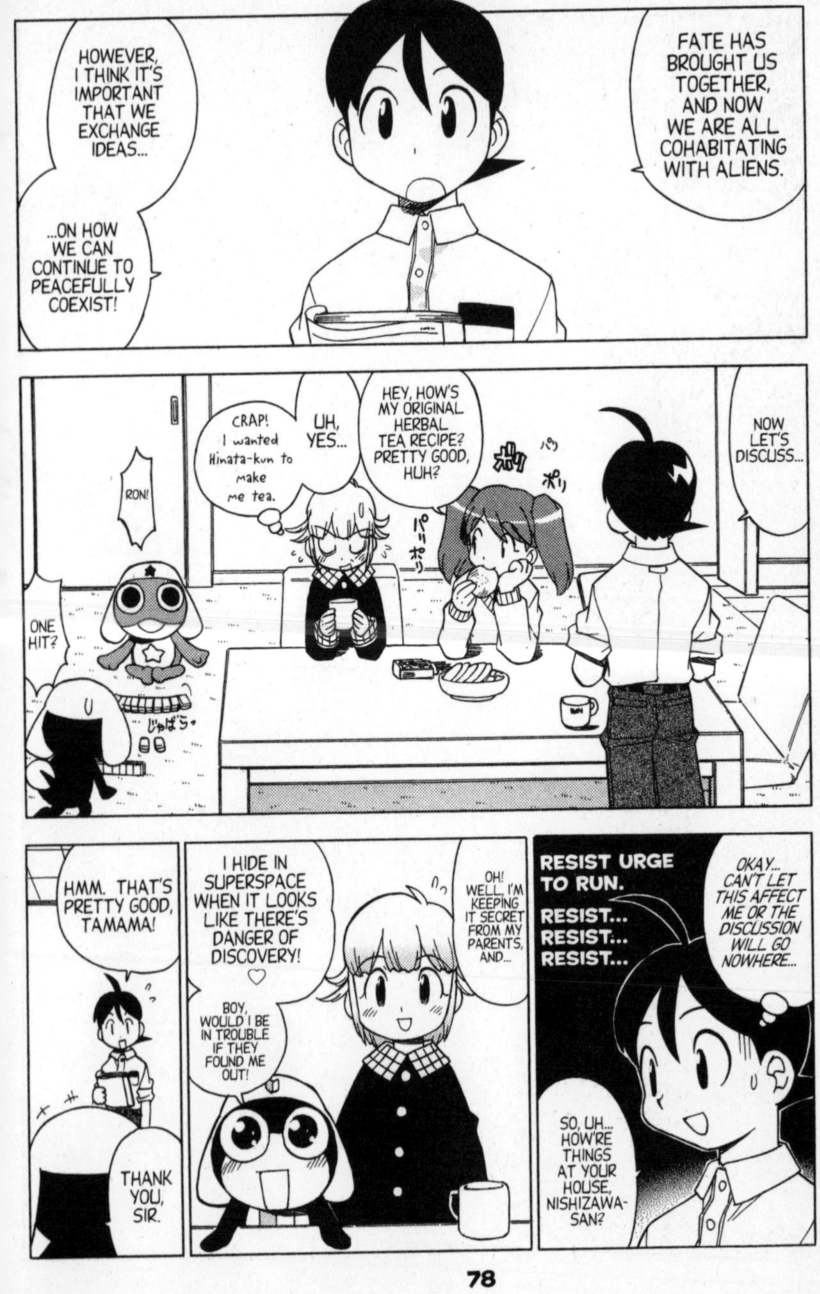
FATE HAS BROUGHT US TOGETHER, AND NOW WE ARE ALL COHABITATING WITH ALIENS.
HOWEVER, I THINK IT'S IMPORTANT THAT WE EXCHANGE IDEAS...
...ON HOW WE CAN CONTINUE TO PEACEFULLY COEXIST!
NOW LET'S DISCUSS...
HEY, HOW'S MY ORIGINAL HERBAL TEA RECIPE? PRETTY GOOD, HUH?
UH, YES...
CRAP! I wanted Hinata-kun to make me tea.
RON!
ONE HIT?
RESIST URGE TO RUN.
RESIST... RESIST... RESIST...
OKAY... CAN'T LET THIS AFFECT ME OR THE DISCUSSION WILL GO NOWHERE...
SO, UH... HOW'RE THINGS AT YOUR HOUSE, NISHIZAWA-SAN?
OH! WELL, I'M KEEPING IT SECRET FROM MY PARENTS, AND...
I HIDE IN SUPERSPACE WHEN IT LOOKS LIKE THERE'S DANGER OF DISCOVERY! ♡
BOY, WOULD I BE IN TROUBLE IF THEY FOUND ME OUT!
HMM. THAT'S PRETTY GOOD, TAMAMA!
THANK YOU, SIR.

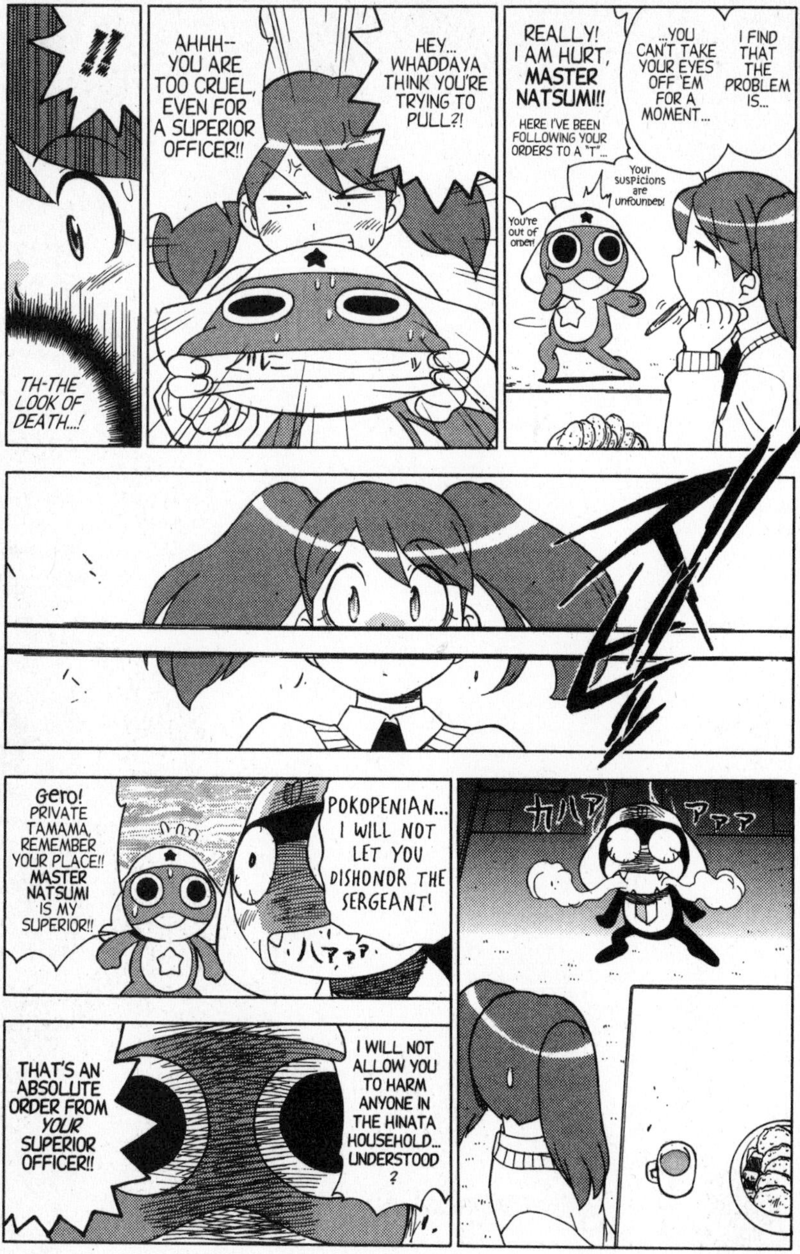
I FIND THAT THE PROBLEM IS...
...YOU CAN'T TAKE YOUR EYES OFF 'EM FOR A MOMENT...
REALLY! I AM HURT, MASTER NATSUMI!!
HERE I'VE BEEN FOLLOWING YOUR ORDERS TO A "T"...
Your suspicions are unfounded!
You're out of order!
HEY... WHADDAYA THINK YOU'RE TRYING TO PULL?!
AHHH-- YOU ARE TOO CRUEL, EVEN FOR A SUPERIOR OFFICER!!
!!
TH-THE LOOK OF DEATH...!
POKOPENIAN... I WILL NOT LET YOU DISHONOR THE SERGEANT!
Gero! PRIVATE TAMAMA, REMEMBER YOUR PLACE!! MASTER NATSUMI IS MY SUPERIOR!!
I WILL NOT ALLOW YOU TO HARM ANYONE IN THE HINATA HOUSEHOLD... UNDERSTOOD?
THAT'S AN ABSOLUTE ORDER FROM YOUR SUPERIOR OFFICER!!

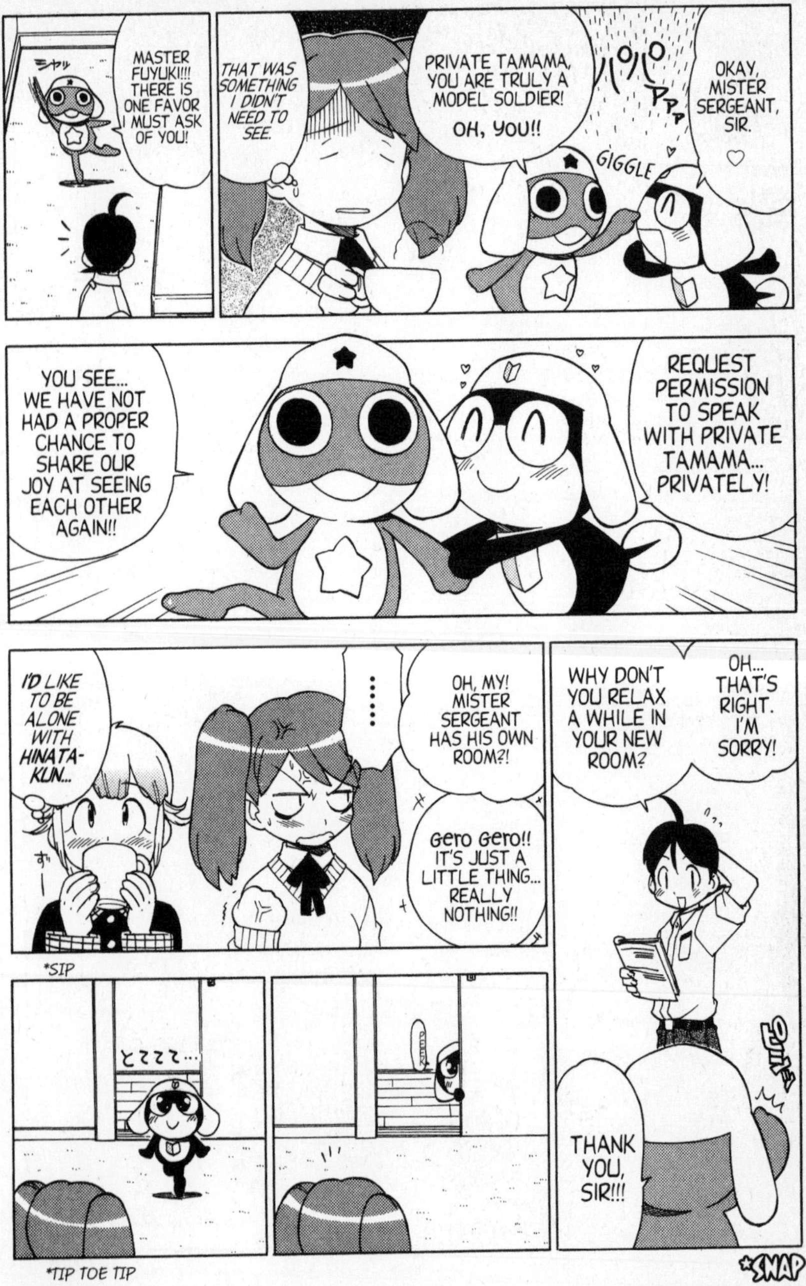
OKAY, MISTER SERGEANT, SIR. ♡
GIGGLE
PRIVATE TAMAMA, YOU ARE TRULY A MODEL SOLDIER!
OH, YOU!!
THAT WAS SOMETHING I DIDN'T NEED TO SEE.
MASTER FUYUKI!!! THERE IS ONE FAVOR I MUST ASK OF YOU!
REQUEST PERMISSION TO SPEAK WITH PRIVATE TAMAMA... PRIVATELY!
YOU SEE... WE HAVE NOT HAD A PROPER CHANCE TO SHARE OUR JOY AT SEEING EACH OTHER AGAIN!!
OH... THAT'S RIGHT. I'M SORRY!
WHY DON'T YOU RELAX A WHILE IN YOUR NEW ROOM?
THANK YOU, SIR!!!
*SNAP
OH, MY! MISTER SERGEANT HAS HIS OWN ROOM?!
Gero Gero!! IT'S JUST A LITTLE THING... REALLY NOTHING!!
......
I'D LIKE TO BE ALONE WITH HINATA-KUN...
*SIP
とととと...
*TIP TOE TIP

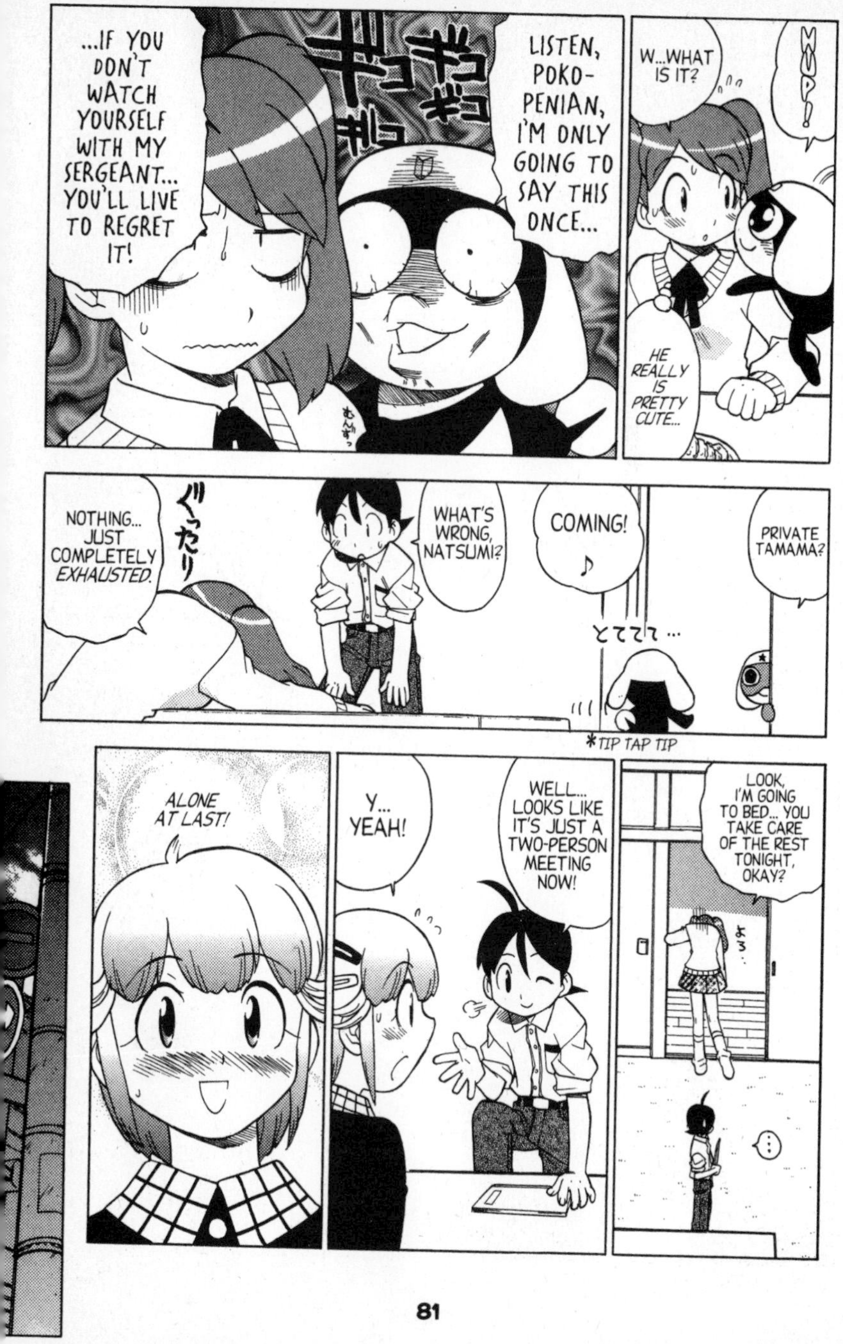
MUP!
W...WHAT IS IT?
HE REALLY IS PRETTY CUTE...
LISTEN, POKO-PENIAN, I'M ONLY GOING TO SAY THIS ONCE...
ギュギュギュ
...IF YOU DON'T WATCH YOURSELF WITH MY SERGEANT... YOU'LL LIVE TO REGRET IT!
むんずっ
PRIVATE TAMAMA?
COMING! ♪
とててて...
*TIP TAP TIP
WHAT'S WRONG, NATSUMI?
ぐったり
NOTHING... JUST COMPLETELY *EXHAUSTED.*
LOOK, I'M GOING TO BED... YOU TAKE CARE OF THE REST TONIGHT, OKAY?
よろ...
...
WELL... LOOKS LIKE IT'S JUST A TWO-PERSON MEETING NOW!
Y... YEAH!
ALONE AT LAST!

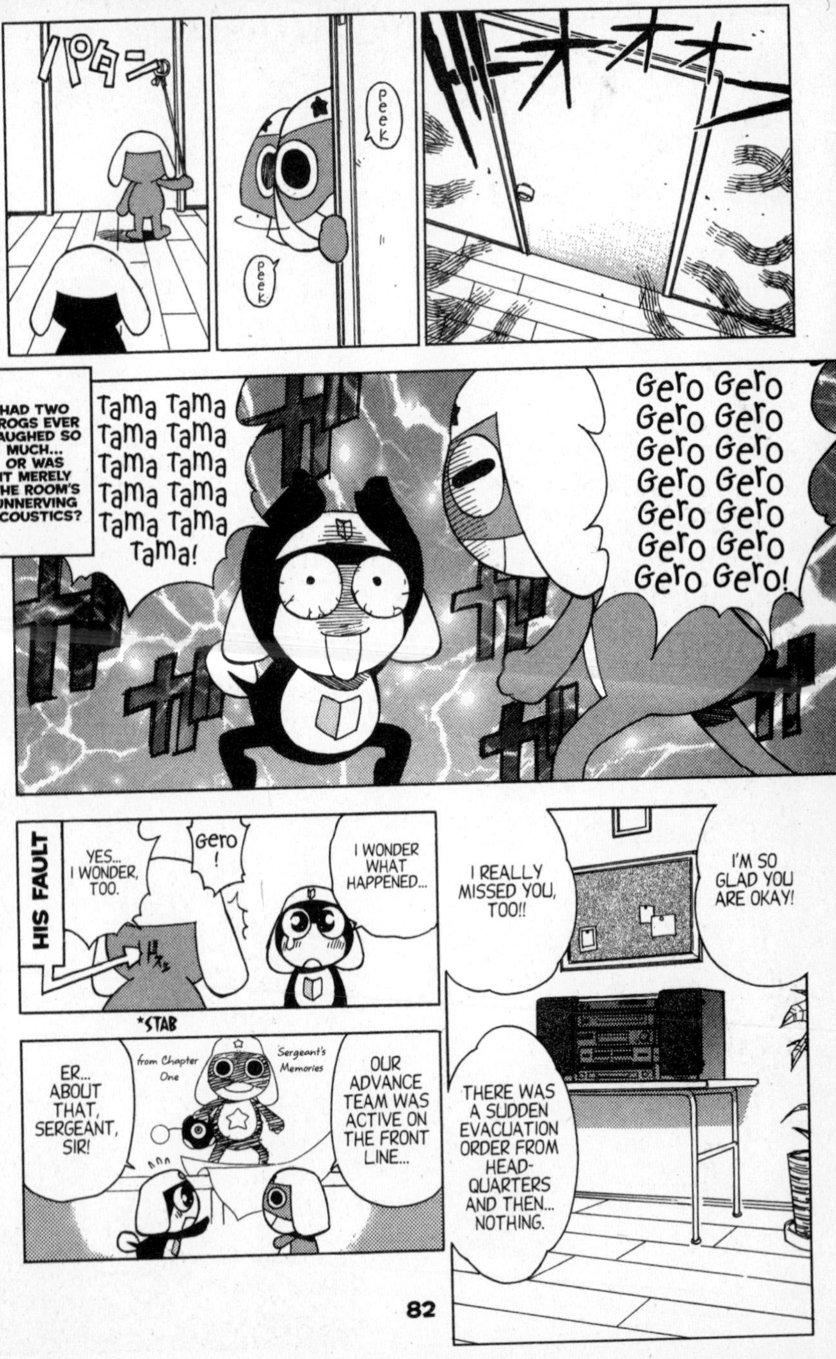
peek
peek
パタン
Gero Gero Gero Gero Gero Gero Gero Gero Gero Gero Gero Gero Gero Gero!
Tama Tama Tama Tama Tama Tama Tama Tama Tama Tama Tama!
HAD TWO FROGS EVER LAUGHED SO MUCH... OR WAS IT MERELY THE ROOM'S UNNERVING ACOUSTICS?
I'M SO GLAD YOU ARE OKAY!
I REALLY MISSED YOU, TOO!!
THERE WAS A SUDDEN EVACUATION ORDER FROM HEAD-QUARTERS AND THEN... NOTHING.
I WONDER WHAT HAPPENED...
Gero!
YES... I WONDER, TOO.
HIS FAULT
*STAB
OUR ADVANCE TEAM WAS ACTIVE ON THE FRONT LINE...
Sergeant's Memories
from Chapter One
ER... ABOUT THAT, SERGEANT, SIR!

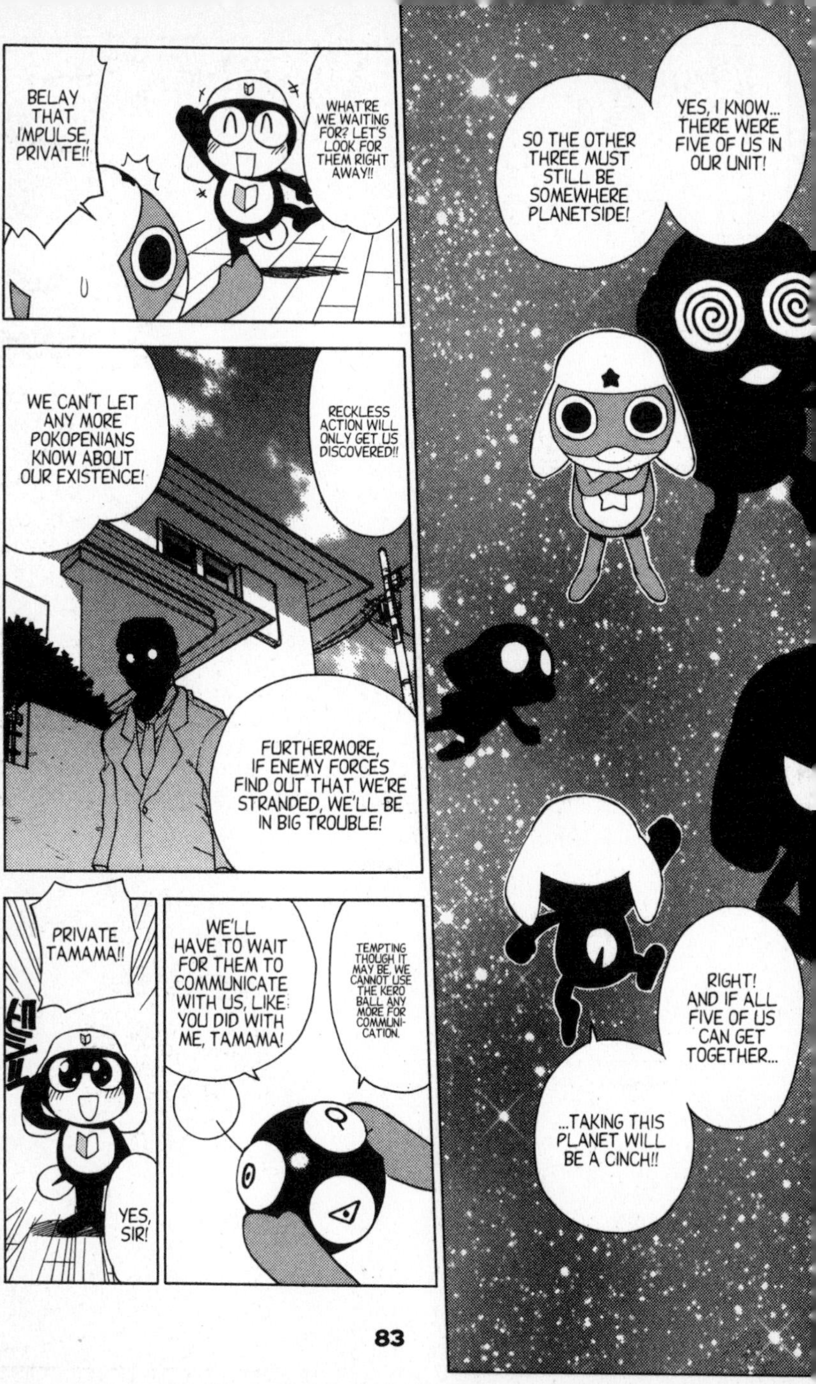
YES, I KNOW... THERE WERE FIVE OF US IN OUR UNIT!
SO THE OTHER THREE MUST STILL BE SOMEWHERE PLANETSIDE!
RIGHT! AND IF ALL FIVE OF US CAN GET TOGETHER...
...TAKING THIS PLANET WILL BE A CINCH!!
WHAT'RE WE WAITING FOR? LET'S LOOK FOR THEM RIGHT AWAY!!
BELAY THAT IMPULSE, PRIVATE!!
RECKLESS ACTION WILL ONLY GET US DISCOVERED!!
WE CAN'T LET ANY MORE POKOPENIANS KNOW ABOUT OUR EXISTENCE!
FURTHERMORE, IF ENEMY FORCES FIND OUT THAT WE'RE STRANDED, WE'LL BE IN BIG TROUBLE!
TEMPTING THOUGH IT MAY BE, WE CANNOT USE THE KERO BALL ANY MORE FOR COMMUNI-CATION.
WE'LL HAVE TO WAIT FOR THEM TO COMMUNICATE WITH US, LIKE YOU DID WITH ME, TAMAMA!
PRIVATE TAMAMA!!
YES, SIR!

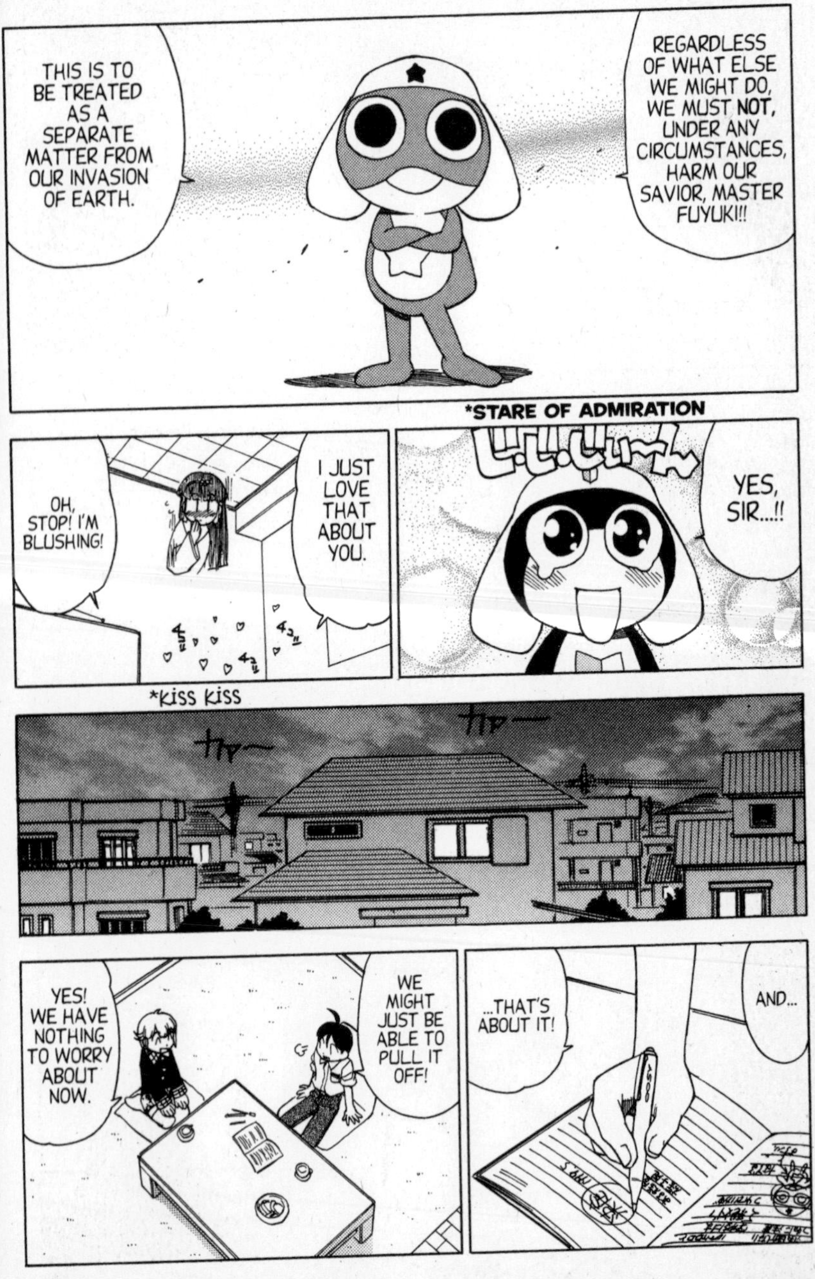
REGARDLESS OF WHAT ELSE WE MIGHT DO, WE MUST NOT, UNDER ANY CIRCUMSTANCES, HARM OUR SAVIOR, MASTER FUYUKI!!
THIS IS TO BE TREATED AS A SEPARATE MATTER FROM OUR INVASION OF EARTH.
*STARE OF ADMIRATION
YES, SIR...!!
I JUST LOVE THAT ABOUT YOU.
OH, STOP! I'M BLUSHING!
*KISS KISS
AND...
...THAT'S ABOUT IT!
WE MIGHT JUST BE ABLE TO PULL IT OFF!
YES! WE HAVE NOTHING TO WORRY ABOUT NOW.

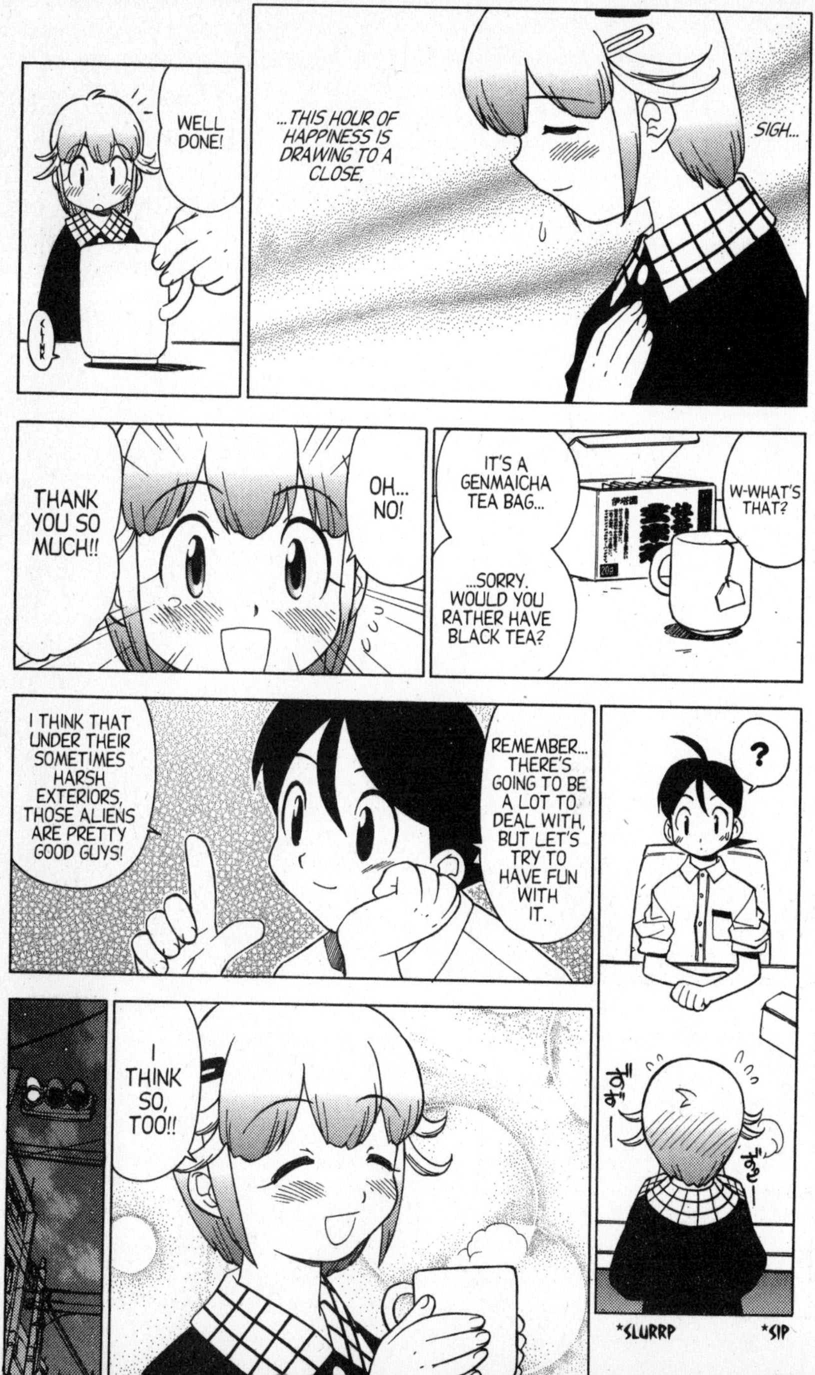
SIGH...
...THIS HOUR OF HAPPINESS IS DRAWING TO A CLOSE.
WELL DONE!
CLINK
W-WHAT'S THAT?
IT'S A GENMAICHA TEA BAG...
...SORRY. WOULD YOU RATHER HAVE BLACK TEA?
OH... NO!
THANK YOU SO MUCH!!
?
*SLURRP
*SIP
REMEMBER... THERE'S GOING TO BE A LOT TO DEAL WITH, BUT LET'S TRY TO HAVE FUN WITH IT.
I THINK THAT UNDER THEIR SOMETIMES HARSH EXTERIORS, THOSE ALIENS ARE PRETTY GOOD GUYS!
I THINK SO, TOO!!

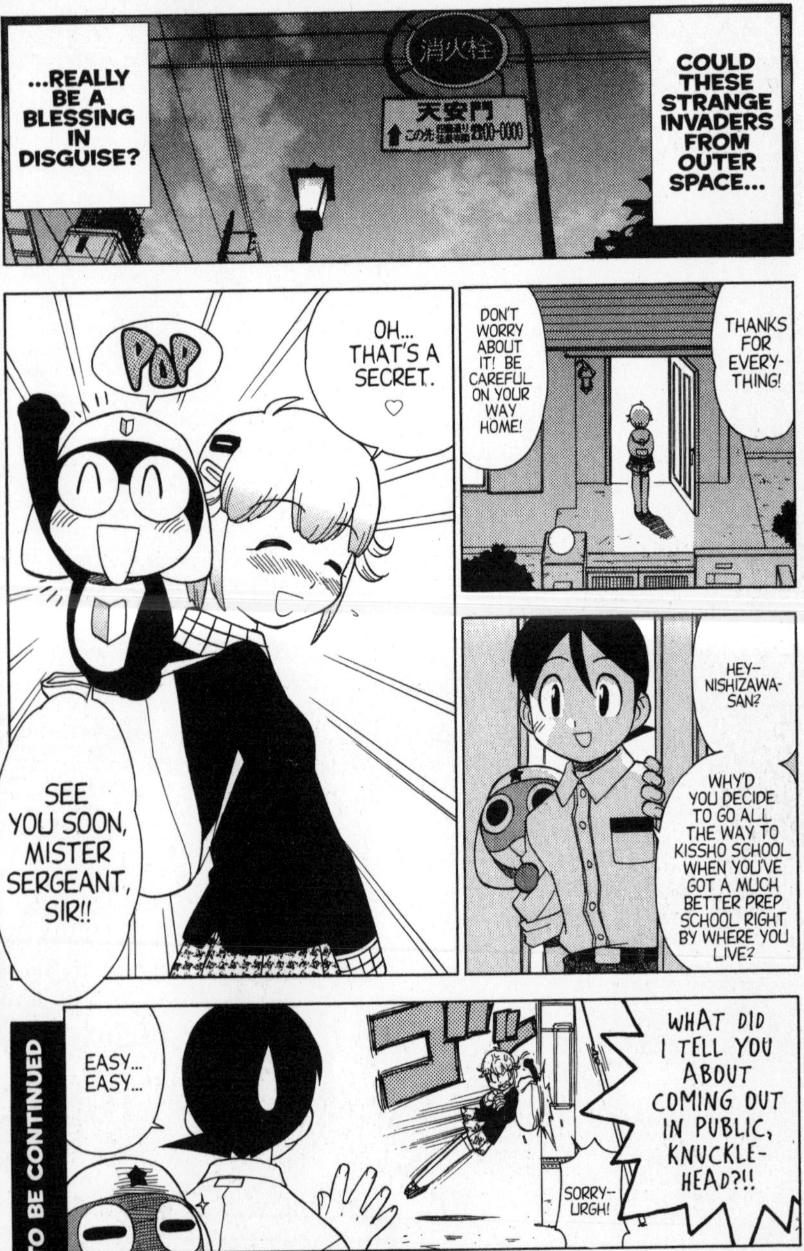
COULD THESE STRANGE INVADERS FROM OUTER SPACE...
消火栓
天安門
...REALLY BE A BLESSING IN DISGUISE?
THANKS FOR EVERY-THING!
DON'T WORRY ABOUT IT! BE CAREFUL ON YOUR WAY HOME!
HEY-- NISHIZAWA-SAN?
WHY'D YOU DECIDE TO GO ALL THE WAY TO KISSHO SCHOOL WHEN YOU'VE GOT A MUCH BETTER PREP SCHOOL RIGHT BY WHERE YOU LIVE?
OH... THAT'S A SECRET. ♡
POP
SEE YOU SOON, MISTER SERGEANT, SIR!!
WHAT DID I TELL YOU ABOUT COMING OUT IN PUBLIC, KNUCKLE-HEAD?!!
SORRY-- URGH!
EASY... EASY...
TO BE CONTINUED

ENCOUNTER VI
ALIEN OBSERVATION JOURNAL

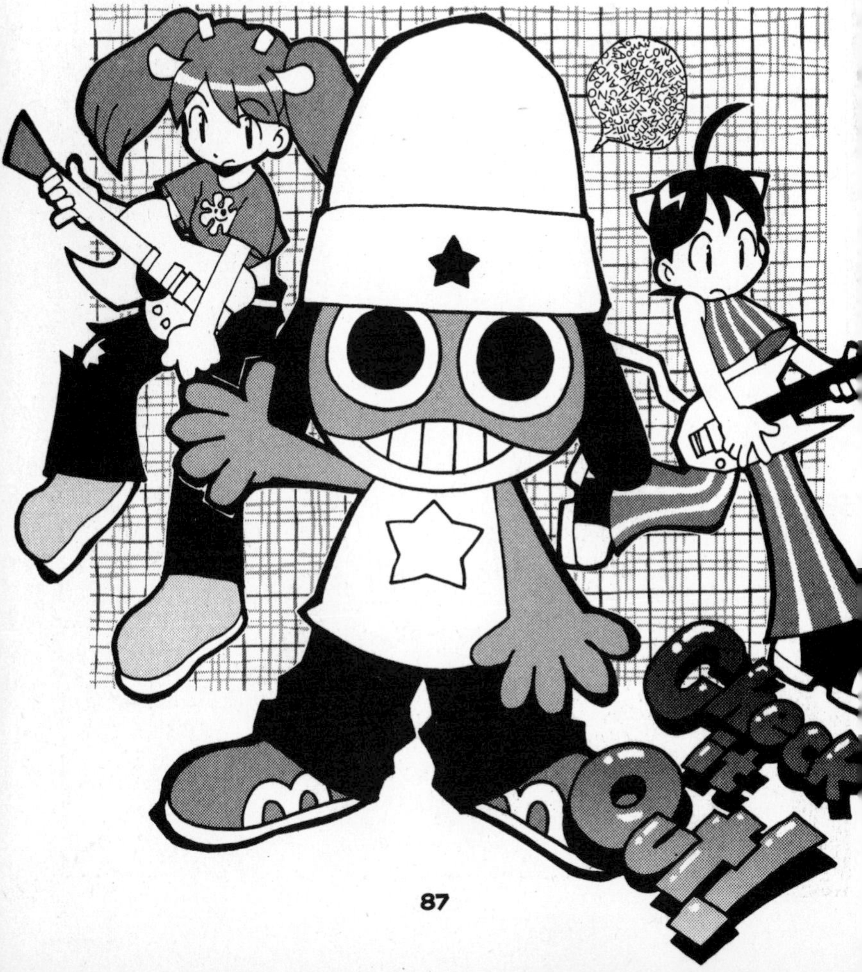
CHECK IT OUT!

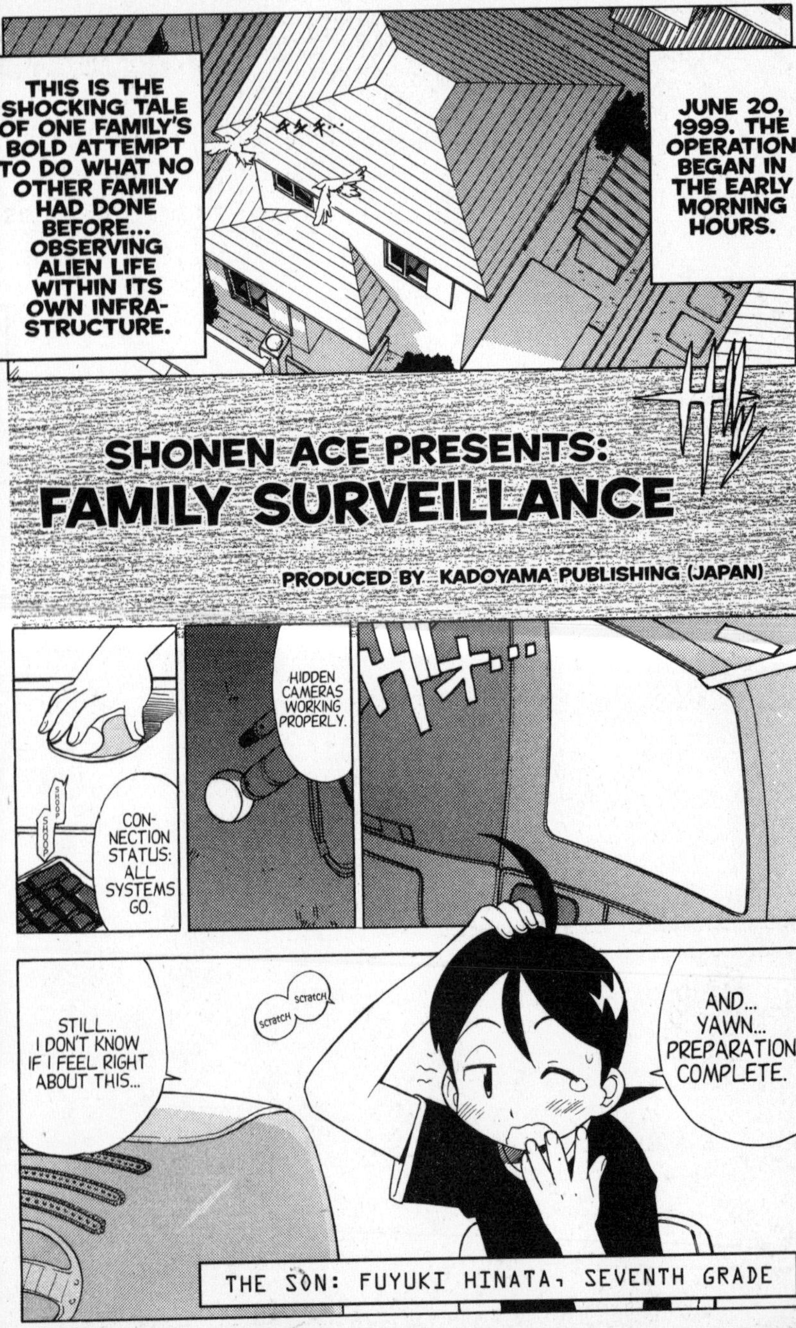
JUNE 20, 1999. THE OPERATION BEGAN IN THE EARLY MORNING HOURS.
THIS IS THE SHOCKING TALE OF ONE FAMILY'S BOLD ATTEMPT TO DO WHAT NO OTHER FAMILY HAD DONE BEFORE... OBSERVING ALIEN LIFE WITHIN ITS OWN INFRA-STRUCTURE.
SHONEN ACE PRESENTS:
FAMILY SURVEILLANCE
PRODUCED BY KADOYAMA PUBLISHING (JAPAN)
HIDDEN CAMERAS WORKING PROPERLY.
SHOOP
SHOOP
CON-NECTION STATUS: ALL SYSTEMS GO.
AND... YAWN... PREPARATION COMPLETE.
scratch
scratch
STILL... I DON'T KNOW IF I FEEL RIGHT ABOUT THIS...
THE SON: FUYUKI HINATA, SEVENTH GRADE

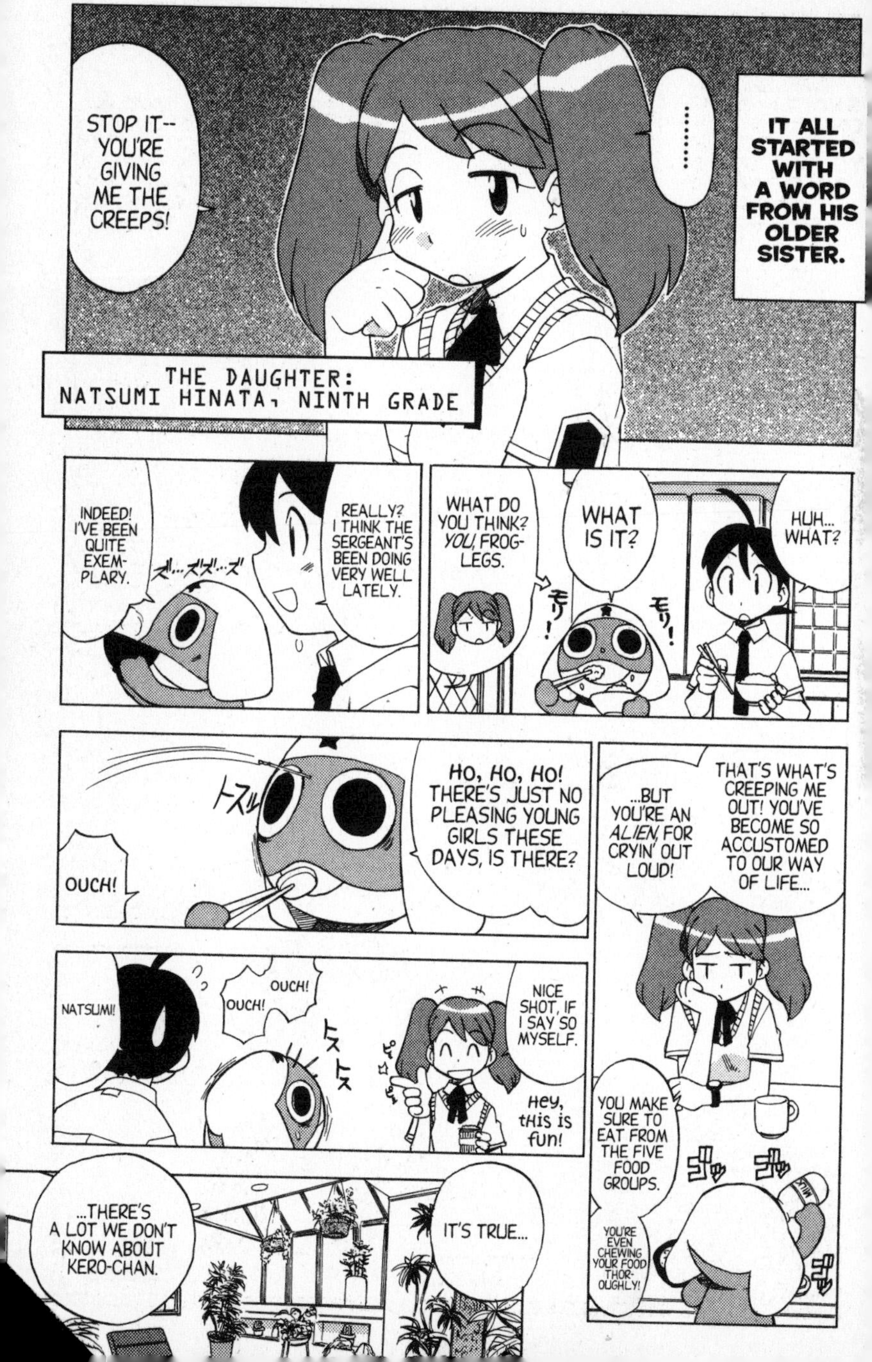
IT ALL STARTED WITH A WORD FROM HIS OLDER SISTER.
......
STOP IT-- YOU'RE GIVING ME THE CREEPS!
THE DAUGHTER: NATSUMI HINATA, NINTH GRADE
HUH... WHAT?
WHAT IS IT?
モリ!
WHAT DO YOU THINK? *YOU*, FROG-LEGS.
モリ!
REALLY? I THINK THE SERGEANT'S BEEN DOING VERY WELL LATELY.
ズ…ズズ…ズ
INDEED! I'VE BEEN QUITE EXEMPLARY.
THAT'S WHAT'S CREEPING ME OUT! YOU'VE BECOME SO ACCUSTOMED TO OUR WAY OF LIFE...
...BUT YOU'RE AN *ALIEN*, FOR CRYIN' OUT LOUD!
YOU MAKE SURE TO EAT FROM THE FIVE FOOD GROUPS.
ゴッ ゴッ
YOU'RE EVEN CHEWING YOUR FOOD THOROUGHLY!
ゴッ
HO, HO, HO! THERE'S JUST NO PLEASING YOUNG GIRLS THESE DAYS, IS THERE?
トスッ
OUCH!
NICE SHOT, IF I SAY SO MYSELF.
Hey, this is fun!
トストス
OUCH!
OUCH!
NATSUMI!
IT'S TRUE...
...THERE'S A LOT WE DON'T KNOW ABOUT KERO-CHAN.

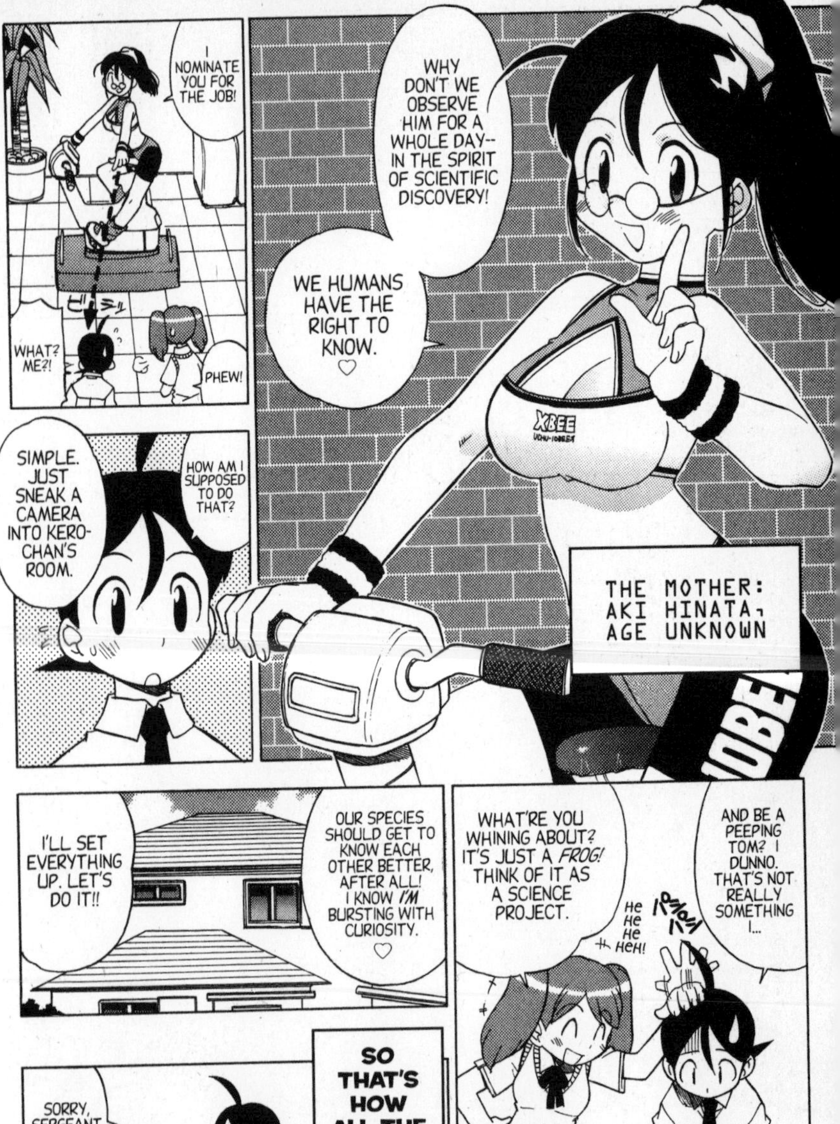
WHY DON'T WE OBSERVE HIM FOR A WHOLE DAY-- IN THE SPIRIT OF SCIENTIFIC DISCOVERY!
WE HUMANS HAVE THE RIGHT TO KNOW. ♡
THE MOTHER: AKI HINATA, AGE UNKNOWN
I NOMINATE YOU FOR THE JOB!
WHAT? ME?!
PHEW!
HOW AM I SUPPOSED TO DO THAT?
SIMPLE. JUST SNEAK A CAMERA INTO KERO-CHAN'S ROOM.
AND BE A PEEPING TOM? I DUNNO. THAT'S NOT REALLY SOMETHING I...
WHAT'RE YOU WHINING ABOUT? IT'S JUST A *FROG!* THINK OF IT AS A SCIENCE PROJECT.
He He He HEH!
OUR SPECIES SHOULD GET TO KNOW EACH OTHER BETTER, AFTER ALL! I KNOW *I'M* BURSTING WITH CURIOSITY. ♡
I'LL SET EVERYTHING UP. LET'S DO IT!!
SO THAT'S HOW ALL THE SPYING STARTED.
SORRY, SERGEANT ...

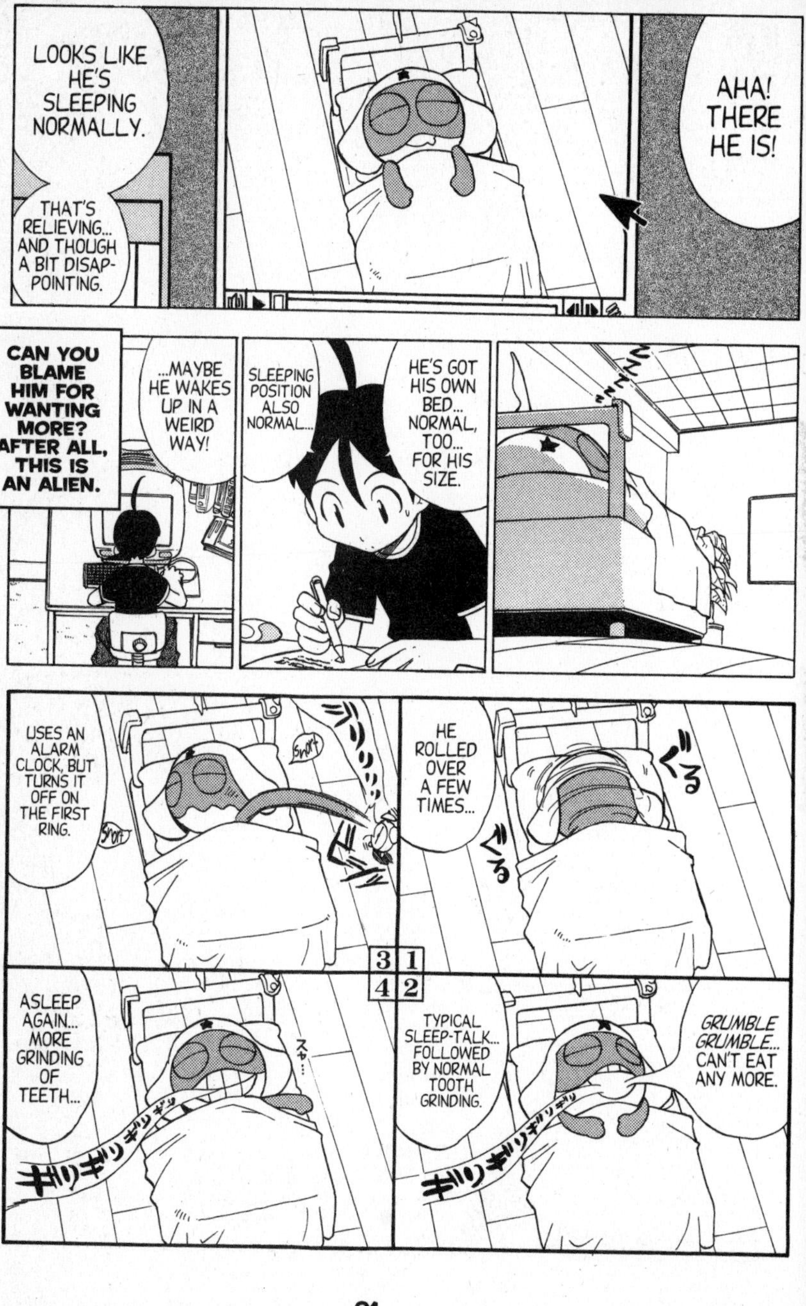

AHA! THERE HE IS!
LOOKS LIKE HE'S SLEEPING NORMALLY.
THAT'S RELIEVING... AND THOUGH A BIT DISAPPOINTING.
HE'S GOT HIS OWN BED... NORMAL, TOO... FOR HIS SIZE.
SLEEPING POSITION ALSO NORMAL...
...MAYBE HE WAKES UP IN A WEIRD WAY!
CAN YOU BLAME HIM FOR WANTING MORE? AFTER ALL, THIS IS AN ALIEN.
1
HE ROLLED OVER A FEW TIMES...
ぐる
ぐる
2
GRUMBLE GRUMBLE... CAN'T EAT ANY MORE.
TYPICAL SLEEP-TALK... FOLLOWED BY NORMAL TOOTH GRINDING.
ギリギリ
3
USES AN ALARM CLOCK, BUT TURNS IT OFF ON THE FIRST RING.
Snort
Snort
4
ASLEEP AGAIN... MORE GRINDING OF TEETH...
スャ…
ギリギリ

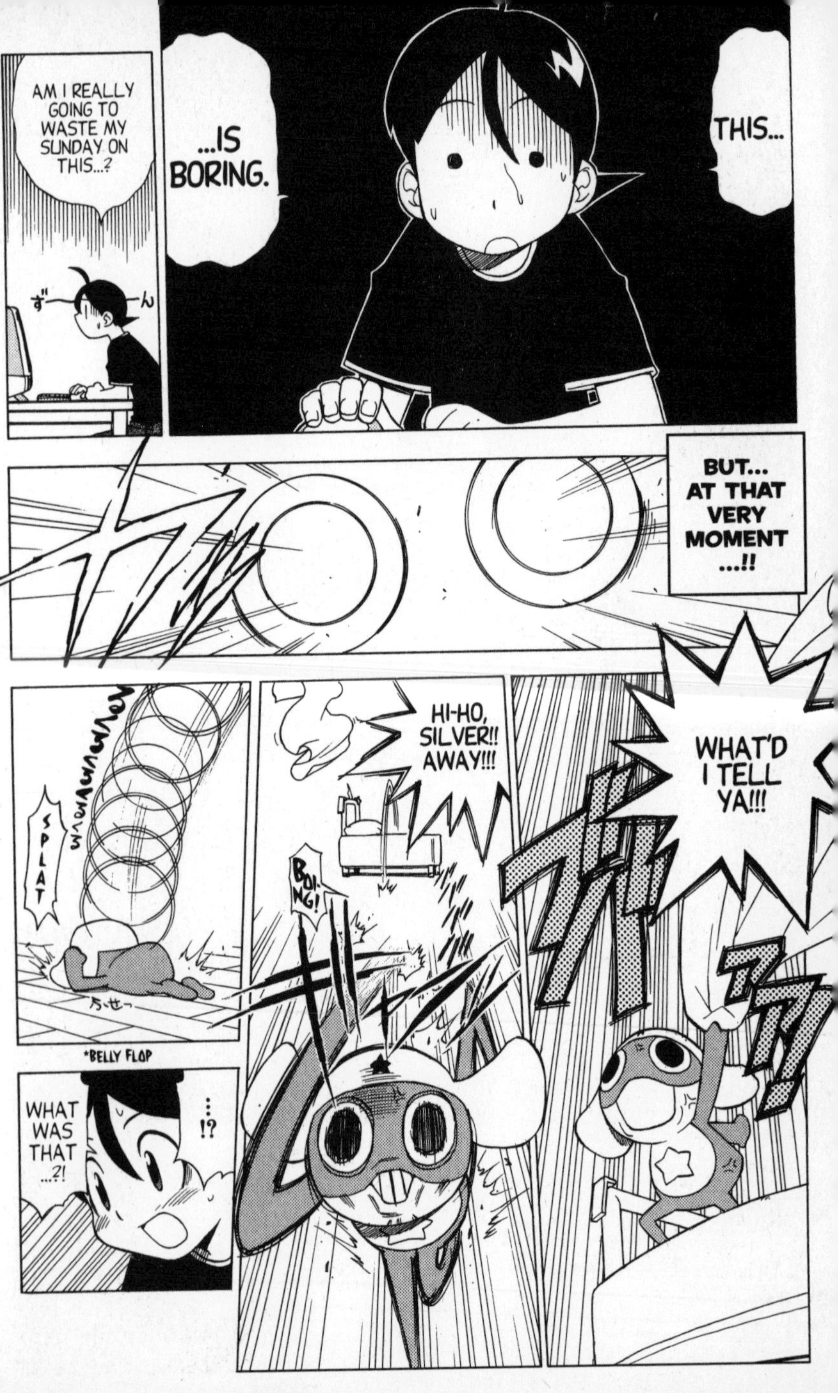
THIS...
...IS BORING.
AM I REALLY GOING TO WASTE MY SUNDAY ON THIS...?
ず―ん
BUT... AT THAT VERY MOMENT...!!
WHAT'D I TELL YA!!!
HI-HO, SILVER!! AWAY!!!
BOING!
SPLAT
*BELLY FLOP
...!?
WHAT WAS THAT...?!

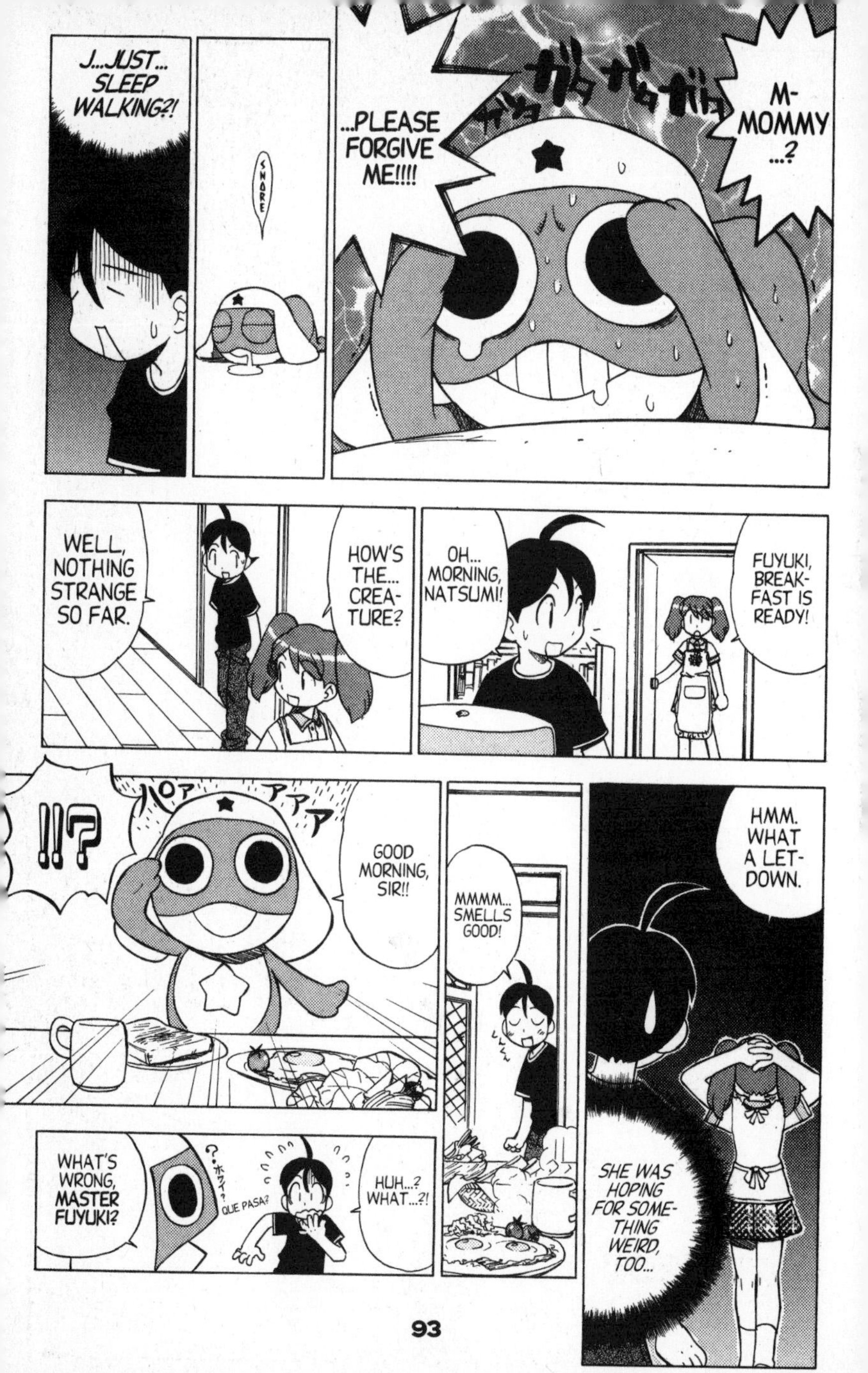
M-
MOMMY
...?
ガタガタガタガタ
...PLEASE
FORGIVE
ME!!!!
SNORE
J...JUST...
SLEEP
WALKING?!
FUYUKI,
BREAK-
FAST IS
READY!
OH...
MORNING,
NATSUMI!
HOW'S
THE...
CREA-
TURE?
WELL,
NOTHING
STRANGE
SO FAR.
HMM.
WHAT
A LET-
DOWN.
SHE WAS
HOPING
FOR SOME-
THING
WEIRD,
TOO...
MMMM...
SMELLS
GOOD!
パアアア
GOOD
MORNING,
SIR!!
!!?
HUH...?
WHAT...?!
?・ホワイ?
QUE PASA?
WHAT'S
WRONG,
MASTER
FUYUKI?

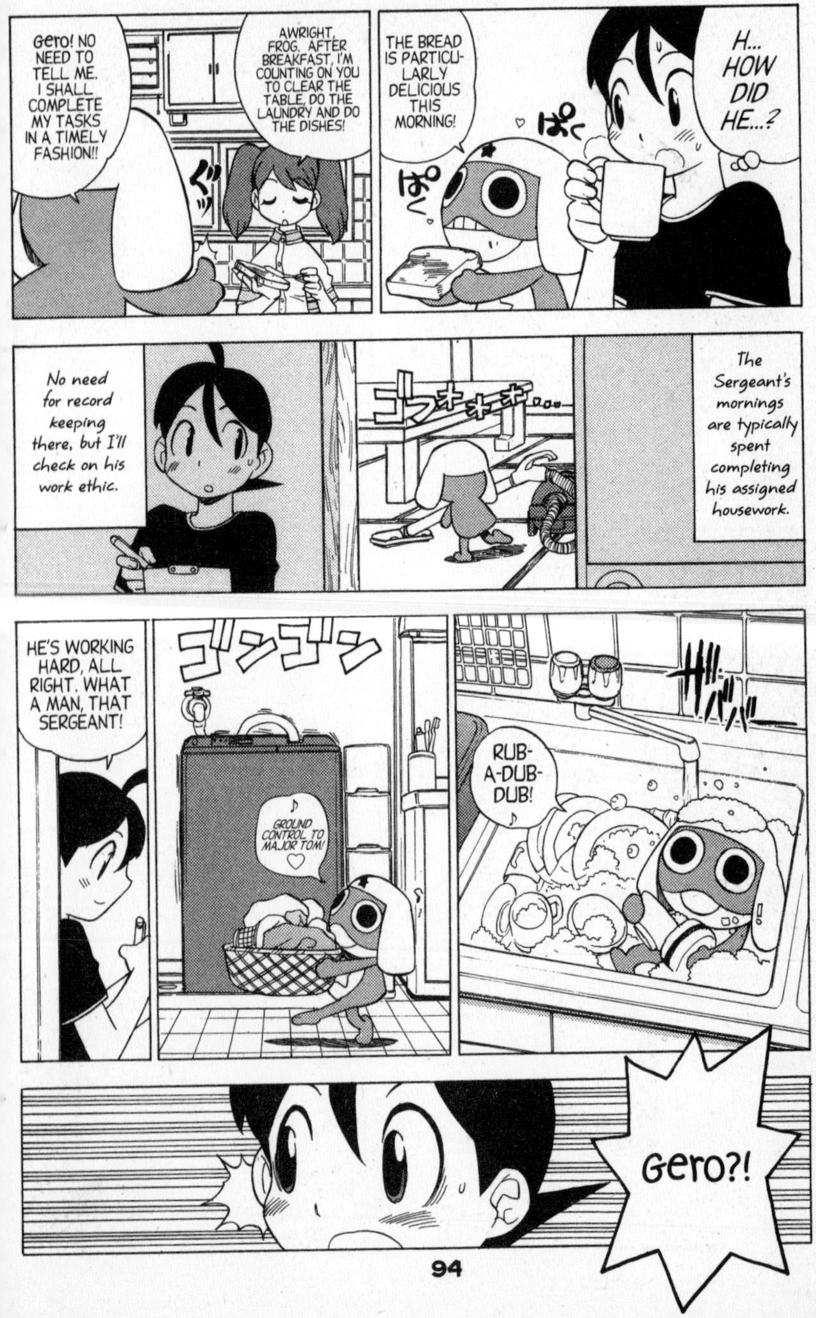
H... HOW DID HE...?
THE BREAD IS PARTICULARLY DELICIOUS THIS MORNING!
ぱく
ぱく
AWRIGHT, FROG. AFTER BREAKFAST, I'M COUNTING ON YOU TO CLEAR THE TABLE, DO THE LAUNDRY AND DO THE DISHES!
Gero! NO NEED TO TELL ME. I SHALL COMPLETE MY TASKS IN A TIMELY FASHION!!
The Sergeant's mornings are typically spent completing his assigned housework.
No need for record keeping there, but I'll check on his work ethic.
RUB-A-DUB-DUB!
GROUND CONTROL TO MAJOR TOM!
HE'S WORKING HARD, ALL RIGHT. WHAT A MAN, THAT SERGEANT!
Gero?!

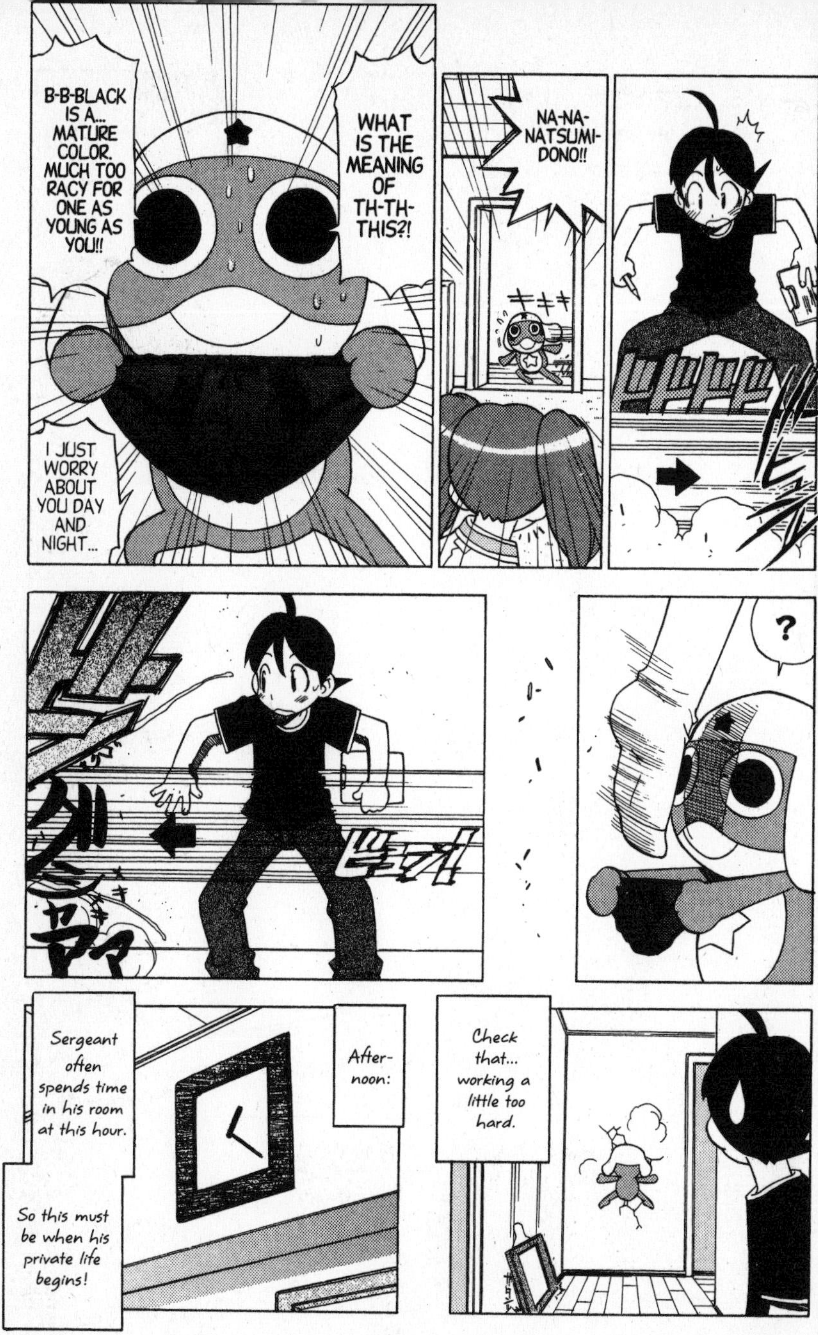
NA-NA-NATSUMI-DONO!!
WHAT IS THE MEANING OF TH-TH-THIS?!
B-B-BLACK IS A... MATURE COLOR. MUCH TOO RACY FOR ONE AS YOUNG AS YOU!!
I JUST WORRY ABOUT YOU DAY AND NIGHT...
?
Check that... working a little too hard.
After-noon:
Sergeant often spends time in his room at this hour.
So this must be when his private life begins!

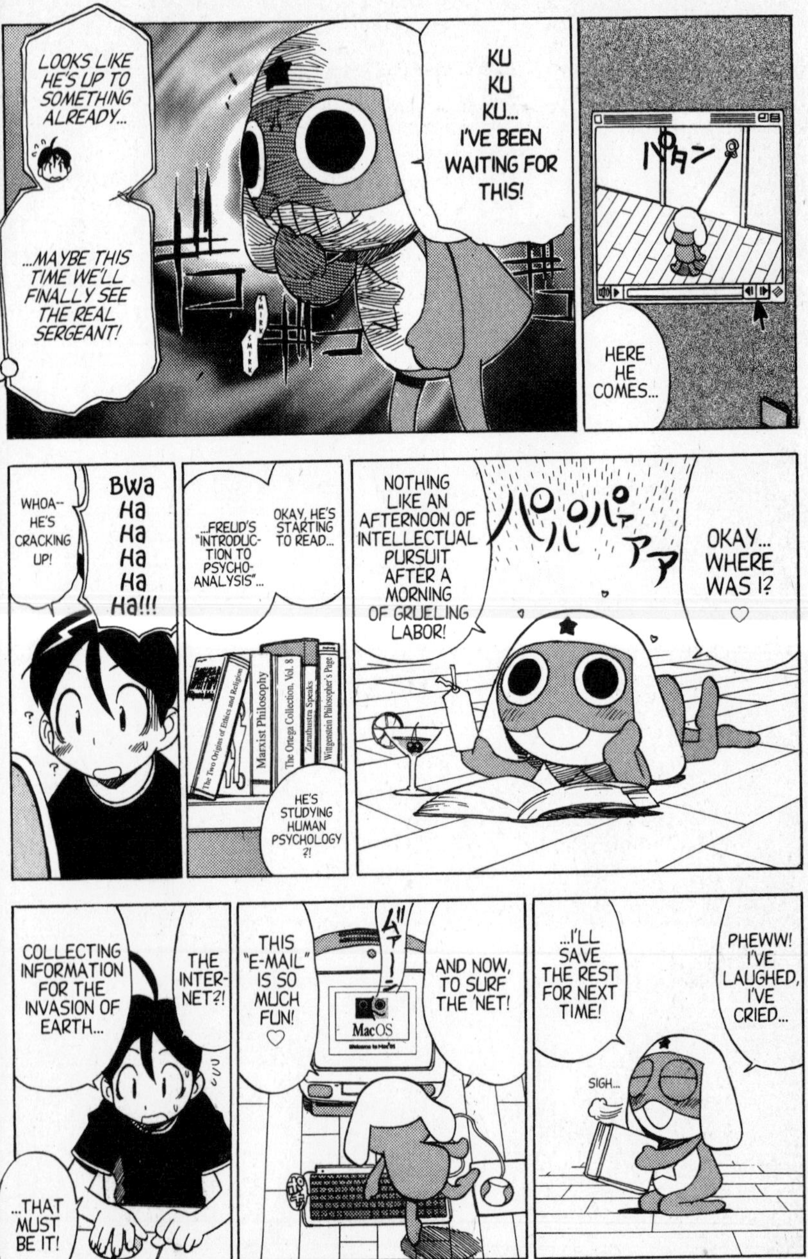
パタン
HERE HE COMES...
KU KU KU... I'VE BEEN WAITING FOR THIS!
LOOKS LIKE HE'S UP TO SOMETHING ALREADY...
...MAYBE THIS TIME WE'LL FINALLY SEE THE REAL SERGEANT!
SMIRK SMIRK
OKAY... WHERE WAS I? ♡
NOTHING LIKE AN AFTERNOON OF INTELLECTUAL PURSUIT AFTER A MORNING OF GRUELING LABOR!
OKAY, HE'S STARTING TO READ...
...FREUD'S "INTRODUCTION TO PSYCHOANALYSIS"...
The Two Origins of Ethics and Religion
Marxist Philosophy
The Ortega Collection, Vol. 8
Zarathustra Speaks
Wittgenstein Philosopher's Page
HE'S STUDYING HUMAN PSYCHOLOGY?!
BWa Ha Ha Ha Ha Ha!!!
WHOA-- HE'S CRACKING UP!
PHEWW! I'VE LAUGHED, I'VE CRIED...
...I'LL SAVE THE REST FOR NEXT TIME!
SIGH...
AND NOW, TO SURF THE 'NET!
THIS "E-MAIL" IS SO MUCH FUN! ♡
MacOS
THE INTER-NET?!
COLLECTING INFORMATION FOR THE INVASION OF EARTH...
...THAT MUST BE IT!

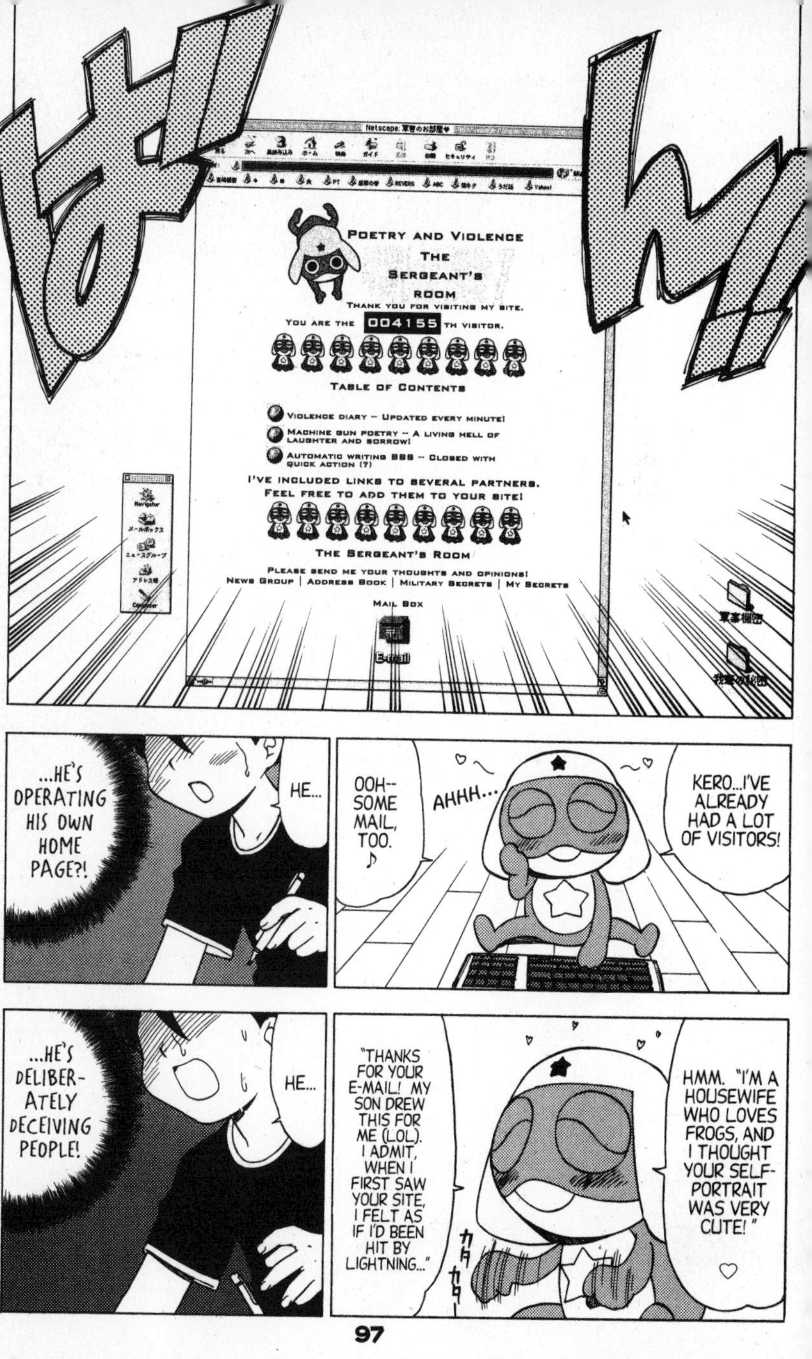
Netscape
POETRY AND VIOLENCE
THE SERGEANT'S ROOM
THANK YOU FOR VISITING MY SITE.
YOU ARE THE 004155 TH VISITOR.
TABLE OF CONTENTS
VIOLENCE DIARY -- UPDATED EVERY MINUTE!
MACHINE GUN POETRY -- A LIVING HELL OF LAUGHTER AND SORROW!
AUTOMATIC WRITING BBS -- CLOSED WITH QUICK ACTION (?)
I'VE INCLUDED LINKS TO SEVERAL PARTNERS.
FEEL FREE TO ADD THEM TO YOUR SITE!
THE SERGEANT'S ROOM
PLEASE SEND ME YOUR THOUGHTS AND OPINIONS!
NEWS GROUP | ADDRESS BOOK | MILITARY SECRETS | MY SECRETS
MAIL BOX
E-mail
Navigator
KERO...I'VE ALREADY HAD A LOT OF VISITORS!
AHHH...
OOH-- SOME MAIL, TOO. ♪
HE...
...HE'S OPERATING HIS OWN HOME PAGE?!
HMM. "I'M A HOUSEWIFE WHO LOVES FROGS, AND I THOUGHT YOUR SELF-PORTRAIT WAS VERY CUTE!" ♡
"THANKS FOR YOUR E-MAIL! MY SON DREW THIS FOR ME (LOL). I ADMIT, WHEN I FIRST SAW YOUR SITE, I FELT AS IF I'D BEEN HIT BY LIGHTNING..."
カタ カタ
HE...
...HE'S DELIBER-ATELY DECEIVING PEOPLE!

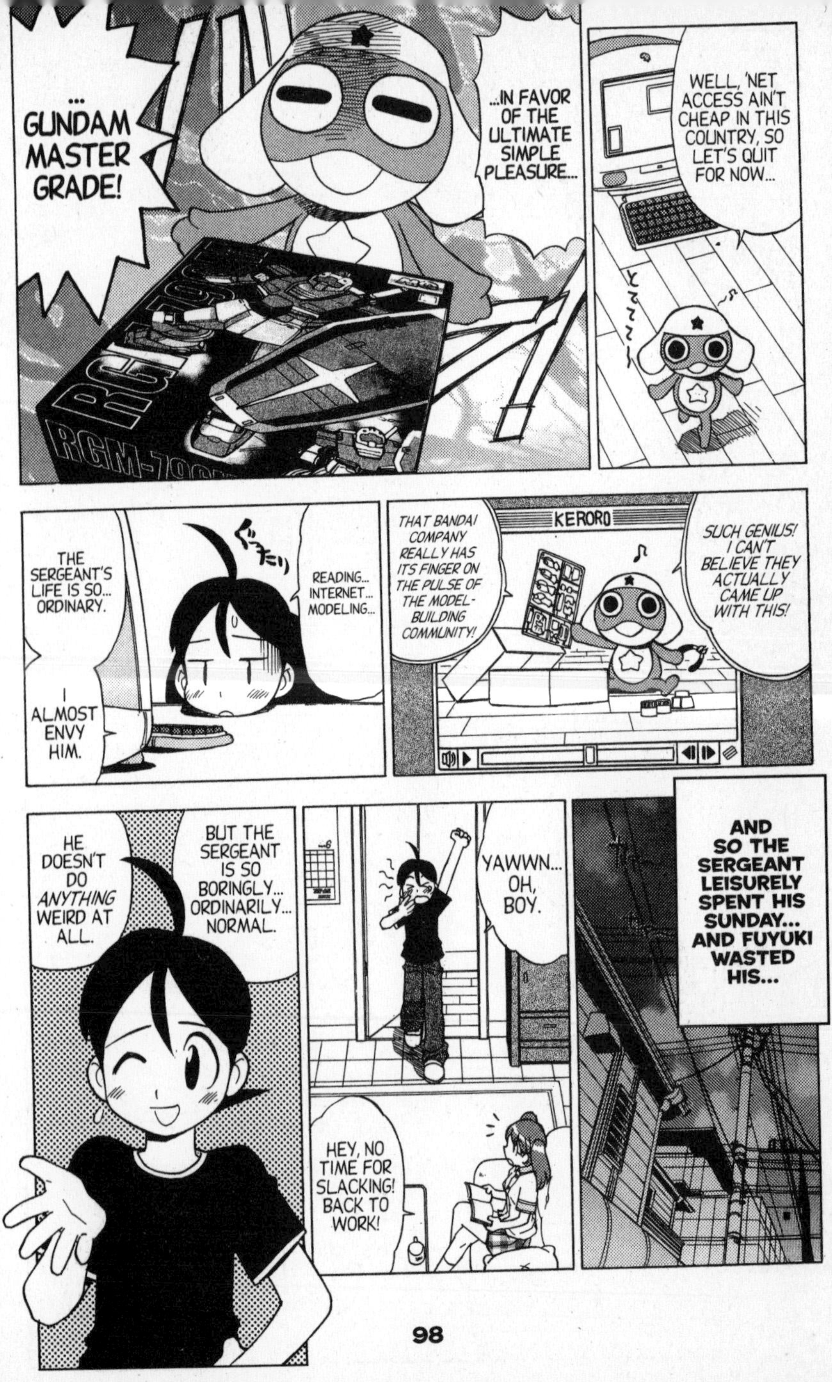
WELL, 'NET ACCESS AIN'T CHEAP IN THIS COUNTRY, SO LET'S QUIT FOR NOW...
...IN FAVOR OF THE ULTIMATE SIMPLE PLEASURE...
... GUNDAM MASTER GRADE!
RGM-79
KERORO
SUCH GENIUS! I CAN'T BELIEVE THEY ACTUALLY CAME UP WITH THIS!
THAT BANDAI COMPANY REALLY HAS ITS FINGER ON THE PULSE OF THE MODEL-BUILDING COMMUNITY!
READING... INTERNET... MODELING...
THE SERGEANT'S LIFE IS SO... ORDINARY.
I ALMOST ENVY HIM.
AND SO THE SERGEANT LEISURELY SPENT HIS SUNDAY... AND FUYUKI WASTED HIS...
YAWWN... OH, BOY.
HEY, NO TIME FOR SLACKING! BACK TO WORK!
BUT THE SERGEANT IS SO BORINGLY... ORDINARILY... NORMAL.
HE DOESN'T DO *ANYTHING* WEIRD AT ALL.

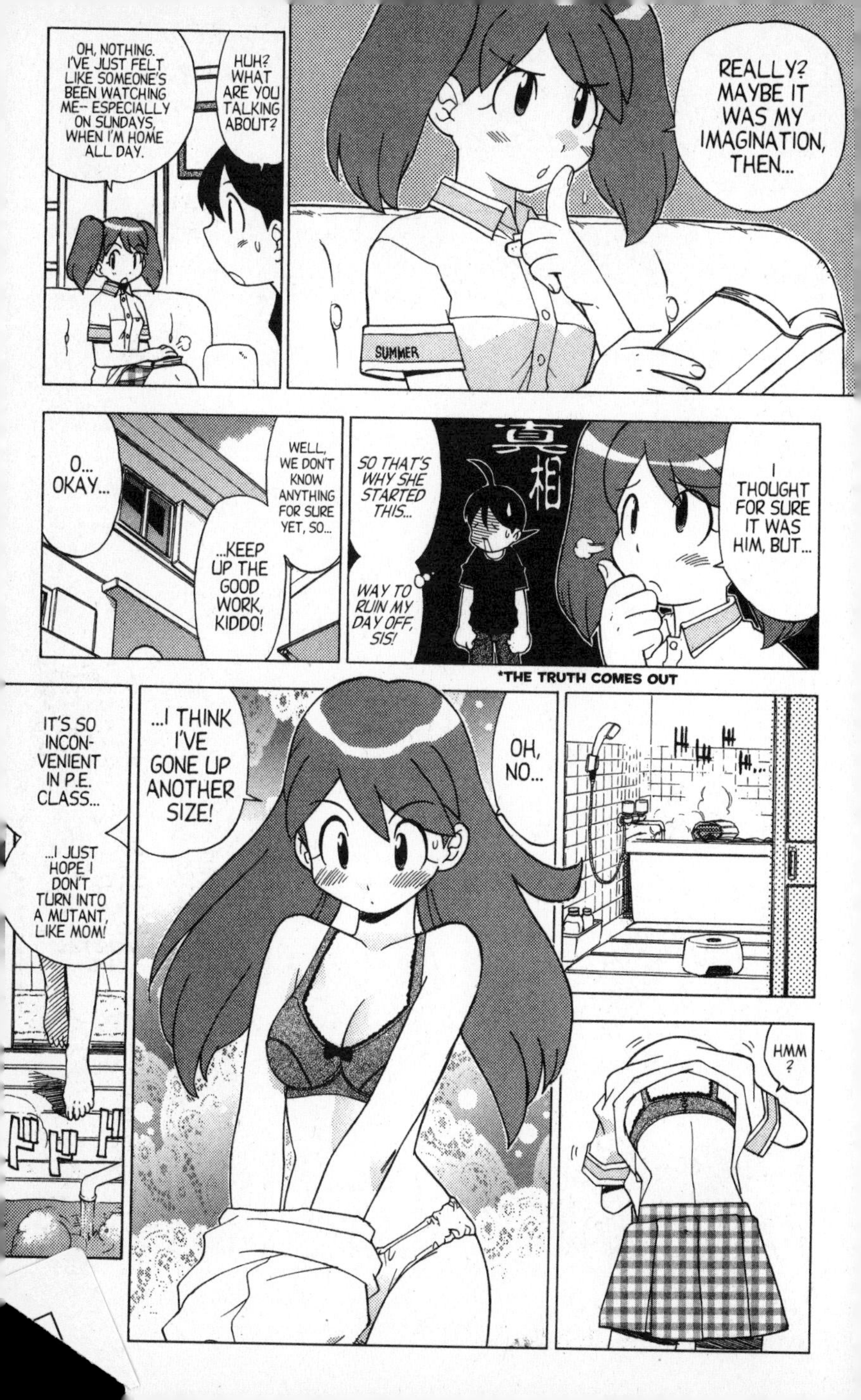
REALLY? MAYBE IT WAS MY IMAGINATION, THEN...
SUMMER
HUH? WHAT ARE YOU TALKING ABOUT?
OH, NOTHING. I'VE JUST FELT LIKE SOMEONE'S BEEN WATCHING ME-- ESPECIALLY ON SUNDAYS, WHEN I'M HOME ALL DAY.
I THOUGHT FOR SURE IT WAS HIM, BUT...
真相
SO THAT'S WHY SHE STARTED THIS...
WAY TO RUIN MY DAY OFF, SIS!
*THE TRUTH COMES OUT
WELL, WE DON'T KNOW ANYTHING FOR SURE YET, SO...
...KEEP UP THE GOOD WORK, KIDDO!
O... OKAY...
HMM?
OH, NO...
...I THINK I'VE GONE UP ANOTHER SIZE!
IT'S SO INCON-VENIENT IN P.E. CLASS...
...I JUST HOPE I DON'T TURN INTO A MUTANT, LIKE MOM!

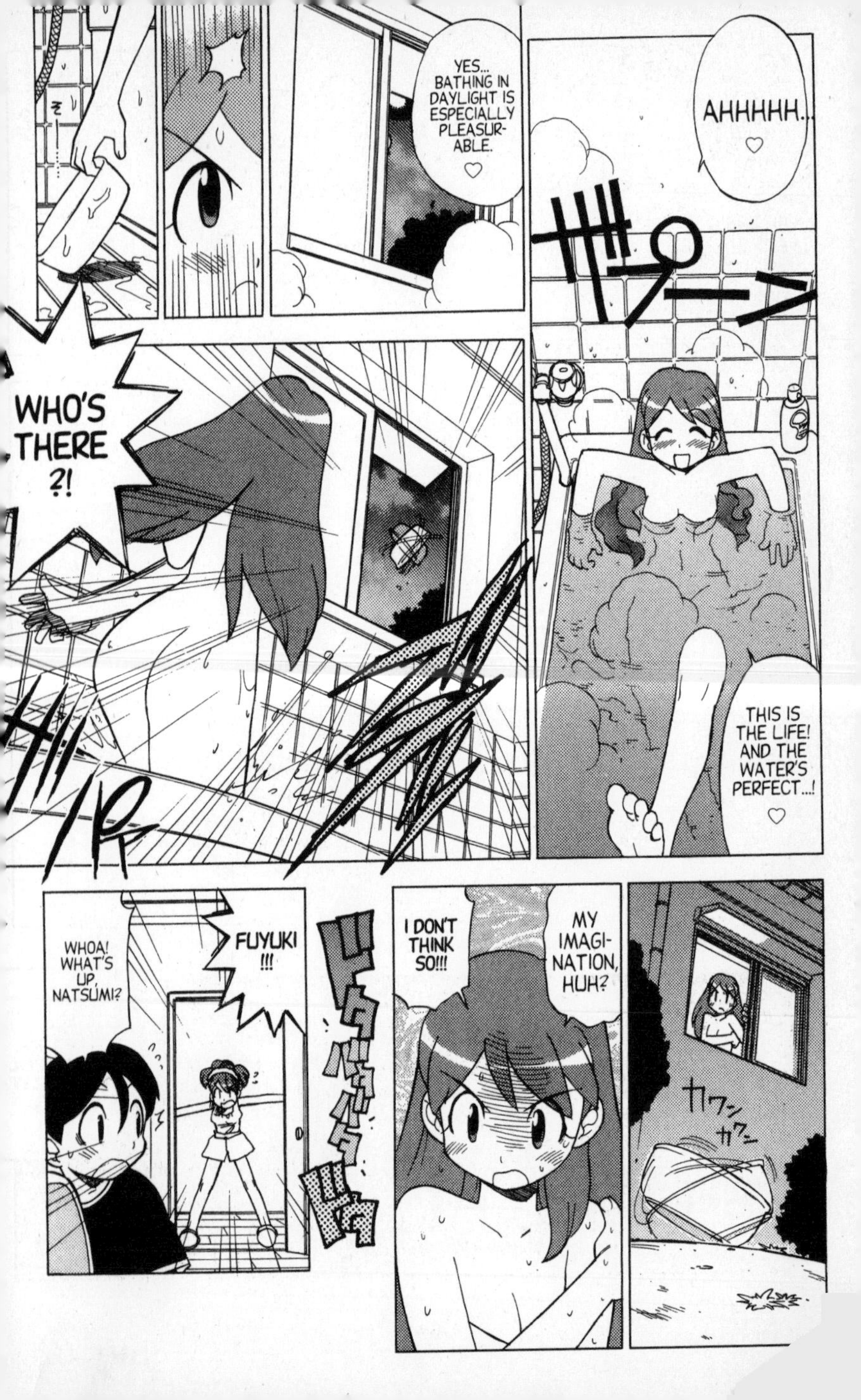
AHHHHH...♡
THIS IS THE LIFE! AND THE WATER'S PERFECT...! ♡
YES... BATHING IN DAYLIGHT IS ESPECIALLY PLEASUR-ABLE. ♡
WHO'S THERE ?!
MY IMAGI-NATION, HUH?
I DON'T THINK SO!!!
FUYUKI !!!
WHOA! WHAT'S UP NATSUMI?

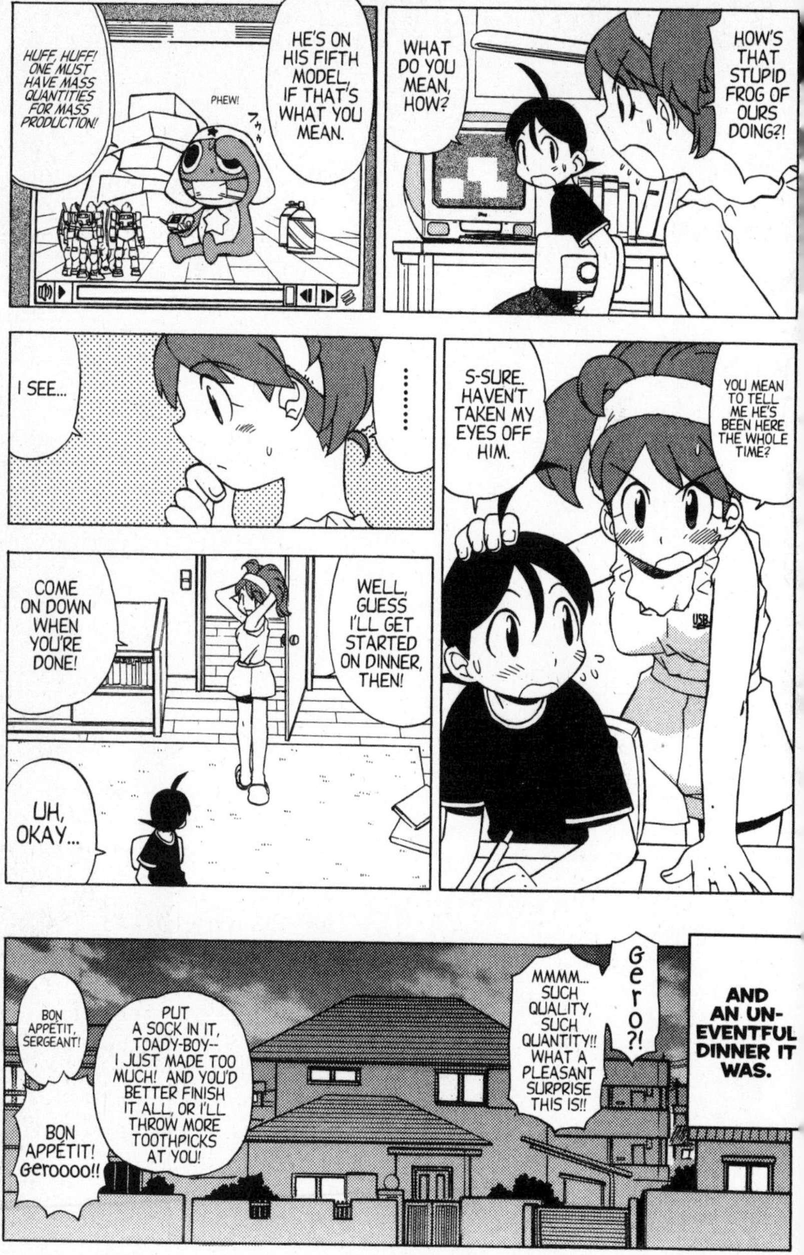
HOW'S THAT STUPID FROG OF OURS DOING?!
WHAT DO YOU MEAN, HOW?
HE'S ON HIS FIFTH MODEL, IF THAT'S WHAT YOU MEAN.
PHEW!
HUFF, HUFF! ONE MUST HAVE MASS QUANTITIES FOR MASS PRODUCTION!
YOU MEAN TO TELL ME HE'S BEEN HERE THE WHOLE TIME?
S-SURE. HAVEN'T TAKEN MY EYES OFF HIM.
....
I SEE...
WELL, GUESS I'LL GET STARTED ON DINNER, THEN!
COME ON DOWN WHEN YOU'RE DONE!
UH, OKAY...
AND AN UN-EVENTFUL DINNER IT WAS.
Gero?!
MMMM... SUCH QUALITY, SUCH QUANTITY!! WHAT A PLEASANT SURPRISE THIS IS!!
PUT A SOCK IN IT, TOADY-BOY-- I JUST MADE TOO MUCH! AND YOU'D BETTER FINISH IT ALL, OR I'LL THROW MORE TOOTHPICKS AT YOU!
BON APPÉTIT, SERGEANT!
BON APPÉTIT! Geroooo!!

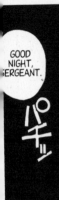

zzZZ
AND... NORMAL TO THE END!
WELL, AT LEAST IT WAS GOOD TO SEE THAT THE SERGEANT REALLY IS TRYING TO COOPERATE!
GOOD NIGHT, SERGEANT.
パチッ
TAP
TAP TAP
TAP ...
6:30: MASTER FUYUKI WAKES UP. 6:24: MASTER NATSUMI WAKES UP...
18:42: MASTER NATSUMI TAKES A BATH. HER BUST MEASUREMENT HAS INCREASED AGAIN. NUMERIC VALUE IS NOW ABOVE THE POKOPENIAN FEMALE AVERAGE.
*TAP
Gero...
FOOLISH POKOPENIANS! THEY'RE A MILLION LIGHT YEARS TOO PRIMITIVE TO MONITOR ME!!!
JUST BECAUSE YOU CALL A CREATURE "PET" DOESN'T MEAN IT SHARES YOUR ILLUSION. PERHAPS, IN THE END, HUMAN VANITY IS THE ONLY REAL BOND BETWEEN YOU...
SHONEN ACE
END
TO BE CONTINUED

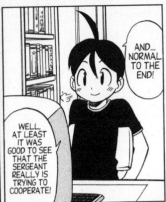

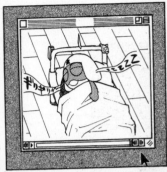

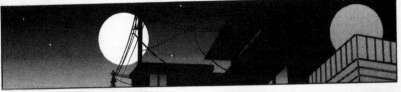

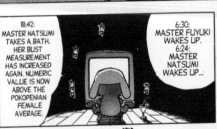

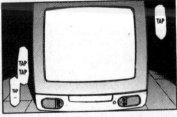

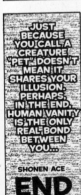

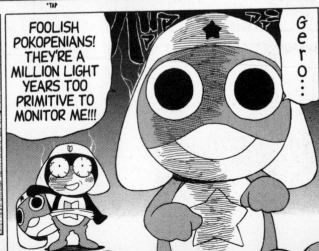

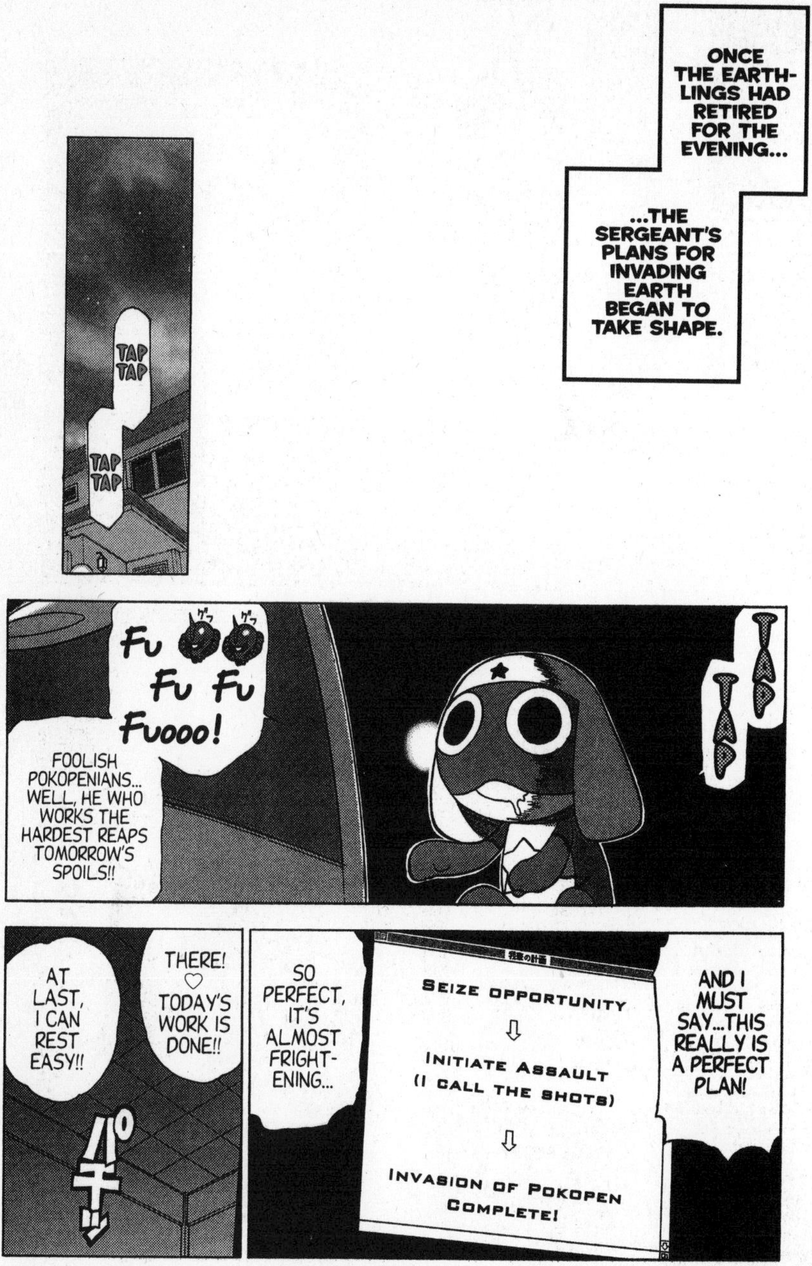

ONCE THE EARTHLINGS HAD RETIRED FOR THE EVENING...
...THE SERGEANT'S PLANS FOR INVADING EARTH BEGAN TO TAKE SHAPE.
TAP TAP
TAP TAP
TAP TAP
Fu Fu Fu Fuooo!
FOOLISH POKOPENIANS... WELL, HE WHO WORKS THE HARDEST REAPS TOMORROW'S SPOILS!!
AND I MUST SAY...THIS REALLY IS A PERFECT PLAN!
SEIZE OPPORTUNITY
⇩
INITIATE ASSAULT (I CALL THE SHOTS)
⇩
INVASION OF POKOPEN COMPLETE!
SO PERFECT, IT'S ALMOST FRIGHTENING...
THERE! ♡ TODAY'S WORK IS DONE!!
AT LAST, I CAN REST EASY!!
パチッ

ZZZZ!

SNORT

HUMMIMNNA

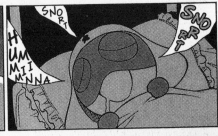

SNORT

VEN--

SMIRK...

V...

*SNORRRRTTTT

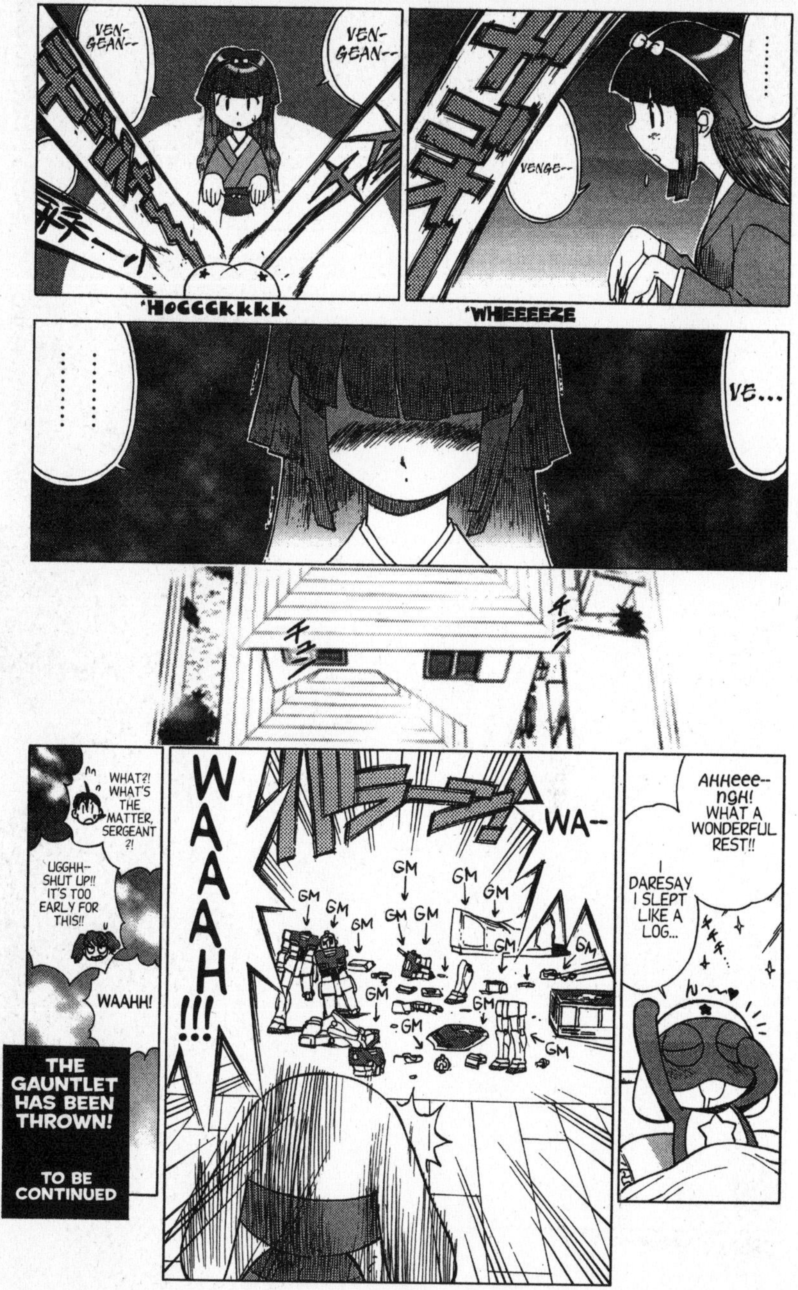
......
VENGE--
*WHEEEEZE
VEN-GEAN--
VEN-GEAN--
*HOGCCKkkkk
VE...
......
AHHeee--ngH! WHAT A WONDERFUL REST!!
I DARESAY I SLEPT LIKE A LOG...
WA--
WAAAAH!!!
WHAT?! WHAT'S THE MATTER, SERGEANT?!
UGGHH--SHUT UP!! IT'S TOO EARLY FOR THIS!!
WAAHH!
THE GAUNTLET HAS BEEN THROWN!
TO BE CONTINUED

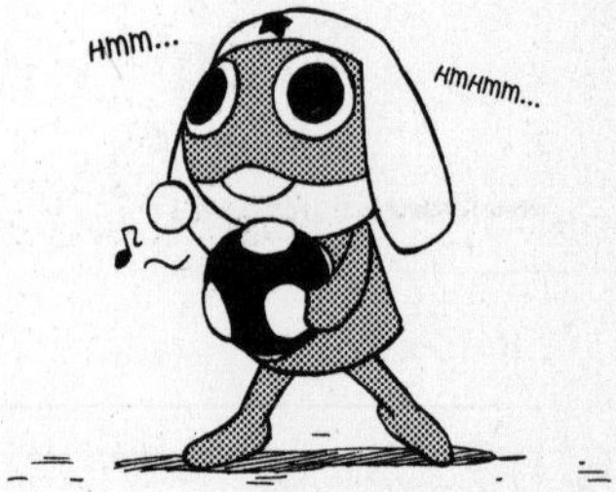
HMM...
HMHMM...

ENCOUNTER VII
CARNAGE IN THE STORM

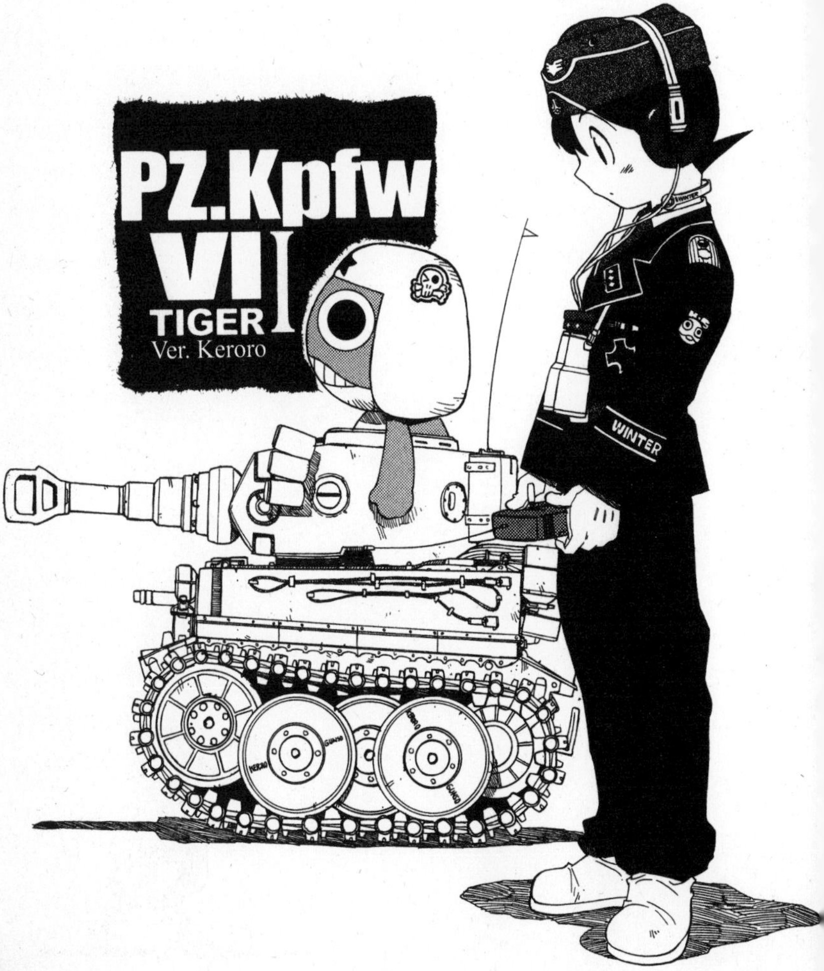
PZ.Kpfw VI TIGER
Ver. Keroro
WINTER

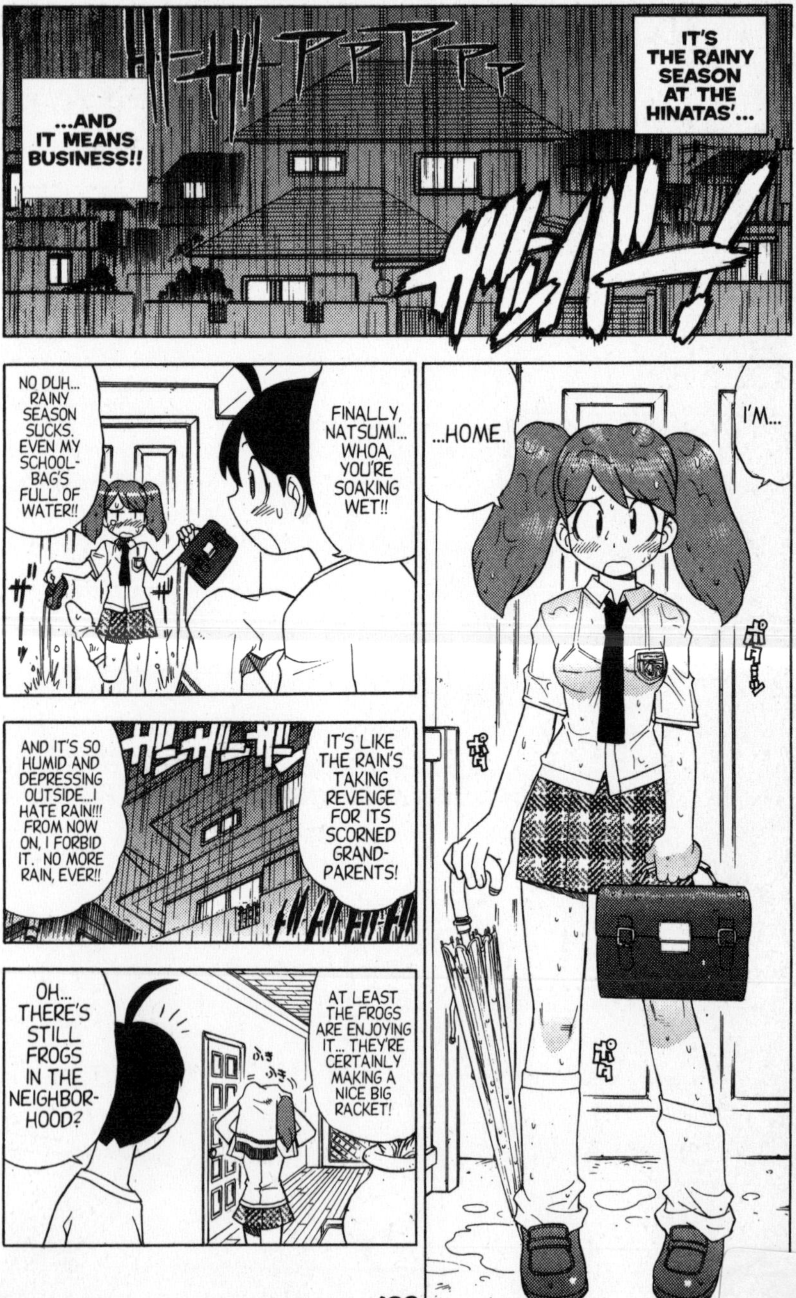

IT'S THE RAINY SEASON AT THE HINATAS'...
...AND IT MEANS BUSINESS!!
I'M...
...HOME.
FINALLY, NATSUMI... WHOA, YOU'RE SOAKING WET!!
NO DUH... RAINY SEASON SUCKS. EVEN MY SCHOOL-BAG'S FULL OF WATER!!
IT'S LIKE THE RAIN'S TAKING REVENGE FOR ITS SCORNED GRAND-PARENTS!
AND IT'S SO HUMID AND DEPRESSING OUTSIDE...I HATE RAIN!!! FROM NOW ON, I FORBID IT. NO MORE RAIN, EVER!!
AT LEAST THE FROGS ARE ENJOYING IT... THEY'RE CERTAINLY MAKING A NICE BIG RACKET!
OH... THERE'S STILL FROGS IN THE NEIGHBOR-HOOD?

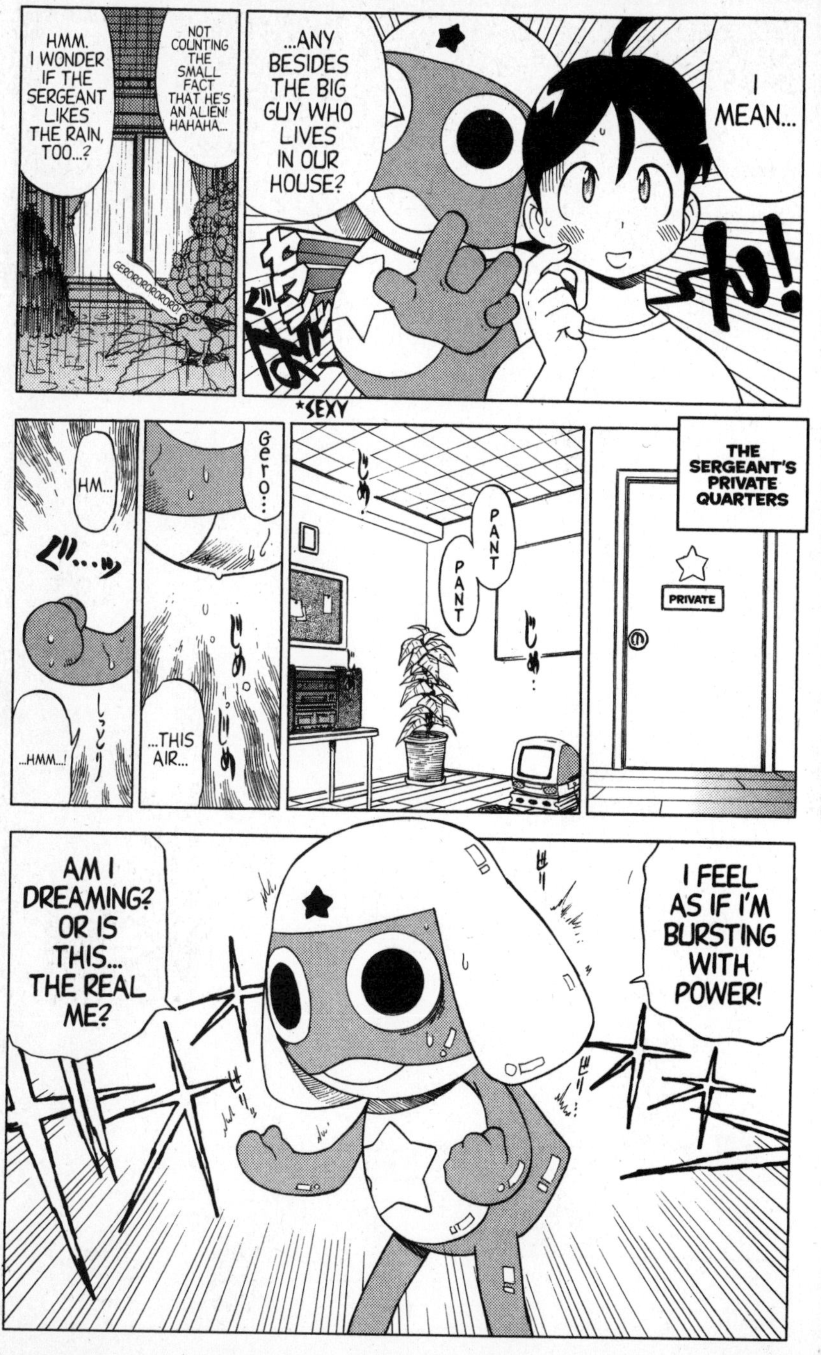
I MEAN...
...ANY BESIDES THE BIG GUY WHO LIVES IN OUR HOUSE?
*SEXY
NOT COUNTING THE SMALL FACT THAT HE'S AN ALIEN! HAHAHA...
HMM. I WONDER IF THE SERGEANT LIKES THE RAIN, TOO...?
GEROROROROROROR!
THE SERGEANT'S PRIVATE QUARTERS
PRIVATE
PANT
PANT
Gero...
...THIS AIR...
HM...
...HMM...!
I FEEL AS IF I'M BURSTING WITH POWER!
AM I DREAMING? OR IS THIS... THE REAL ME?

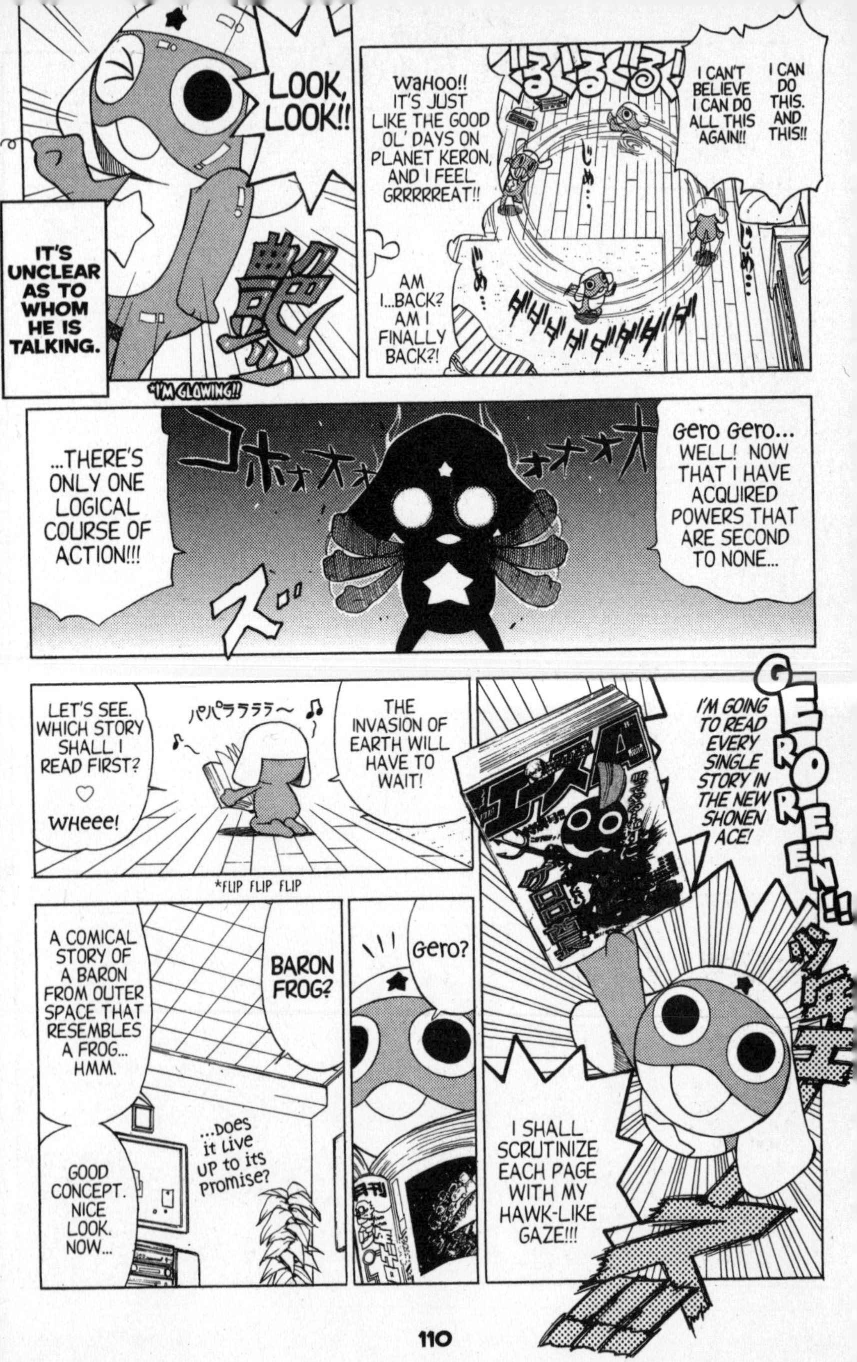
I CAN DO THIS. AND THIS!!
I CAN'T BELIEVE I CAN DO ALL THIS AGAIN!!
WaHoo!! IT'S JUST LIKE THE GOOD OL' DAYS ON PLANET KERON, AND I FEEL GRRRRREAT!!
AM I...BACK? AM I FINALLY BACK?!
LOOK, LOOK!!
IT'S UNCLEAR AS TO WHOM HE IS TALKING.
*I'M GLOWING!!
Gero Gero... WELL! NOW THAT I HAVE ACQUIRED POWERS THAT ARE SECOND TO NONE...
...THERE'S ONLY ONE LOGICAL COURSE OF ACTION!!!
GERO-RE-N!!
I'M GOING TO READ EVERY SINGLE STORY IN THE NEW SHONEN ACE!
I SHALL SCRUTINIZE EACH PAGE WITH MY HAWK-LIKE GAZE!!!
THE INVASION OF EARTH WILL HAVE TO WAIT!
LET'S SEE. WHICH STORY SHALL I READ FIRST? ♡ WHeee!
*FLIP FLIP FLIP
Gero?
BARON FROG?
A COMICAL STORY OF A BARON FROM OUTER SPACE THAT RESEMBLES A FROG... HMM.
...does it live up to its promise?
GOOD CONCEPT. NICE LOOK. NOW...

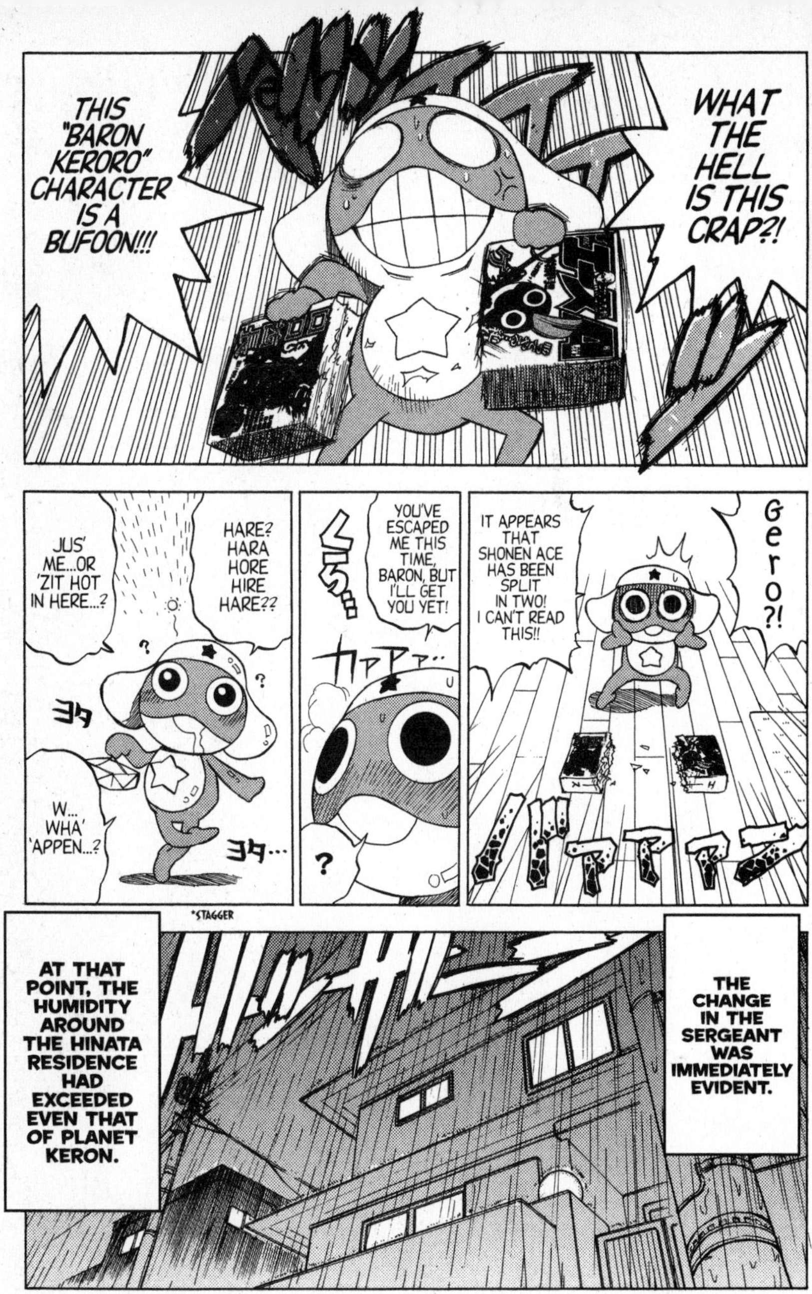
WHAT THE HELL IS THIS CRAP?!
THIS "BARON KERORO" CHARACTER IS A BUFOON!!!
Gero?!
IT APPEARS THAT SHONEN ACE HAS BEEN SPLIT IN TWO! I CAN'T READ THIS!!
YOU'VE ESCAPED ME THIS TIME, BARON, BUT I'LL GET YOU YET!
?
HARE? HARA HORE HIRE HARE??
JUS' ME...OR 'ZIT HOT IN HERE...?
W... WHA' 'APPEN...?
*STAGGER
THE CHANGE IN THE SERGEANT WAS IMMEDIATELY EVIDENT.
AT THAT POINT, THE HUMIDITY AROUND THE HINATA RESIDENCE HAD EXCEEDED EVEN THAT OF PLANET KERON.

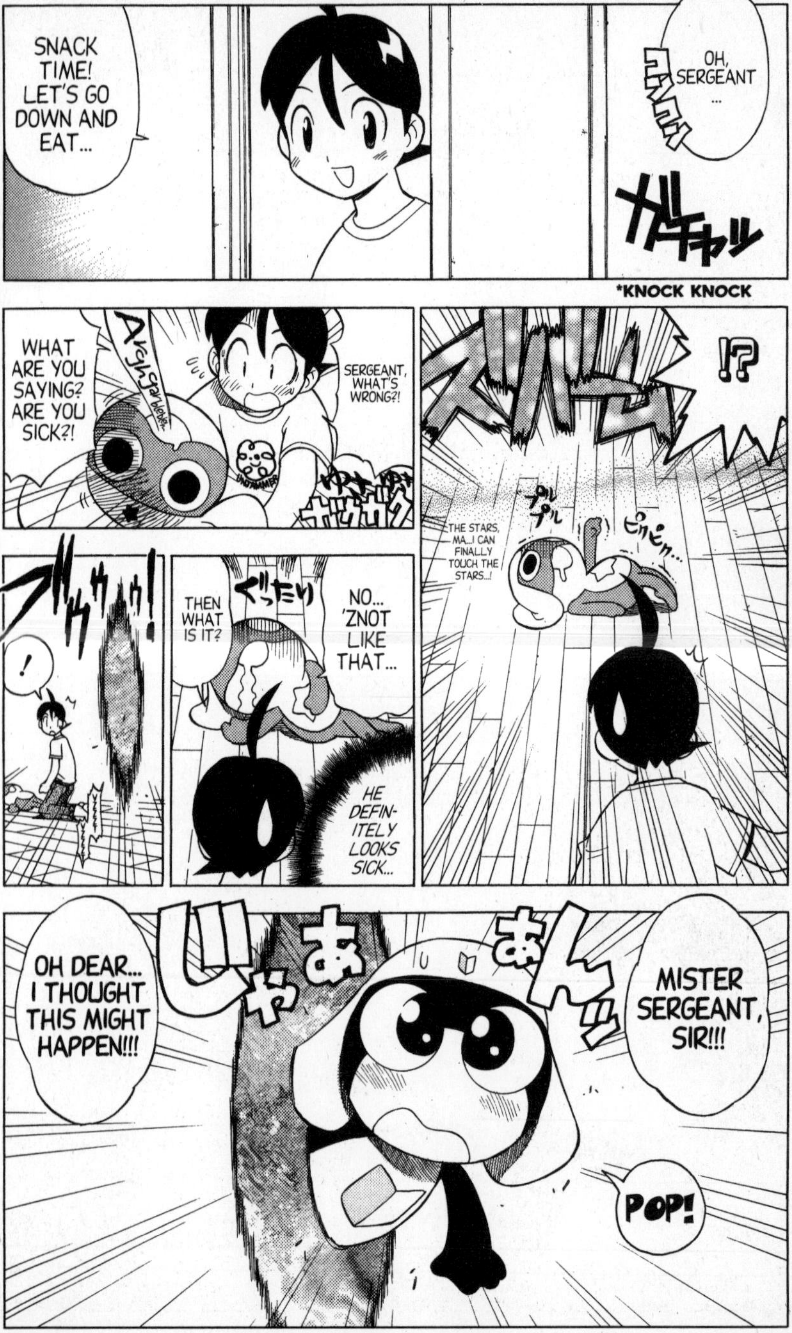
OH, SERGEANT ...
SNACK TIME! LET'S GO DOWN AND EAT...
*KNOCK KNOCK
!?
THE STARS, MA...I CAN FINALLY TOUCH THE STARS...!
SERGEANT, WHAT'S WRONG?!
Arghgarblebla...
WHAT ARE YOU SAYING? ARE YOU SICK?!
NO... 'ZNOT LIKE THAT...
THEN WHAT IS IT?
HE DEFIN-ITELY LOOKS SICK...
!
MISTER SERGEANT, SIR!!!
POP!
OH DEAR... I THOUGHT THIS MIGHT HAPPEN!!!

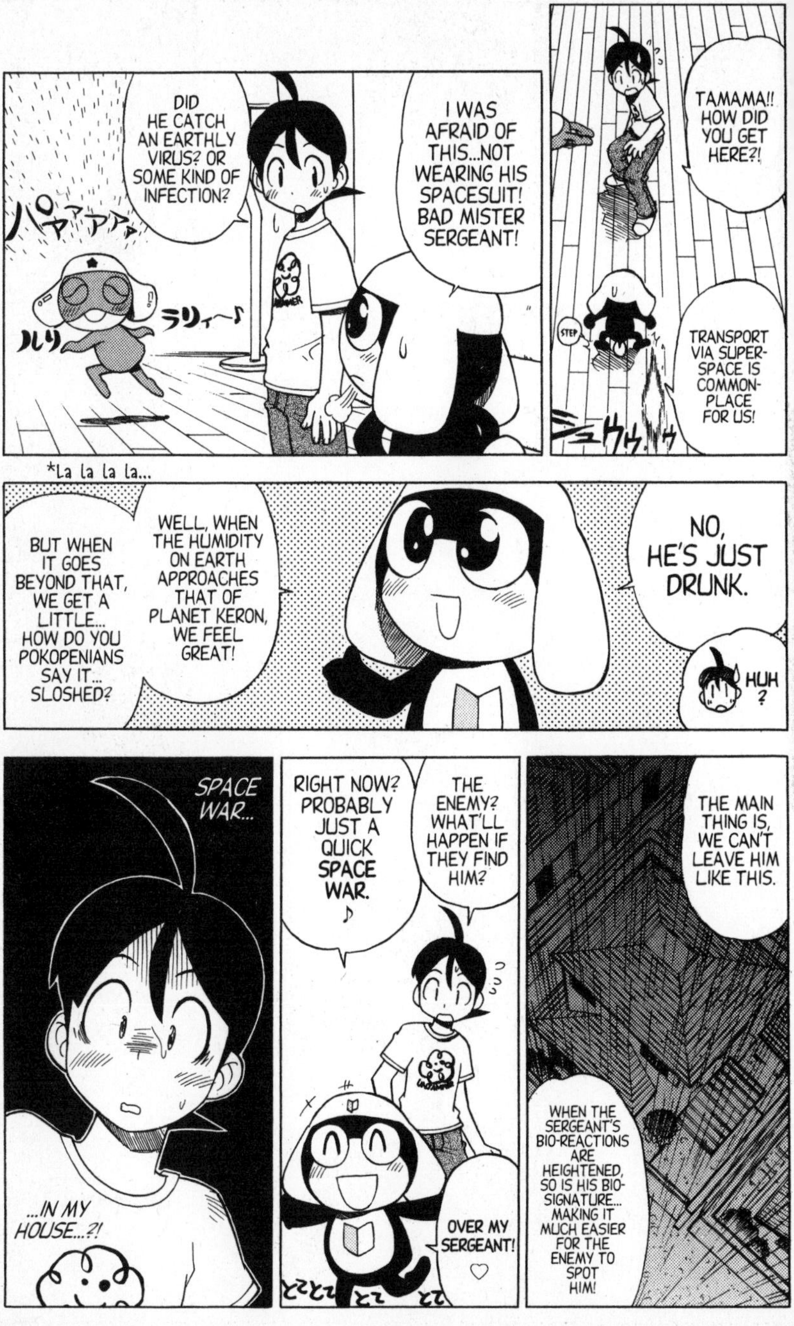
TAMAMA!! HOW DID YOU GET HERE?!
STEP
TRANSPORT VIA SUPER-SPACE IS COMMONPLACE FOR US!
I WAS AFRAID OF THIS...NOT WEARING HIS SPACESUIT! BAD MISTER SERGEANT!
DID HE CATCH AN EARTHLY VIRUS? OR SOME KIND OF INFECTION?
*La la la la...
NO, HE'S JUST DRUNK.
HUH?
WELL, WHEN THE HUMIDITY ON EARTH APPROACHES THAT OF PLANET KERON, WE FEEL GREAT!
BUT WHEN IT GOES BEYOND THAT, WE GET A LITTLE... HOW DO YOU POKOPENIANS SAY IT... SLOSHED?
THE MAIN THING IS, WE CAN'T LEAVE HIM LIKE THIS.
WHEN THE SERGEANT'S BIO-REACTIONS ARE HEIGHTENED, SO IS HIS BIO-SIGNATURE... MAKING IT MUCH EASIER FOR THE ENEMY TO SPOT HIM!
THE ENEMY? WHAT'LL HAPPEN IF THEY FIND HIM?
RIGHT NOW? PROBABLY JUST A QUICK SPACE WAR. ♪
OVER MY SERGEANT! ♡
SPACE WAR...
...IN MY HOUSE...?!

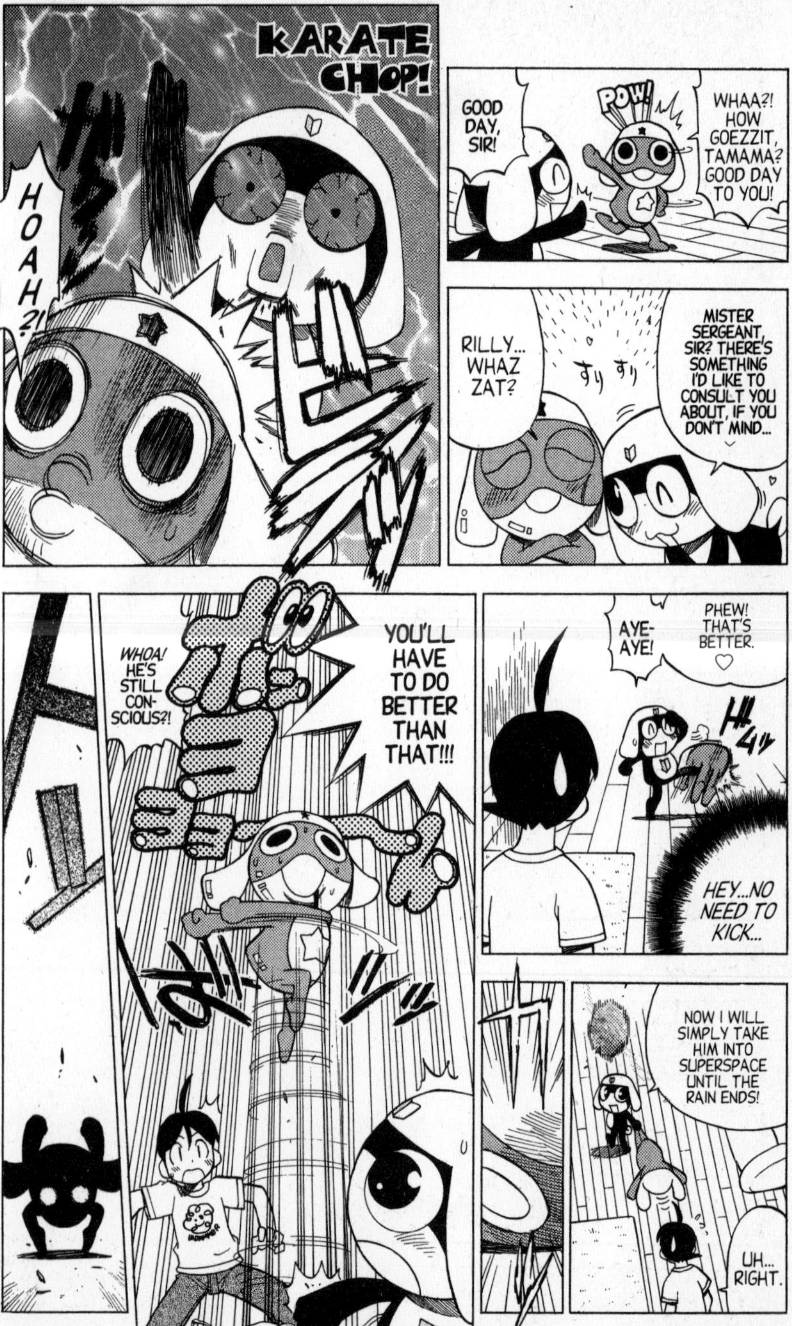
WHAA?! HOW GOEZZIT, TAMAMA? GOOD DAY TO YOU!
POW!
GOOD DAY, SIR!
MISTER SERGEANT, SIR? THERE'S SOMETHING I'D LIKE TO CONSULT YOU ABOUT, IF YOU DON'T MIND...
すり すり
RILLY... WHAZ ZAT?
KARATE CHOP!
HOAH?!
PHEW! THAT'S BETTER.
AYE-AYE!
HEY...NO NEED TO KICK...
NOW I WILL SIMPLY TAKE HIM INTO SUPERSPACE UNTIL THE RAIN ENDS!
UH... RIGHT.
YOU'LL HAVE TO DO BETTER THAN THAT!!!
WHOA! HE'S STILL CON-SCIOUS?!

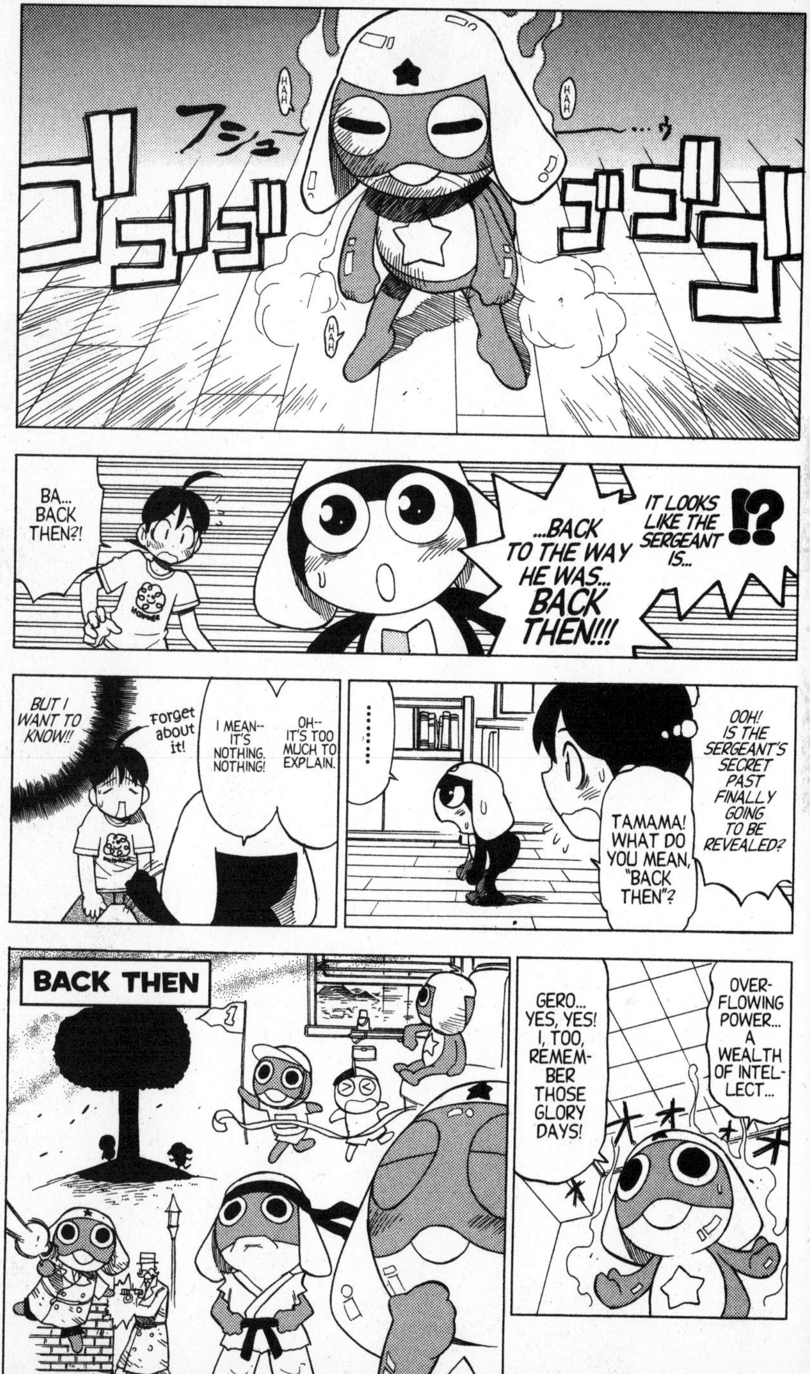
HAH
フシュ
HAH
HAH
...ウ
IT LOOKS LIKE THE SERGEANT IS... !?
...BACK TO THE WAY HE WAS... BACK THEN!!!
BA... BACK THEN?!
OOH! IS THE SERGEANT'S SECRET PAST FINALLY GOING TO BE REVEALED?
TAMAMA! WHAT DO YOU MEAN, "BACK THEN"?
....
OH-- IT'S TOO MUCH TO EXPLAIN.
I MEAN-- IT'S NOTHING. NOTHING!
Forget about it!
BUT I WANT TO KNOW!!
OVER-FLOWING POWER... A WEALTH OF INTEL-LECT...
GERO... YES, YES! I, TOO, REMEM-BER THOSE GLORY DAYS!
BACK THEN

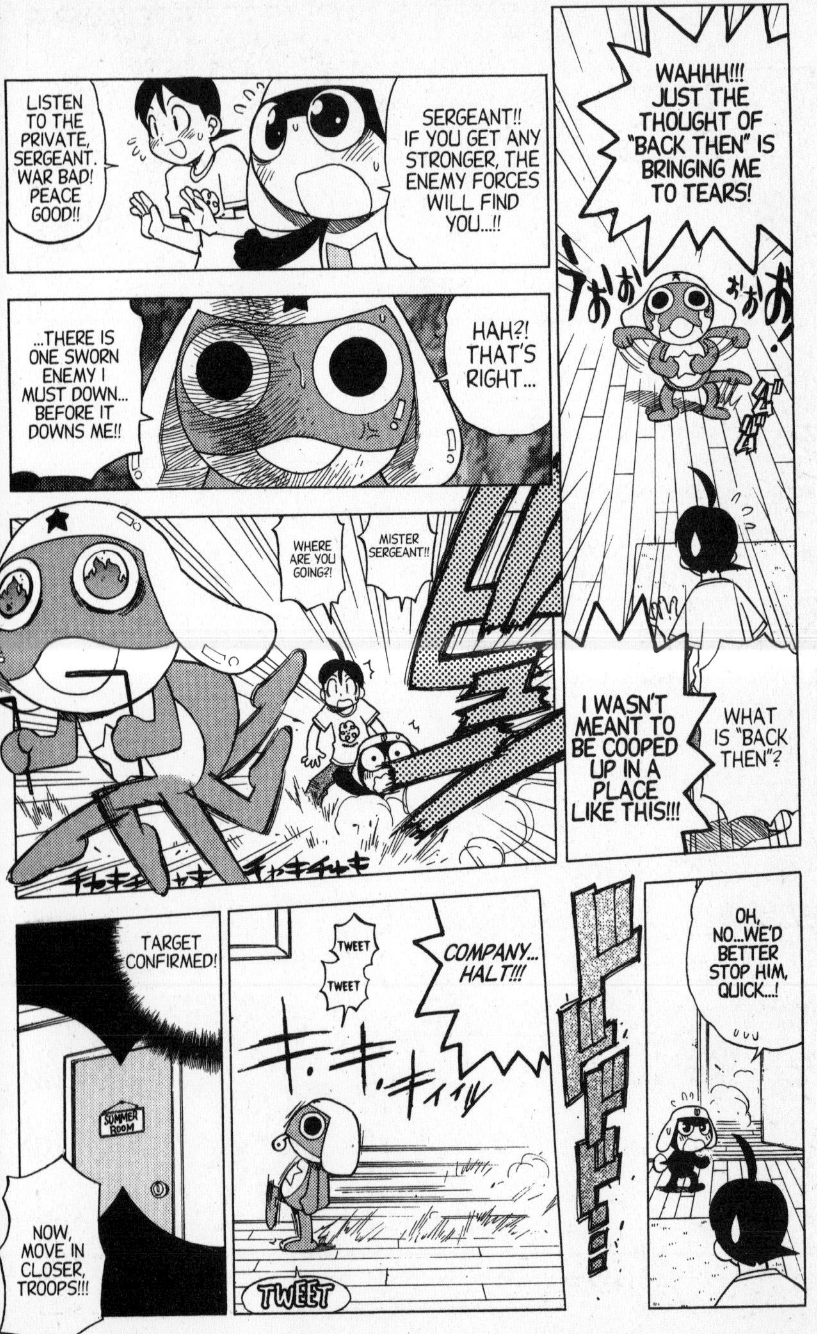
WAHHH!!! JUST THE THOUGHT OF "BACK THEN" IS BRINGING ME TO TEARS!
WHAT IS "BACK THEN"?
I WASN'T MEANT TO BE COOPED UP IN A PLACE LIKE THIS!!!
SERGEANT!! IF YOU GET ANY STRONGER, THE ENEMY FORCES WILL FIND YOU...!!
LISTEN TO THE PRIVATE, SERGEANT. WAR BAD! PEACE GOOD!!
HAH?! THAT'S RIGHT...
...THERE IS ONE SWORN ENEMY I MUST DOWN... BEFORE IT DOWNS ME!!
MISTER SERGEANT!!
WHERE ARE YOU GOING?!
OH, NO...WE'D BETTER STOP HIM, QUICK...!
COMPANY... HALT!!!
TWEET
TWEET
TWEET
TARGET CONFIRMED!
SUMMER ROOM
NOW, MOVE IN CLOSER, TROOPS!!!

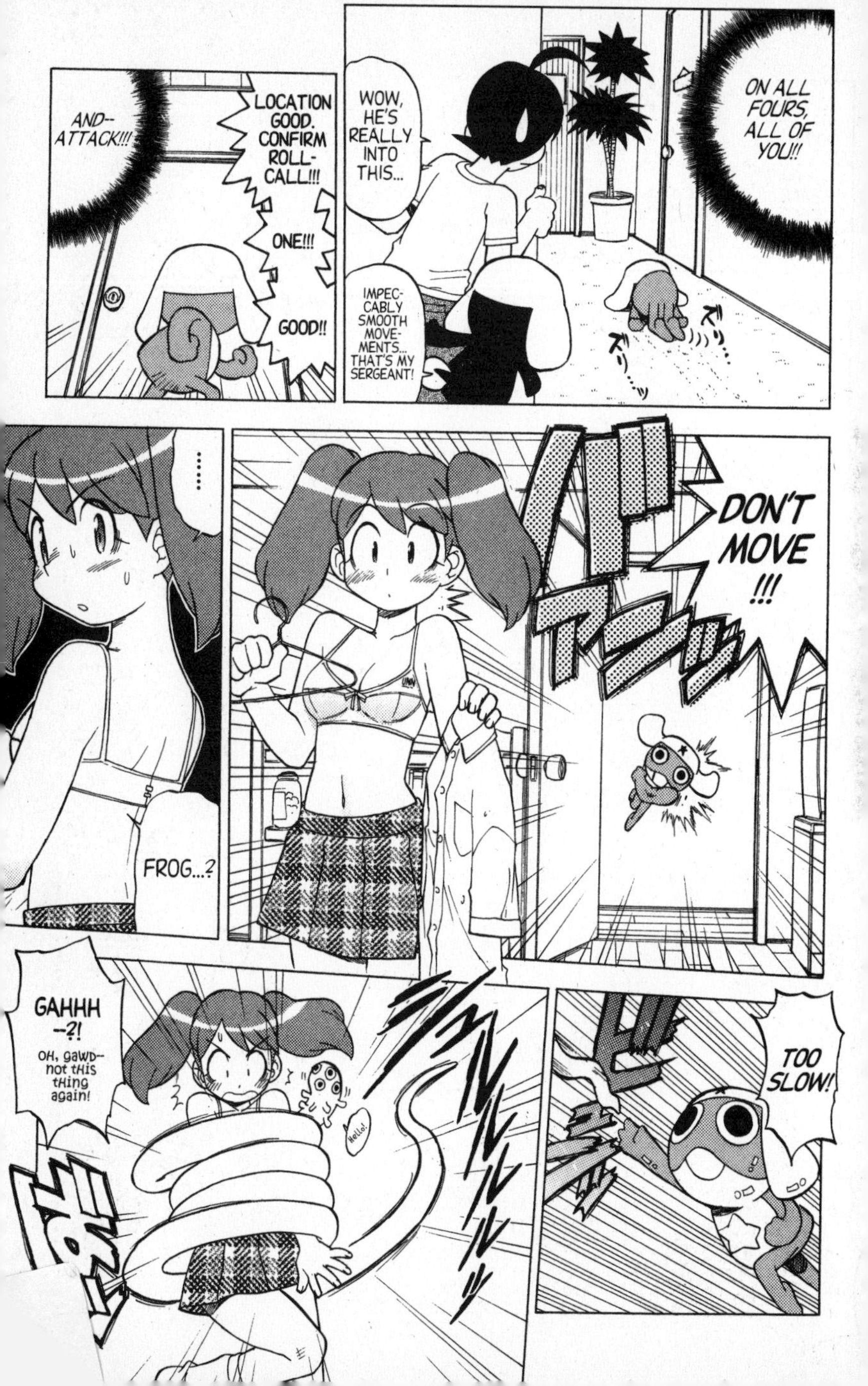
ON ALL FOURS, ALL OF YOU!!
WOW, HE'S REALLY INTO THIS...
IMPECCABLY SMOOTH MOVEMENTS... THAT'S MY SERGEANT!
LOCATION GOOD. CONFIRM ROLL-CALL!!!
ONE!!!
GOOD!!
AND-- ATTACK!!!
DON'T MOVE!!!
......
FROG...?
TOO SLOW!
GAHHH --?!
OH, GAWD-- not this thing again!
Hello!

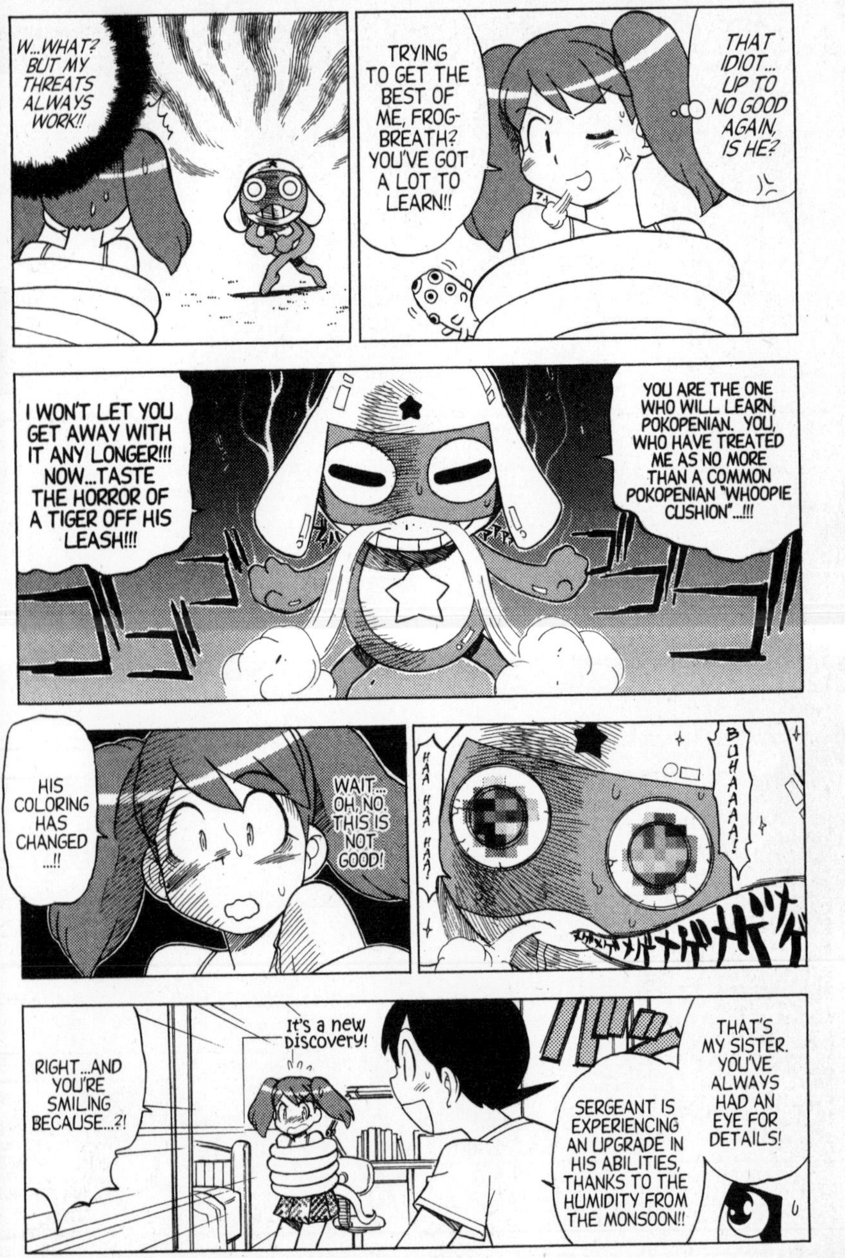
THAT IDIOT... UP TO NO GOOD AGAIN, IS HE?
TRYING TO GET THE BEST OF ME, FROG-BREATH? YOU'VE GOT A LOT TO LEARN!!
W...WHAT? BUT MY THREATS ALWAYS WORK!!
YOU ARE THE ONE WHO WILL LEARN, POKOPENIAN. YOU, WHO HAVE TREATED ME AS NO MORE THAN A COMMON POKOPENIAN "WHOOPIE CUSHION"...!!!
I WON'T LET YOU GET AWAY WITH IT ANY LONGER!!! NOW...TASTE THE HORROR OF A TIGER OFF HIS LEASH!!!
BUHAAAAAA!
HAA HAA HAA HAA?
WAIT... OH, NO. THIS IS NOT GOOD!
HIS COLORING HAS CHANGED ...!!
THAT'S MY SISTER. YOU'VE ALWAYS HAD AN EYE FOR DETAILS!
SERGEANT IS EXPERIENCING AN UPGRADE IN HIS ABILITIES, THANKS TO THE HUMIDITY FROM THE MONSOON!!
It's a new discovery!
RIGHT...AND YOU'RE SMILING BECAUSE...?!

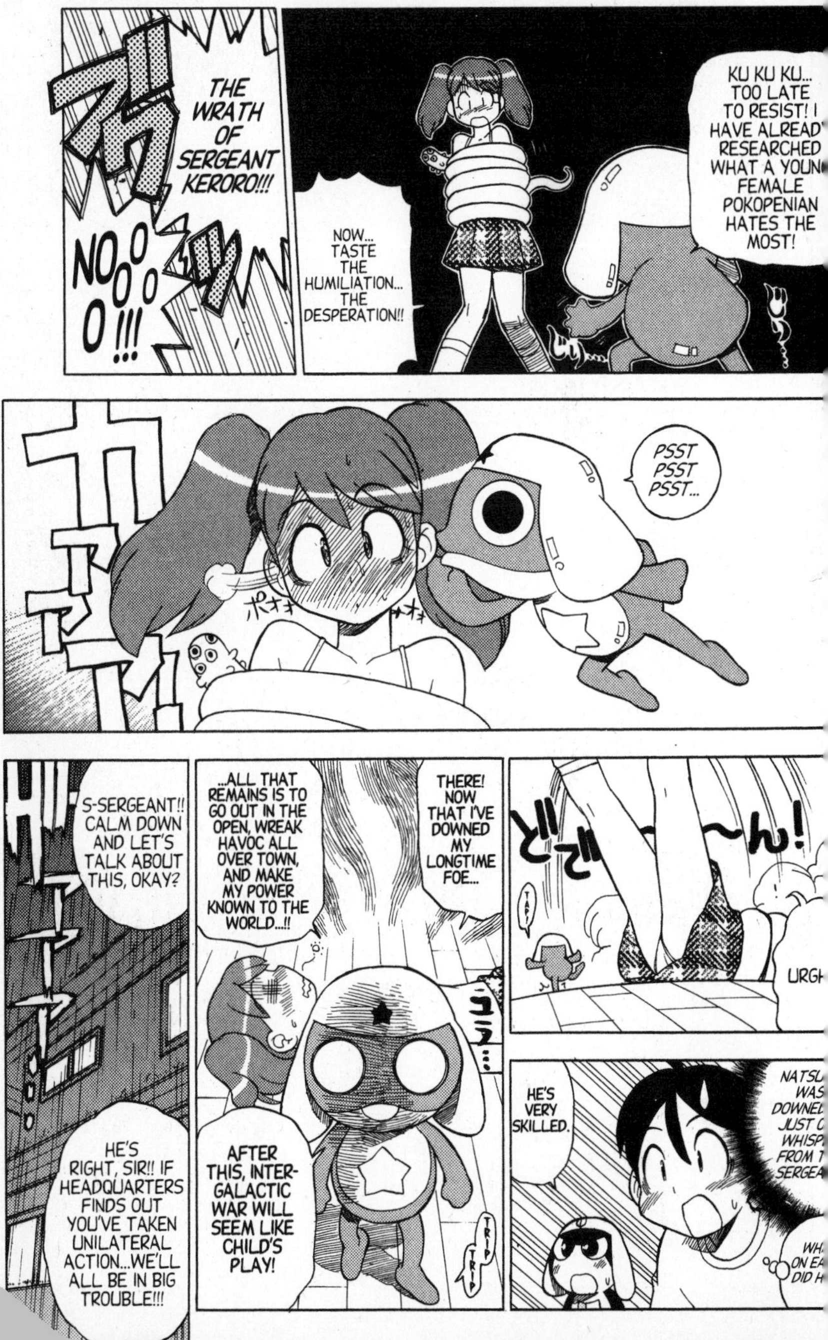
KU KU KU... TOO LATE TO RESIST! I HAVE ALREAD RESEARCHED WHAT A YOUN FEMALE POKOPENIAN HATES THE MOST!
NOW... TASTE THE HUMILIATION... THE DESPERATION!!
THE WRATH OF SERGEANT KERORO!!!
NOOOOO!!!
PSST PSST PSST...
TAP!
URGH
NATSU WAS DOWNEL JUST C WHISP FROM T SERGEA
HE'S VERY SKILLED.
WHA ON EA DID H
THERE! NOW THAT I'VE DOWNED MY LONGTIME FOE...
...ALL THAT REMAINS IS TO GO OUT IN THE OPEN, WREAK HAVOC ALL OVER TOWN, AND MAKE MY POWER KNOWN TO THE WORLD...!!
AFTER THIS, INTER-GALACTIC WAR WILL SEEM LIKE CHILD'S PLAY!
TRIP TRIP
S-SERGEANT!! CALM DOWN AND LET'S TALK ABOUT THIS, OKAY?
HE'S RIGHT, SIR!! IF HEADQUARTERS FINDS OUT YOU'VE TAKEN UNILATERAL ACTION...WE'LL ALL BE IN BIG TROUBLE!!!

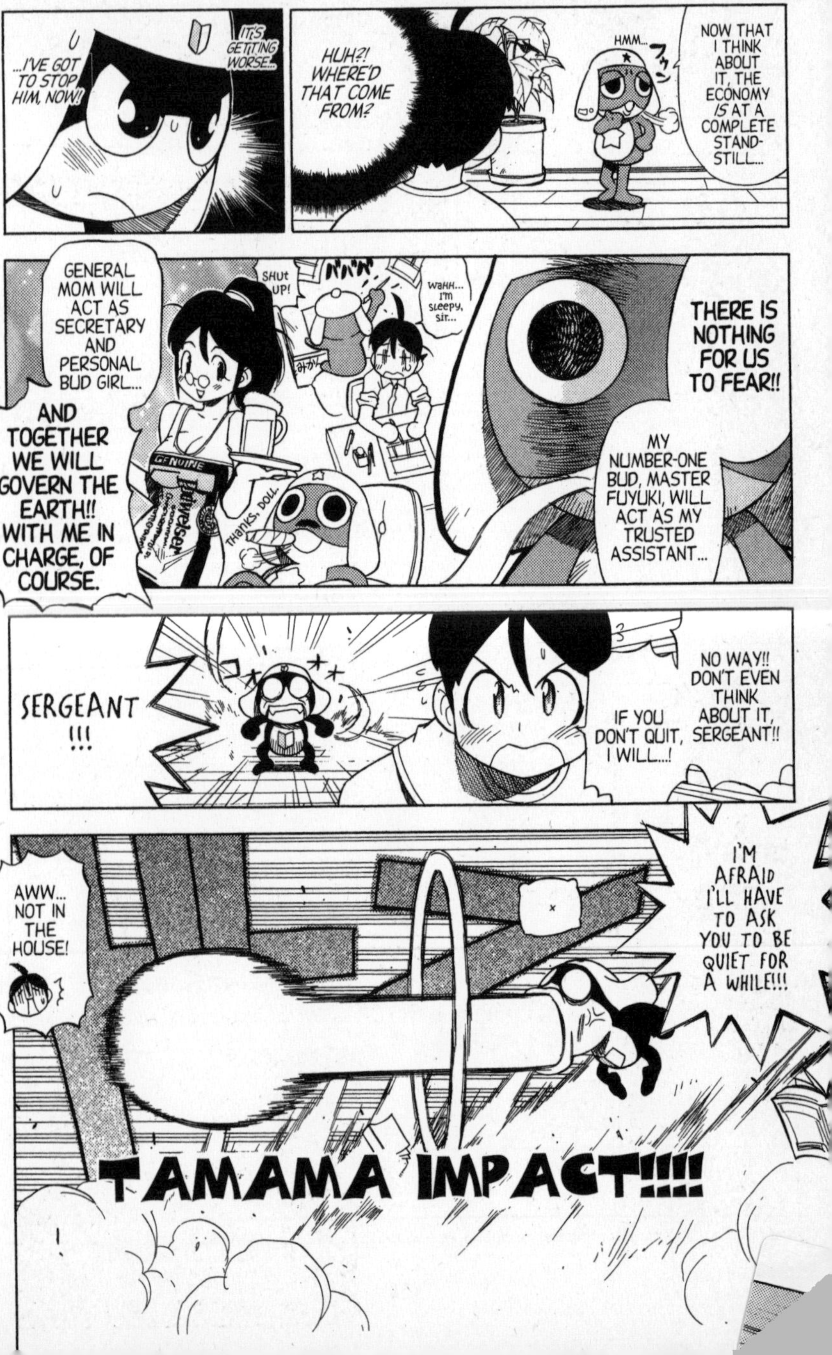
NOW THAT I THINK ABOUT IT, THE ECONOMY IS AT A COMPLETE STAND-STILL...
HMM...
HUH?! WHERE'D THAT COME FROM?
IT'S GETTING WORSE...
...I'VE GOT TO STOP HIM, NOW!
THERE IS NOTHING FOR US TO FEAR!!
MY NUMBER-ONE BUD, MASTER FUYUKI, WILL ACT AS MY TRUSTED ASSISTANT...
WAHH... I'm sleepy, sir...
SHUT UP!
GENERAL MOM WILL ACT AS SECRETARY AND PERSONAL BUD GIRL...
GENUINE
Budweiser
THANKS, DOLL.
AND TOGETHER WE WILL GOVERN THE EARTH!! WITH ME IN CHARGE, OF COURSE.
NO WAY!! DON'T EVEN THINK ABOUT IT, SERGEANT!!
IF YOU DON'T QUIT, I WILL...!
SERGEANT!!!
I'M AFRAID I'LL HAVE TO ASK YOU TO BE QUIET FOR A WHILE!!!
AWW... NOT IN THE HOUSE!
TAMAMA IMPACT!!!!

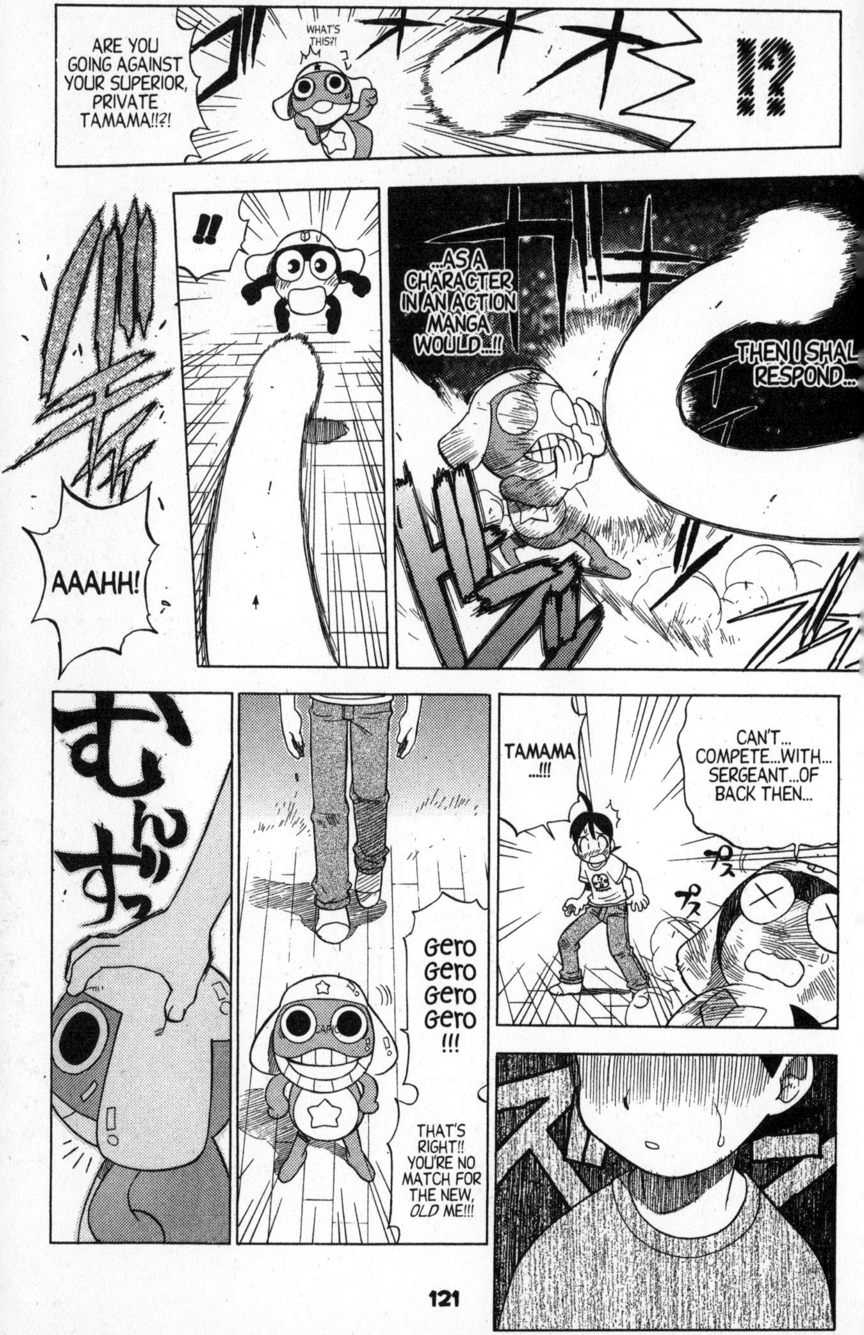
!?
WHAT'S THIS?!
ARE YOU GOING AGAINST YOUR SUPERIOR, PRIVATE TAMAMA!!?!
THEN I SHAL RESPOND...
...AS A CHARACTER IN AN ACTION MANGA WOULD...!!
!!
AAAHH!
CAN'T... COMPETE...WITH... SERGEANT...OF BACK THEN...
TAMAMA ...!!!
Gero Gero Gero Gero !!!
THAT'S RIGHT!! YOU'RE NO MATCH FOR THE NEW, *OLD* ME!!!
むんずっ

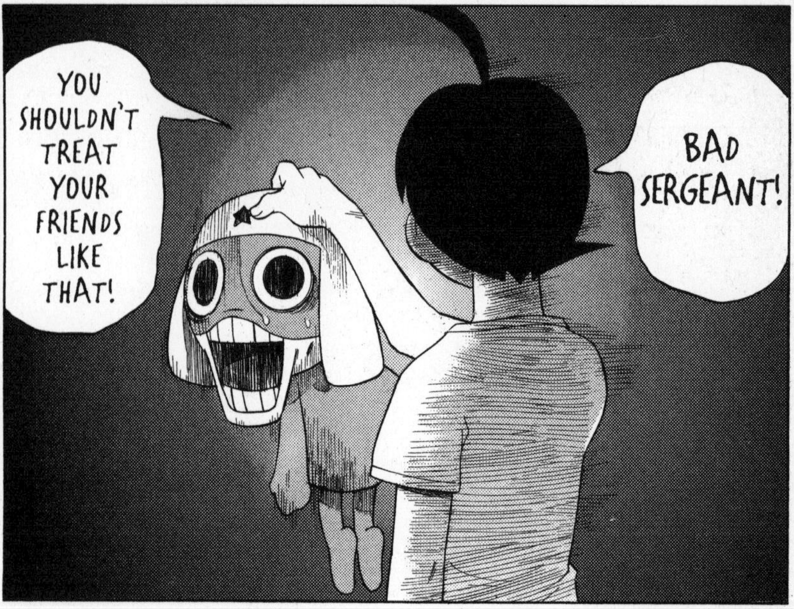
BAD SERGEANT!
YOU SHOULDN'T TREAT YOUR FRIENDS LIKE THAT!

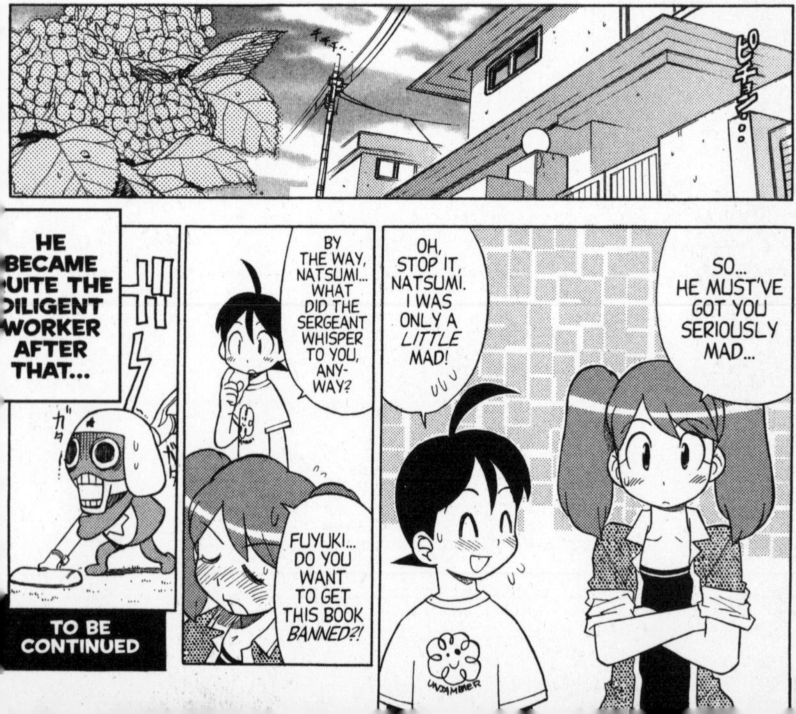
ピチュン…
SO... HE MUST'VE GOT YOU SERIOUSLY MAD...
OH, STOP IT, NATSUMI. I WAS ONLY A *LITTLE* MAD!
BY THE WAY, NATSUMI... WHAT DID THE SERGEANT WHISPER TO YOU, ANYWAY?
FUYUKI... DO YOU WANT TO GET THIS BOOK *BANNED*?!
HE BECAME QUITE THE DILIGENT WORKER AFTER THAT...
TO BE CONTINUED

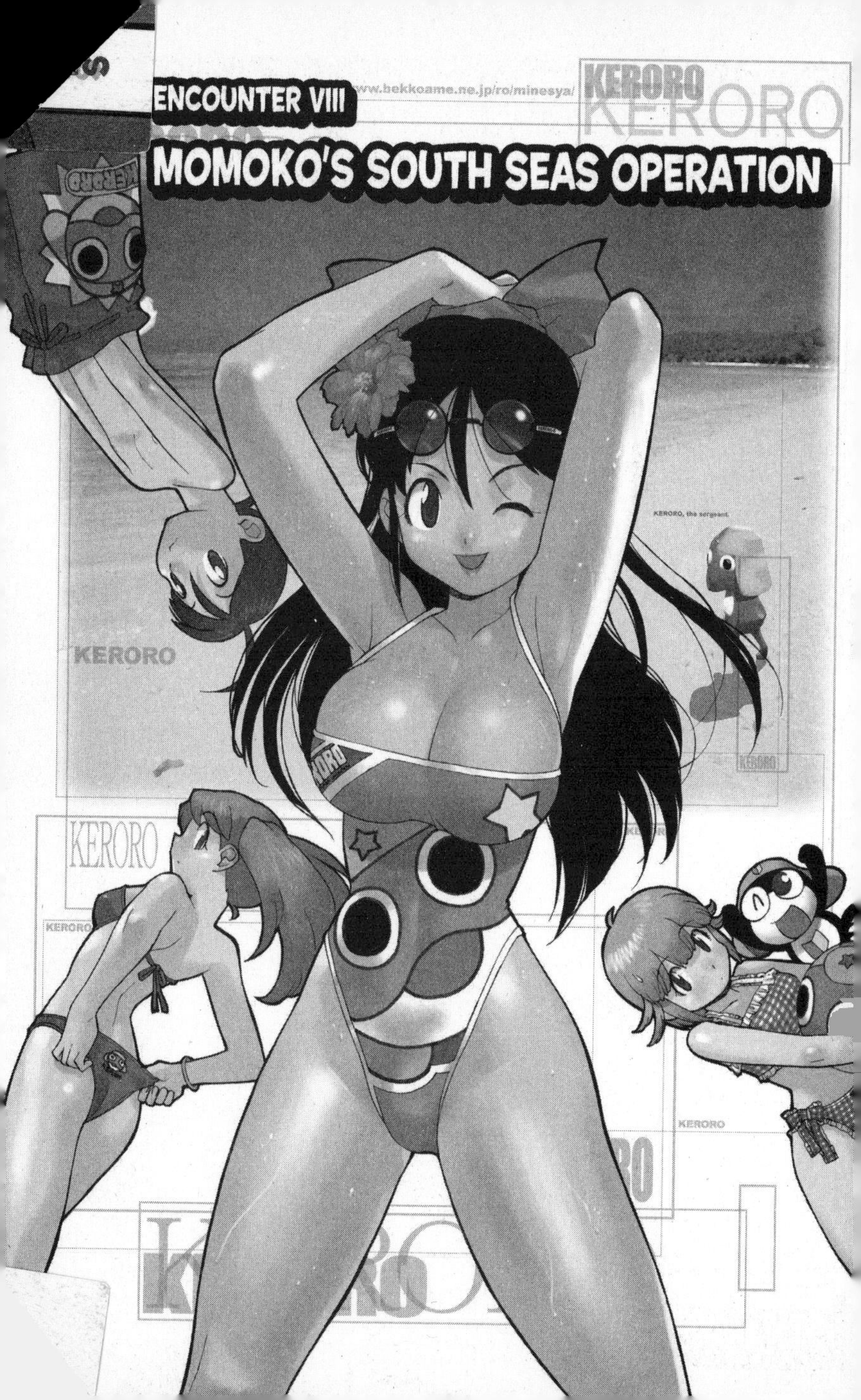
ENCOUNTER VIII
MOMOKO'S SOUTH SEAS OPERATION
www.bekkoame.ne.jp/ro/minesya/
KERORO
KERORO
KERORO, the sergeant.
KERORO
KERORO
KERORO
KERORO

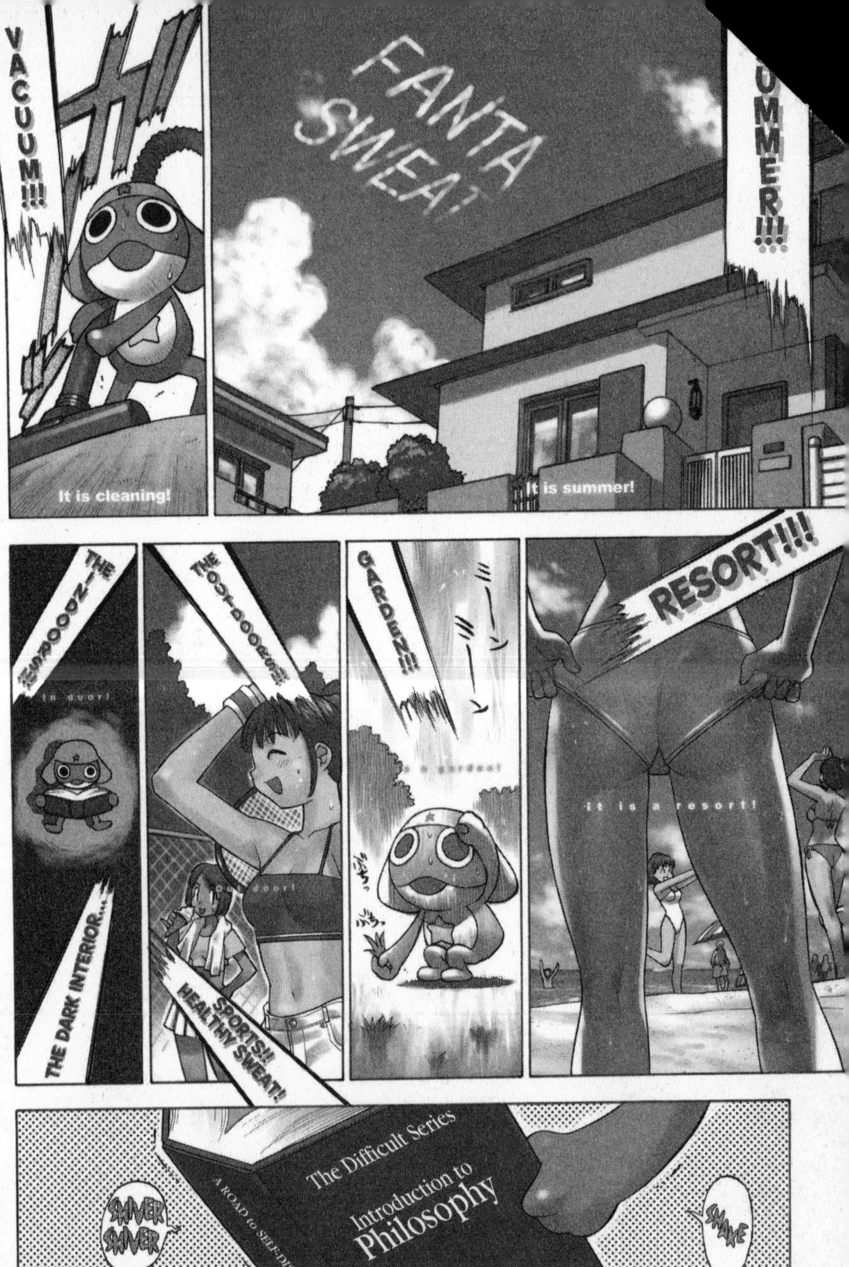
SUMMER!!!
FANTA SWEAT
It is summer!
VACUUM!!!
It is cleaning!
RESORT!!!
it is a resort!
GARDEN!!!
ミーン
ミーン
THE OUT-DOORS!!!
SPORTS!!! HEALTHY SWEAT!
THE INDOORS!!
in door!
THE DARK INTERIOR...
SHAKE
The Difficult Series
Introduction to Philosophy
A ROAD to SELF-DISCOVERY
SHIVER SHIVER

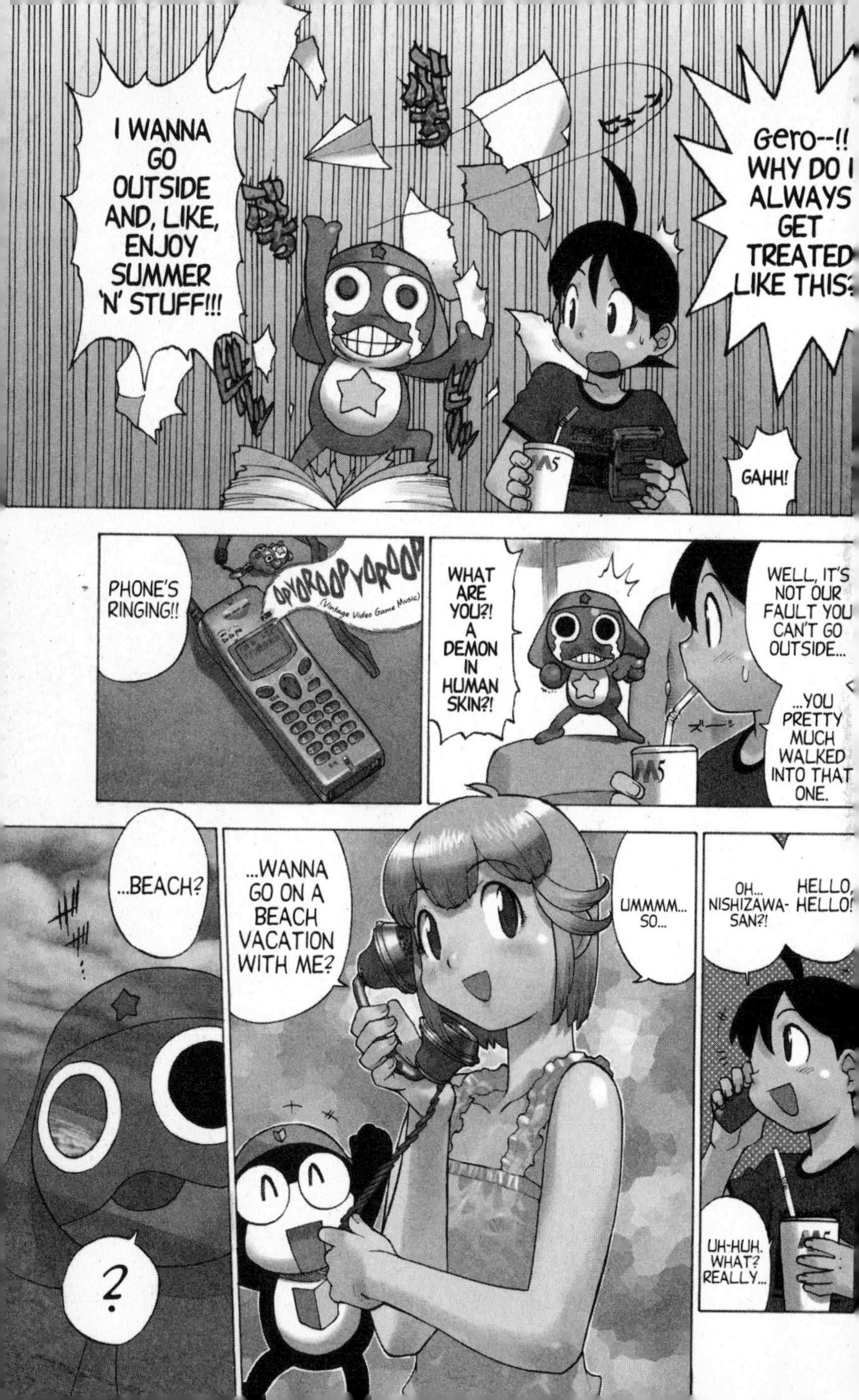
Gero--!! WHY DO I ALWAYS GET TREATED LIKE THIS?
I WANNA GO OUTSIDE AND, LIKE, ENJOY SUMMER 'N' STUFF!!!
GAHH!
WELL, IT'S NOT OUR FAULT YOU CAN'T GO OUTSIDE...
WHAT ARE YOU?! A DEMON IN HUMAN SKIN?!
...YOU PRETTY MUCH WALKED INTO THAT ONE.
OPYOROOPYOROOP
(Vintage Video Game Music)
PHONE'S RINGING!!
HELLO, HELLO!
OH... NISHIZAWA-SAN?!
UH-HUH. WHAT? REALLY...
UMMMM... SO...
...WANNA GO ON A BEACH VACATION WITH ME?
...BEACH?
?

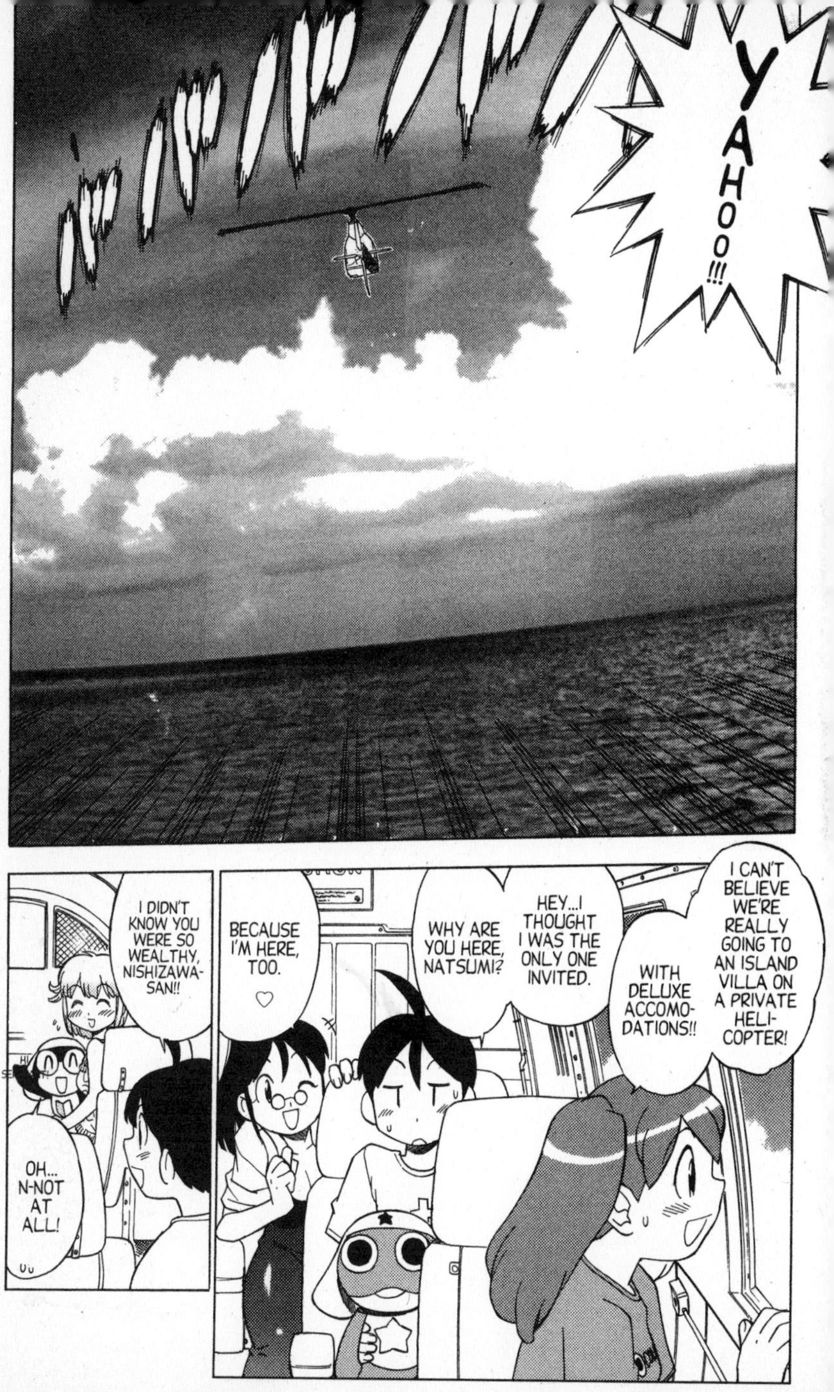
YAHOO!!!
I CAN'T BELIEVE WE'RE REALLY GOING TO AN ISLAND VILLA ON A PRIVATE HELI-COPTER!
WITH DELUXE ACCOMO-DATIONS!!
HEY...I THOUGHT I WAS THE ONLY ONE INVITED.
WHY ARE YOU HERE, NATSUMI?
BECAUSE I'M HERE, TOO. ♡
I DIDN'T KNOW YOU WERE SO WEALTHY, NISHIZAWA-SAN!!
OH... N-NOT AT ALL!

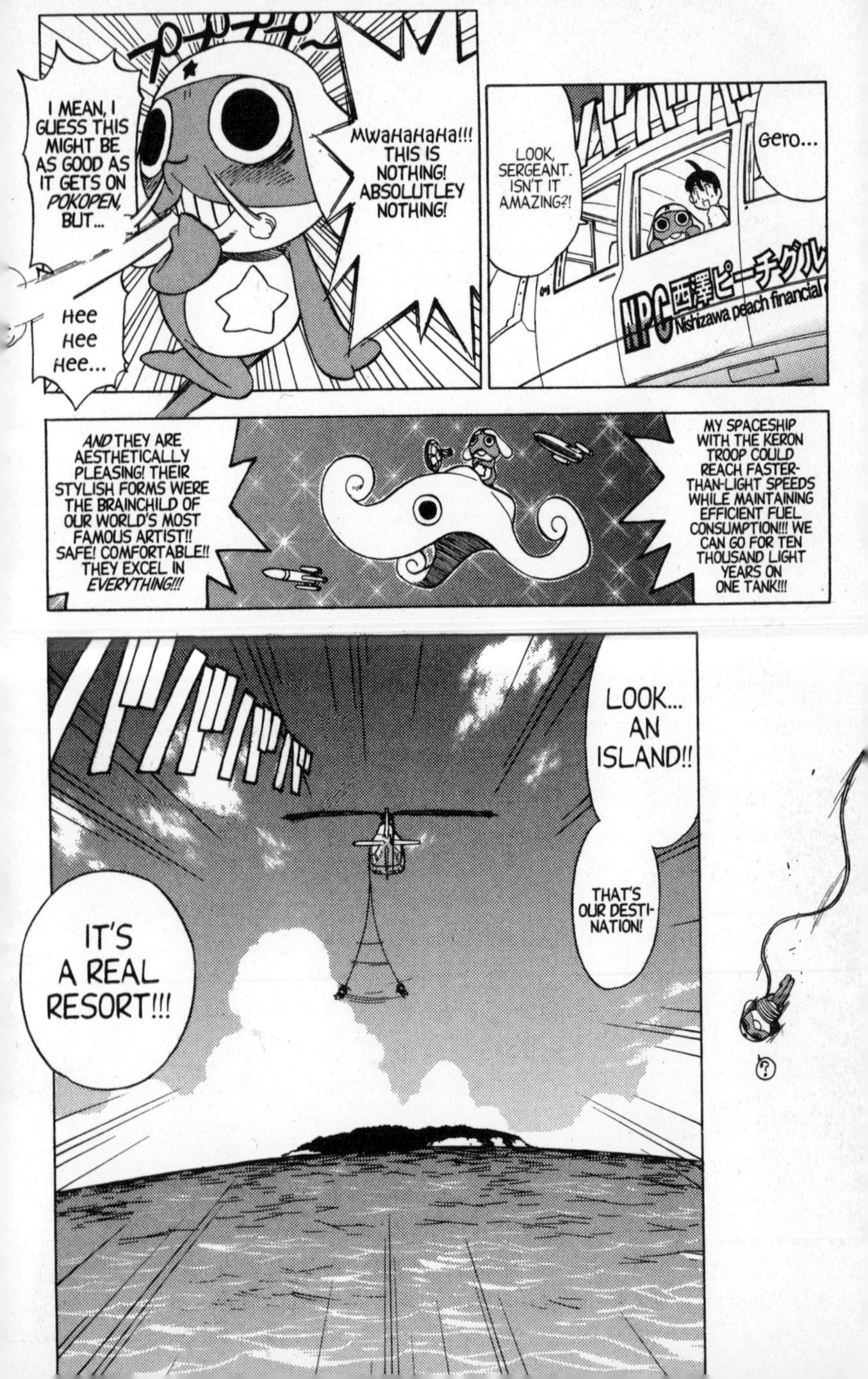
Gero...
LOOK, SERGEANT. ISN'T IT AMAZING?!
NPC 西澤ピーチグル
Nishizawa peach financial
MWAHAHAHA!!! THIS IS NOTHING! ABSOLUTLEY NOTHING!
I MEAN, I GUESS THIS MIGHT BE AS GOOD AS IT GETS ON *POKOPEN*, BUT...
Hee Hee Hee...
MY SPACESHIP WITH THE KERON TROOP COULD REACH FASTER-THAN-LIGHT SPEEDS WHILE MAINTAINING EFFICIENT FUEL CONSUMPTION!!! WE CAN GO FOR TEN THOUSAND LIGHT YEARS ON ONE TANK!!!
AND THEY ARE AESTHETICALLY PLEASING! THEIR STYLISH FORMS WERE THE BRAINCHILD OF OUR WORLD'S MOST FAMOUS ARTIST!! SAFE! COMFORTABLE!! THEY EXCEL IN *EVERYTHING!!!*
LOOK... AN ISLAND!!
THAT'S OUR DESTINATION!
IT'S A REAL RESORT!!!

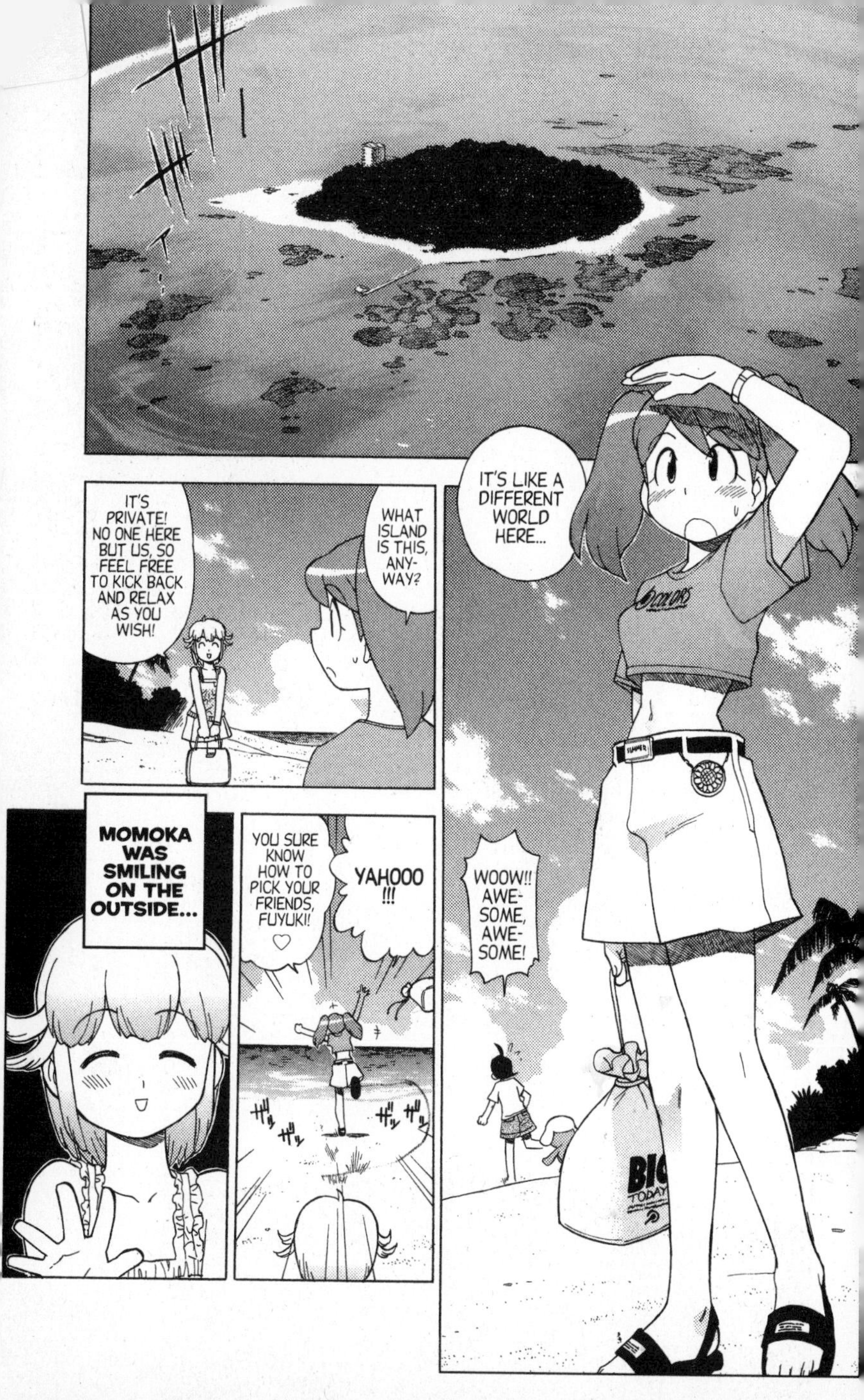
IT'S LIKE A DIFFERENT WORLD HERE...
WOOW!! AWESOME, AWESOME!
WHAT ISLAND IS THIS, ANYWAY?
IT'S PRIVATE! NO ONE HERE BUT US, SO FEEL FREE TO KICK BACK AND RELAX AS YOU WISH!
YAHOOO!!!
YOU SURE KNOW HOW TO PICK YOUR FRIENDS, FUYUKI! ♡
MOMOKA WAS SMILING ON THE OUTSIDE...

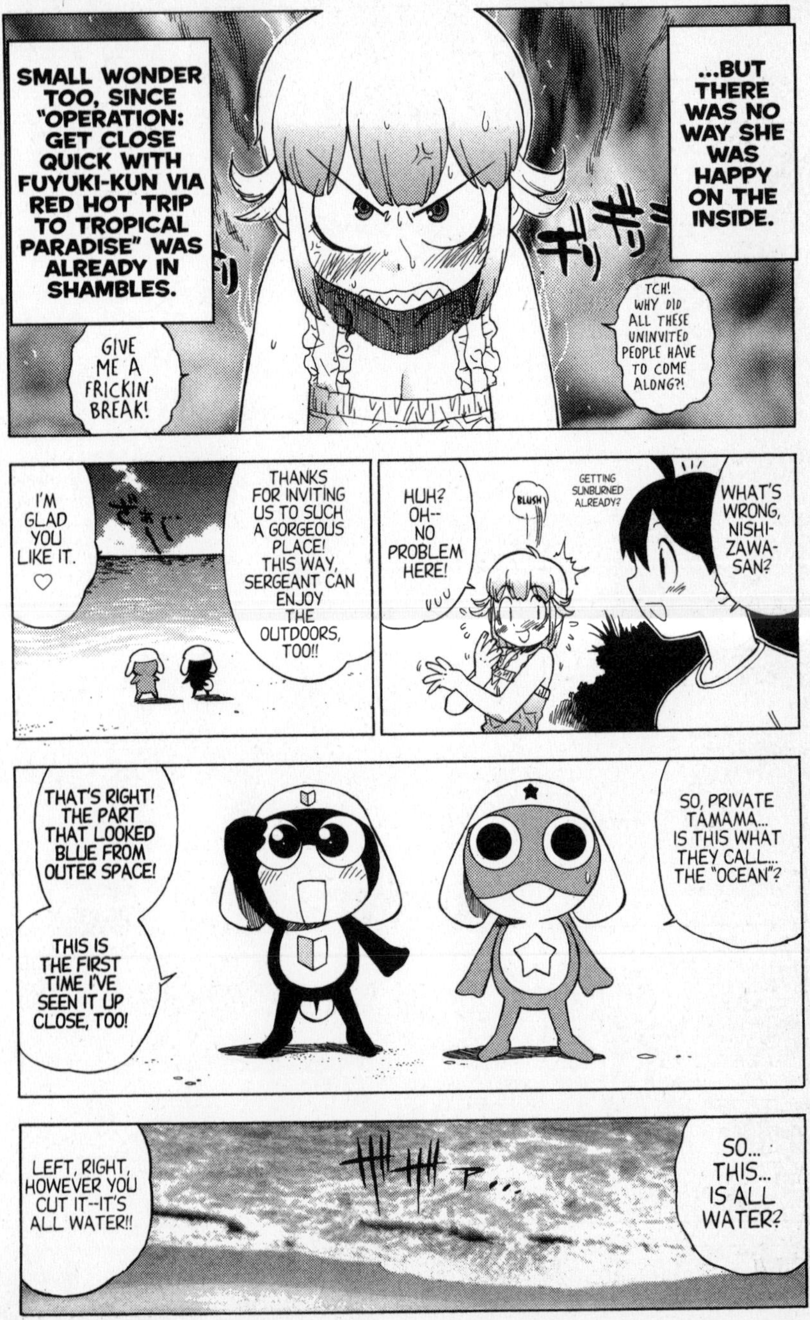
...BUT THERE WAS NO WAY SHE WAS HAPPY ON THE INSIDE.
SMALL WONDER TOO, SINCE "OPERATION: GET CLOSE QUICK WITH FUYUKI-KUN VIA RED HOT TRIP TO TROPICAL PARADISE" WAS ALREADY IN SHAMBLES.
TCH! WHY DID ALL THESE UNINVITED PEOPLE HAVE TO COME ALONG?!
GIVE ME A FRICKIN' BREAK!
WHAT'S WRONG, NISHI-ZAWA-SAN?
GETTING SUNBURNED ALREADY?
BLUSH
HUH? OH-- NO PROBLEM HERE!
THANKS FOR INVITING US TO SUCH A GORGEOUS PLACE! THIS WAY, SERGEANT CAN ENJOY THE OUTDOORS, TOO!!
I'M GLAD YOU LIKE IT. ♡
SO, PRIVATE TAMAMA... IS THIS WHAT THEY CALL... THE "OCEAN"?
THAT'S RIGHT! THE PART THAT LOOKED BLUE FROM OUTER SPACE!
THIS IS THE FIRST TIME I'VE SEEN IT UP CLOSE, TOO!
SO... THIS... IS ALL WATER?
LEFT, RIGHT, HOWEVER YOU CUT IT--IT'S ALL WATER!!

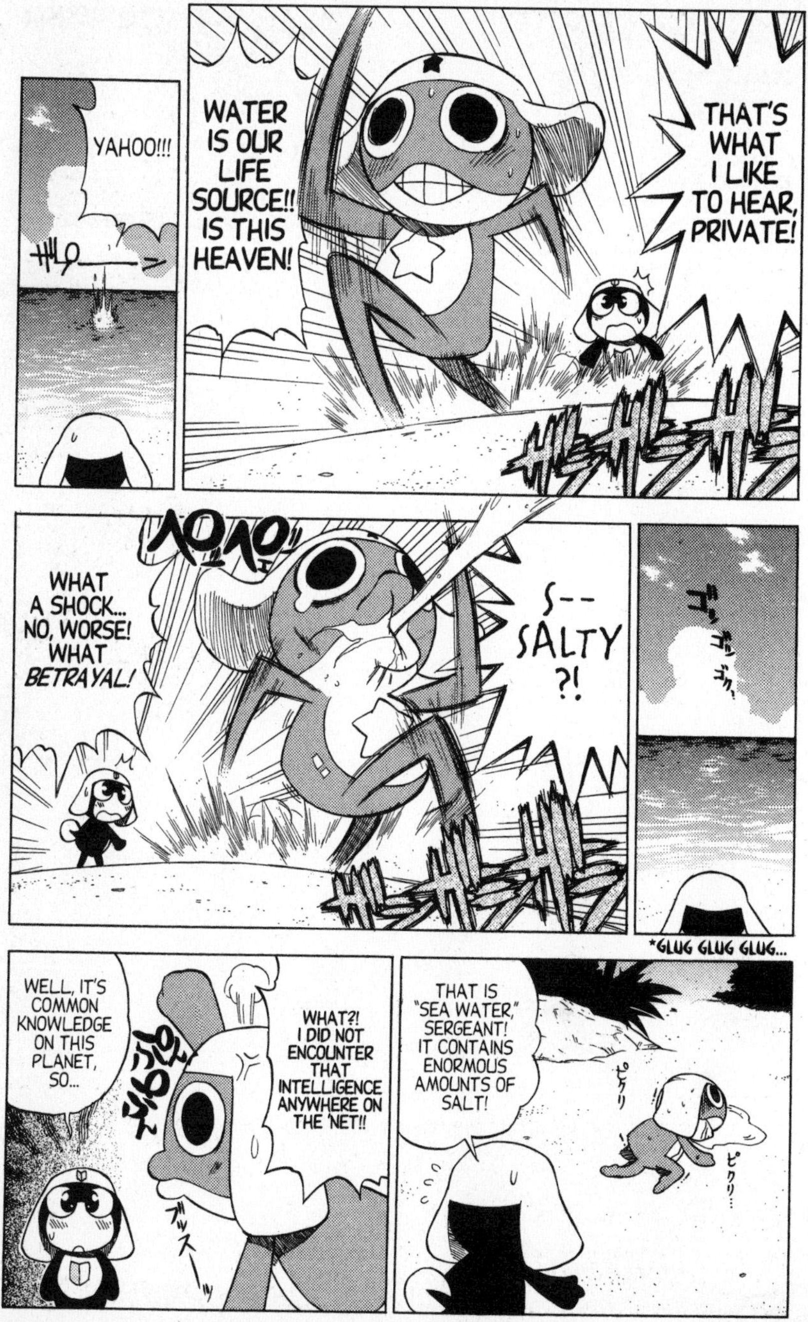
THAT'S WHAT I LIKE TO HEAR, PRIVATE!
WATER IS OUR LIFE SOURCE!! IS THIS HEAVEN!
YAHOO!!!
S-- SALTY?!
WHAT A SHOCK... NO, WORSE! WHAT *BETRAYAL!*
*GLUG GLUG GLUG...
THAT IS "SEA WATER," SERGEANT! IT CONTAINS ENORMOUS AMOUNTS OF SALT!
WHAT?! I DID NOT ENCOUNTER THAT INTELLIGENCE ANYWHERE ON THE 'NET!!
WELL, IT'S COMMON KNOWLEDGE ON THIS PLANET, SO...

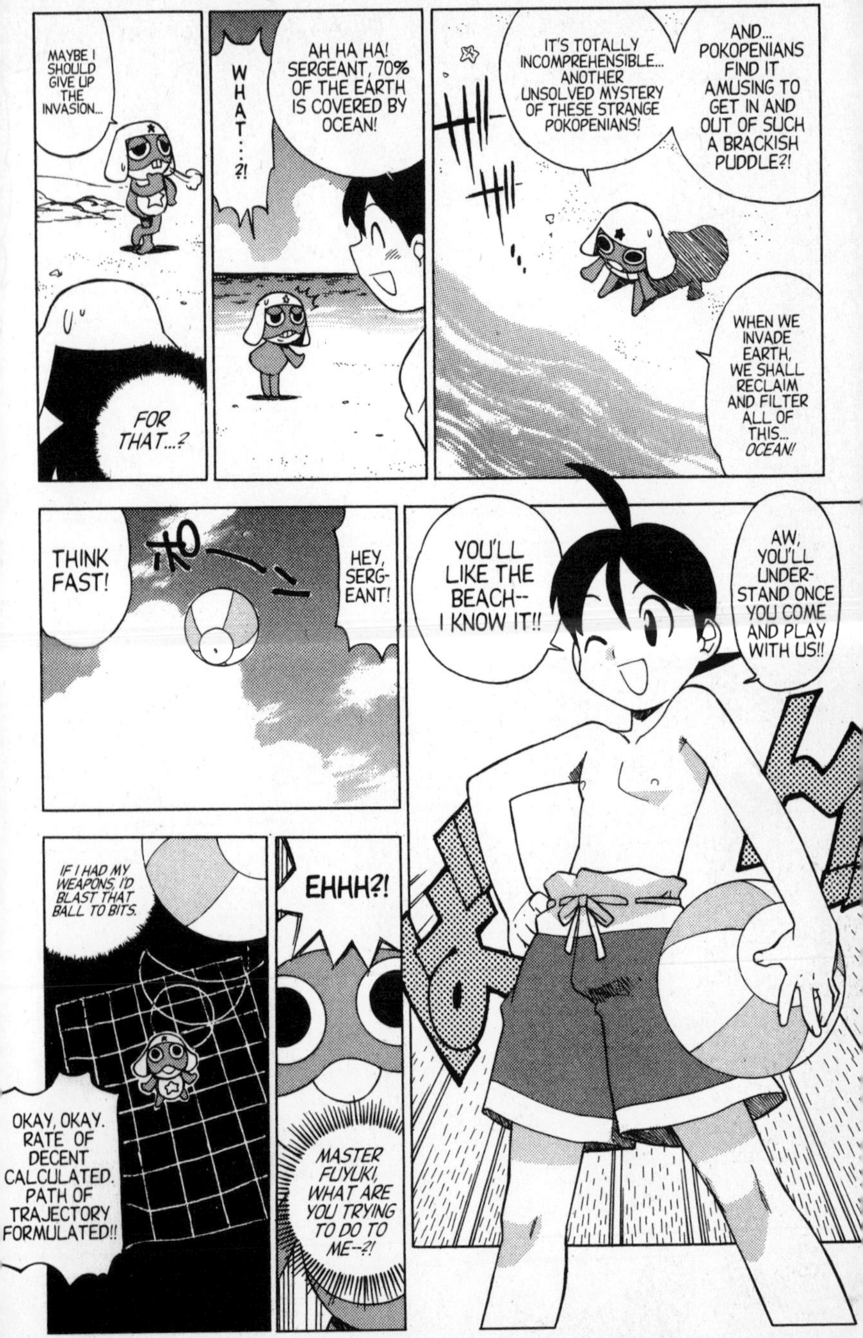
IT'S TOTALLY INCOMPREHENSIBLE... ANOTHER UNSOLVED MYSTERY OF THESE STRANGE POKOPENIANS!
AND... POKOPENIANS FIND IT AMUSING TO GET IN AND OUT OF SUCH A BRACKISH PUDDLE?!
WHEN WE INVADE EARTH, WE SHALL RECLAIM AND FILTER ALL OF THIS... OCEAN!
AH HA HA! SERGEANT, 70% OF THE EARTH IS COVERED BY OCEAN!
WHAT...?!
MAYBE I SHOULD GIVE UP THE INVASION...
FOR THAT...?
AW, YOU'LL UNDER-STAND ONCE YOU COME AND PLAY WITH US!!
YOU'LL LIKE THE BEACH-- I KNOW IT!!
HEY, SERG-EANT!
THINK FAST!
EHHH?!
MASTER FUYUKI, WHAT ARE YOU TRYING TO DO TO ME--?!
IF I HAD MY WEAPONS, I'D BLAST THAT BALL TO BITS.
OKAY, OKAY. RATE OF DECENT CALCULATED. PATH OF TRAJECTORY FORMULATED!!

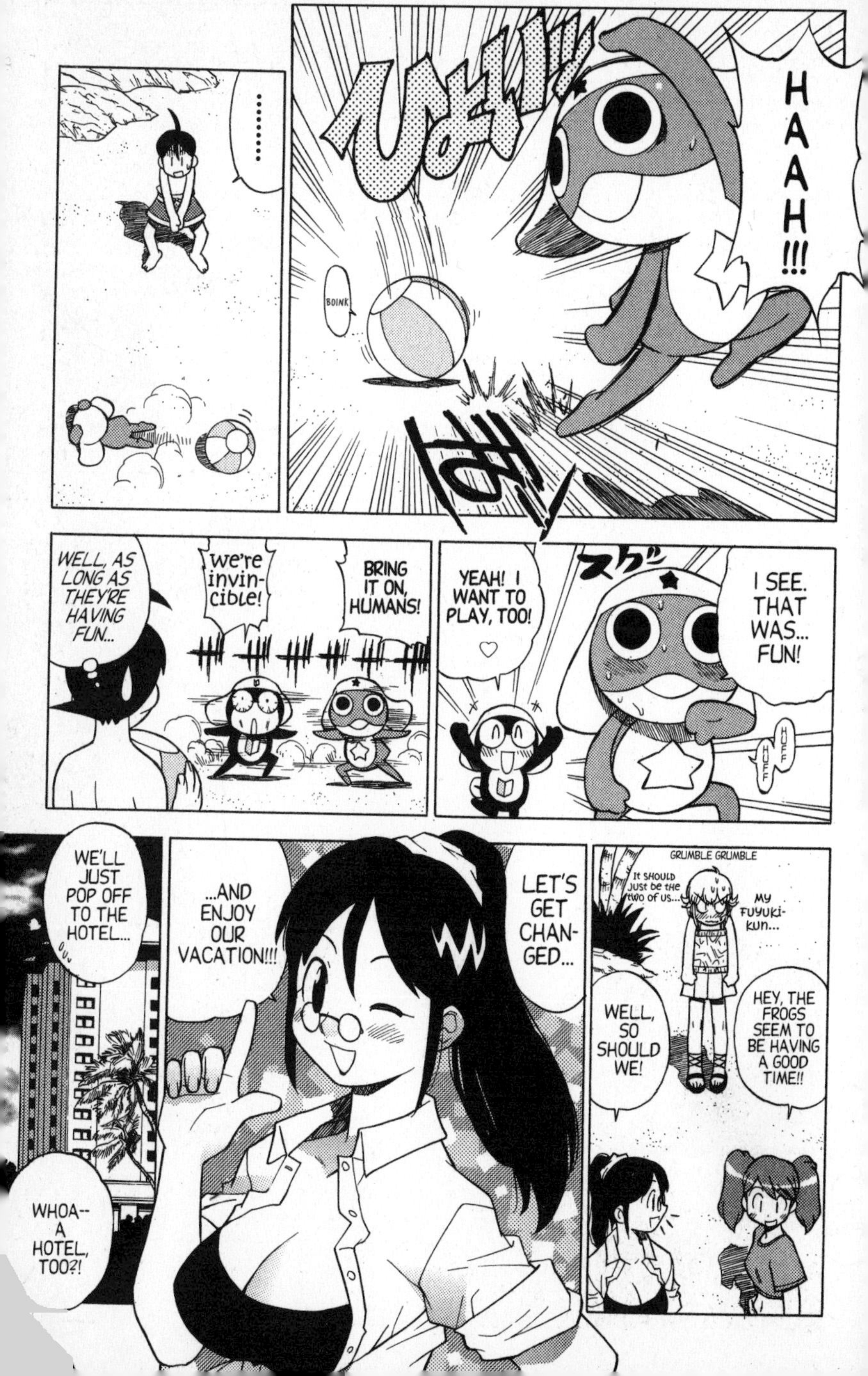
HAAH!!!
BOINK
....
I SEE. THAT WAS... FUN!
HUFF HUFF
YEAH! I WANT TO PLAY, TOO!
BRING IT ON, HUMANS!
We're invincible!
WELL, AS LONG AS THEY'RE HAVING FUN...
GRUMBLE GRUMBLE
It SHOULD JUST be the two of us...
MY FUYUKI-KUN...
HEY, THE FROGS SEEM TO BE HAVING A GOOD TIME!!
WELL, SO SHOULD WE!
LET'S GET CHANGED...
...AND ENJOY OUR VACATION!!!
WE'LL JUST POP OFF TO THE HOTEL...
WHOA-- A HOTEL, TOO?!

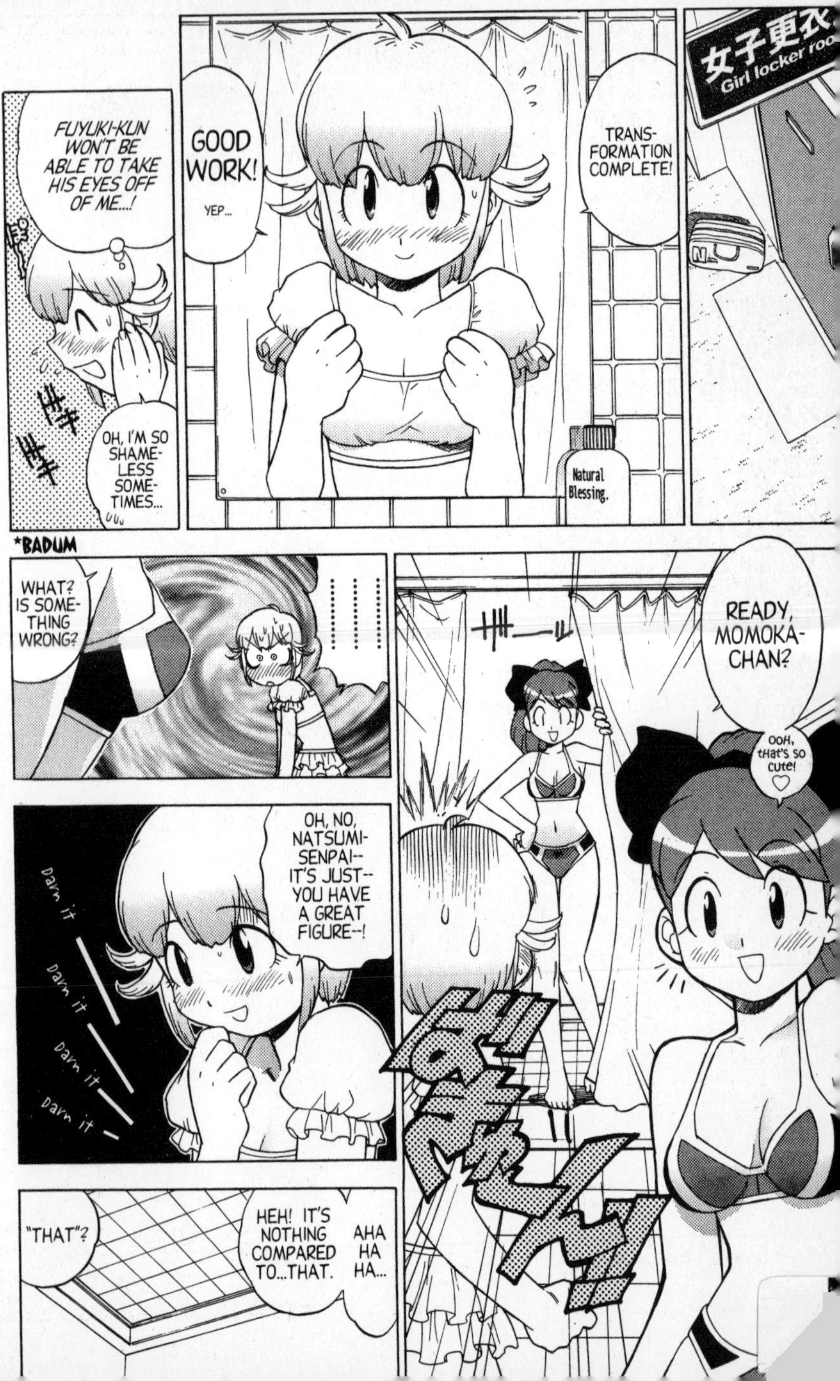
女子更衣
Girl locker roo
TRANS-FORMATION COMPLETE!
GOOD WORK!
YEP...
FUYUKI-KUN WON'T BE ABLE TO TAKE HIS EYES OFF OF ME...!
OH, I'M SO SHAME-LESS SOME-TIMES...
*BADUM
READY, MOMOKA-CHAN?
OOH, THAT'S SO CUTE! ♡
WHAT? IS SOME-THING WRONG?
....
OH, NO, NATSUMI-SENPAI-- IT'S JUST-- YOU HAVE A GREAT FIGURE--!
Darn it
Darn it
Darn it
Darn it
HEH! IT'S NOTHING COMPARED TO...THAT.
AHA HA HA...
"THAT"?

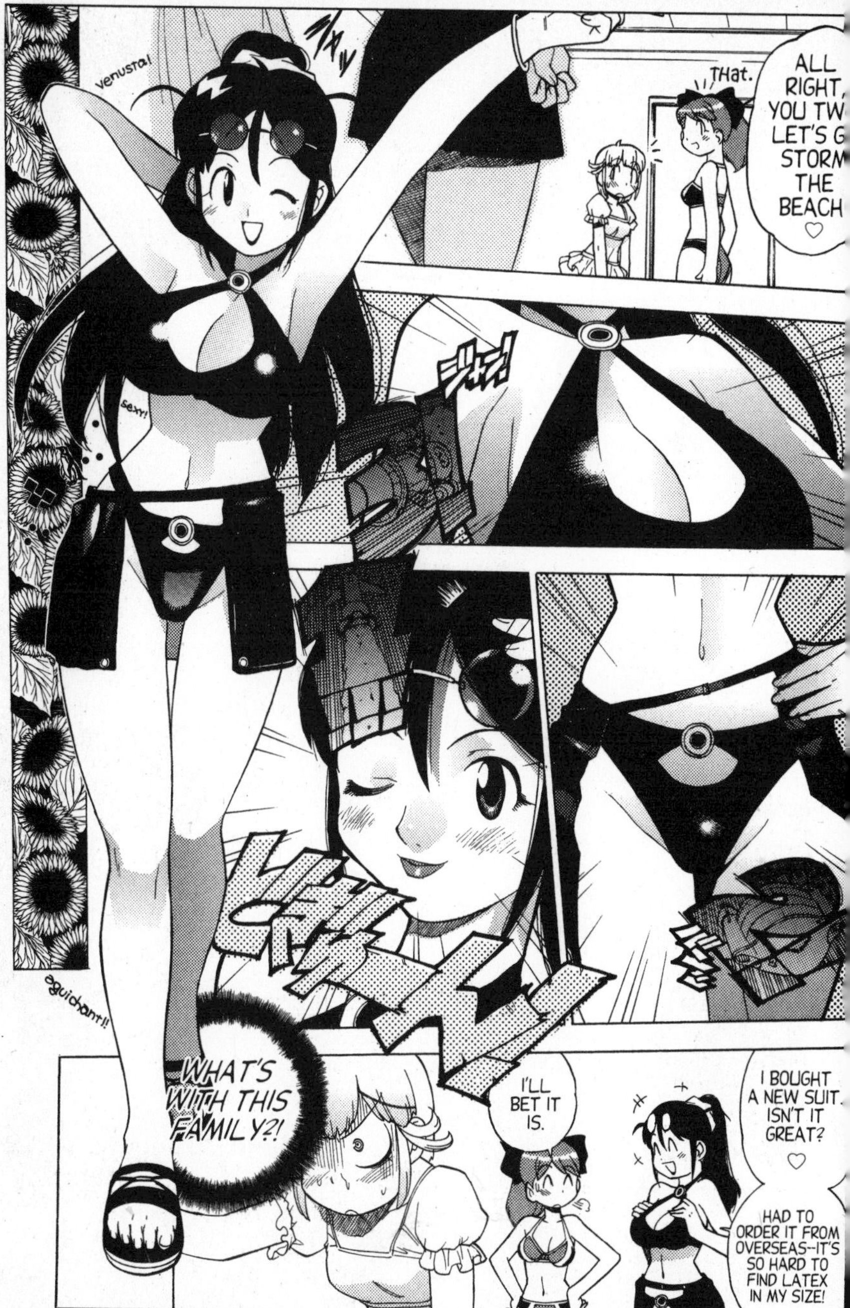
ALL RIGHT, YOU TW LET'S G STORM THE BEACH ♡
THat.
venusta!
sexy!
aguichant!!
I BOUGHT A NEW SUIT. ISN'T IT GREAT? ♡
HAD TO ORDER IT FROM OVERSEAS--IT'S SO HARD TO FIND LATEX IN MY SIZE!
I'LL BET IT IS.
WHAT'S WITH THIS FAMILY?!

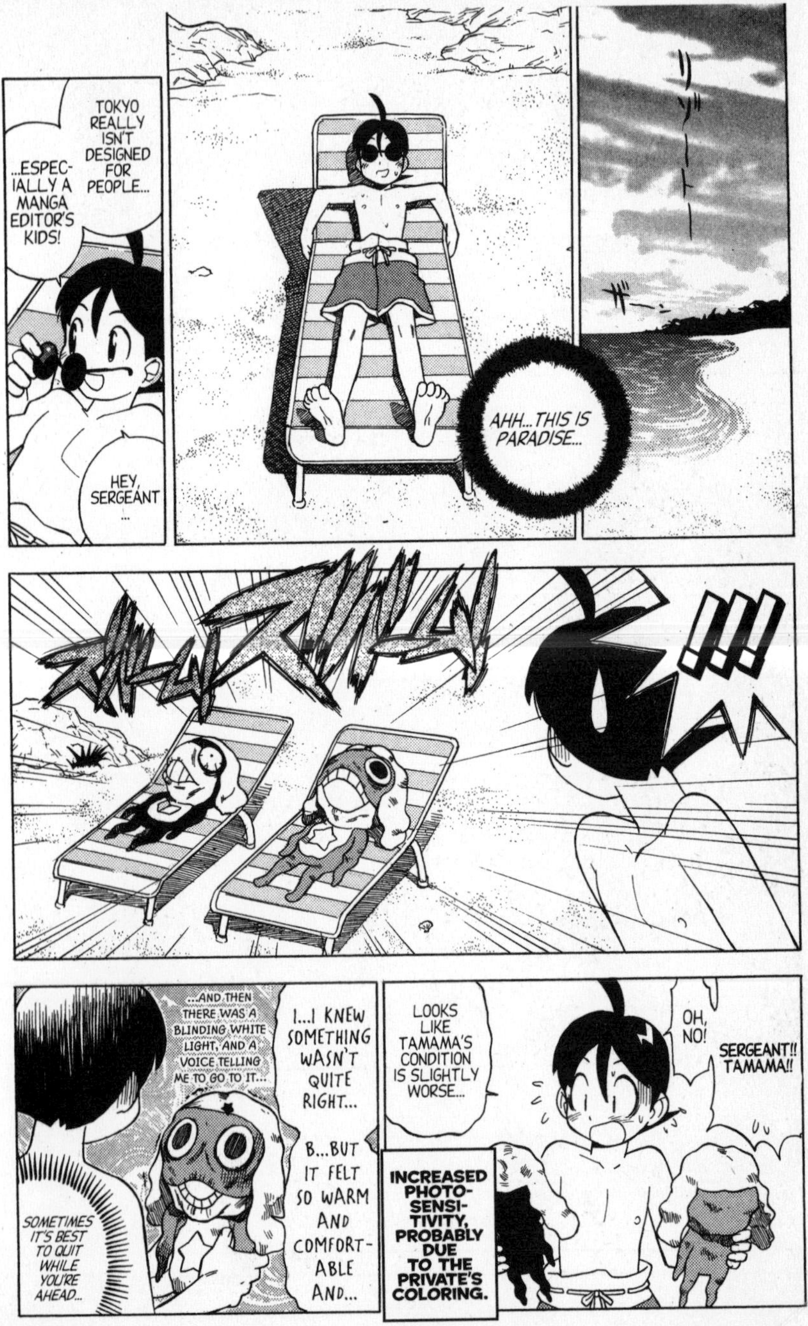
AHH...THIS IS PARADISE...
TOKYO REALLY ISN'T DESIGNED FOR PEOPLE...
...ESPECIALLY A MANGA EDITOR'S KIDS!
HEY, SERGEANT...
OH, NO!
SERGEANT!! TAMAMA!!
LOOKS LIKE TAMAMA'S CONDITION IS SLIGHTLY WORSE...
INCREASED PHOTOSENSITIVITY, PROBABLY DUE TO THE PRIVATE'S COLORING.
I...I KNEW SOMETHING WASN'T QUITE RIGHT...
B...BUT IT FELT SO WARM AND COMFORTABLE AND...
...AND THEN THERE WAS A BLINDING WHITE LIGHT, AND A VOICE TELLING ME TO GO TO IT...
SOMETIMES IT'S BEST TO QUIT WHILE YOU'RE AHEAD...

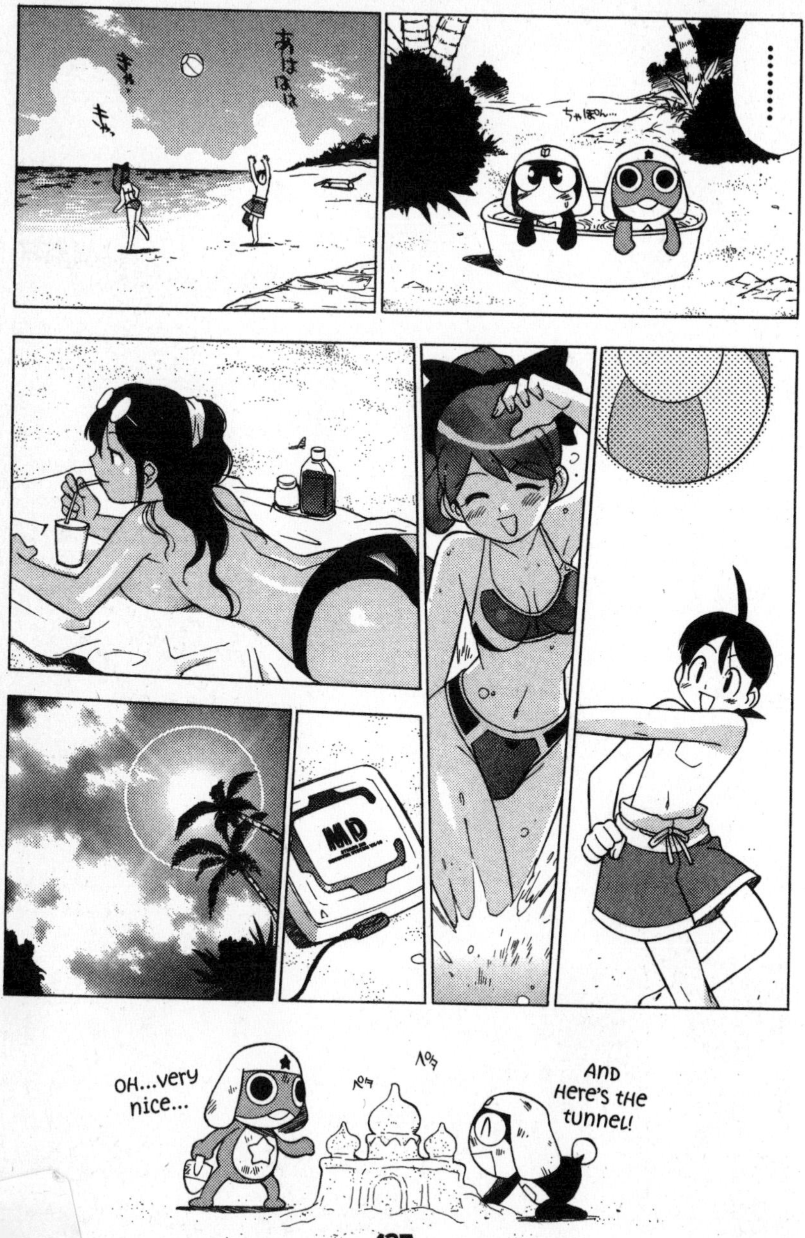
……
ちゃぽん…
あははは
きゃ、
きゃ、
AND Here's tHe tunnel!
ペタ
ペタ
OH...very nice...

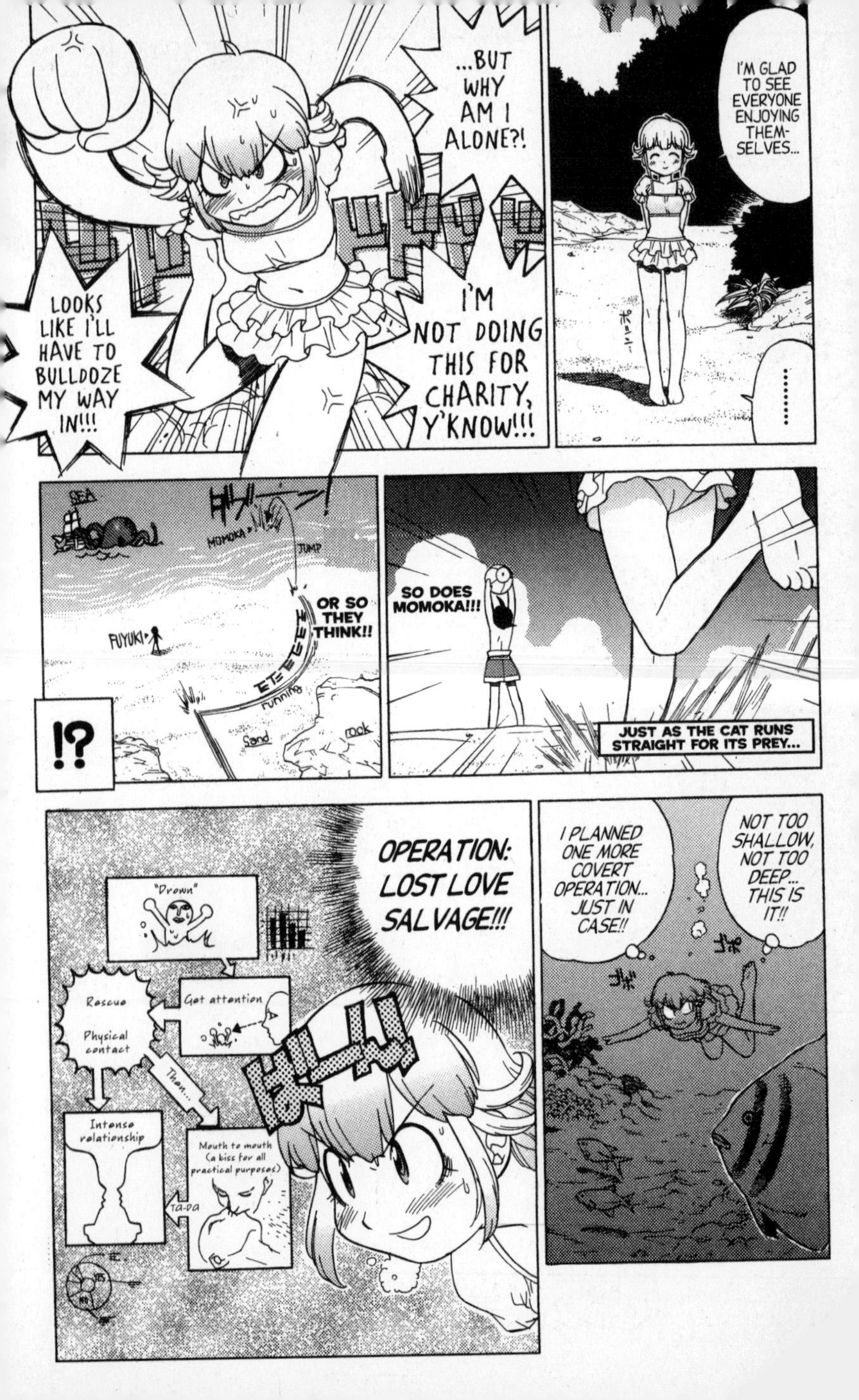
I'M GLAD TO SEE EVERYONE ENJOYING THEM-SELVES...
......
...BUT WHY AM I ALONE?!
I'M NOT DOING THIS FOR CHARITY, Y'KNOW!!!
LOOKS LIKE I'LL HAVE TO BULLDOZE MY WAY IN!!!
JUST AS THE CAT RUNS STRAIGHT FOR ITS PREY...
SO DOES MOMOKA!!!
SEA
MOMOKA
JUMP
OR SO THEY THINK!!
FUYUKI
running
sand
rock
!?
NOT TOO SHALLOW, NOT TOO DEEP... THIS IS IT!!
I PLANNED ONE MORE COVERT OPERATION... JUST IN CASE!!
OPERATION: LOST LOVE SALVAGE!!!
"Drown"
Get attention
Rescue
Physical contact
Then...
Intense relationship
Mouth to mouth (a kiss for all practical purposes)
TA-DA
YES
NO

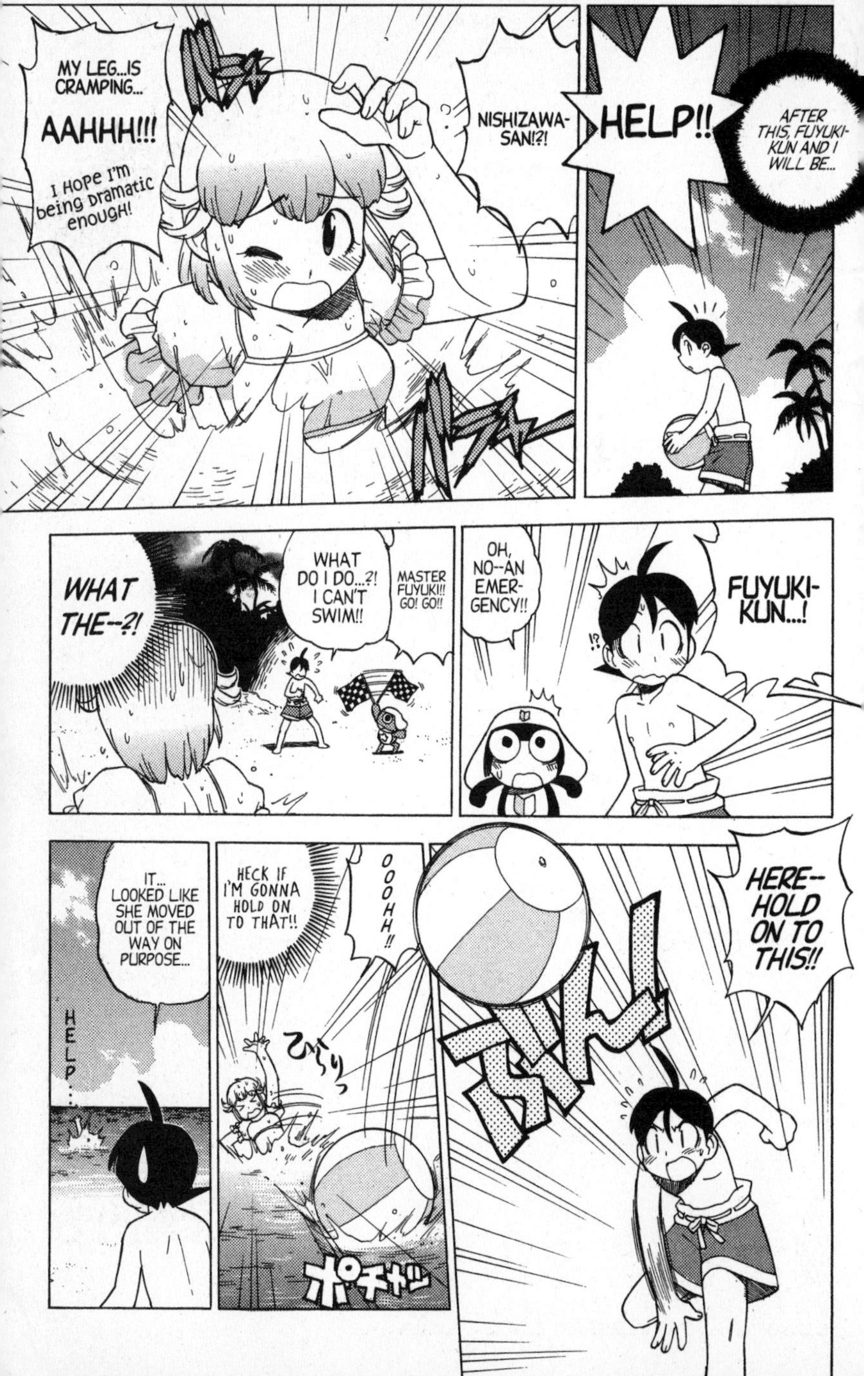
AFTER THIS, FUYUKI-KUN AND I WILL BE...
HELP!!
NISHIZAWA-SAN!?!
MY LEG...IS CRAMPING...
AAHHH!!!
I Hope I'm being Dramatic enough!
FUYUKI-KUN...!
OH, NO--AN EMERGENCY!!
MASTER FUYUKI!!! GO! GO!!
WHAT DO I DO...?! I CAN'T SWIM!!
WHAT THE--?!
HERE--HOLD ON TO THIS!!
OOOHH!!
HECK IF I'M GONNA HOLD ON TO THAT!!
IT... LOOKED LIKE SHE MOVED OUT OF THE WAY ON PURPOSE...
HELP...

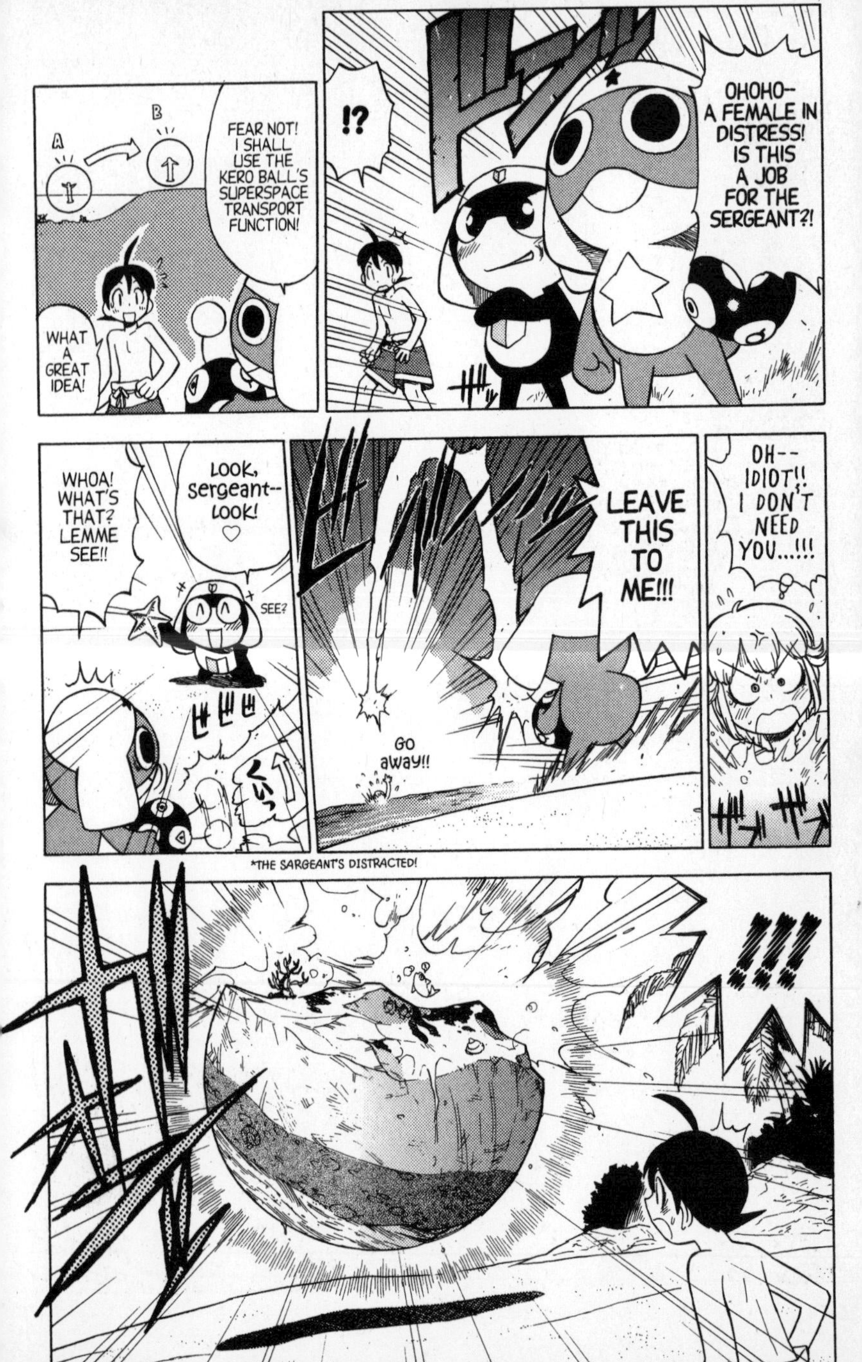
OHOHO- A FEMALE IN DISTRESS! IS THIS A JOB FOR THE SERGEANT?!
!?
FEAR NOT! I SHALL USE THE KERO BALL'S SUPERSPACE TRANSPORT FUNCTION!
B
A
WHAT A GREAT IDEA!
OH-- IDIOT!! I DON'T NEED YOU...!!!
LEAVE THIS TO ME!!!
GO away!!
LOOK, sergeant-- LOOK! ♡
WHOA! WHAT'S THAT? LEMME SEE!!
SEE?
くいっ
*THE SARGEANT'S DISTRACTED!
!!!

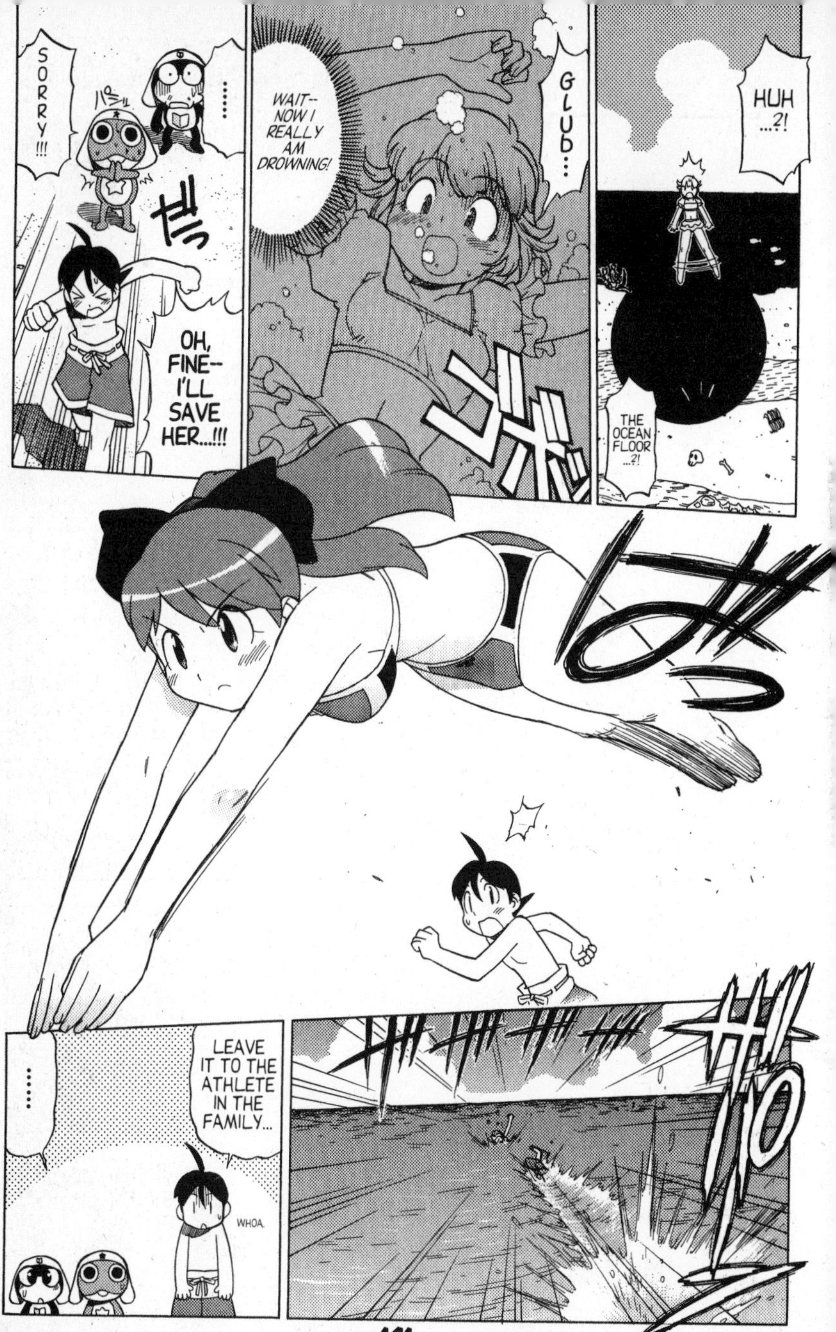
HUH ...?!
THE OCEAN FLOOR ...?!
GLUB...
WAIT-- NOW I REALLY AM DROWNING!
SORRY!!!
......
OH, FINE-- I'LL SAVE HER...!!!
LEAVE IT TO THE ATHLETE IN THE FAMILY...
......
WHOA.

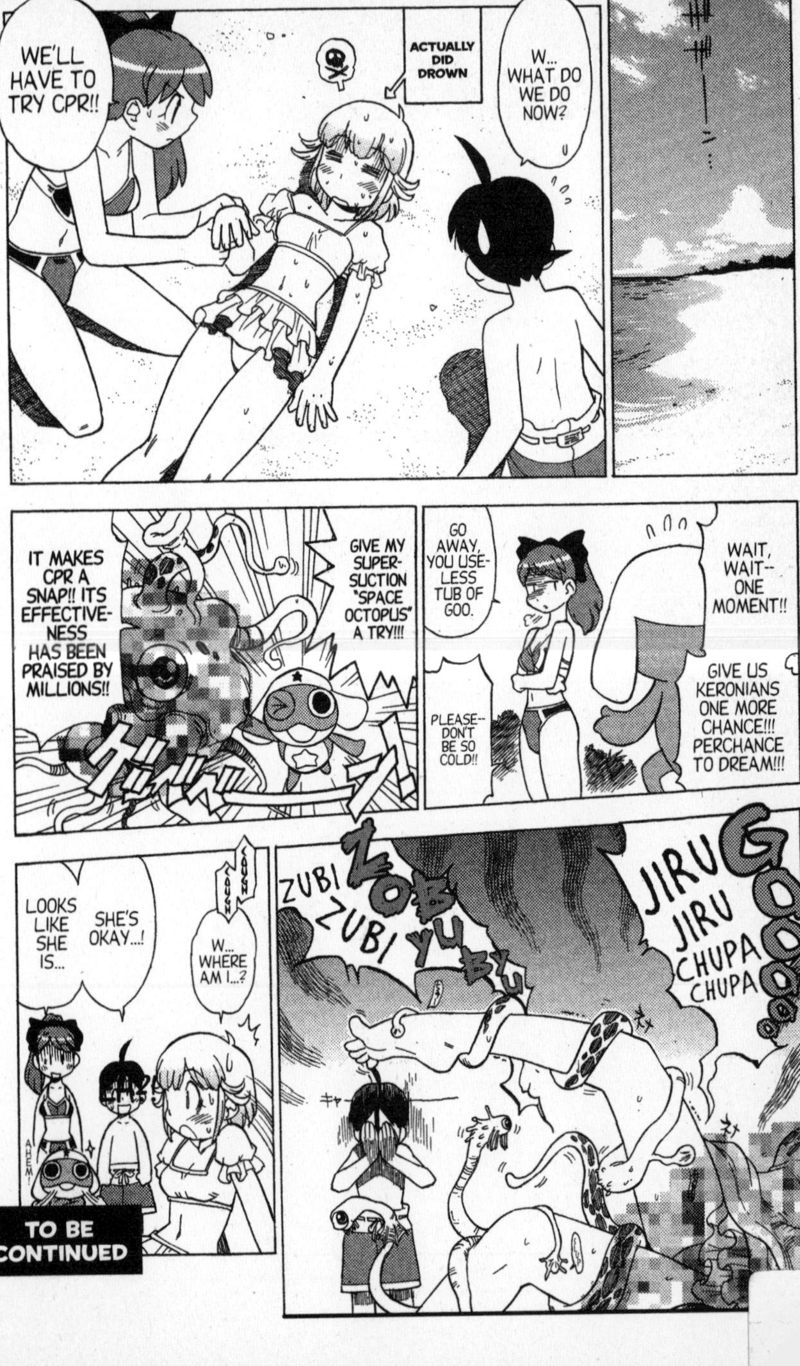
W... WHAT DO WE DO NOW?
ACTUALLY DID DROWN
WE'LL HAVE TO TRY CPR!!
WAIT, WAIT-- ONE MOMENT!!
GO AWAY, YOU USELESS TUB OF GOO.
GIVE US KERONIANS ONE MORE CHANCE!!! PERCHANCE TO DREAM!!!
PLEASE-- DON'T BE SO COLD!!
GIVE MY SUPER-SUCTION "SPACE OCTOPUS" A TRY!!!
IT MAKES CPR A SNAP!! ITS EFFECTIVENESS HAS BEEN PRAISED BY MILLIONS!!
JIRU JIRU CHUPA CHUPA
GOOOO...
ZOB
ZUBI ZUBI
YUBU
COUGH COUGH
W... WHERE AM I...?
SHE'S OKAY...!
LOOKS LIKE SHE IS...
AHEM!
TO BE CONTINUED

ENCOUNTER IX
EXTENDED SHORE LEAVE

Sunflower

Momoka
Nishizawa

Tamama

Keroro~Gunso

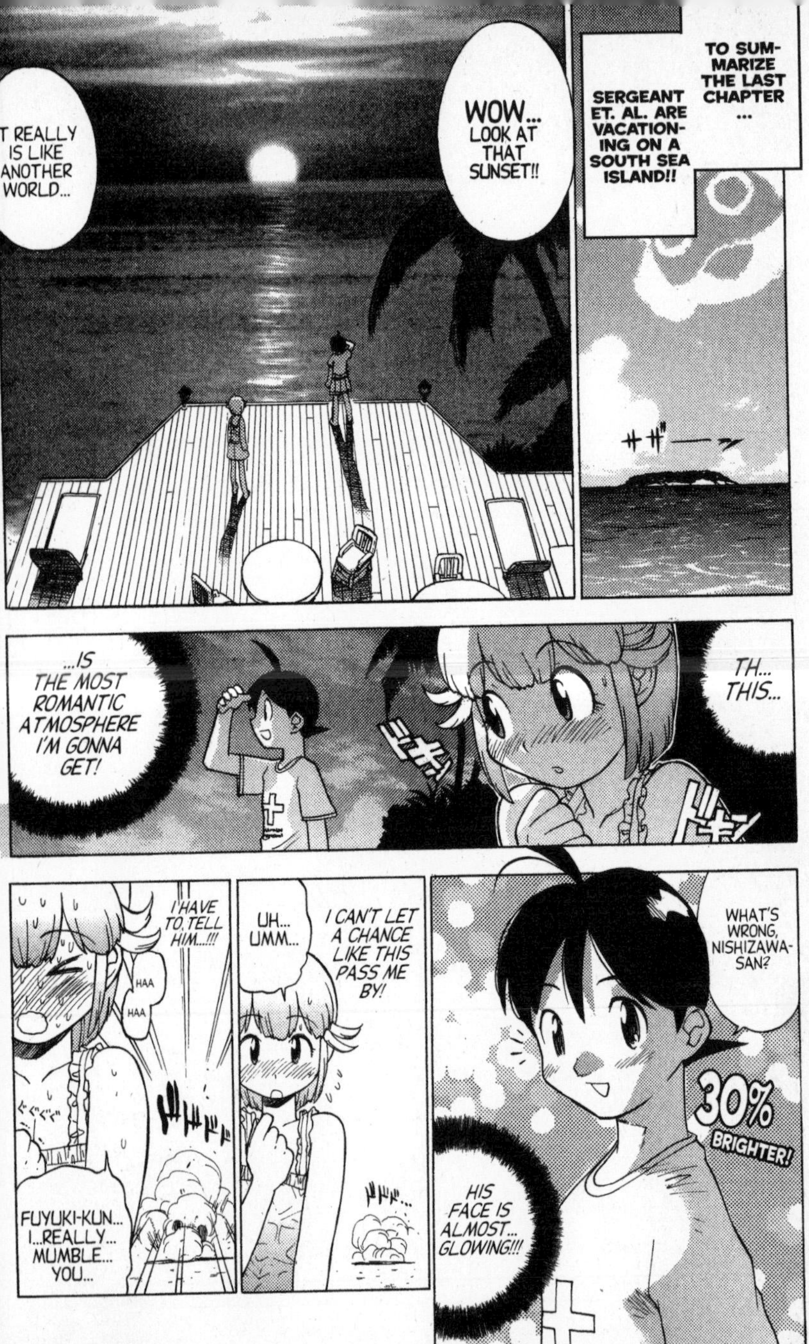
TO SUMMARIZE THE LAST CHAPTER...
SERGEANT ET. AL. ARE VACATIONING ON A SOUTH SEA ISLAND!!
WOW... LOOK AT THAT SUNSET!!
T REALLY IS LIKE ANOTHER WORLD...
TH... THIS...
...IS THE MOST ROMANTIC ATMOSPHERE I'M GONNA GET!
WHAT'S WRONG, NISHIZAWA-SAN?
30% BRIGHTER!
HIS FACE IS ALMOST... GLOWING!!!
UH... UMM...
I CAN'T LET A CHANCE LIKE THIS PASS ME BY!
I HAVE TO TELL HIM...!!!
HAA
HAA
FUYUKI-KUN... I...REALLY... MUMBLE... YOU...

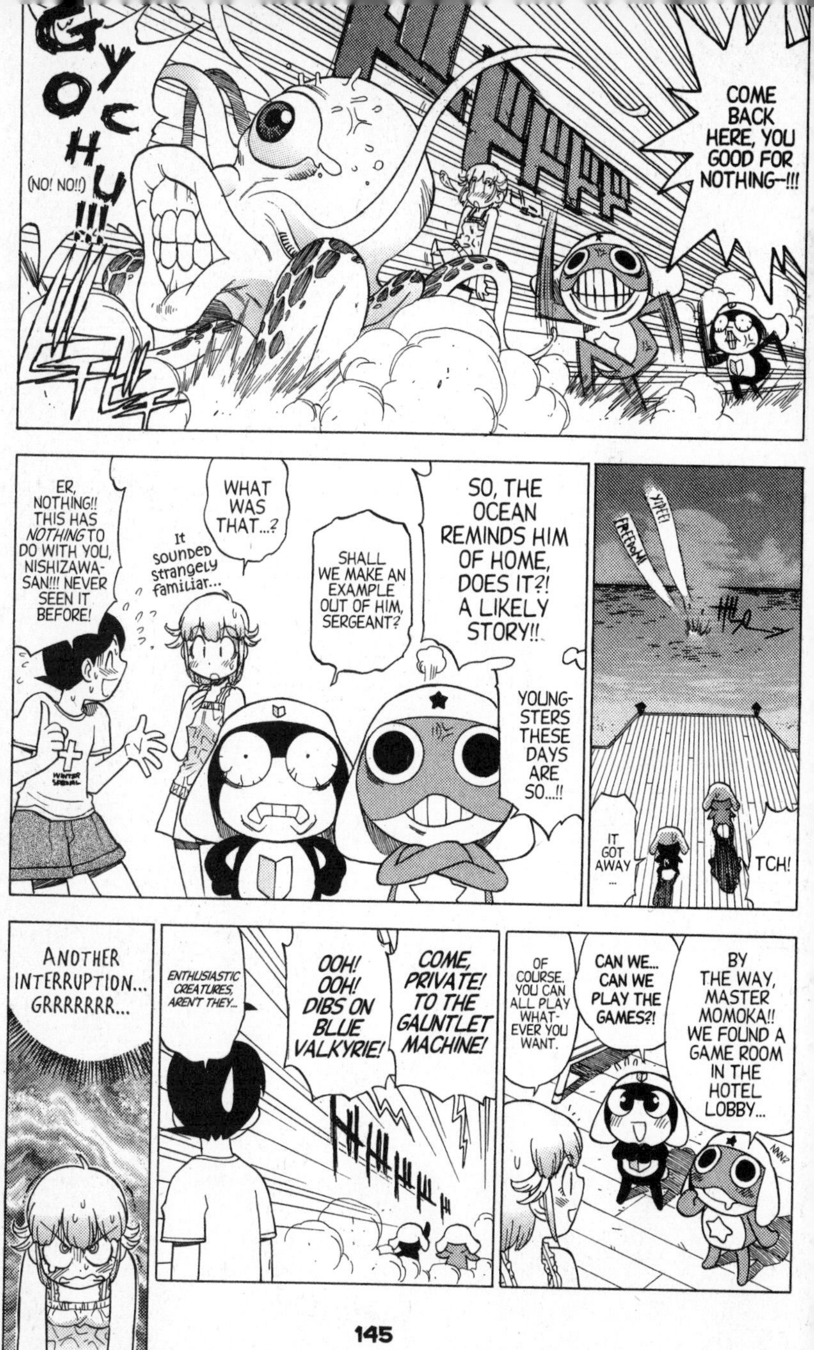
COME BACK HERE, YOU GOOD FOR NOTHING--!!!
GYOCHU!!!
(NO! NO!!)
YIPEE!
FREEDOM!
TCH!
IT GOT AWAY ...
SO, THE OCEAN REMINDS HIM OF HOME, DOES IT?! A LIKELY STORY!!
YOUNGSTERS THESE DAYS ARE SO...!!
SHALL WE MAKE AN EXAMPLE OUT OF HIM, SERGEANT?
WHAT WAS THAT...?
It sounded strangely familiar...
ER, NOTHING!! THIS HAS *NOTHING* TO DO WITH YOU, NISHIZAWA-SAN!!! NEVER SEEN IT BEFORE!
WINTER SPECIAL
BY THE WAY, MASTER MOMOKA!! WE FOUND A GAME ROOM IN THE HOTEL LOBBY...
NNN?
CAN WE... CAN WE PLAY THE GAMES?!
OF COURSE. YOU CAN ALL PLAY WHATEVER YOU WANT.
COME, PRIVATE! TO THE GAUNTLET MACHINE!
OOH! OOH! DIBS ON BLUE VALKYRIE!
ENTHUSIASTIC CREATURES, AREN'T THEY...
ANOTHER INTERRUPTION... GRRRRRRR...

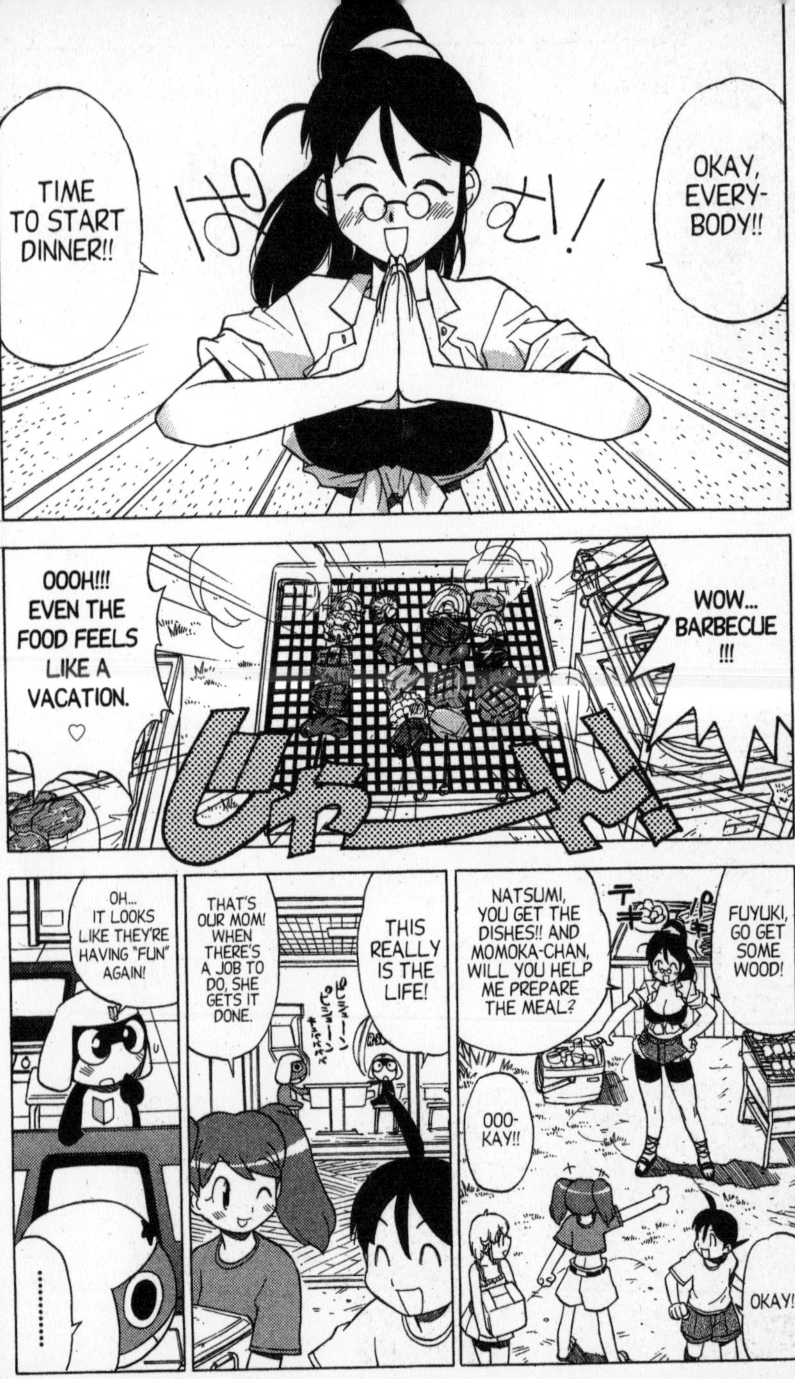
OKAY, EVERY-BODY!!
TIME TO START DINNER!!
WOW... BARBECUE !!!
OOOH!!! EVEN THE FOOD FEELS LIKE A VACATION. ♡
FUYUKI, GO GET SOME WOOD!
NATSUMI, YOU GET THE DISHES!! AND MOMOKA-CHAN, WILL YOU HELP ME PREPARE THE MEAL?
OKAY!
OOO-KAY!!
THIS REALLY IS THE LIFE!
THAT'S OUR MOM! WHEN THERE'S A JOB TO DO, SHE GETS IT DONE.
OH... IT LOOKS LIKE THEY'RE HAVING "FUN" AGAIN!
....

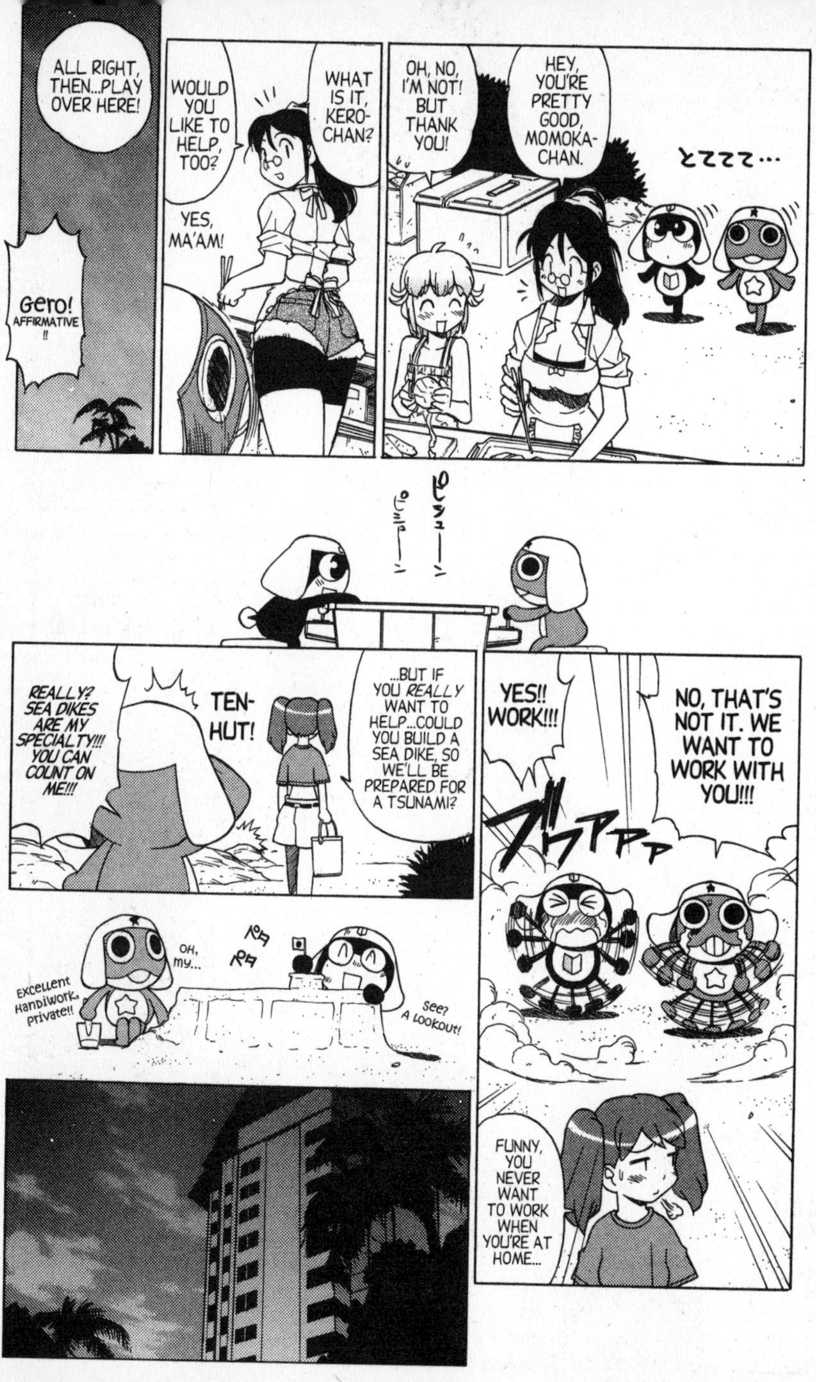
とととと…
HEY, YOU'RE PRETTY GOOD, MOMOKA-CHAN.
OH, NO, I'M NOT! BUT THANK YOU!
WHAT IS IT, KERO-CHAN?
WOULD YOU LIKE TO HELP, TOO?
YES, MA'AM!
ALL RIGHT, THEN...PLAY OVER HERE!
Gero! AFFIRMATIVE!!
NO, THAT'S NOT IT. WE WANT TO WORK WITH YOU!!!
YES!! WORK!!!
FUNNY, YOU NEVER WANT TO WORK WHEN YOU'RE AT HOME...
...BUT IF YOU *REALLY* WANT TO HELP...COULD YOU BUILD A SEA DIKE, SO WE'LL BE PREPARED FOR A TSUNAMI?
TEN-HUT!
REALLY? SEA DIKES ARE MY SPECIALTY!!! YOU CAN COUNT ON ME!!!
See? A LOOKOUT!
OH, my...
Excellent Handiwork, Private!!

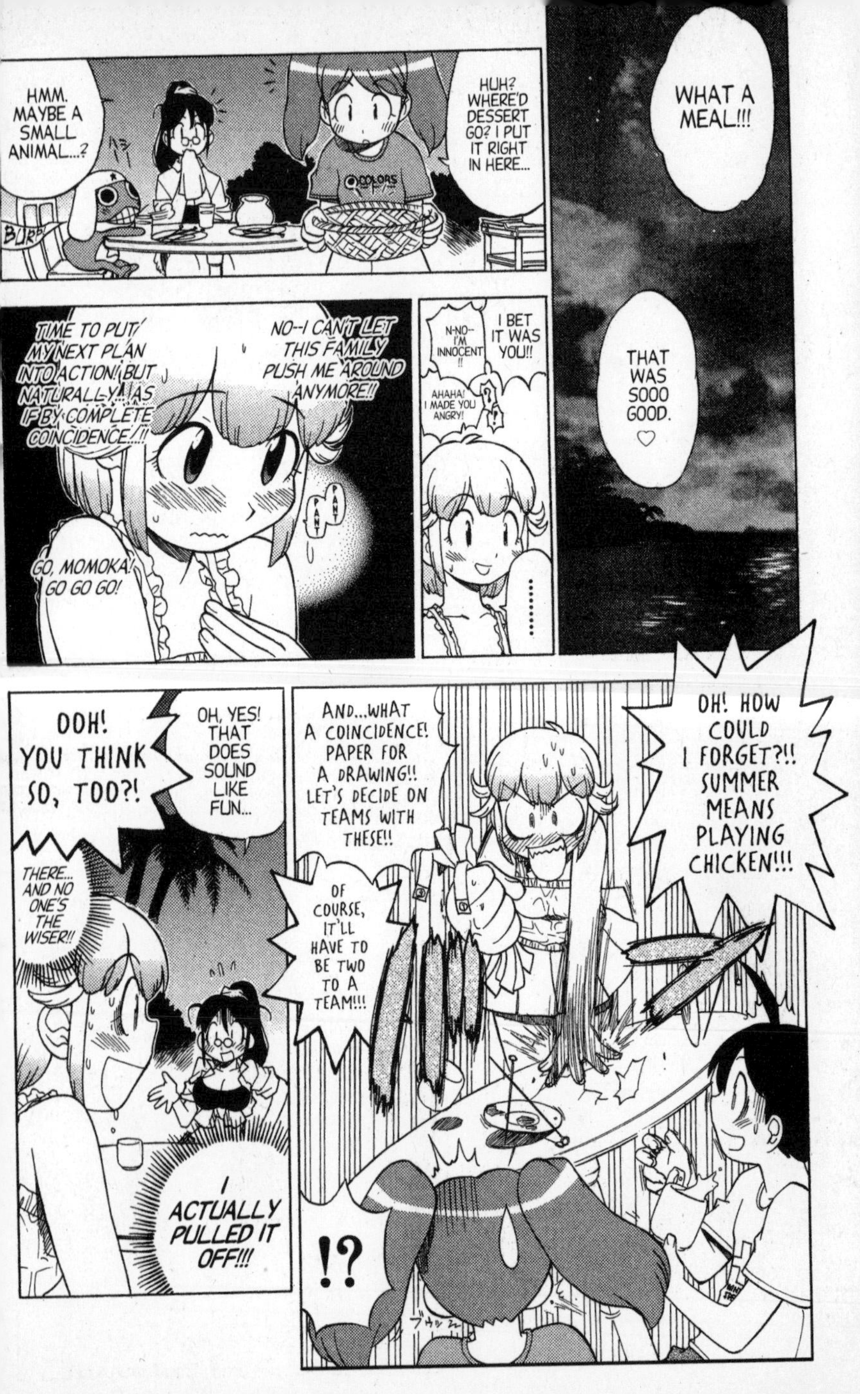
WHAT A MEAL!!!
THAT WAS SOOO GOOD. ♡
HUH? WHERE'D DESSERT GO? I PUT IT RIGHT IN HERE...
HMM. MAYBE A SMALL ANIMAL...?
BURP
I BET IT WAS YOU!!
N-NO-- I'M INNOCENT !!
AHAHA! I MADE YOU ANGRY!
......
NO--I CAN'T LET THIS FAMILY PUSH ME AROUND ANYMORE!!
TIME TO PUT MY NEXT PLAN INTO ACTION! BUT NATURALLY...AS IF BY COMPLETE COINCIDENCE...!!
PANT PANT
GO, MOMOKA! GO GO GO!
OH! HOW COULD I FORGET?!! SUMMER MEANS PLAYING CHICKEN!!!
AND...WHAT A COINCIDENCE! PAPER FOR A DRAWING!! LET'S DECIDE ON TEAMS WITH THESE!!
OF COURSE, IT'LL HAVE TO BE TWO TO A TEAM!!!
!?
OH, YES! THAT DOES SOUND LIKE FUN...
OOH! YOU THINK SO, TOO?!
THERE... AND NO ONE'S THE WISER!!
I ACTUALLY PULLED IT OFF!!!

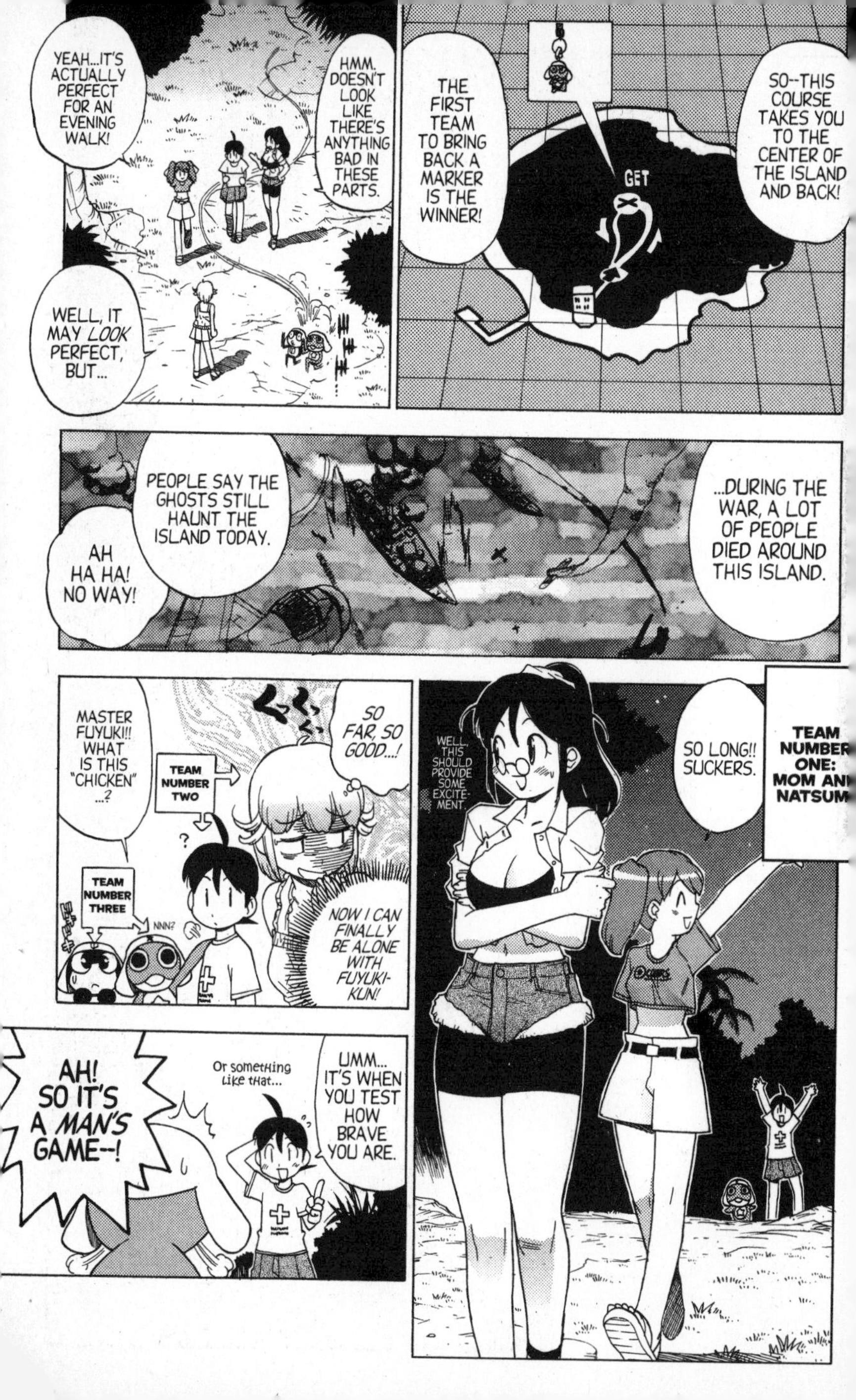
SO--THIS COURSE TAKES YOU TO THE CENTER OF THE ISLAND AND BACK!
THE FIRST TEAM TO BRING BACK A MARKER IS THE WINNER!
GET
HMM. DOESN'T LOOK LIKE THERE'S ANYTHING BAD IN THESE PARTS.
YEAH...IT'S ACTUALLY PERFECT FOR AN EVENING WALK!
WELL, IT MAY *LOOK* PERFECT, BUT...
...DURING THE WAR, A LOT OF PEOPLE DIED AROUND THIS ISLAND.
PEOPLE SAY THE GHOSTS STILL HAUNT THE ISLAND TODAY.
AH HA HA! NO WAY!
TEAM NUMBER ONE: MOM AN NATSUM
SO LONG!! SUCKERS.
WELL, THIS SHOULD PROVIDE SOME EXCITEMENT.
SO FAR, SO GOOD...!
TEAM NUMBER TWO
MASTER FUYUKI!! WHAT IS THIS "CHICKEN" ...?
?
NOW I CAN FINALLY BE ALONE WITH FUYUKI-KUN!
TEAM NUMBER THREE
NNN?
UMM... IT'S WHEN YOU TEST HOW BRAVE YOU ARE.
Or something like that...
AH! SO IT'S A *MAN'S* GAME--!

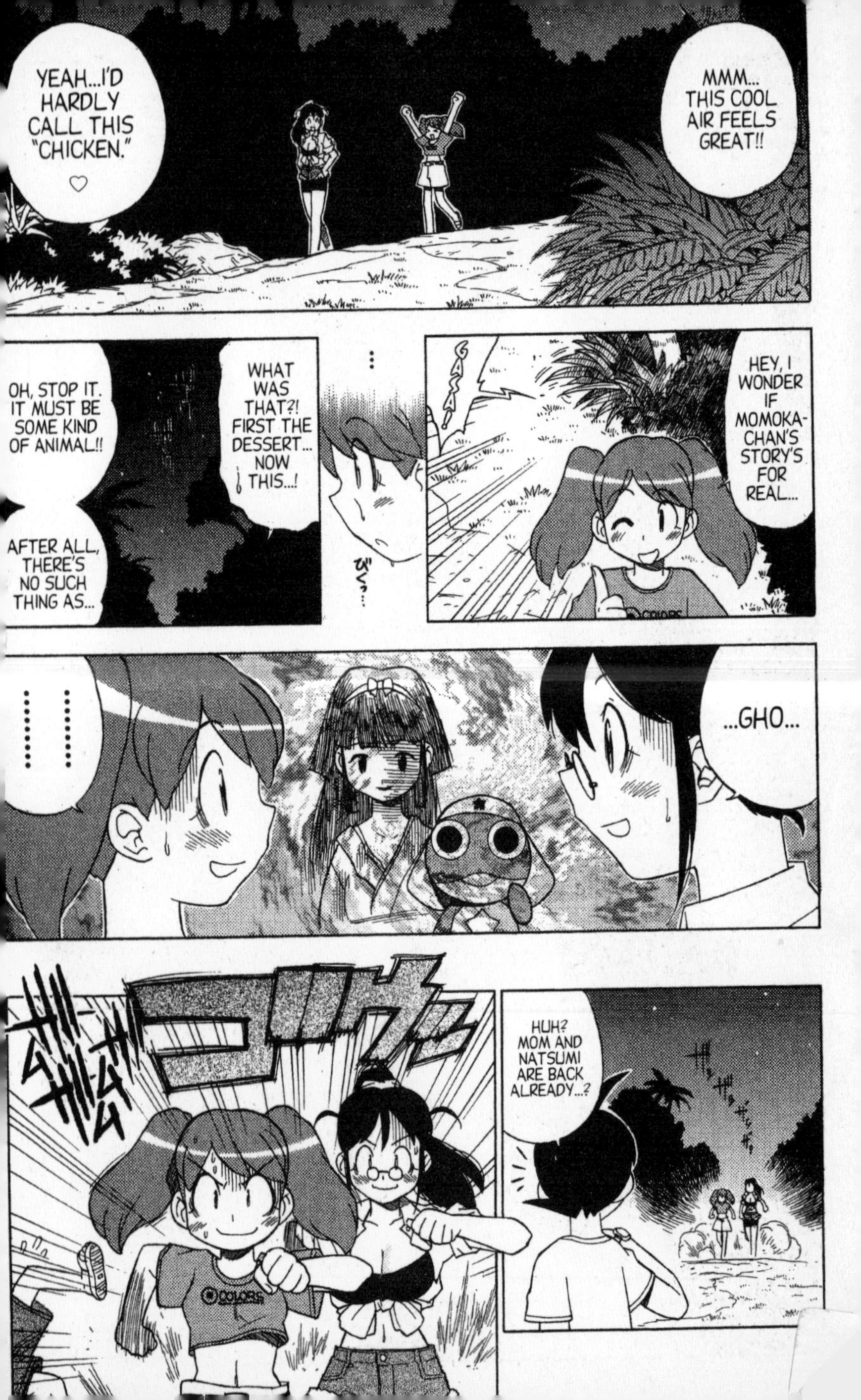
MMM... THIS COOL AIR FEELS GREAT!!
YEAH...I'D HARDLY CALL THIS "CHICKEN." ♡
GASA!
HEY, I WONDER IF MOMOKA-CHAN'S STORY'S FOR REAL...
...
WHAT WAS THAT?! FIRST THE DESSERT... NOW THIS...!
びくっ...
OH, STOP IT. IT MUST BE SOME KIND OF ANIMAL!!
AFTER ALL, THERE'S NO SUCH THING AS...
...GHO...
......
......
HUH? MOM AND NATSUMI ARE BACK ALREADY...?

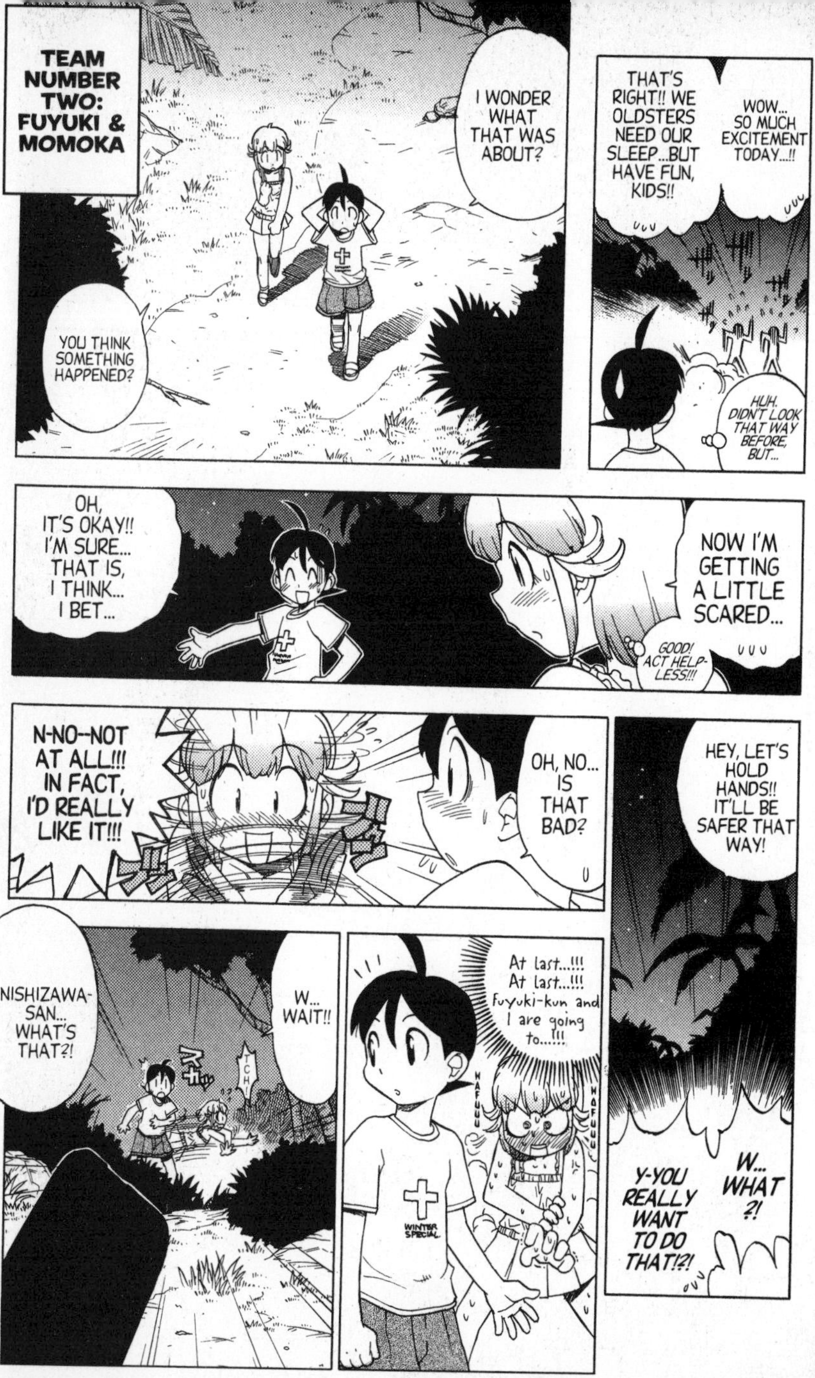
WOW... SO MUCH EXCITEMENT TODAY...!!
THAT'S RIGHT!! WE OLDSTERS NEED OUR SLEEP...BUT HAVE FUN, KIDS!!
HUH. DIDN'T LOOK THAT WAY BEFORE, BUT...
TEAM NUMBER TWO: FUYUKI & MOMOKA
I WONDER WHAT THAT WAS ABOUT?
YOU THINK SOMETHING HAPPENED?
NOW I'M GETTING A LITTLE SCARED...
GOOD! ACT HELPLESS!!!
OH, IT'S OKAY!! I'M SURE... THAT IS, I THINK... I BET...
HEY, LET'S HOLD HANDS!! IT'LL BE SAFER THAT WAY!
W... WHAT?!
Y-YOU REALLY WANT TO DO THAT!?!
OH, NO... IS THAT BAD?
N-NO--NOT AT ALL!!! IN FACT, I'D REALLY LIKE IT!!!
At last...!!! At last...!!! Fuyuki-kun and I are going to...!!!
HAFUUU
HAFUUU
WINTER SPECIAL
W... WAIT!!
TCH!
NISHIZAWA-SAN... WHAT'S THAT?!

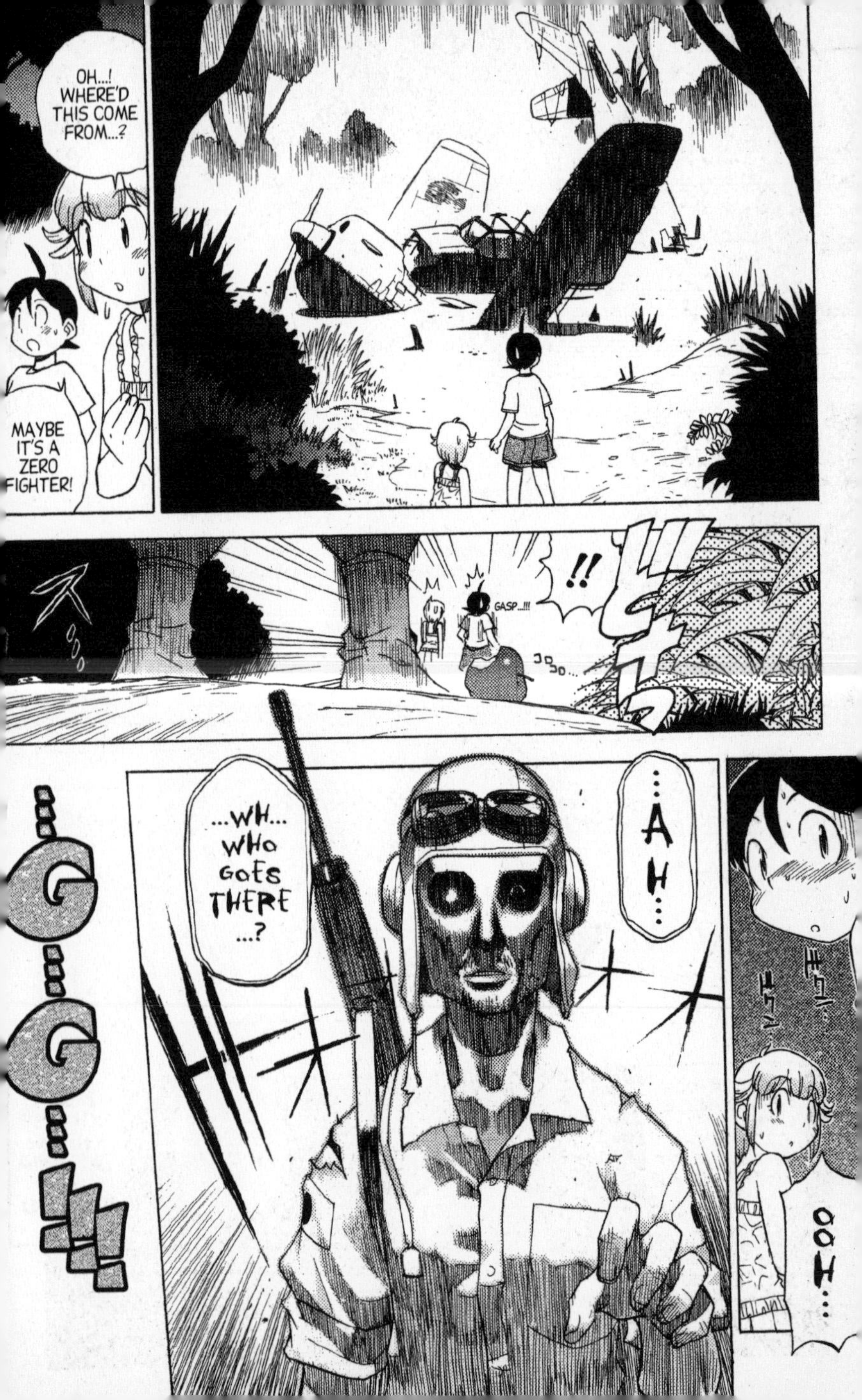
OH...! WHERE'D THIS COME FROM...?
MAYBE IT'S A ZERO FIGHTER!
!!
GASP...!!!
OOH...
...AH...
...WH... WHO GOES THERE ...?
...G...G...G...

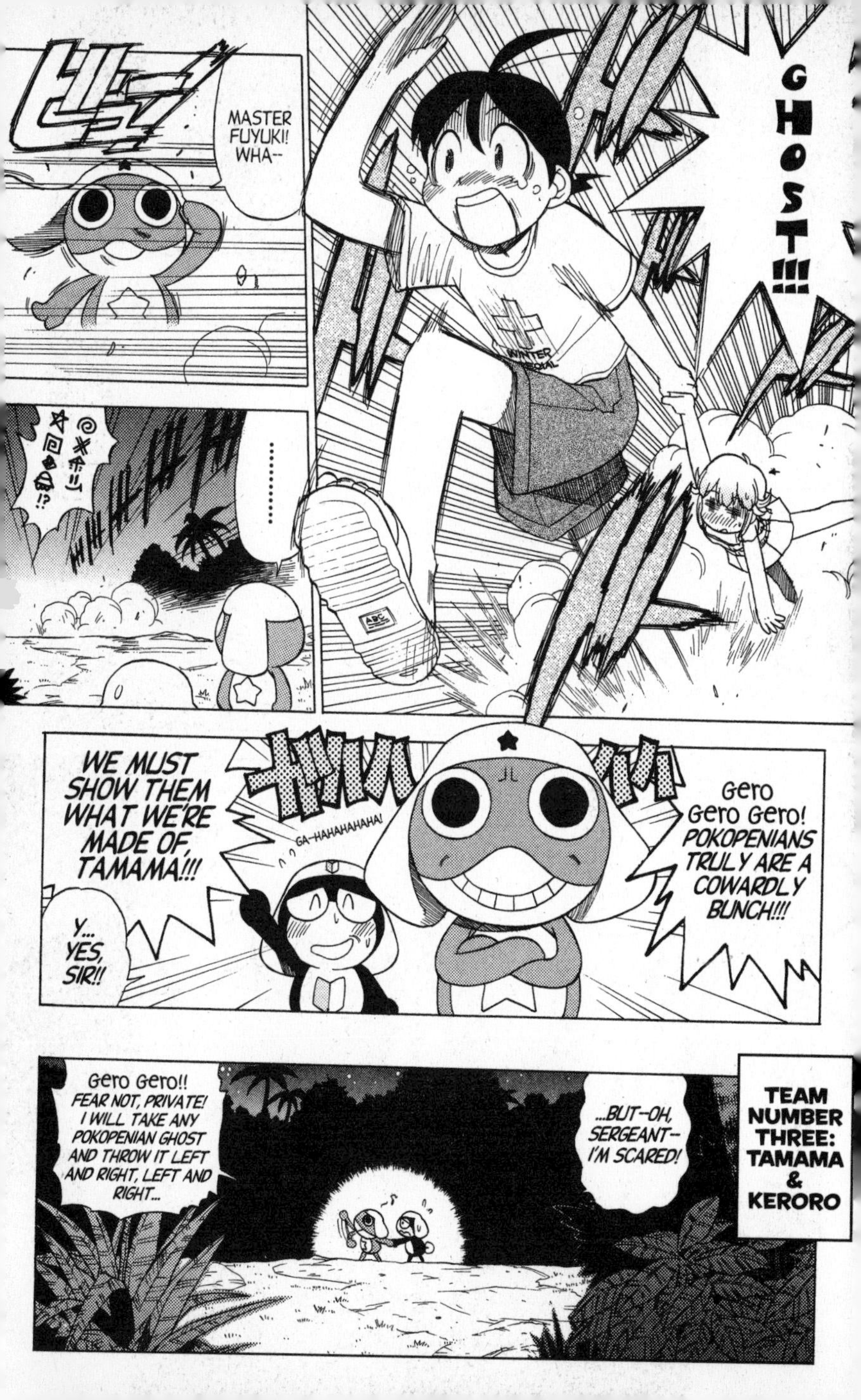
GHOST!!!
MASTER FUYUKI! WHA--
......
Gero Gero Gero! POKOPENIANS TRULY ARE A COWARDLY BUNCH!!!
GA-HAHAHAHAHA!
WE MUST SHOW THEM WHAT WE'RE MADE OF, TAMAMA!!!
Y... YES, SIR!!
TEAM NUMBER THREE: TAMAMA & KERORO
...BUT--OH, SERGEANT-- I'M SCARED!
Gero Gero!! FEAR NOT, PRIVATE! I WILL TAKE ANY POKOPENIAN GHOST AND THROW IT LEFT AND RIGHT, LEFT AND RIGHT...

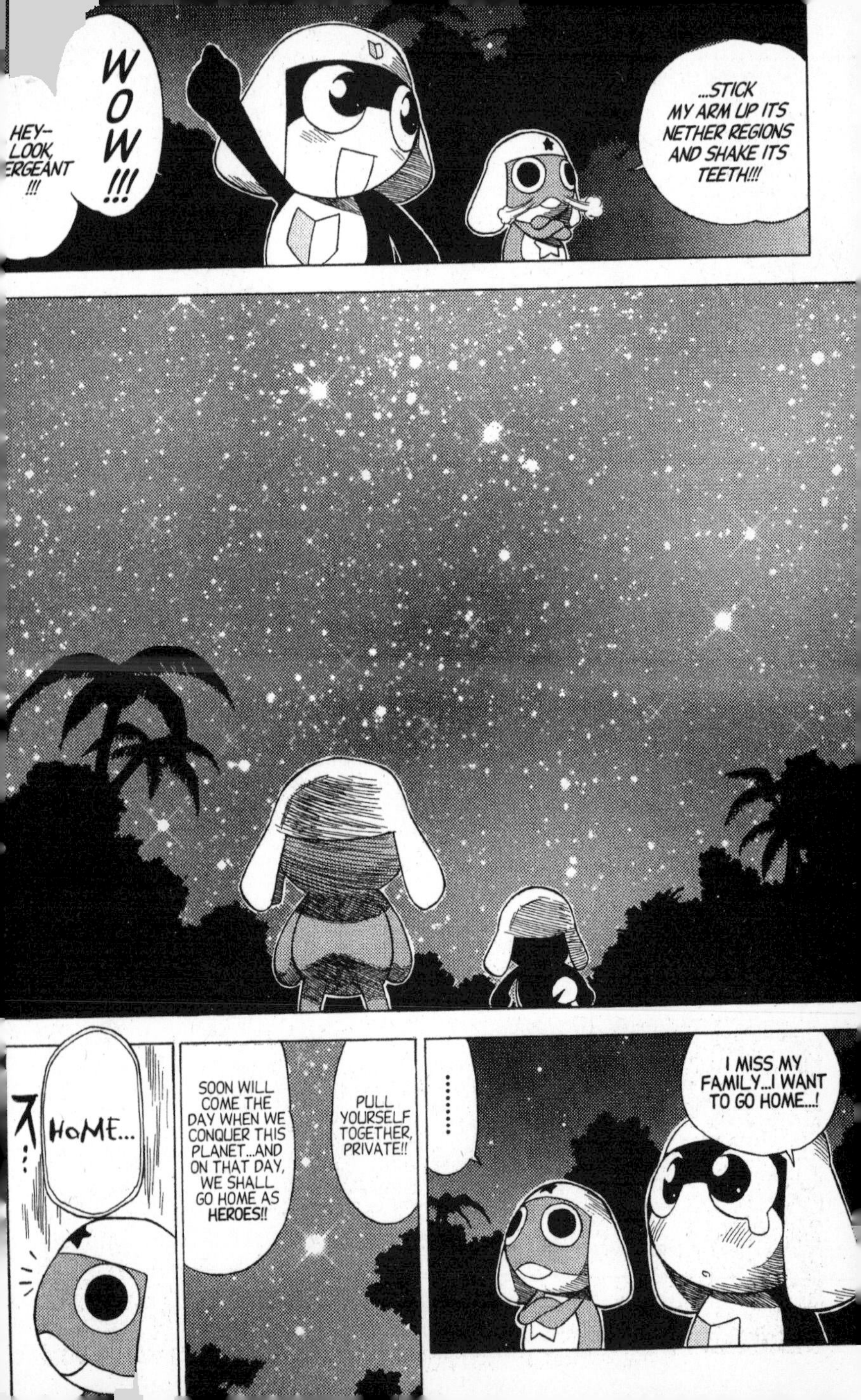
...STICK MY ARM UP ITS NETHER REGIONS AND SHAKE ITS TEETH!!!
WOW!!!
HEY— LOOK, ERGEANT !!!
I MISS MY FAMILY...I WANT TO GO HOME...!
....
PULL YOURSELF TOGETHER, PRIVATE!!
SOON WILL COME THE DAY WHEN WE CONQUER THIS PLANET...AND ON THAT DAY, WE SHALL GO HOME AS **HEROES!!**
HOME...
ス...

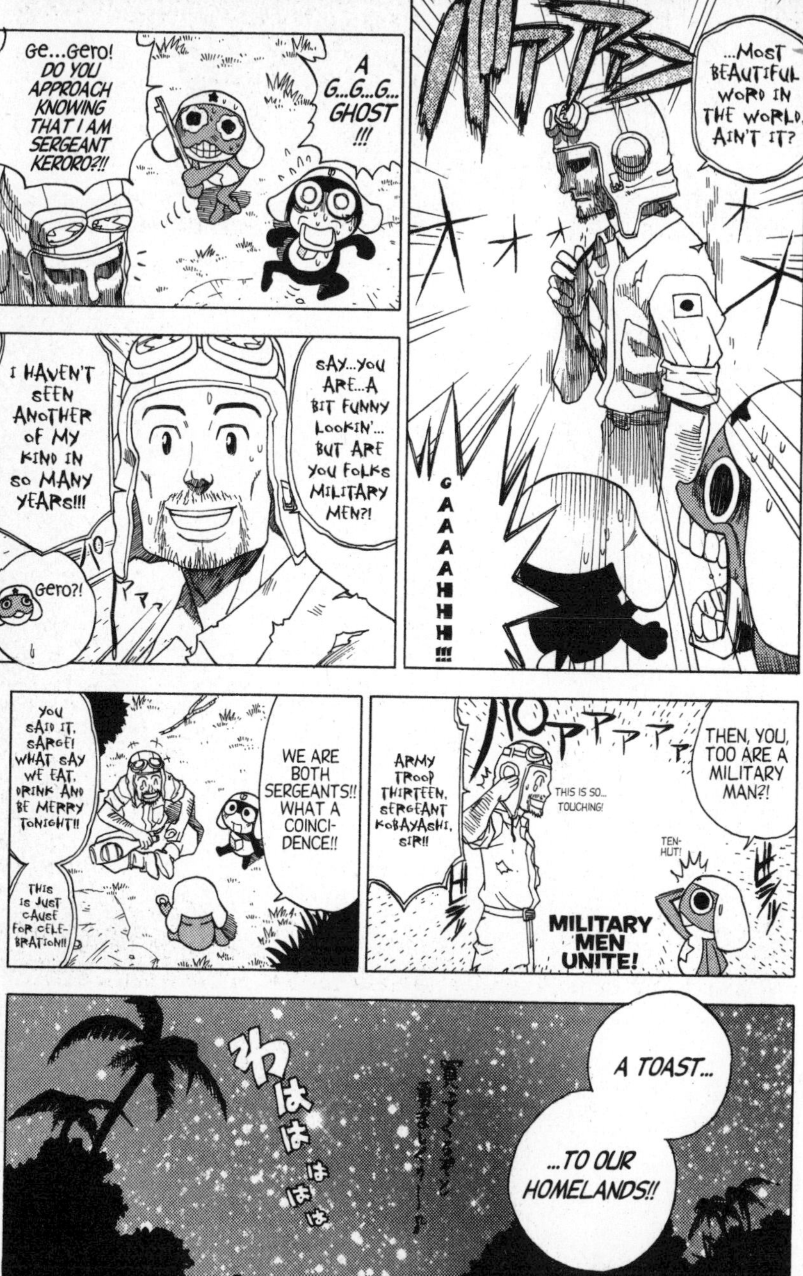
...Most beautiful word in the world, ain't it?
GAAAAAAHHH!!!
A G...G...G... GHOST!!!
Ge...Gero! Do you approach knowing that I am Sergeant Keroro?!!
Say...you are...a bit funny lookin'... but are you folks military men?!
I haven't seen another of my kind in so many years!!!
Gero?!
Then, you, too are a military man?!
Ten-hut!
This is so... touching!
Army troop thirteen, Sergeant Kobayashi, sir!!
MILITARY MEN UNITE!
We are both sergeants!! What a coincidence!!
You said it, sarge! What say we eat, drink and be merry tonight!!
This is just cause for celebration!!
A toast...
...to our homelands!!
わはははは

*THEY'RE SINGING A JAPANESE WWII SONG

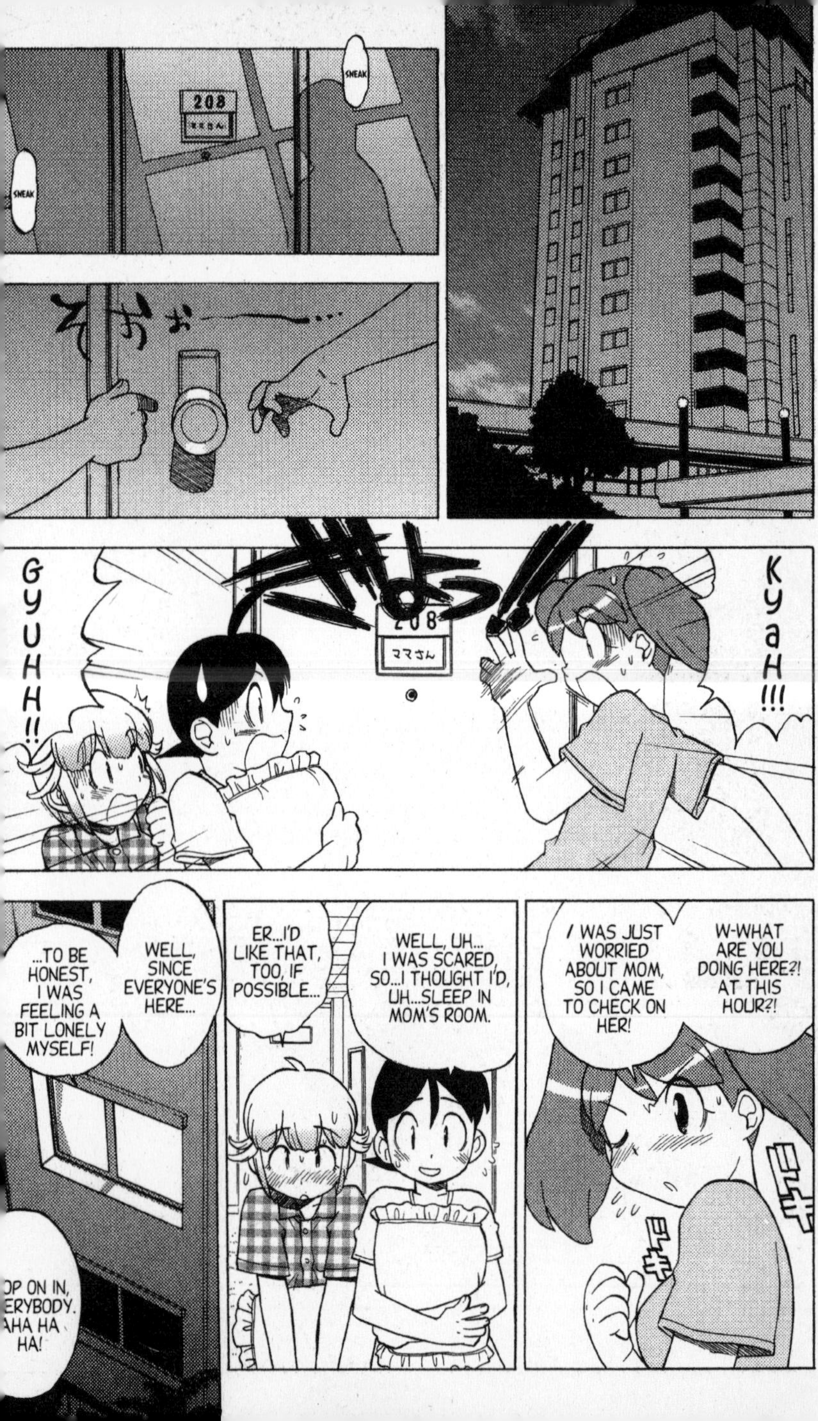
SNEAK
SNEAK
KyaH!!!
208
ママさん
GYUHH!!
W-WHAT ARE YOU DOING HERE?! AT THIS HOUR?!
I WAS JUST WORRIED ABOUT MOM, SO I CAME TO CHECK ON HER!
ドキ
ドキ
WELL, UH... I WAS SCARED, SO...I THOUGHT I'D, UH...SLEEP IN MOM'S ROOM.
ER...I'D LIKE THAT, TOO, IF POSSIBLE...
WELL, SINCE EVERYONE'S HERE...
...TO BE HONEST, I WAS FEELING A BIT LONELY MYSELF!
OP ON IN, ERYBODY. AHA HA HA!

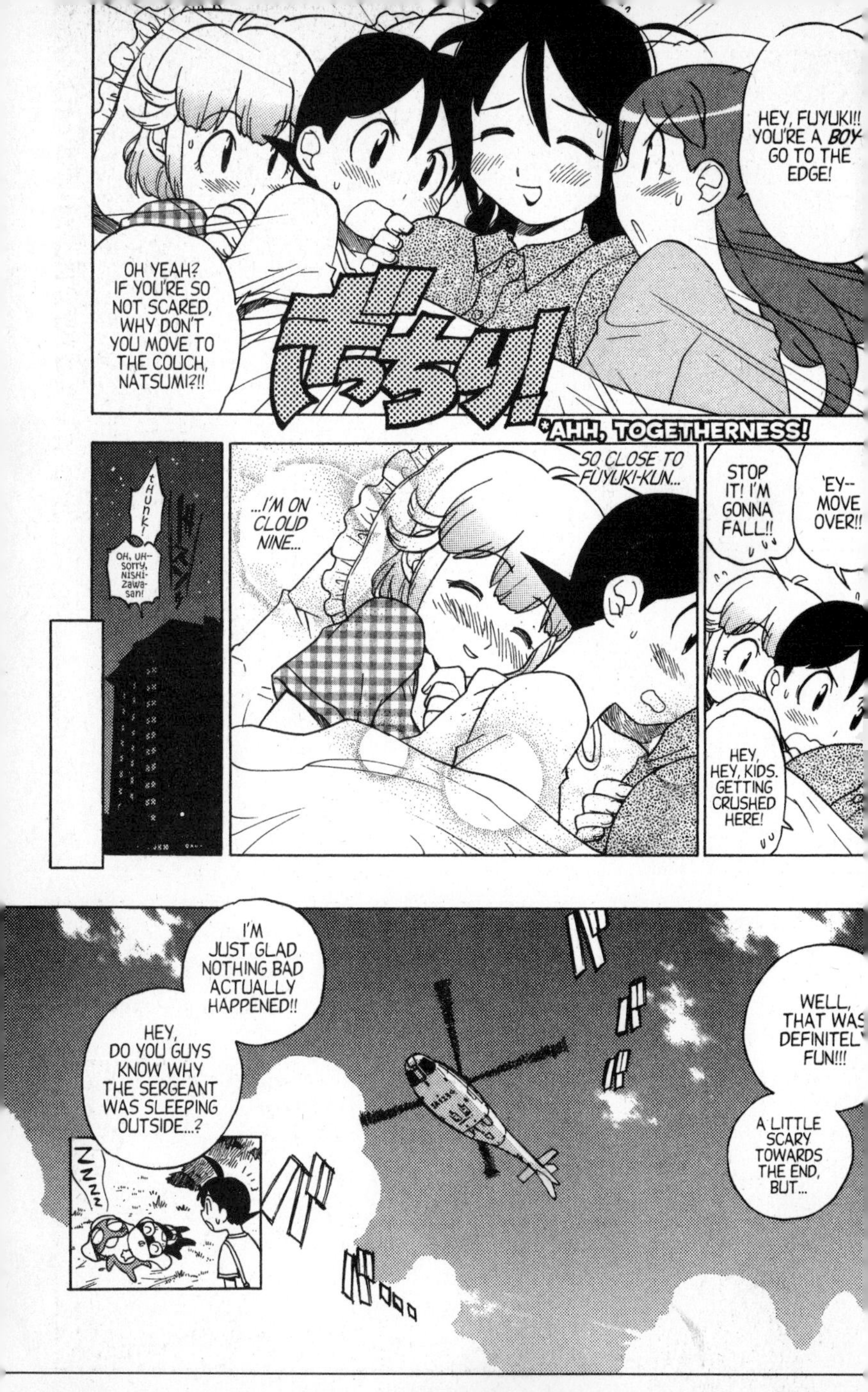
HEY, FUYUKI!! YOU'RE A BOY GO TO THE EDGE!
OH YEAH? IF YOU'RE SO NOT SCARED, WHY DON'T YOU MOVE TO THE COUCH, NATSUMI?!!
*AHH, TOGETHERNESS!
'EY-- MOVE OVER!!
STOP IT! I'M GONNA FALL!!
HEY, HEY, KIDS. GETTING CRUSHED HERE!
SO CLOSE TO FUYUKI-KUN...
...I'M ON CLOUD NINE...
THUNK!
OH, UH-- SORRY, NISHIZAWA-SAN!
WELL, THAT WAS DEFINITEL FUN!!!
A LITTLE SCARY TOWARDS THE END, BUT...
I'M JUST GLAD NOTHING BAD ACTUALLY HAPPENED!!
HEY, DO YOU GUYS KNOW WHY THE SERGEANT WAS SLEEPING OUTSIDE...?

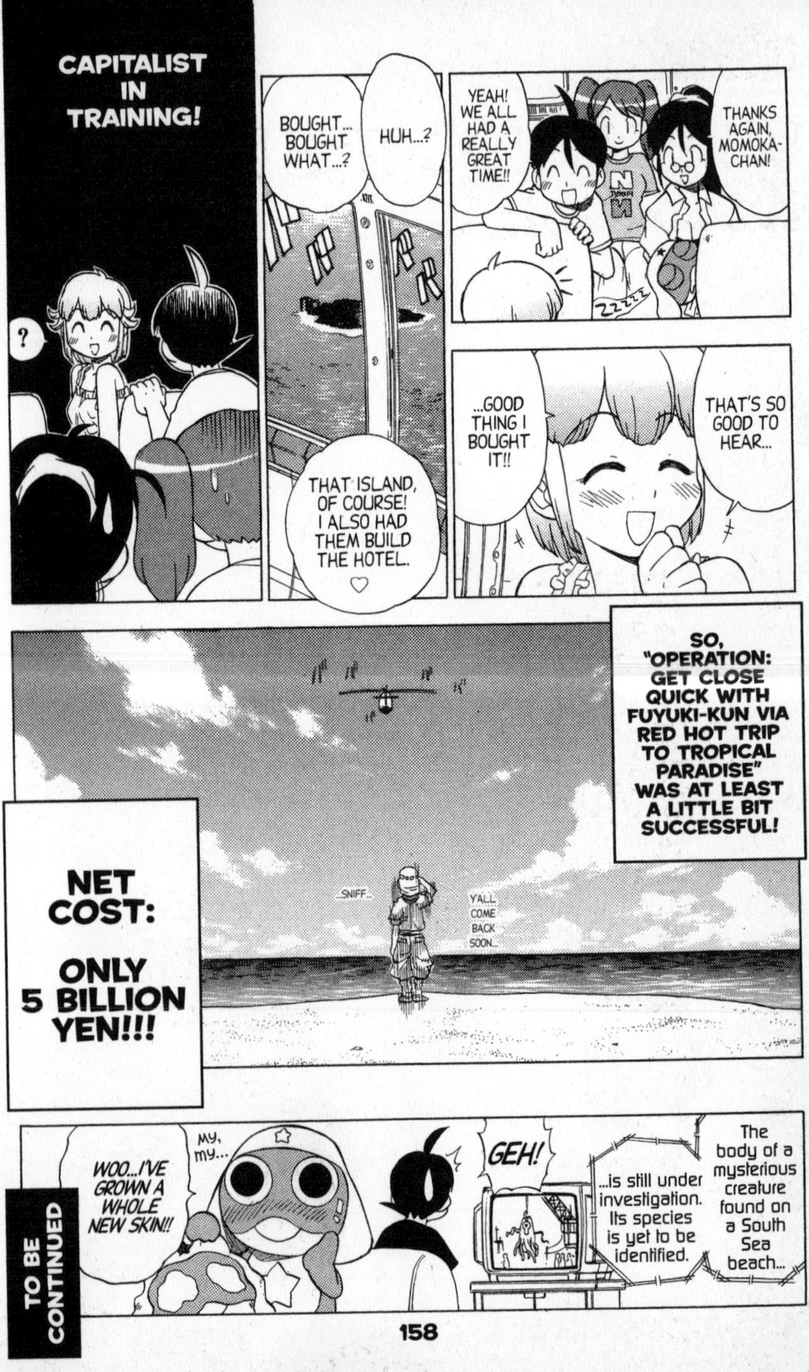
CAPITALIST IN TRAINING!
THANKS AGAIN, MOMOKA-CHAN!
YEAH! WE ALL HAD A REALLY GREAT TIME!!
THAT'S SO GOOD TO HEAR...
...GOOD THING I BOUGHT IT!!
HUH...?
BOUGHT... BOUGHT WHAT...?
THAT ISLAND, OF COURSE! I ALSO HAD THEM BUILD THE HOTEL. ♡
?
SO, "OPERATION: GET CLOSE QUICK WITH FUYUKI-KUN VIA RED HOT TRIP TO TROPICAL PARADISE" WAS AT LEAST A LITTLE BIT SUCCESSFUL!
Y'ALL COME BACK SOON...
...SNIFF...
NET COST: ONLY 5 BILLION YEN!!!
The body of a mysterious creature found on a South Sea beach...
...is still under investigation. Its species is yet to be identified.
GEH!
My, my...
WOO...I'VE GROWN A WHOLE NEW SKIN!!
TO BE CONTINUED

ENCOUNTER X

BEHOLD THE LORD OF TERROR! APOCALYPSE NOW!

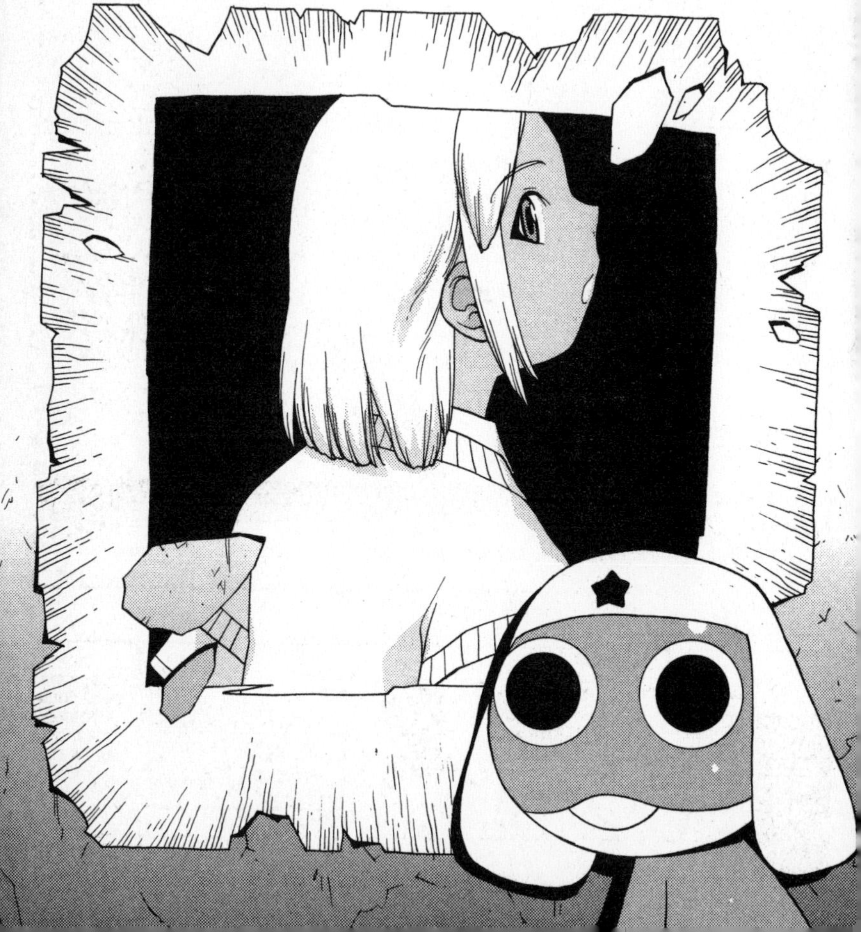

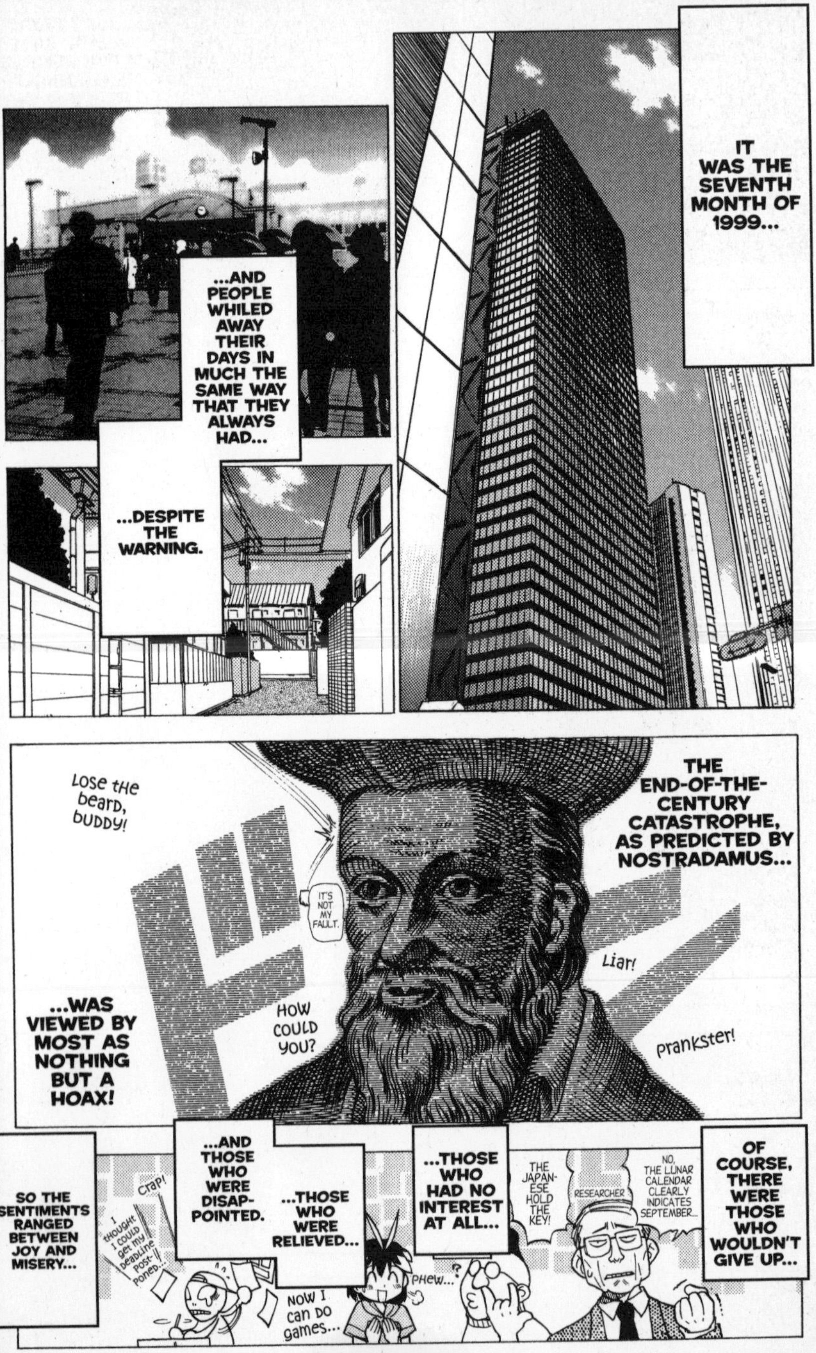
IT WAS THE SEVENTH MONTH OF 1999...
...AND PEOPLE WHILED AWAY THEIR DAYS IN MUCH THE SAME WAY THAT THEY ALWAYS HAD...
...DESPITE THE WARNING.
THE END-OF-THE-CENTURY CATASTROPHE, AS PREDICTED BY NOSTRADAMUS...
Lose the beard, buddy!
IT'S NOT MY FAULT.
Liar!
Prankster!
HOW COULD YOU?
...WAS VIEWED BY MOST AS NOTHING BUT A HOAX!
OF COURSE, THERE WERE THOSE WHO WOULDN'T GIVE UP...
NO, THE LUNAR CALENDAR CLEARLY INDICATES SEPTEMBER...
RESEARCHER
THE JAPANESE HOLD THE KEY!
...THOSE WHO HAD NO INTEREST AT ALL...
PHEW...
...THOSE WHO WERE RELIEVED...
NOW I can do games...
...AND THOSE WHO WERE DISAPPOINTED.
Crap!
I thought I could get my deadline post-poned...
SO THE SENTIMENTS RANGED BETWEEN JOY AND MISERY...

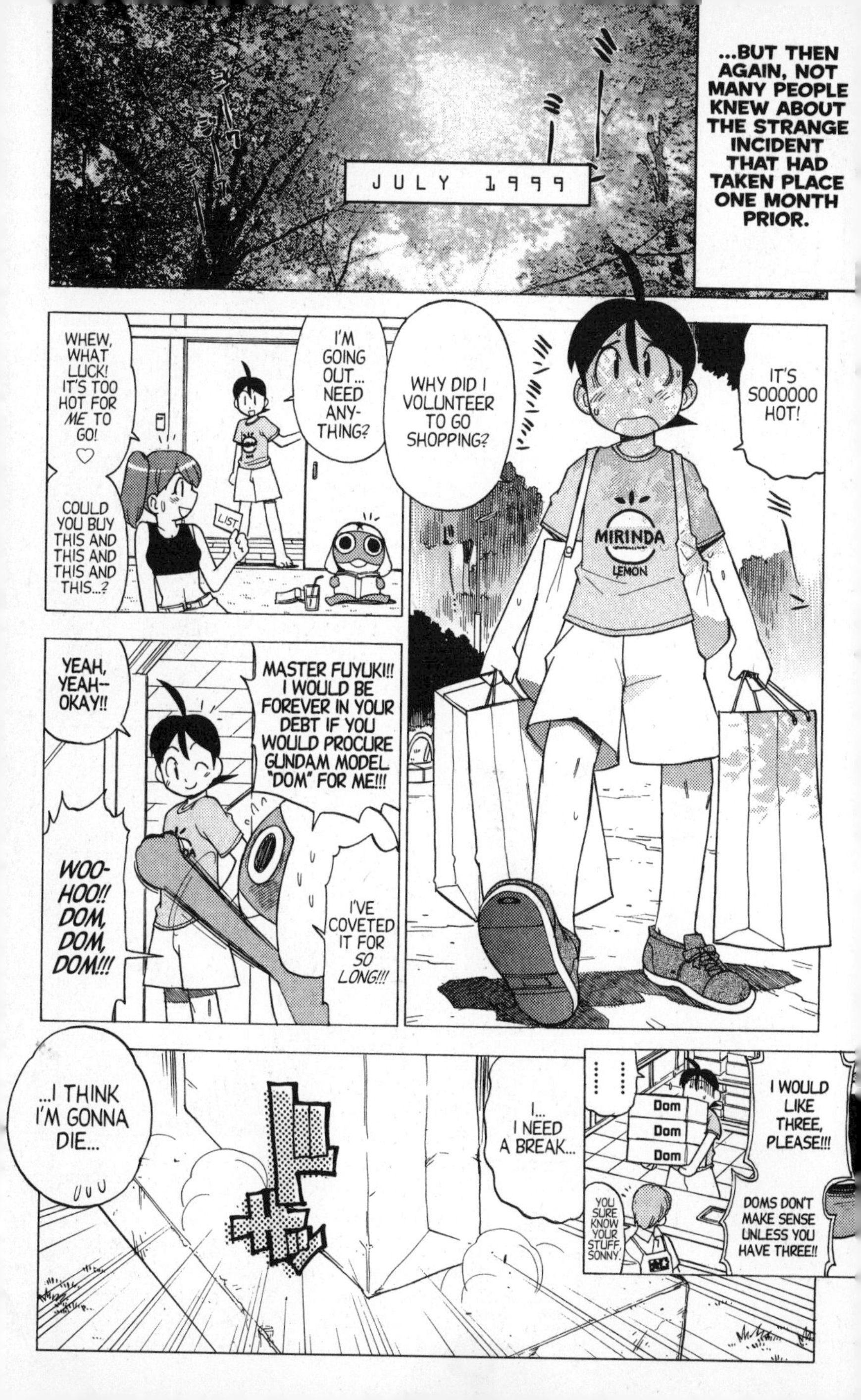

...BUT THEN AGAIN, NOT MANY PEOPLE KNEW ABOUT THE STRANGE INCIDENT THAT HAD TAKEN PLACE ONE MONTH PRIOR.
JULY 1999
IT'S SOOOOOO HOT!
WHY DID I VOLUNTEER TO GO SHOPPING?
MIRINDA
LEMON
I'M GOING OUT... NEED ANY-THING?
WHEW, WHAT LUCK! IT'S TOO HOT FOR *ME* TO GO! ♡
COULD YOU BUY THIS AND THIS AND THIS AND THIS...?
LIST
MASTER FUYUKI!! I WOULD BE FOREVER IN YOUR DEBT IF YOU WOULD PROCURE GUNDAM MODEL "DOM" FOR ME!!!
YEAH, YEAH-- OKAY!!
I'VE COVETED IT FOR *SO LONG!!!*
WOO-HOO!! DOM, DOM, DOM!!!
......
I WOULD LIKE THREE, PLEASE!!!
Dom
Dom
Dom
DOMS DON'T MAKE SENSE UNLESS YOU HAVE THREE!!
YOU SURE KNOW YOUR STUFF, SONNY.
I... I NEED A BREAK...
...I THINK I'M GONNA DIE...

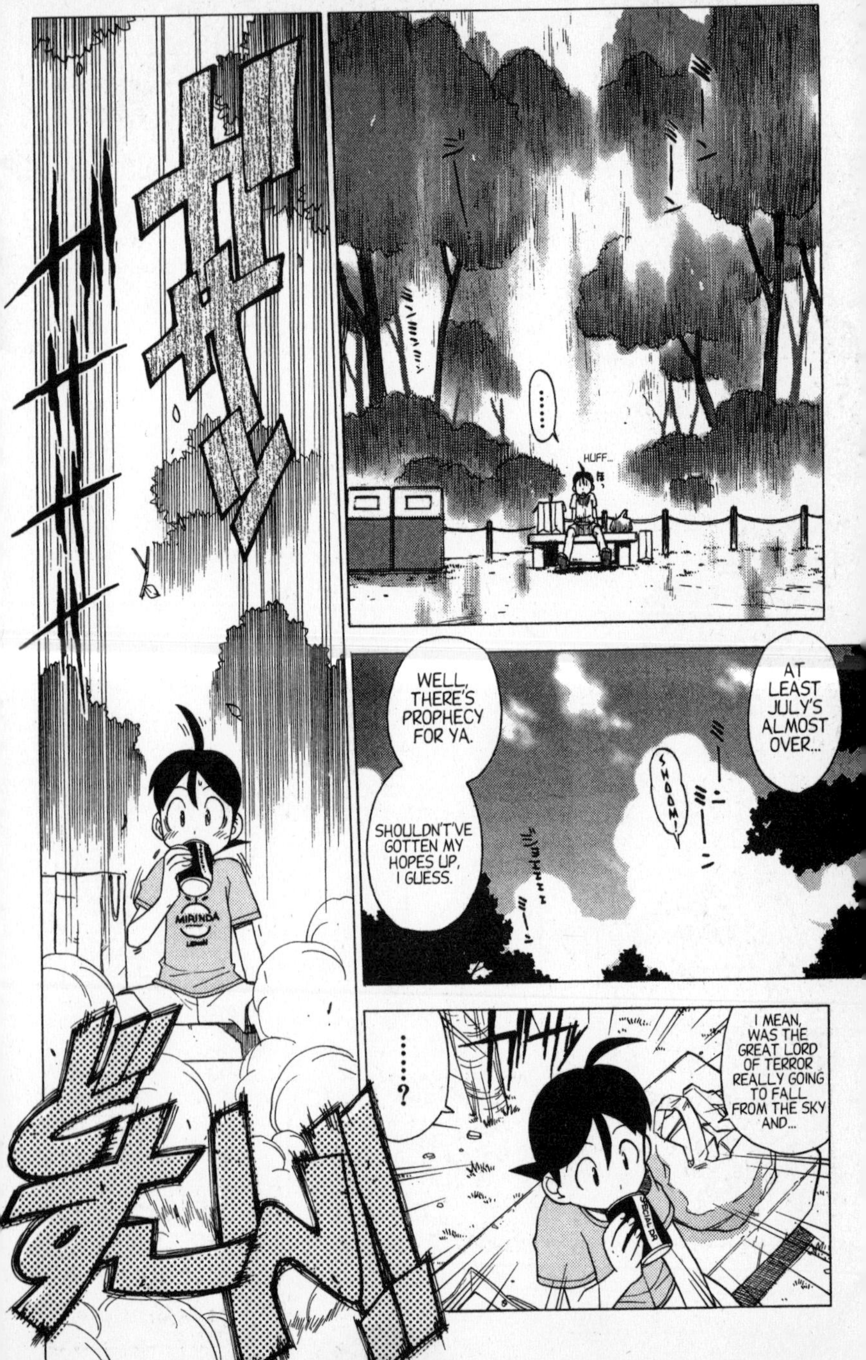
......
HUFF...
AT LEAST JULY'S ALMOST OVER...
SHOOM!
WELL, THERE'S PROPHECY FOR YA.
SHOULDN'T'VE GOTTEN MY HOPES UP, I GUESS.
I MEAN, WAS THE GREAT LORD OF TERROR REALLY GOING TO FALL FROM THE SKY AND...
......?
MIRINDA

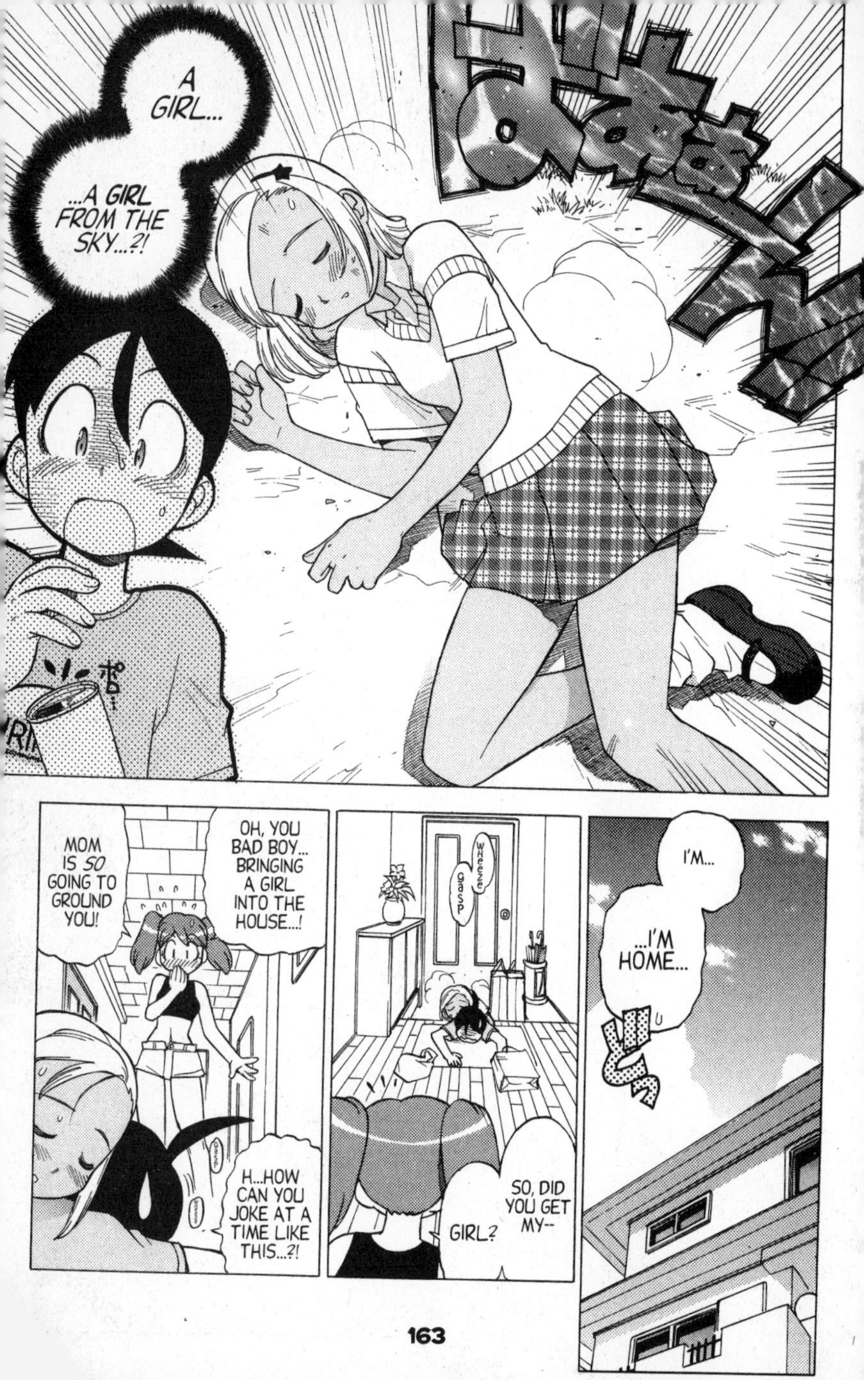
A GIRL...
...A GIRL FROM THE SKY...?!
I'M...
...I'M HOME...
WHEEZE
GASP
SO, DID YOU GET MY--
GIRL?
OH, YOU BAD BOY... BRINGING A GIRL INTO THE HOUSE...!
MOM IS *SO* GOING TO GROUND YOU!
H...HOW CAN YOU JOKE AT A TIME LIKE THIS...?!

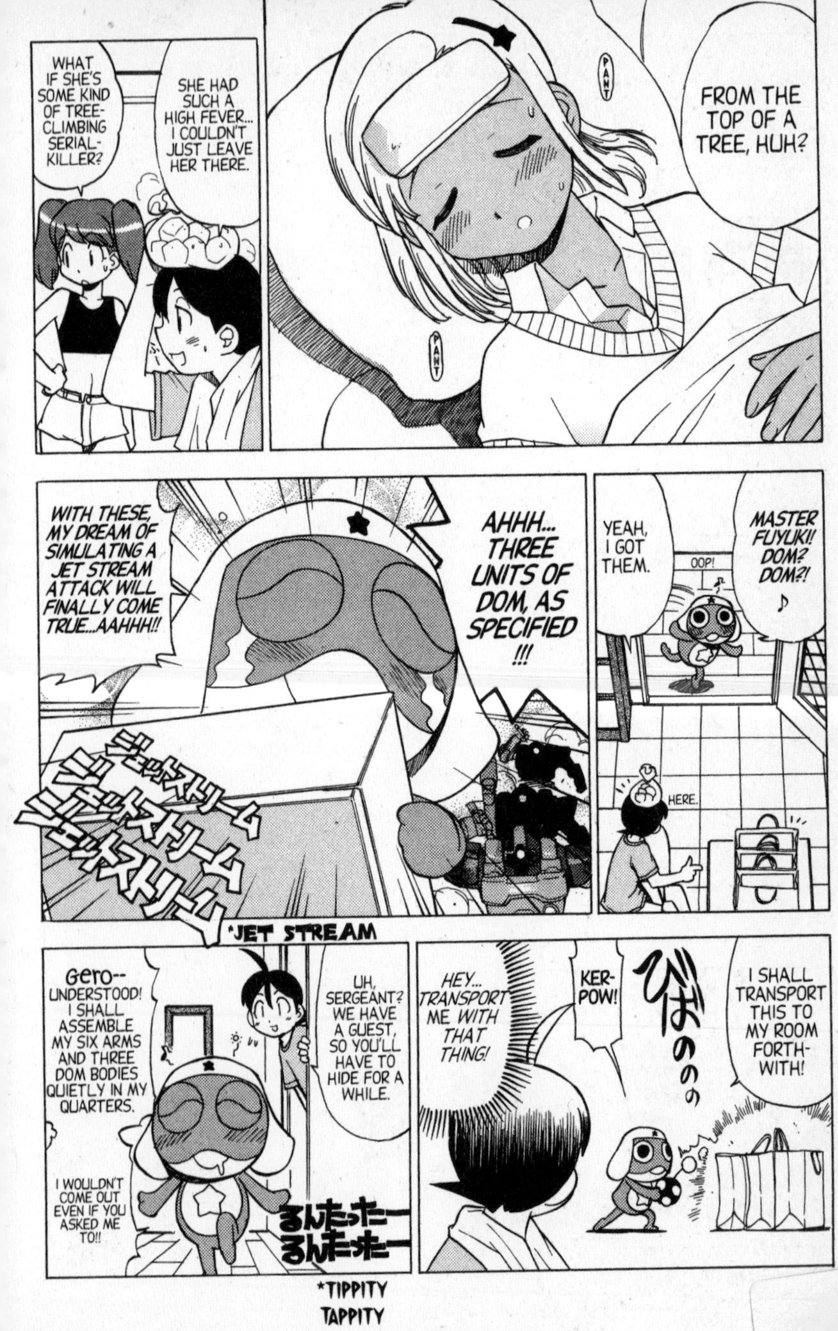
FROM THE TOP OF A TREE, HUH?
PANT
PANT
SHE HAD SUCH A HIGH FEVER... I COULDN'T JUST LEAVE HER THERE.
WHAT IF SHE'S SOME KIND OF TREE-CLIMBING SERIAL-KILLER?
MASTER FUYUKI!! DOM? DOM?! ♪
OOP!
YEAH, I GOT THEM.
HERE.
AHHH... THREE UNITS OF DOM, AS SPECIFIED !!!
WITH THESE, MY DREAM OF SIMULATING A JET STREAM ATTACK WILL FINALLY COME TRUE...AAHHH!!
ジェットストリーム
ジェットストリーム
ジェットストリーム
*JET STREAM
I SHALL TRANSPORT THIS TO MY ROOM FORTH-WITH!
ぴぱののの
KER-POW!
HEY... TRANSPORT ME WITH THAT THING!
UH, SERGEANT? WE HAVE A GUEST, SO YOU'LL HAVE TO HIDE FOR A WHILE.
Gero-- UNDERSTOOD! I SHALL ASSEMBLE MY SIX ARMS AND THREE DOM BODIES QUIETLY IN MY QUARTERS.
I WOULDN'T COME OUT EVEN IF YOU ASKED ME TO!!
るんたったー
るんたったー

*TIPPITY TAPPITY

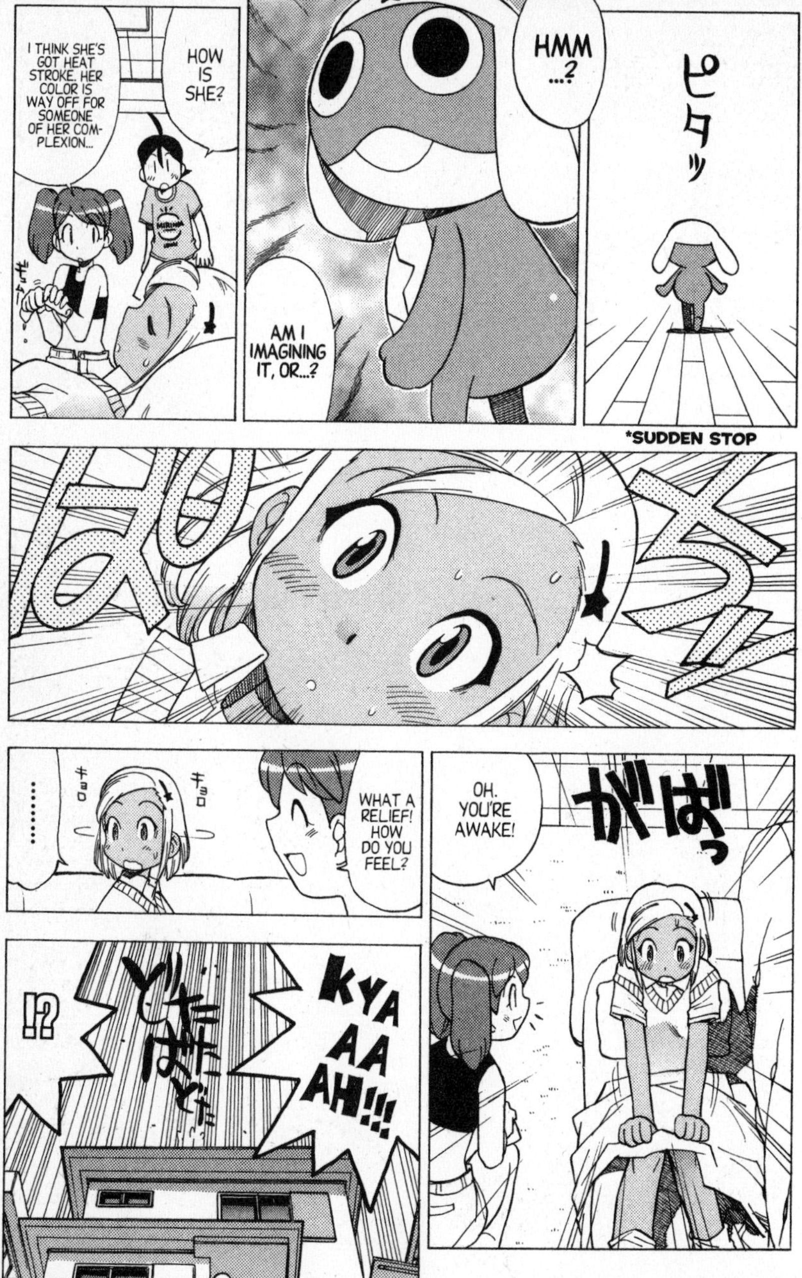
ピタッ
HMM ...?
AM I IMAGINING IT, OR...?
HOW IS SHE?
I THINK SHE'S GOT HEAT STROKE. HER COLOR IS WAY OFF FOR SOMEONE OF HER COMPLEXION...
がばっ
OH. YOU'RE AWAKE!
WHAT A RELIEF! HOW DO YOU FEEL?
キョロ
キョロ
....
KYAAAAH!!!
!?
*SUDDEN STOP

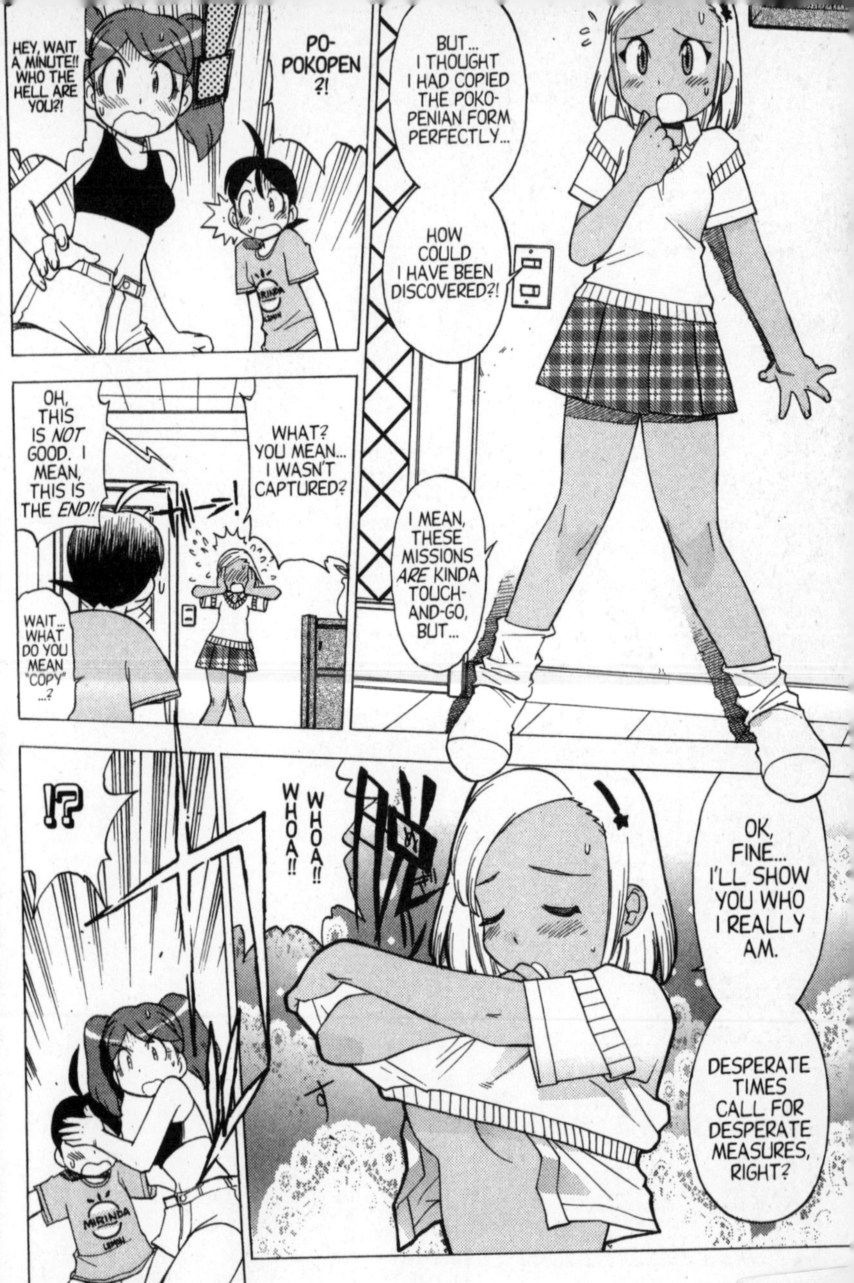
BUT... I THOUGHT I HAD COPIED THE POKO-PENIAN FORM PERFECTLY...
HOW COULD I HAVE BEEN DISCOVERED?!
I MEAN, THESE MISSIONS *ARE* KINDA TOUCH-AND-GO, BUT...
PO-POKOPEN?!
HEY, WAIT A MINUTE!! WHO THE HELL ARE YOU?!
WHAT? YOU MEAN... I WASN'T CAPTURED?
OH, THIS IS *NOT* GOOD. I MEAN, THIS IS THE *END*!!
WAIT... WHAT DO YOU MEAN "COPY" ...?
OK, FINE... I'LL SHOW YOU WHO I REALLY AM.
DESPERATE TIMES CALL FOR DESPERATE MEASURES, RIGHT?
WHOA!!
WHOA!!
!?

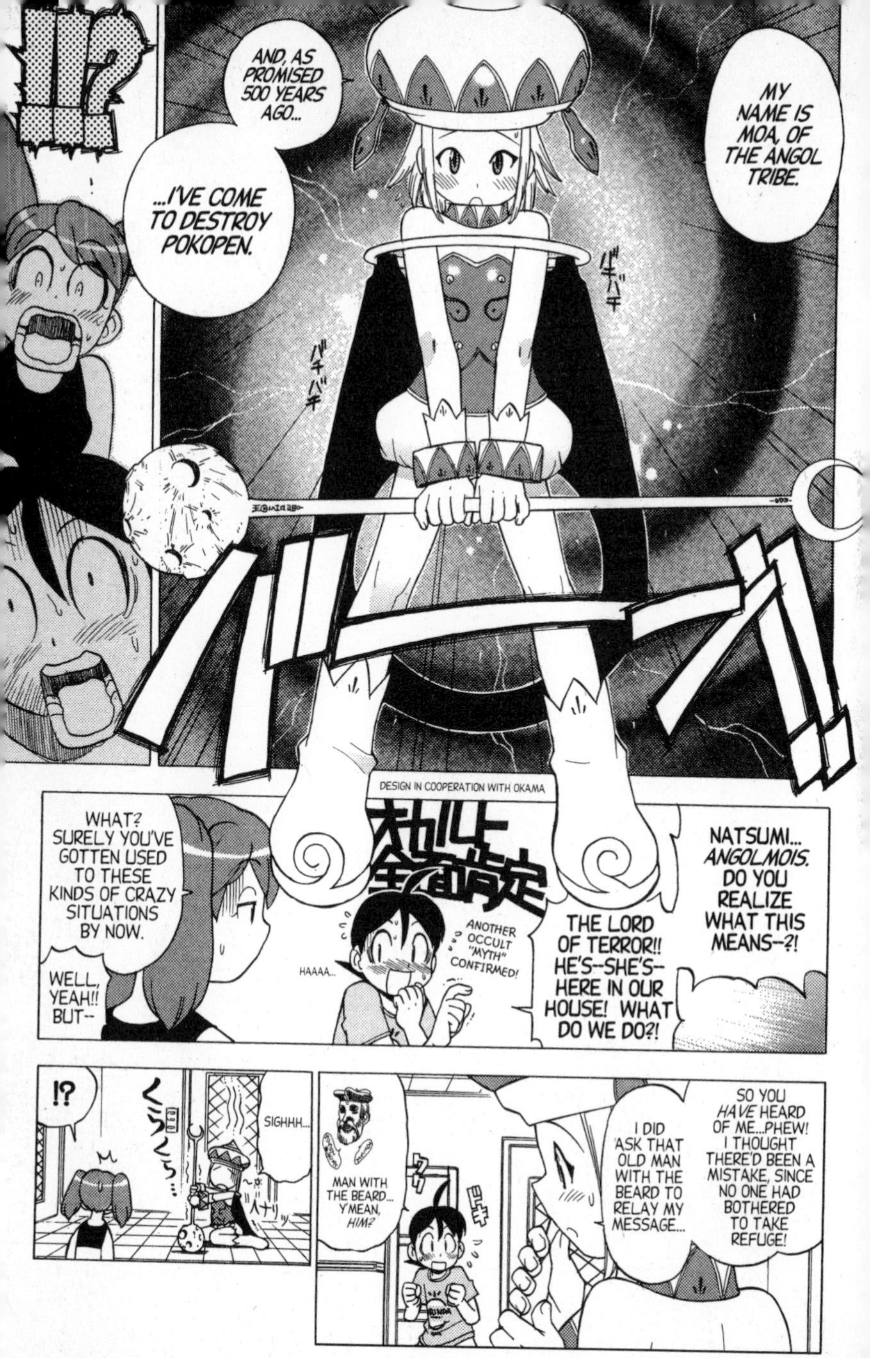
MY NAME IS MOA, OF THE ANGOL TRIBE.
AND, AS PROMISED 500 YEARS AGO...
...I'VE COME TO DESTROY POKOPEN.
!?
DESIGN IN COOPERATION WITH OKAMA
NATSUMI... ANGOLMOIS. DO YOU REALIZE WHAT THIS MEANS--?!
THE LORD OF TERROR!! HE'S--SHE'S--HERE IN OUR HOUSE! WHAT DO WE DO?!
ANOTHER OCCULT "MYTH" CONFIRMED!
HAAAA...
WHAT? SURELY YOU'VE GOTTEN USED TO THESE KINDS OF CRAZY SITUATIONS BY NOW.
WELL, YEAH!! BUT--
SO YOU HAVE HEARD OF ME...PHEW! I THOUGHT THERE'D BEEN A MISTAKE, SINCE NO ONE HAD BOTHERED TO TAKE REFUGE!
I DID ASK THAT OLD MAN WITH THE BEARD TO RELAY MY MESSAGE...
MAN WITH THE BEARD... Y'MEAN, HIM?
SIGHHH...
!?

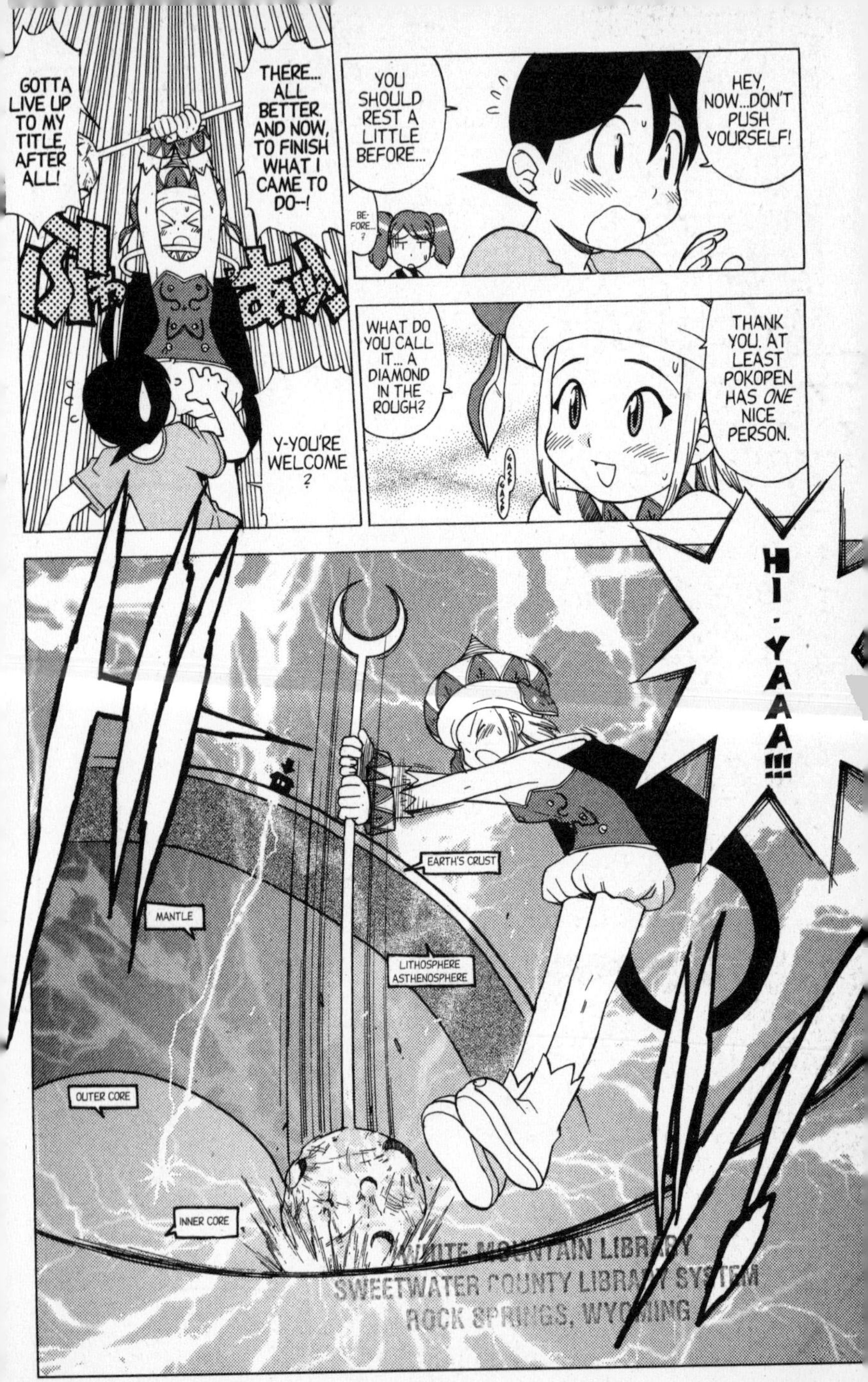
HEY, NOW...DON'T PUSH YOURSELF!
YOU SHOULD REST A LITTLE BEFORE...
BE-FORE...?
THANK YOU. AT LEAST POKOPEN HAS *ONE* NICE PERSON.
WHAT DO YOU CALL IT... A DIAMOND IN THE ROUGH?
GASP GASP
THERE... ALL BETTER. AND NOW, TO FINISH WHAT I CAME TO DO--!
GOTTA LIVE UP TO MY TITLE, AFTER ALL!
Y-YOU'RE WELCOME?
HI-YAAA!!!
EARTH'S CRUST
MANTLE
LITHOSPHERE ASTHENOSPHERE
OUTER CORE
INNER CORE

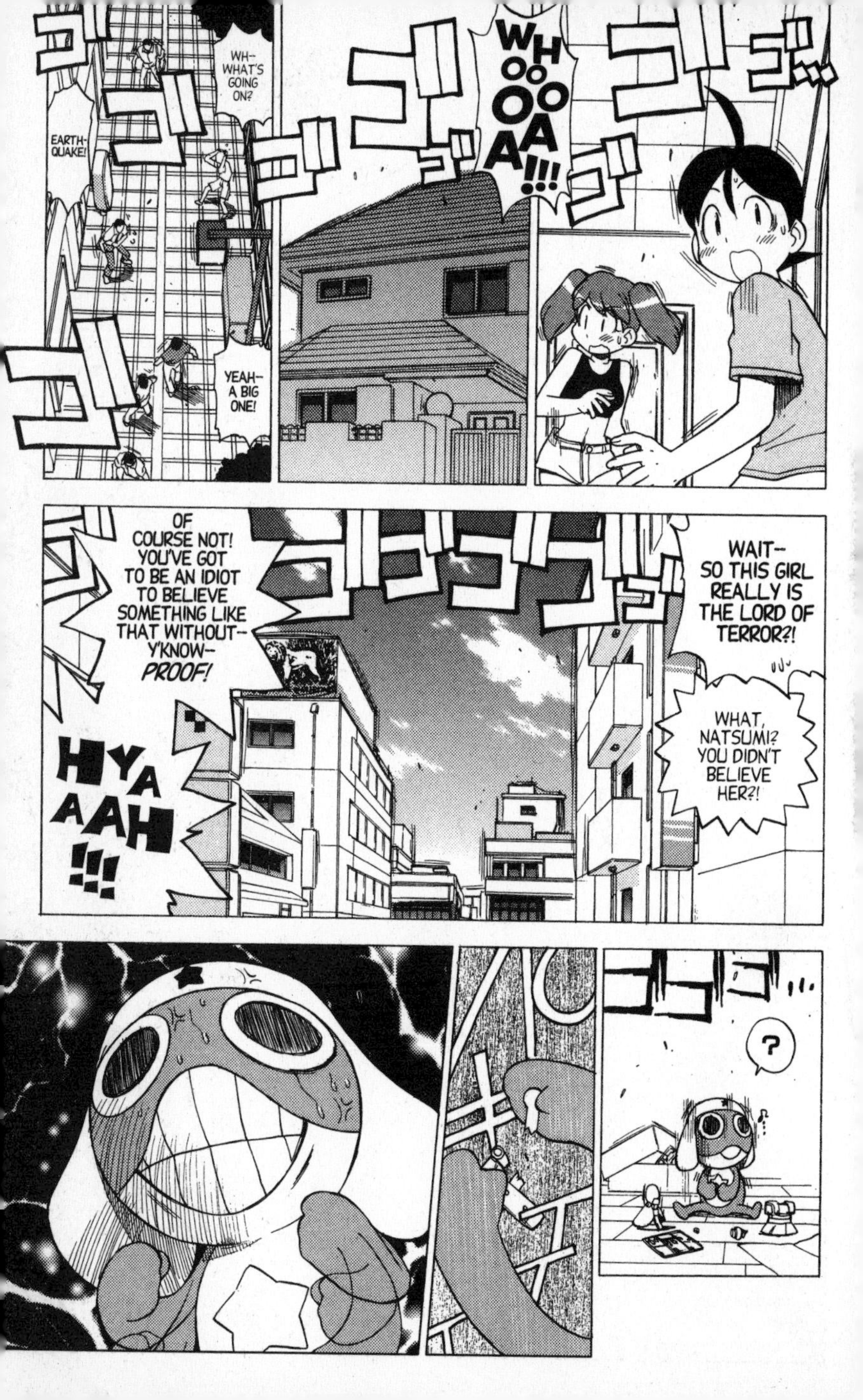
WHOOOOOAA!!!
WH-- WHAT'S GOING ON?
EARTH-QUAKE!
YEAH-- A BIG ONE!
WAIT-- SO THIS GIRL REALLY IS THE LORD OF TERROR?!
WHAT, NATSUMI? YOU DIDN'T BELIEVE HER?!
OF COURSE NOT! YOU'VE GOT TO BE AN IDIOT TO BELIEVE SOMETHING LIKE THAT WITHOUT-- Y'KNOW-- PROOF!
HYAAAH!!!
?

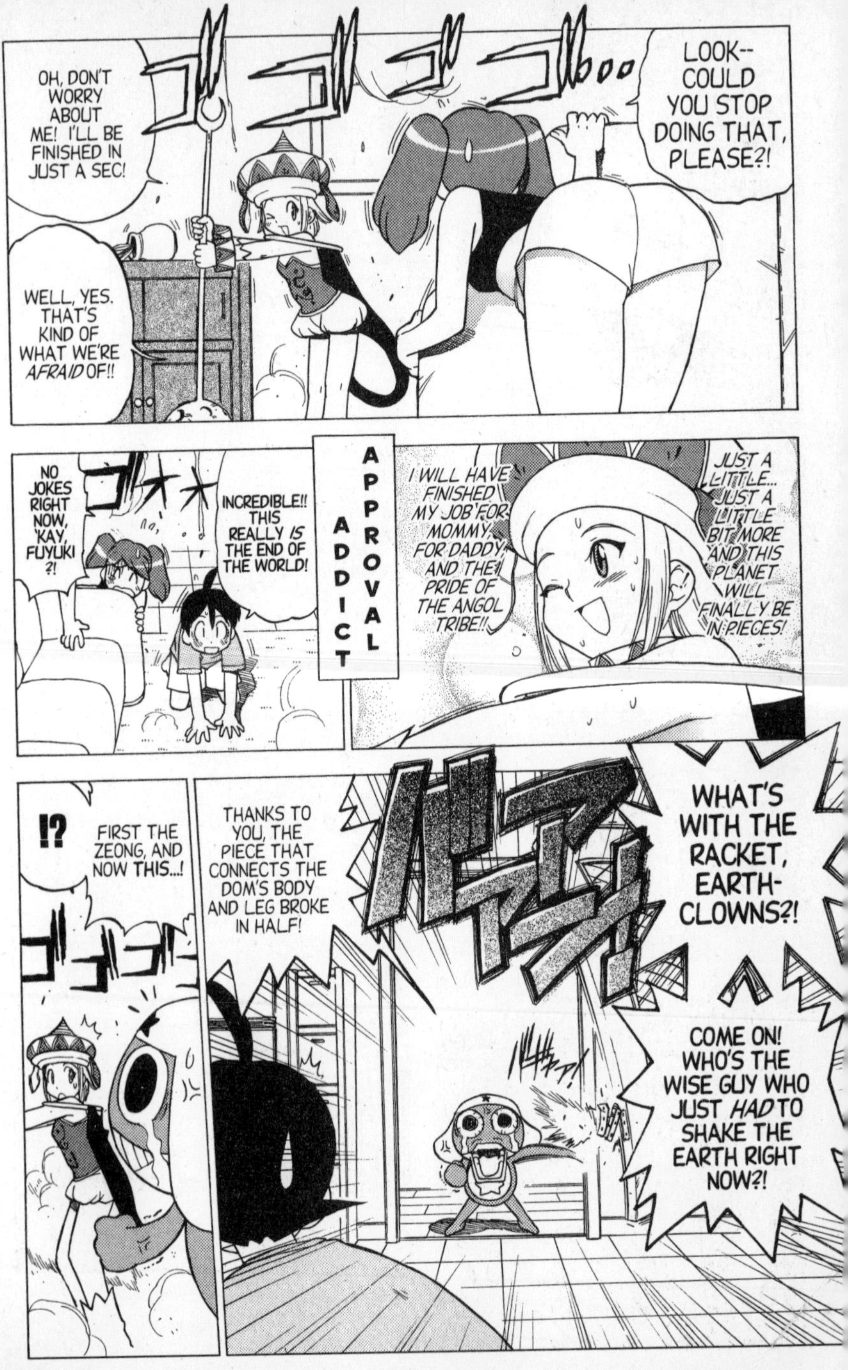

LOOK-- COULD YOU STOP DOING THAT, PLEASE?!
OH, DON'T WORRY ABOUT ME! I'LL BE FINISHED IN JUST A SEC!
WELL, YES. THAT'S KIND OF WHAT WE'RE *AFRAID* OF!!
JUST A LITTLE... JUST A LITTLE BIT MORE AND THIS PLANET WILL FINALLY BE IN PIECES!
I WILL HAVE FINISHED MY JOB FOR MOMMY, FOR DADDY, AND THE PRIDE OF THE ANGOL TRIBE!!
APPROVAL ADDICT
INCREDIBLE!! THIS REALLY *IS* THE END OF THE WORLD!
NO JOKES RIGHT NOW, 'KAY, FUYUKI?!
WHAT'S WITH THE RACKET, EARTH-CLOWNS?!
COME ON! WHO'S THE WISE GUY WHO JUST *HAD* TO SHAKE THE EARTH RIGHT NOW?!
THANKS TO YOU, THE PIECE THAT CONNECTS THE DOM'S BODY AND LEG BROKE IN HALF!
FIRST THE ZEONG, AND NOW **THIS**...!
!?

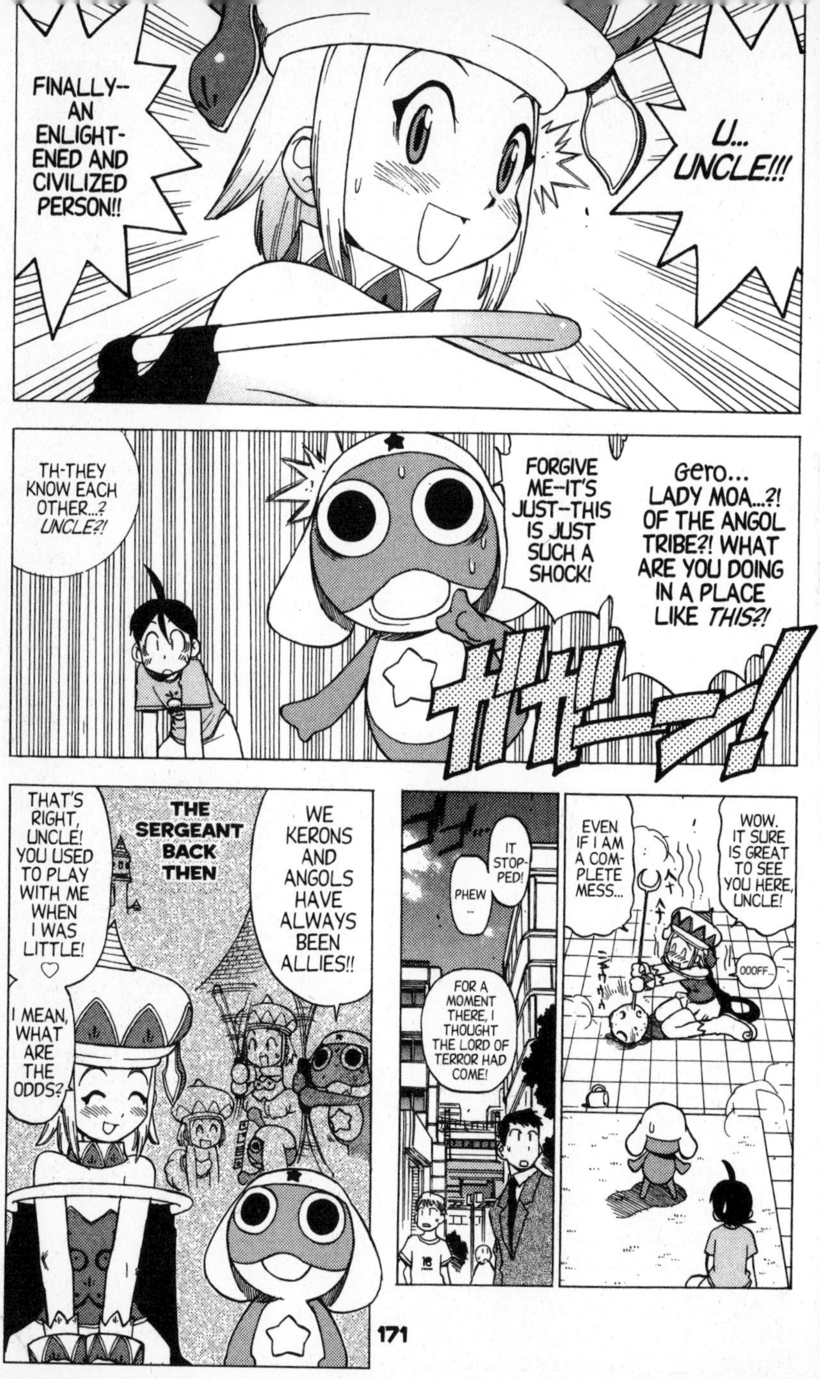
U... UNCLE!!!
FINALLY-- AN ENLIGHT-ENED AND CIVILIZED PERSON!!
Gero... LADY MOA...?! OF THE ANGOL TRIBE?! WHAT ARE YOU DOING IN A PLACE LIKE *THIS*?!
FORGIVE ME--IT'S JUST--THIS IS JUST SUCH A SHOCK!
TH-THEY KNOW EACH OTHER...? *UNCLE?!*
WOW. IT SURE IS GREAT TO SEE YOU HERE, UNCLE!
EVEN IF I AM A COM-PLETE MESS...
OOOFF...
IT STOP-PED!
PHEW...
FOR A MOMENT THERE, I THOUGHT THE LORD OF TERROR HAD COME!
WE KERONS AND ANGOLS HAVE ALWAYS BEEN ALLIES!!
THE SERGEANT BACK THEN
THAT'S RIGHT, UNCLE! YOU USED TO PLAY WITH ME WHEN I WAS LITTLE! ♡
I MEAN, WHAT ARE THE ODDS?

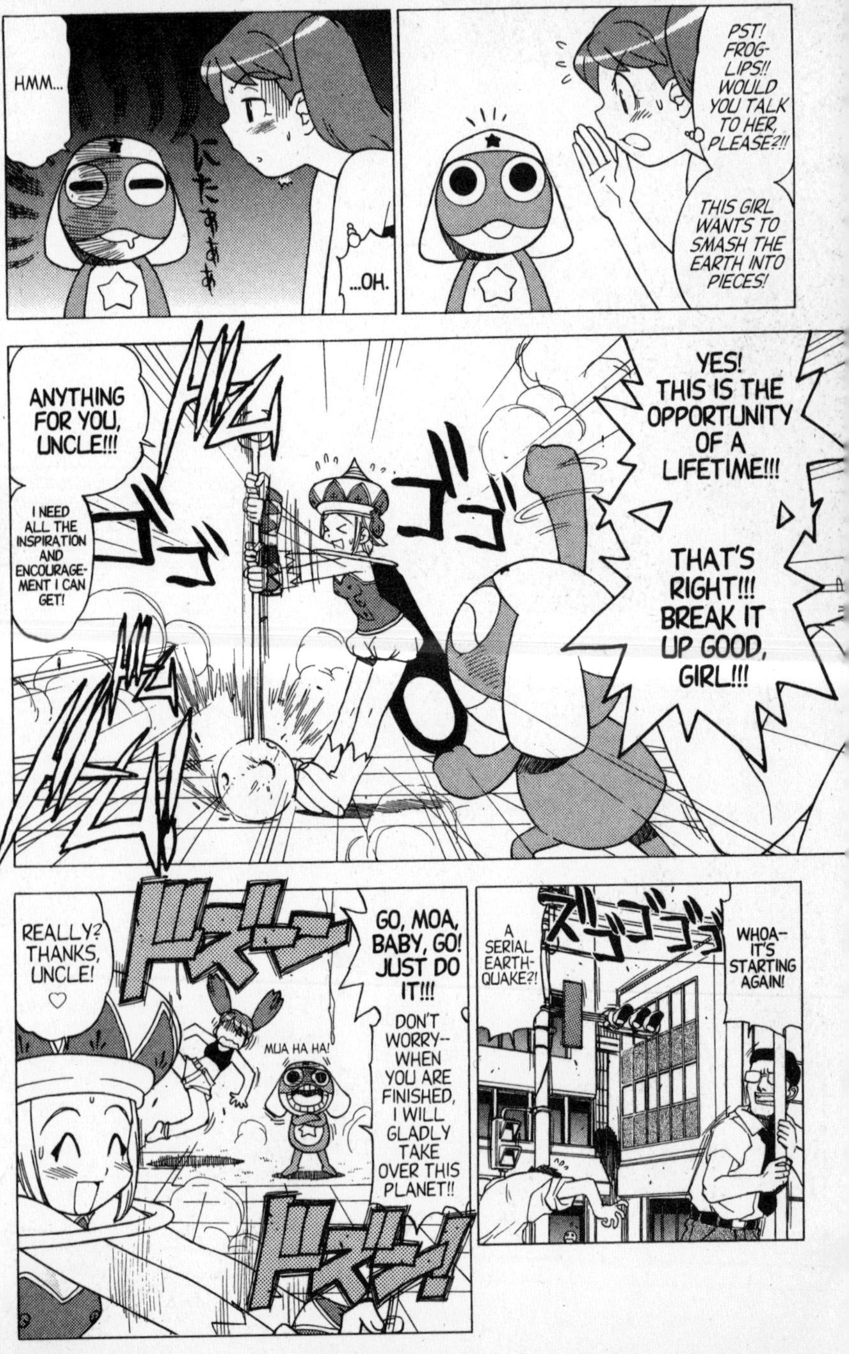
PST! FROG-LIPS!! WOULD YOU TALK TO HER, PLEASE?!!
THIS GIRL WANTS TO SMASH THE EARTH INTO PIECES!
...OH.
にたあああ
HMM...
YES! THIS IS THE OPPORTUNITY OF A LIFETIME!!!
THAT'S RIGHT!!! BREAK IT UP GOOD, GIRL!!!
ゴゴ
ANYTHING FOR YOU, UNCLE!!!
I NEED ALL THE INSPIRATION AND ENCOURAGE-MENT I CAN GET!
WHOA-IT'S STARTING AGAIN!
ズゴゴゴゴ
A SERIAL EARTH-QUAKE?!
GO, MOA, BABY, GO! JUST DO IT!!!
DON'T WORRY-- WHEN YOU ARE FINISHED, I WILL GLADLY TAKE OVER THIS PLANET!!
MUA HA HA!
REALLY? THANKS, UNCLE! ♡

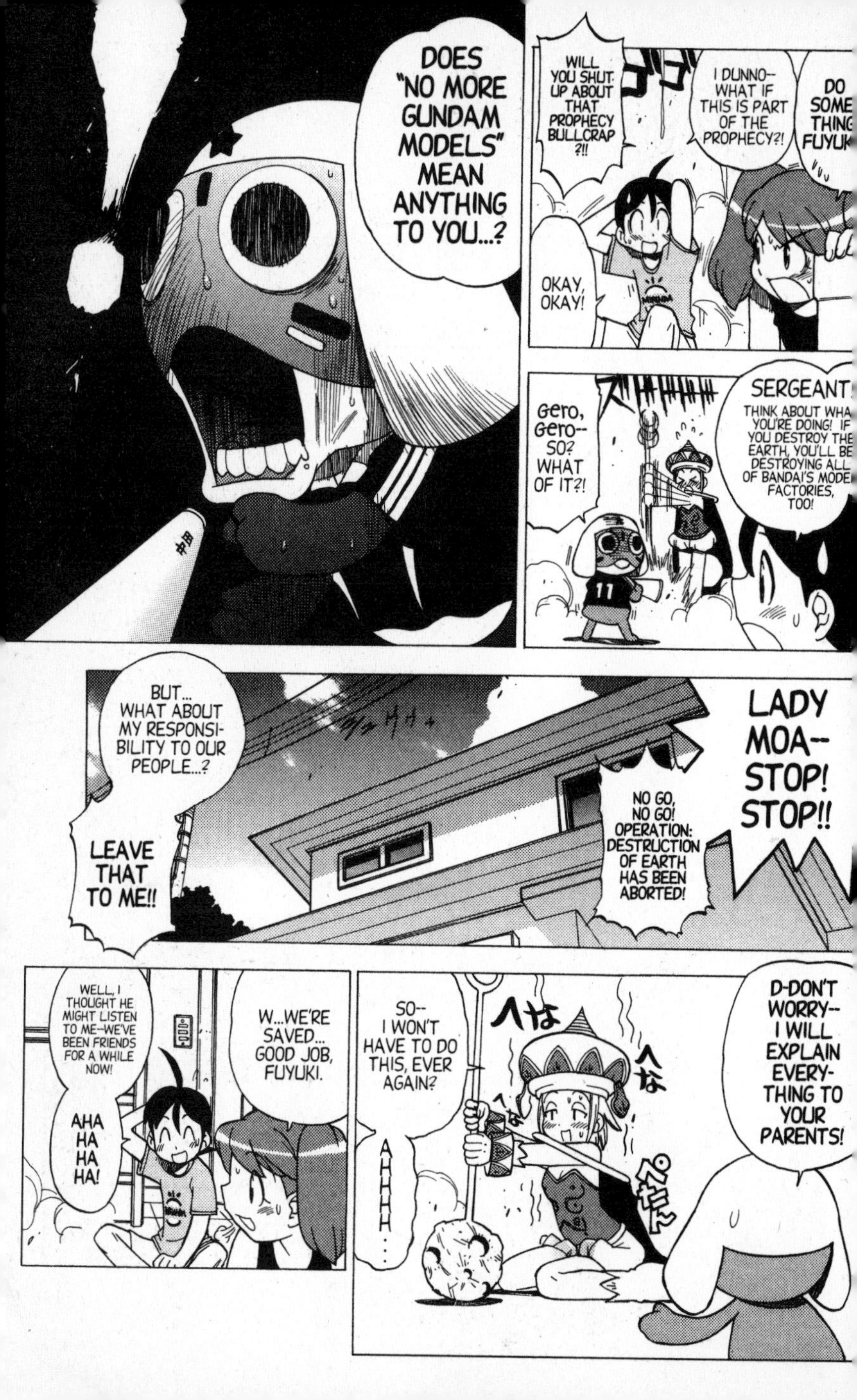
DO SOME THING FUYUK
I DUNNO-- WHAT IF THIS IS PART OF THE PROPHECY?!
WILL YOU SHUT UP ABOUT THAT PROPHECY BULLCRAP?!!
OKAY, OKAY!
SERGEANT! THINK ABOUT WHA YOU'RE DOING! IF YOU DESTROY THE EARTH, YOU'LL BE DESTROYING ALL OF BANDAI'S MODEL FACTORIES, TOO!
Gero, Gero-- SO? WHAT OF IT?!
DOES "NO MORE GUNDAM MODELS" MEAN ANYTHING TO YOU...?
LADY MOA-- STOP! STOP!!
NO GO, NO GO! OPERATION: DESTRUCTION OF EARTH HAS BEEN ABORTED!
BUT... WHAT ABOUT MY RESPONSI-BILITY TO OUR PEOPLE...?
LEAVE THAT TO ME!!
D-DON'T WORRY-- I WILL EXPLAIN EVERY-THING TO YOUR PARENTS!
へな
へな
SO-- I WON'T HAVE TO DO THIS, EVER AGAIN?
ぺたん
AHHHH...
W...WE'RE SAVED... GOOD JOB, FUYUKI.
WELL, I THOUGHT HE MIGHT LISTEN TO ME--WE'VE BEEN FRIENDS FOR A WHILE NOW!
AHA HA HA HA!

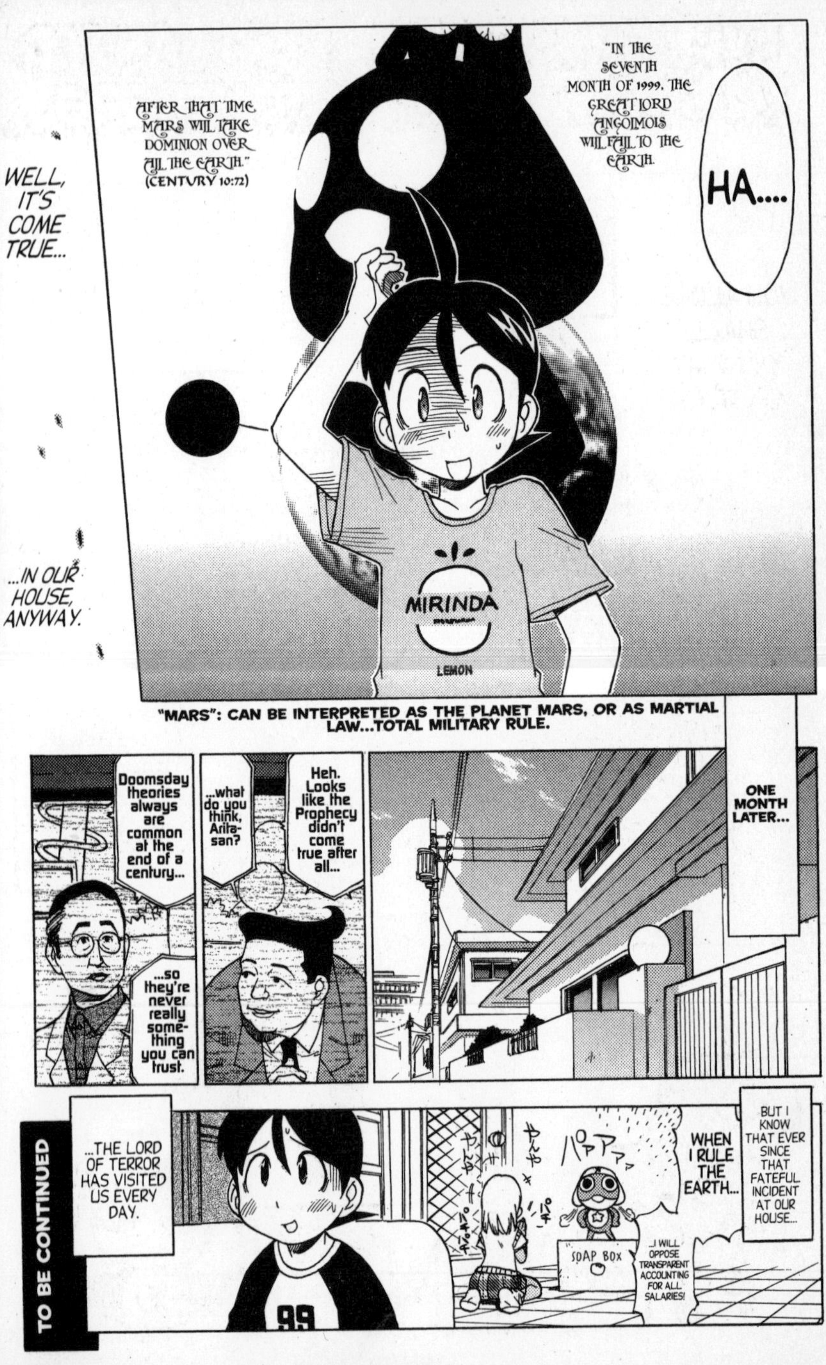
HA....
"IN THE SEVENTH MONTH OF 1999, THE GREAT LORD ANGOLMOIS WILL FALL TO THE EARTH.
AFTER THAT TIME MARS WILL TAKE DOMINION OVER ALL THE EARTH." (CENTURY 10:72)
WELL, IT'S COME TRUE...
...IN OUR HOUSE, ANYWAY.
MIRINDA
LEMON
"MARS": CAN BE INTERPRETED AS THE PLANET MARS, OR AS MARTIAL LAW...TOTAL MILITARY RULE.
ONE MONTH LATER...
Heh. Looks like the Prophecy didn't come true after all...
...what do you think, Arita-san?
Doomsday theories always are common at the end of a century...
...so they're never really something you can trust.
BUT I KNOW THAT EVER SINCE THAT FATEFUL INCIDENT AT OUR HOUSE...
WHEN I RULE THE EARTH...
...I WILL OPPOSE TRANSPARENT ACCOUNTING FOR ALL SALARIES!
SOAP BOX
...THE LORD OF TERROR HAS VISITED US EVERY DAY.
99
TO BE CONTINUED

EVERYTHING YOU EVER WANTED TO KNOW ABOUT SGT. KERORO...

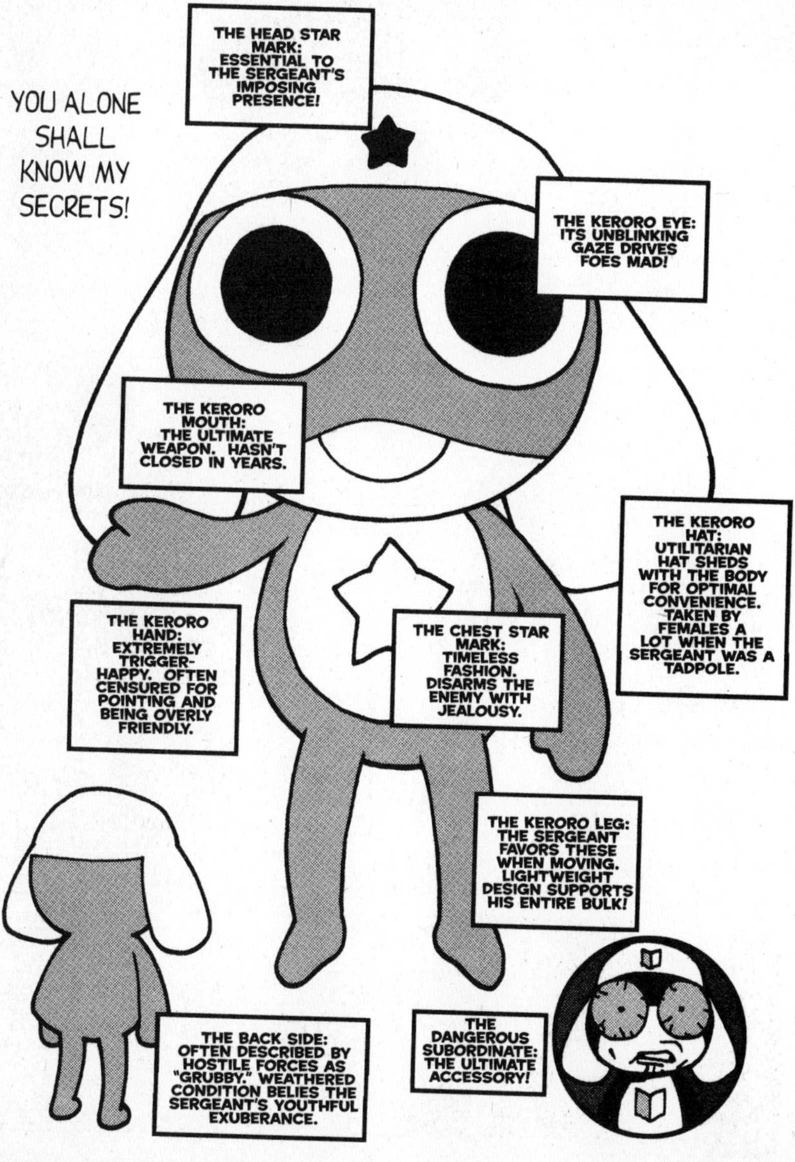
THE HEAD STAR MARK: ESSENTIAL TO THE SERGEANT'S IMPOSING PRESENCE!
YOU ALONE SHALL KNOW MY SECRETS!
THE KERORO EYE: ITS UNBLINKING GAZE DRIVES FOES MAD!
THE KERORO MOUTH: THE ULTIMATE WEAPON. HASN'T CLOSED IN YEARS.
THE KERORO HAT: UTILITARIAN HAT SHEDS WITH THE BODY FOR OPTIMAL CONVENIENCE. TAKEN BY FEMALES A LOT WHEN THE SERGEANT WAS A TADPOLE.
THE CHEST STAR MARK: TIMELESS FASHION. DISARMS THE ENEMY WITH JEALOUSY.
THE KERORO HAND: EXTREMELY TRIGGER-HAPPY. OFTEN CENSURED FOR POINTING AND BEING OVERLY FRIENDLY.
THE KERORO LEG: THE SERGEANT FAVORS THESE WHEN MOVING. LIGHTWEIGHT DESIGN SUPPORTS HIS ENTIRE BULK!
THE DANGEROUS SUBORDINATE: THE ULTIMATE ACCESSORY!
THE BACK SIDE: OFTEN DESCRIBED BY HOSTILE FORCES AS "GRUBBY." WEATHERED CONDITION BELIES THE SERGEANT'S YOUTHFUL EXUBERANCE.

SERGEANT SIGHTINGS... IN THE STATES!

"Pappy, would you move over a tiny tittle? I think I see somethin' in them bushes up yonder...!"

On his drive home in rural Ohio, Mike Richards suddenly came upon a life form so strange that it temporarily reduced him to gibberish. Authorities officially confirmed the sighting of the UMA (Unidentified Moving Animal) later that evening.

Mr. Richards' wife, also in the vehicle at the time, retained her senses long enough to quickly draw a crude rendering of the UMA. Pointing at her sketchbook, she vividly recounted the scene.

"I was so scared. Strangely large eyes...long arms and legs. The entire body was green, with a star on both the head and chest area...almost like a little outfit. It also had two flaps dangling on either side of its head, like ears. That was actually kind of cute...but I remembered that appearance is frequently the devil's servant, so I didn't let it put me off guard. What I remember most is its tail. It was long and thin and slimy. I had a feeling that if it were caught, it'd just drop the darn thing and slip right away."

The couple was so frightened that they considered running the UMA over with their car and leaving the scene for a weekend party, Roberts said. However, they reconsidered and simply drove off.

SERGEANT SIGHTINGS... IN THE STATES

(CONTINUED FROM PREVIOUS PAGE)

The Monster Speaks!

A similar sighting was reported shortly thereafter in rural Kentucky. One Mr. Gertlich Strongfire Black Montblanc Stanley Vanilago Zandez, who successfully took a clear picture of the creature, stated that the monster actually spoke to him.

"I couldn't move. I mean there was an alien in front of me! And, well, what're you supposed to say to an alien? "Hey, bro, how's it hangin?" Then, lo and behold, he starts talkin' to me!"

According to Zandez, what the alien actually said was, "Pokopenion! State the location of the nearest facility that sells Gundam models!"

Of all the wonders of the Earth, the alien seemed to have an abnormal interest in Japanese model kits!

"Hey, I like them, too. I mean, I understand how he might have felt, not being able to get his hands on the new Gundam Seed kits, so I told him I reckoned that as they were in short supply he'd best reserve one, just in case. I guess he wanted one right away though, 'cause he looked real disappointed and headed back into the trees. Matter of fact, I had just bought the last kit at a store nearby and was on my way home to build it. But I don't know...what if he came all the way from outer space just to get one? I feel kinda bad."

Authorities speculate that if the alien were indeed on Earth specifically to procure the Gundam model, it could give rise to a whole new theory on extraterrestrial life.

(Article: Fuyuki Hinata)

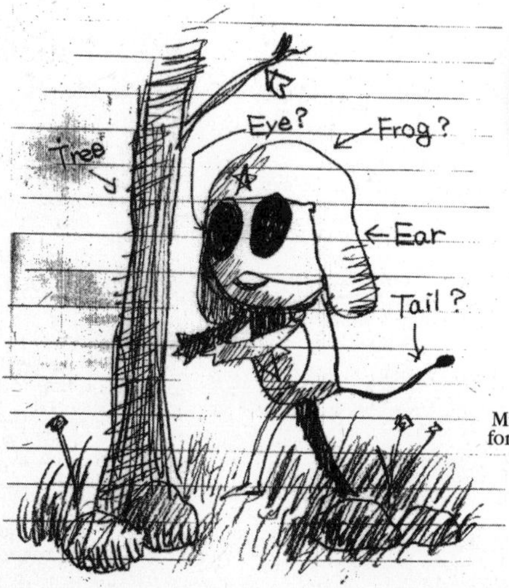
Eye?
Frog?
Tree
Ear
Tail?

Sightings in multiple regions? What could this mean?

PREVIOUS PAGE:
The alien does look "real disappointed" as he slinks out of the clearing.
(Photo confirmed as authentic.)

LEFT:
Mrs. Richards' sketch of the life form. Its resemblance to that of other sightings is uncanny.

JAPAN STAFF

**MINE YOSHIZAKI
OYSTER
GOMOKU AKATSUKI
RYOICHI KOGA
MADARA
TAKEDA**

**ANGOLMOIS DESIGN
CREATED IN
COOPERATION WITH
OKAMA**

KICHIJOJI

吉祥寺

**TO BE CONTINUED IN
VOLUME 2**

NATSUMI-CHAN

LA DEE DA...

 ~♪ LA DA DEE...

Translator - Yuko Fukami
English Adaptation - Carol Fox
Copy Editor - Tim Beedle
Retouch and Lettering - Eric Botero & James Lee
Cover Colors - Pauline Sims
Cover Layout - Chy Lin
Graphic Designer - Jose Macasocol, Jr.

Editor - Paul Morrissey
Digital Imaging Manager - Chris Buford
Pre-Press Manager - Antonio DePietro
Production Managers - Jennifer Miller and Mutsumi Miyazaki
Art Director - Matt Alford
Managing Editor - Jill Freshney
VP of Production - Ron Klamert
President & C.O.O. - John Parker
Publisher & C.E.O. - Stuart Levy

E-mail: info@TOKYOPOP.com

Come visit us online at www.TOKYOPOP.com

A  Manga

TOKYOPOP Inc.
5900 Wilshire Blvd. Suite 2000
Los Angeles, CA 90036

SGT. Frog Vol. 1

KERORO GUNSO © 1999 MINE YOSHIZAKI
First published in Japan in 1999 by KADOKAWA SHOTEN PUBLISHING CO., LTD., Tokyo.
English translation rights arranged with KADOKAWA SHOTEN PUBLISHING CO., LTD., Tokyo
through TUTTLE-MORI AGENCY, INC., Tokyo.

English text copyright ©2004 TOKYOPOP Inc.

ISBN: 1-59182-703-5

First TOKYOPOP printing: March 2004

10 9 8 7 6 5 4 3 2
Printed in the USA

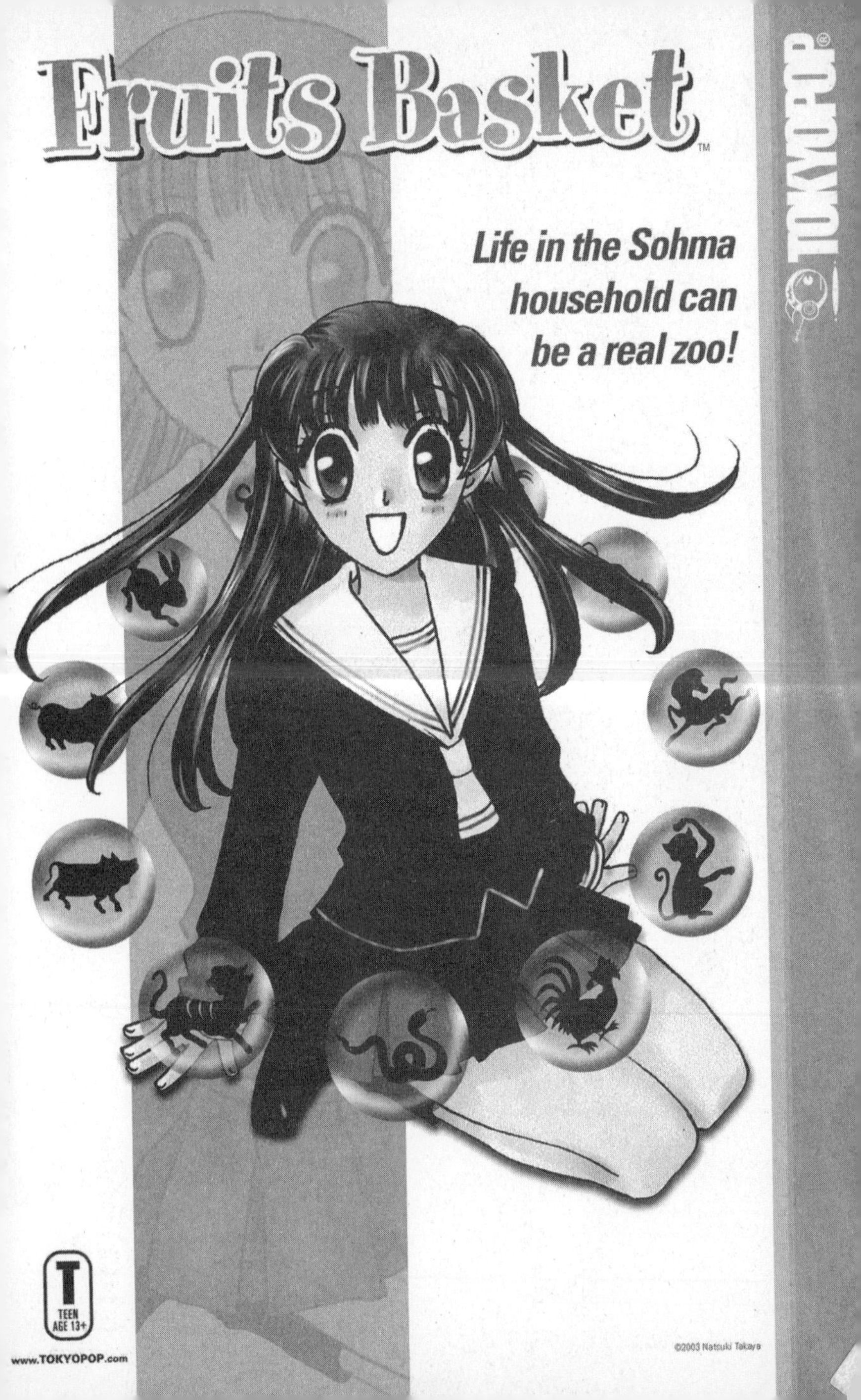

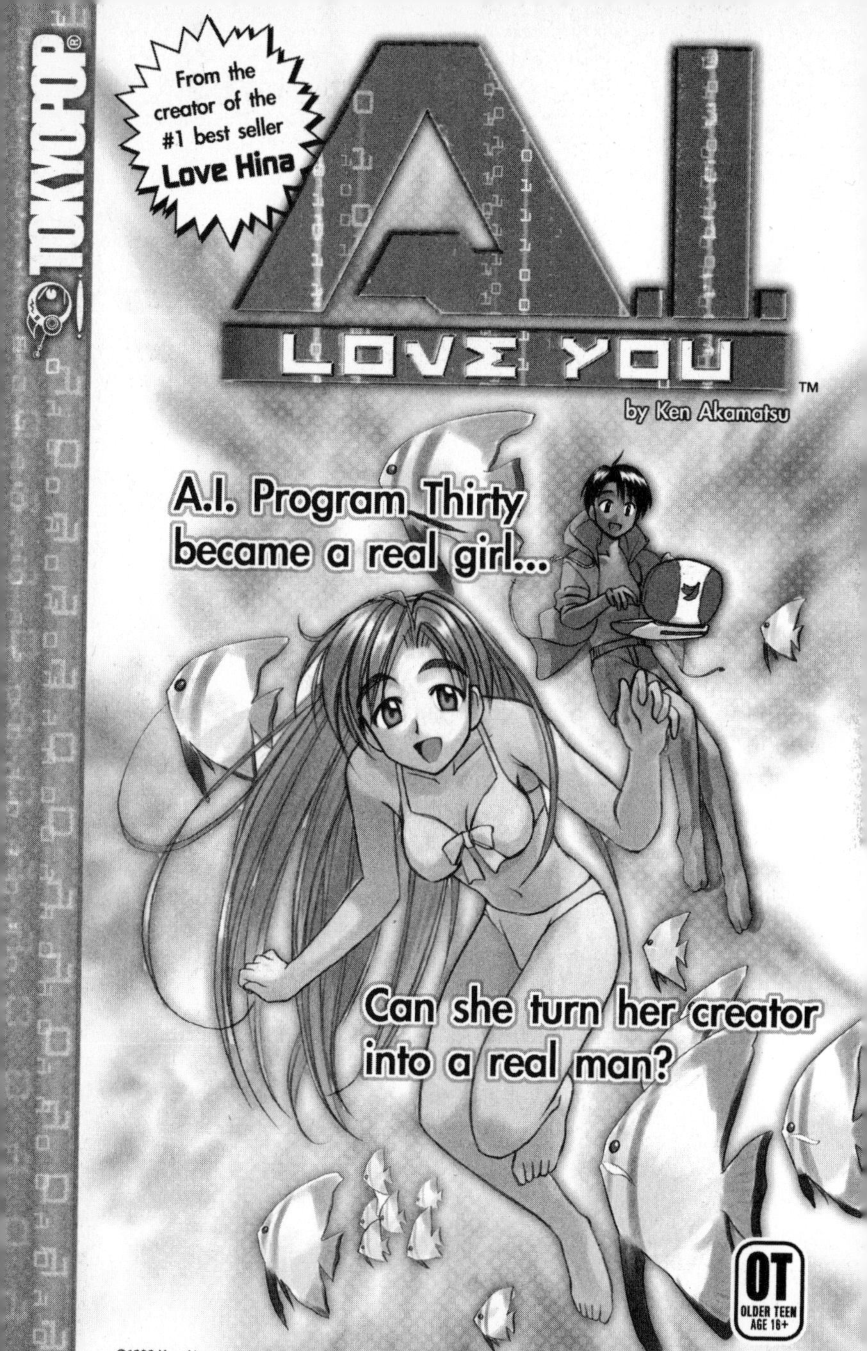
TOKYOPOP
From the creator of the #1 best seller Love Hina
A.I. LOVE YOU™
by Ken Akamatsu
A.I. Program Thirty became a real girl...
Can she turn her creator into a real man?
OT
OLDER TEEN AGE 16+

CYBORG009

THE MANGA

™

THE CYBORGS HAVE ARRIVED!

A CLASSIC SERIES FROM MANGA LEGEND SHOTARO ISHINOMORI

TOKYOPOP

VINTAGE

TEEN
AGE 13+

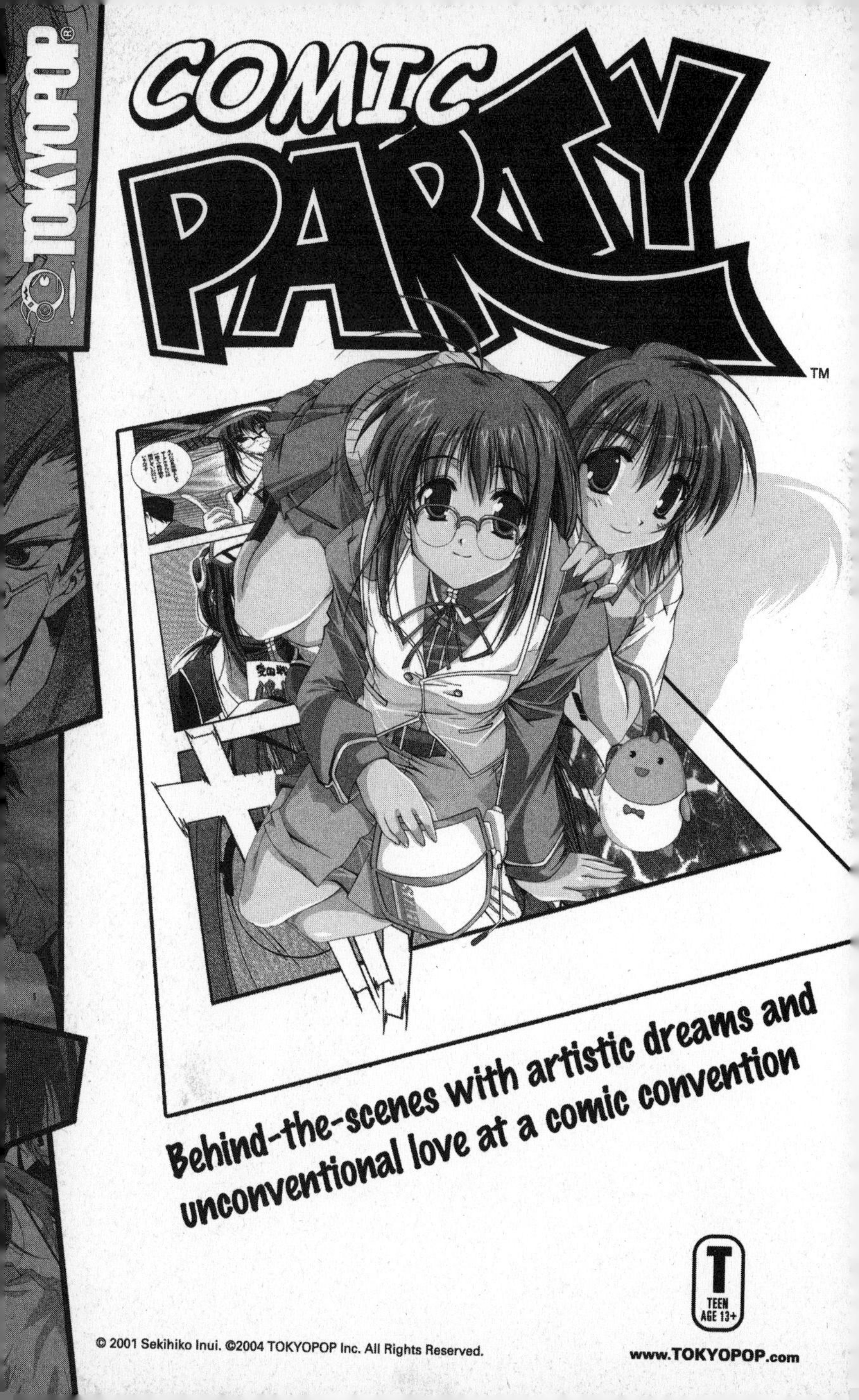
TOKYOPOP®
COMIC PARTY™
Behind-the-scenes with artistic dreams and unconventional love at a comic convention
T TEEN AGE 13+
© 2001 Sekihiko Inui. ©2004 TOKYOPOP Inc. All Rights Reserved.
www.TOKYOPOP.com

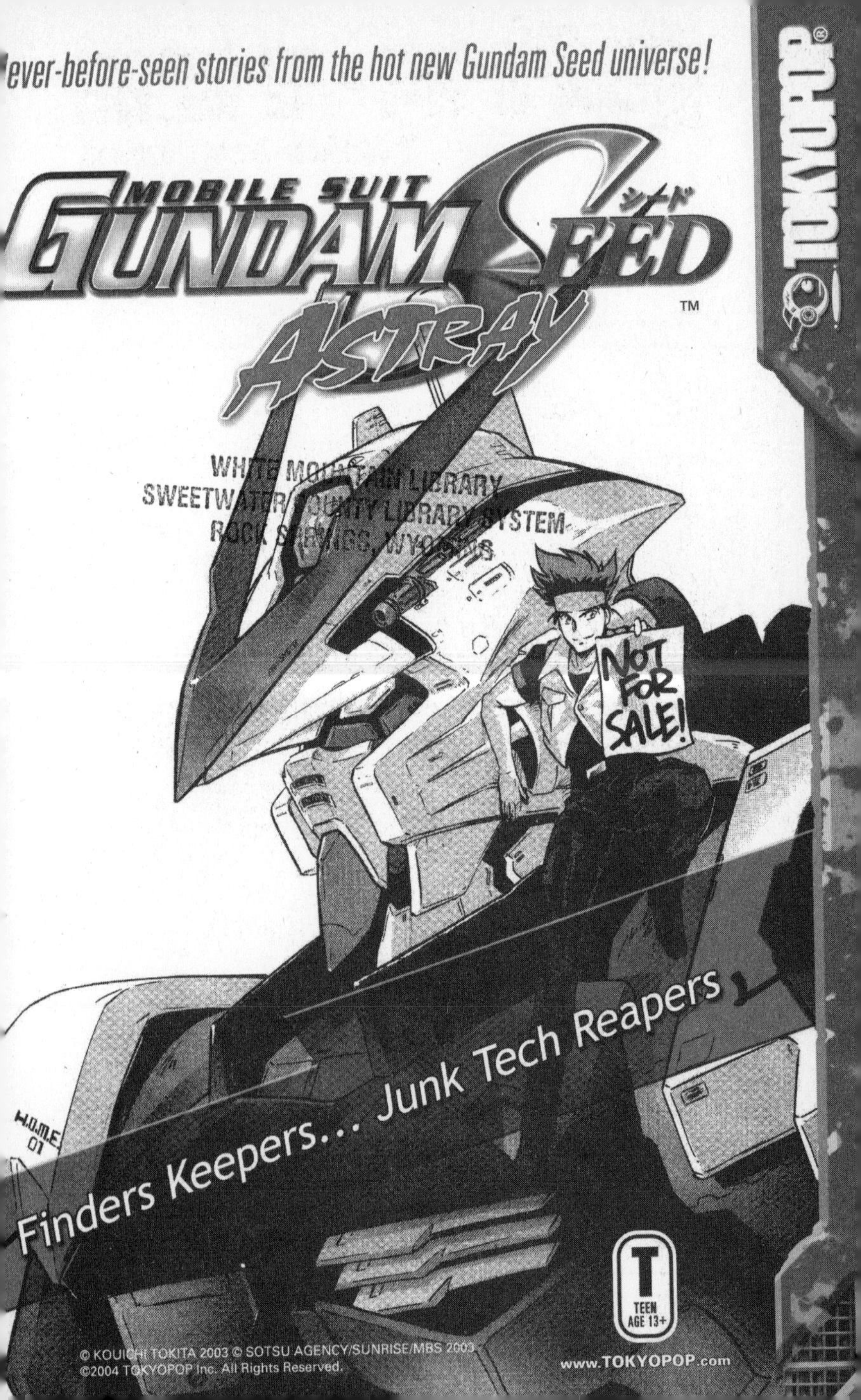
Never-before-seen stories from the hot new Gundam Seed universe!
MOBILE SUIT GUNDAM SEED ASTRAY™
シード
NOT FOR SALE!
H.O.M.E. 01
Finders Keepers... Junk Tech Reapers
T TEEN AGE 13+
© KOUICHI TOKITA 2003 © SOTSU AGENCY/SUNRISE/MBS 2003
©2004 TOKYOPOP Inc. All Rights Reserved.
www.TOKYOPOP.com
TOKYOPOP

ALSO AVAILABLE FROM TOKYOPOP

You want it? We got it!
A full range of TOKYOPOP
products are available now at:
www.TOKYOPOP.com/shop

04.23.04T

ALSO AVAILABLE FROM TOKYOPOP

MANGA

.HACK//LEGEND OF THE TWILIGHT
@LARGE
ABENOBASHI: MAGICAL SHOPPING ARCADE
A.I. LOVE YOU
AI YORI AOSHI
ANGELIC LAYER
ARM OF KANNON
BABY BIRTH
BATTLE ROYALE
BATTLE VIXENS
BRAIN POWERED
BRIGADOON
B'TX
CANDIDATE FOR GODDESS, THE
CARDCAPTOR SAKURA
CARDCAPTOR SAKURA - MASTER OF THE CLOW
CHOBITS
CHRONICLES OF THE CURSED SWORD
CLAMP SCHOOL DETECTIVES
CLOVER
COMIC PARTY
CONFIDENTIAL CONFESSIONS
CORRECTOR YUI
COWBOY BEBOP
COWBOY BEBOP: SHOOTING STAR
CRAZY LOVE STORY
CRESCENT MOON
CROSS
CULDCEPT
CYBORG 009
D•N•ANGEL
DEMON DIARY
DEMON ORORON, THE
DEUS VITAE
DIABOLO
DIGIMON
DIGIMON TAMERS
DIGIMON ZERO TWO
DOLL
DRAGON HUNTER
DRAGON KNIGHTS
DRAGON VOICE
DREAM SAGA
DUKLYON: CLAMP SCHOOL DEFENDERS
EERIE QUEERIE!
ERICA SAKURAZAWA: COLLECTED WORKS
ET CETERA
ETERNITY
EVIL'S RETURN
FAERIES' LANDING
FAKE
FLCL
FLOWER OF THE DEEP SLEEP
FORBIDDEN DANCE
FRUITS BASKET
G GUNDAM

GATEKEEPERS
GETBACKERS
GIRL GOT GAME
GIRLS' EDUCATIONAL CHARTER
GRAVITATION
GTO
GUNDAM BLUE DESTINY
GUNDAM SEED ASTRAY
GUNDAM WING
GUNDAM WING: BATTLEFIELD OF PACIFISTS
GUNDAM WING: ENDLESS WALTZ
GUNDAM WING: THE LAST OUTPOST (G-UNIT)
GUYS' GUIDE TO GIRLS
HANDS OFF!
HAPPY MANIA
HARLEM BEAT
I.N.V.U.
IMMORTAL RAIN
INITIAL D
INSTANT TEEN: JUST ADD NUTS
ISLAND
JING: KING OF BANDITS
JING: KING OF BANDITS - TWILIGHT TALES
JULINE
KARE KANO
KILL ME, KISS ME
KINDAICHI CASE FILES, THE
KING OF HELL
KODOCHA: SANA'S STAGE
LAMENT OF THE LAMB
LEGAL DRUG
LEGEND OF CHUN HYANG, THE
LES BIJOUX
LOVE HINA
LUPIN III
LUPIN III: WORLD'S MOST WANTED
MAGIC KNIGHT RAYEARTH I
MAGIC KNIGHT RAYEARTH II
MAHOROMATIC: AUTOMATIC MAIDEN
MAN OF MANY FACES
MARMALADE BOY
MARS
MARS: HORSE WITH NO NAME
MINK
MIRACLE GIRLS
MIYUKI-CHAN IN WONDERLAND
MODEL
MY LOVE
NECK AND NECK
ONE
ONE I LOVE, THE
PARADISE KISS
PARASYTE
PASSION FRUIT
PEACH GIRL
PEACH GIRL: CHANGE OF HEART
PET SHOP OF HORRORS
PITA-TEN

04.23.04T

STOP!

This is the back of the book.
You wouldn't want to spoil a great ending!

This book is printed "manga-style," in the authentic Japanese right-to-left format. Since none of the artwork has been flipped or altered, readers get to experience the story just as the creator intended. You've been asking for it, so TOKYOPOP® delivered: authentic, hot-off-the-press, and far more fun!

DIRECTIONS

If this is your first time reading manga-style, here's a quick guide to help you understand how it works.

It's easy... just start in the top right panel and follow the numbers. Have fun, and look for more 100% authentic manga from TOKYOPOP®!